The Battle of Valle Giulia

The Battle of Valle Giulia

ORAL HISTORY AND THE ART OF DIALOGUE

Alessandro Portelli

THE UNIVERSITY OF WISCONSIN PRESS

The University of Wisconsin Press
1930 Monroe Street
Madison, Wisconsin 53711

3 Henrietta Street
London WC2E 8LU, England

www.wisc.edu\wisconsinpress

Library of Congress Cataloging-in-Publication Data
Portelli, Alessandro.
The battle of Valle Giulia: oral history and the art of dialogue /
Alessandro Portelli.
376 pp.   cm.
Includes bibliographical references and index.
ISBN 0-299-15370-3 (cloth: alk. paper).
ISBN 0-299-15374-6 (pbk.: alk. paper).
1. Oral history. 2. Youth movement—History. I. Title.
D16.14.P66   1997
907.2—dc21   96-36474

Contents

PART III. MOVEMENTS

Introduction

WHAT DID YOU DO IN THE WAR?

Sometime in the fall of 1995 I thought I would try to break myself of the habit of reading only books and articles directly pertinent to my current research and teaching interests, and retrieve the pleasure of reading for its own sake, too often lost on us professional readers. So I picked up some novels by Ian McEwan that I had laid aside for just such a moment, and started reading and enjoying my mental leisure—until a passage near the end of *Black Dogs* frustrated the evasion and jolted me back to my concerns.

As they travel through the South of France, the two central characters see an iron cross on a stone base, a memorial to the victims of war, on which a blue-clothed mason is engraving names. Standing perfectly still by the monument is a pale woman in black.

> As they drank from their water bottles he was struck by the recently concluded war not as a historical, geopolitical fact, but as a multiplicity, a near-infinity of private sorrows, as a boundless grief minutely subdivided without diminishment among individuals who covered the continent like dust, like spores whose separate identities would remain unknown, and borne in silence by hundreds of thousands, millions, like the woman in black for a husband and two brothers, each grief a particular, intricate, keening love story that might have been otherwise. It seemed as though he had never thought about the war before, not about its cost. He had been so busy with the details of his work, of doing it well, and his widest view had been of war aims, of winning, of statistical deaths, statistical destruction, and of postwar reconstruction. For the first time he sensed the scale of the catastrophe in terms of feeling; all those unique and solitary deaths, all that consequent sorrow, unique and solitary too, which had no place in conferences, headlines, history, and which had quietly retired to houses, kitchens, unshared beds, and anguished memories.[1]

Ian McEwan's epiphany illuminates the dramatic distance and the indissoluble bond between "history" and personal experience, between the private unique and solitary spores of sorrow in houses, kitchens, and anguished memories, and the historian's perception and reconstruction of broad, public historical events. This passage showed me with surprising clarity what I was trying to do. The task and theme of oral history—an art dealing with the individual in social and historical context—is to explore this distance and this bond, to search out the memories in the private, enclosed space of houses and kitchens and—without violating that space, without cracking the uniqueness of each spore with an arrogant need to scrutinize, to know, and to classify—to connect them with "history" and in turn force history to listen to them. This is what I have tried to say in methodological terms in the first part of this book, which is dedicated to the practice, experience, and method of oral history, and in more concrete terms in the thematic parts that follow: part 2 on war narratives and part 3 on youth movements.

McEwan's page reminded me of a passage in an interview that Giovanni Contini held in Civitella Val di Chiana with the local partisan chief Edoardo Succhielli (see chapter 10). After years of silence, Succhielli was finally speaking of the effects of the partisan war and the German reprisal it brought on the uncommitted village, whose entire male population was exterminated.

> We brought, unfortunately, ruin to that village. I'll tell you the truth: unintentionally, with good intentions; but unfortunately. . . .
> Unfortunately, even the Resistance is not made only of well thought-out, well planned, well carried out actions. That action was a mistake. Unfortunately . . . for all those people who had the family destroyed, their sons dead, their husbands, and so on: for them, the war, win or lose—practically the war, as far as they're concerned, they lost it.[2]

In history, France and anti-Fascist Italy are technically among the winners of World War II. The woman by the monument who lost "Trois. Mari et deux frères" and the women survivors at Civitella who witnessed the massacre of all their men signify how partial and limited that history is. They are the price paid for this victory they do not share, and they are its meaning. History has no content without their stories.

To my surprise, I found that over the years I had written a number of essays that had to do with war. When I got them all together and looked back at them, I realized that this was the link I had been looking for. I have never been especially concerned with or even interested in war narratives; I never sought them out, barely listened when interviewees insisted on telling them, and all but skipped them altogether in my transcriptions. But the stories kept coming back—in the use of war as a metaphor for labor or student struggle (chapters 7, 12), in the conferences in which I was asked to take part (chapters 8, 10), in the books I read (chapter 11), and in the unsolved contradictions that the memory of war still generates in the minds of the witnesses and the narrators—and in my own (chapter 9).

One of the themes of this book, therefore, is the relationship between private and public histories, experiences, and narratives as a specific task and realm of oral history. War keeps coming back in narratives and memories as the most dramatic point of encounter between the personal and public, between biography and history. For generations we have been taught in school that history is a narrative of kings and wars; the child's question—"Daddy, what did you do in the war?"—is an embryonic way of phrasing the larger question: What is our place in history, and what is the place of history in our lives? The naive picture of the schoolchild interviewing a grandparent about World War I, so often used to belittle the whole enterprise of oral history, is in fact a clue to its meaning. Of course, oral history is by no means the only way to approach the question of the individual's relationship to history, but it cannot exist without dealing with it, because it begins with individual narratives and with encounters between individuals.

Yet I also found that in these chapters I often dealt less with the victims than with the perpetrators. Again, I found a clue in an unrelated text, Richard Slotkin's preface to James Fenimore Cooper's *The Last of the Mohicans*. Cooper's aim, Slotkin writes, was "to pose a question about the moral character of man in an uncivil or precivilized condition. This character is revealed in historical action, and the characteristic form of historical action for Cooper is warfare, or warlike acts of violence."[3] War—the act of killing as much as the experience of loss and the vision of death—challenges our definition of what is human, pushes everyone's humanity to the limit: the "state of nature" represented by the jungles of Vietnam (chapter 11) or the refugee experience (chapter 8) becomes a metaphor for the "uncivil or precivilized condition" that reveals what human nature is capable of doing.

While the victims, like the women of Civitella, uncomprehendingly reiterate the question, "How could they do such a thing to us?" the perpetrators—both war criminals like the Nazi veterans who return to Civitella or some of the American soldiers in Vietnam, and those we might consider war heroes, like the partisans at Poggio Bustone—ask another question:

"How could we do such a thing? What had we become?" (chapters 9, 11). This question, explicit or not, marks the difference between the time of the events and the time of the telling, the time of history and the time of discourse, highlighting through memory and storytelling the changing historical and narrative subject. War, then, draws together thematic as well as formal concerns that are both general and very specific to oral history.

WHAT DID WE DO?

The essays gathered in part 3 are also concerned with the memory and narrative of changing subjects, and with the relationship of the public and the private. The politics of private life were the central discovery and theme of youth and student movements, especially in the 1970s (chapter 14). Hair and clothes became contested terrain of political struggle as emotionally charged as land reform or union organizing, as young people became aware of how history and social relationships impinge on personal life and feelings, and how the private sphere is itself a terrain of political experiment and struggle. Youth and student movements became bridges from private adolescence to public youth, as their protagonists for the first time took personal responsibility for the changing of society. These movements brought the first person to the foreground of social and historical discourse. Without the youth movements, the factory worker Bruno Andreoli might not have been able to formulate the question about his generation's role in history: "And what did we do?" (chapter 7).

In these essays, however, the relationship between the general and the particular is also explored from another angle: the impact of a worldwide movement of generally middle-class young people on rural peripheries that had no significant student population to speak of and whose youth was mostly of working-class origins. Just as war "comes" to the noncombatant refugees of Terni (chapter 8), so do "the sixties" come to Harlan and Giulianello (chapters 13, 14). On the other hand, the experience of leaving home became relevant, often for the first time, to large numbers of young people who left either to go to school in Velletri or Lexington, or to go to war in Vietnam (could we conceive of youth culture in the sixties without Vietnam?). Indeed, the expression *movements* is to be also taken literally, to include travel and migration as expressions and locations of contemporary youth cultures (chapters 15, 16). These dialectics of invasion and evasion between the local and the worldwide are another variant of the dialectics of the general and the specific, of history and stories, that runs through the book.

Both in the youth narratives and in the war stories, what strikes me is the distance between the narrated and the narrating self, the time of history and the time of the telling. By definition, narratives of youth are concerned with changing subjects, especially in a time of rapid historical change such as the last twenty or thirty years. Yet, the sense of openness, of multiple possible identities found in these narratives (chapter 15, 16) provides a telling contrast with the sense of annihilation of identity that dominates the war stories.

Going to war, as Alistair Thomson reminds us, is primarily a youth experience: war myths and war narratives are one way of shaping ideas of manhood and identity. Old men may tell war stories, but young men fight the wars (Ferruccio Mauri in chapter 4 is an example of how these functions are illustrated in one narrative), and boys and adolescents grow up hearing about them and imagining them. One does not have to be an army officer's son to have a "military childhood" and to "relish . . . the warrior culture of Australian boyhood" or any other boyhood for that matter.[4] Perhaps because they grew up playing warriors on the one hand and reacting to cautionary tales of wartime privation on the other (chapter 14), postwar youth cultivate an ambiguous relationship between war narratives and their own. While they are suspicious of their parents' narratives, they generate "war" narratives of their own. On the one hand, they exorcise the heroic legend by inventing ironic parodies in the mock-heroic mode about themselves as "bold and daring young men . . . heroic, in quotes" (chapter 12, 15). On the other hand, since both war and movements are final goodbyes to that childhood, unrepeatable turning points in personal biographies, movement narratives often reflect the same nostalgia as war stories, ironically projecting the narrators as future veterans who "will remember [the movement] ten years from now and tell about it like grandfather's tales."[5] Finally, of course, the theme of violence and the vision of revolution as war have been central to the imagination of the movements. All these implications are present in the event that gives the title to this book: the "battle" of Valle Giulia.

I had already chosen this title when a symbolic event intensified its meaning for me. In the summer of 1995, as I was working on the chapter on the Nazi massacre at Civitella and the contradictions of anti-Fascist memory, the mayor of Rome, Francesco Rutelli (a "Green" politician elected as the progressive candidate over a Fascist antagonist), announced that the city would name a street after Luigi Bottai, a cabinet member of Mussolini's Fascist government in the 1930s and early 1940s. Bottai was to be honored as a benefactor to Italian culture because, as an intellectual, he had allowed a certain tolerance in the regime's cultural politics. On the other hand, as Secretary of Education, Bottai had zealously enforced the most odious of Fascist laws: the racial discrimination that excluded all Jewish teachers and students from the public school and university system. Quite a contribution to Italian culture, indeed. To compound the insult, Rutelli planned to name after him the square of Valle Giulia, the birthplace of the student movement in 1968. In one stroke, in the name of a dubious reconciliation (in the fiftieth anniversary of the Resistance!), official "progressive" memory was erasing both anti-Fascism and the radical movements of 1968.

Ultimately, Rutelli had to back down. But the message remained: both memories, the student rebellion of 1968 and the anti-Fascist rebellion during World War II, were under siege. This book is also a critical defense and vindication of both.

WHAT AM I DOING?

My earlier collection of oral history essays, *The Death of Luigi Trastulli,*[6] was primarily a study of working-class cultures, to which I came as a friendly neighbor and a sympathetic outsider, but an outsider all the same. Listening to steelworkers and coal miners, I was primarily learning about realms of which I had no firsthand experience. In this book, I deal with events and memories in which I have been directly involved. Although for a number of reasons I was always somewhat on the periphery, yet the movements of the 1960s and 1970s turned my life around; either I was closely involved with their cultural politics (chapters 3, 12), or they took place directly in my own everyday space (chapters 15, 16).

By writing about these events, I am inevitably writing about myself. My own memories as well as those of others are involved. Indeed, after I began to be aware of this difference, I also realized that I, too, have grown up listening to parental narratives of wartime privations on the one hand and playing war on the other. Working on these materials actually revived my own vague childhood memories of the war: the refugee narratives of Terni suddenly brought back shadows from my own recollection, which in turn gave me a better feeling for the tone of those narratives. Ultimately, what I discovered was, indeed, "what I did in the war," both as a toddler during World War II and as a young adult in the politics of 1968 and after.

This personal sense of connectedness is one reason why the first person is prominent in this book, though I never eschewed it in my work. Self-reflexivity is one of the things that help make a book out of a collection of essays: while the individual chapters remain distinct, the voice that speaks in them is the same. The voice also asks another unifying question: not only What did I do in the war and the movement? but also What am I doing, and how, in interrogating their history?

This is not a very interesting question if it remains autobiographical, but it becomes relevant as it offers access to a broader range of self-reflexivity concerning the work of oral history in general. This is why, while my earlier collection was about "*form and meaning* in oral history," I view this one as essays on the *practice* of oral history. Meaning and practice, of course, are inseparable: the interpretation begins at the moment of collection, and all presentation—including the most "objective" one—is an interpretation. Yet they are logically distinct aspects of a complex work. The difference between the two approaches, therefore, reflects a shift in emphasis from the *materials* of oral history, the narratives and their interpretation, to the *process* by which they come into being *as* oral history narratives and are presented as such.

Each interview is an *experience* before it becomes a *text*. The chapter that seems to me the key to the whole book—chapter 2, "There's Gonna Always Be a Line"—shows that it is one thing to analyze the verbal structure and form of a narrative (as I do in the first part of the essay), and quite another to suddenly feel the narrative's impact on one's own subjectivity (as in the final sections). Many of the essays in this book hinge on encounters that were also experiences in my own self-definition as white (Mrs. Cowans, chapter 2), Italian (Shackleford, chapter 4) middle class (Giulio R., chapter 3), and intellectual (Annamaria Di Marco, chapter 15). Although much of the book is about a supposedly very male experience, war (but chapters 8, 10, and parts of 7 are essentially women's narratives), the fact that the majority of these epiphanies of otherness involved conversations with women means that gender is also an implicit and pervasive subtext.

These essays, therefore, are intended as a contribution to the growing self-awareness of oral history as an established field of intellectual research and social involvement. To a greater extent than in the past, I find myself engaging in dialogue with other oral historians, discussing their work, and using interviews collected by others (chapters 1, 10, 12, 13), working with others (chapter 16). This is, at one level, a sign of the maturity of oral history. We are no longer confined to the stage of gathering data, but are also able to treat them *as* data; the methods of analysis and interpretation have been considerably refined; and the interpretations and analyses of oral historians are now consolidated to the point where they may bear critical scrutiny on a par with any other intellectual practice, and serve as springboards for further intellectual development. Oral history has gone well beyond that pioneering stage of primary field work that Gianni Bosio used to call "hermetic discovery."[7]

Self-awareness and self-reflexivity, on the other hand, may not be exclusively unmixed goods. While they indicate a heightened maturity and sense of responsibility in the discipline as a whole, these attitudes may also include a degree of self-enclosed narcissism; a healthy recognition of partiality and limits may slide into an acceptance of irrelevance and irresponsibility. Indeed—and this is by no means exclusive to oral history— the increasing attention to metadiscourse (history of historiography, anthropology of anthropologists, theory of theory, etc.) also signals the weakening of the relationship between our intellectual practices and the world outside. To be aware of ourselves is essential to a delineation of otherness, but to confine our conversation to our own self-reflexivity is a way to erase the other from our discourse and negate the very reason for the discourse itself. This is why by *practice* I refer to oral history both as an *intellectual* and as a *social* endeavor.

Methodological sophistication and social practice combine today in much of the oral history work that goes on outside the so-called Western world. The 1994 New York conference organized by Ronald Grele and the Oral History Office of Columbia University clearly indicated that Western Europe and the United States no longer hold the central position that they did in earlier stages of the development of oral history. While I do not know enough of Asia, Africa, or even Eastern Europe, I have been impressed by what I have seen of the work of colleagues in Latin America. Those working with oral sources in Brazil, Mexico, Argentina, and other Latin American countries avail themselves fully of the experience and work of European and U.S. oral history, but they also possess rich and fascinating bibliographies of their own, of which European and U.S. historians are but dimly aware, and not only for linguistic reasons. Also, Latin American (and, perhaps, Asian and African) oral history has the advantage of a much closer contact with thriving oral cultures of ethnic, native, and immigrant communities, and of a still tangible context of social struggle.

On the other hand, an increased awareness of the world context also results in a further questioning of my own position in this international discourse. One of the "epiphanies" referred to in this book has to do with myself as an Italian working in a U.S. context (Mildred Shackleford, chapter 4) or involved in American studies (and, on this and other occasions, addressing a primarily American and broadly international audience). In previous work, I took advantage of a comparative perspective, speaking about two different and yet comparable cultures. In this collection, speaking as an Italian is less incidental and somewhat more thematized. For instance, after interpreting the war refugee experience with reference to American literary works (John Steinbeck and Margaret Mitchell), I purposely sought out the work of Alberto Moravia to place these narratives not only in the comparative American perspective but also in their Italian cultural context (chapter 8).

Once again, this is less interesting as autobiography than as it places this book in the strangely paradoxical context of the international visibility and national invisibility of Italian oral history. On the one hand, beginning with the international recognition of the work of Luisa Passerini, there is a general recognition of the international significance of Italian oral history. Italian scholars fill more than their share of committees and editorial boards, appear prominently in most international occasions, and are almost routinely translated. Though it is doubtful whether Italian oral history can be described as a homogeneous or even coherent discourse, yet it has become widely identified with theoretical sophistication, and its influence has been welcomed as a sign of methodological maturity.[8]

On the other hand, the Italian intellectual community is almost entirely unaware of all this. Oral history in Italy began and developed largely independently from the university and with reference to social and political movements. None of its founders—Gianni Bosio, Danilo Montaldi, Cesare Bermani, Rocco Scotellaro—ever had an academic career. This fact has enabled anthropologist Pietro Clemente recently to criticize—with reference to debates of the 1970s and early 1980s—the so-called anti-intellectual implications and political dogmatism of the Italian oral history "movement."[9] From the perspective of the 1990s, I am convinced that things are quite the opposite: there is a definite and obdurate intellectual and political resistance to oral history among the Italian academics including professional anthropologists and general historians. Though born outside the academy, oral history ought not necessarily to have remained there if the academy had been less afraid to deal with an intellectual enterprise it could not entirely own and control. Rather than oral history's hostility to the university, the scandal is that *not one person* is employed in any public or private institution in Italy as an oral historian; *not one person* in Italy makes a living primarily from oral history either as teacher, field worker, or archivist.

Among the better known and active Italian oral historians, I am the only one who has a tenured university chair—but in another discipline,

outside the field of history. Luisa Passerini was already known and admired internationally when she was being refused associate professorships
in Italian universities (she has worked primarily in international institutions for the last several years, and in other areas of historical research).
A promising young historian had to omit all her oral history publications
from her résumé (and asked me to drop her name from our magazine) in
order to get into graduate school in urban history, and she has not done
any oral history since. Alfredo Martini, Giovanni Contini, Mimmo Bo-
ninelli, very active and productive in oral history, are otherwise employed;
Nuto Revelli is a retired army officer; Cesare Bermani, who all but created the whole enterprise in the 1960s, is literally unemployed. (Within
one month, he was refused both an associate professorship in history and
a job as a janitor in the local elementary school. He was better qualified
for the former.) There have been recent signs of interest from the state
archives and other institutions, but I think I may safely claim that, insti-
tutionally, oral history in Italy does not exist.

Its intellectual impact nationally is also quite out of proportion with
its international visibility. Whatever its merits, *The Death of Luigi Trastulli* is routinely referred to by oral and other historians internationally;
on the other hand, it does not exist in Italian other than in the form of a
few essays scattered in obscure publications (and the same will hold for
this book). The Italian historians and anthropologists who are aware of
The Death of Luigi Trastulli are the handful to whom I personally gave
copies (judging from their bibliographies, not all of them have managed
to read it). Luisa Passerini has fared a little better both because she is a
professional historian, and because of her important conversation with
the women's movement (in and out of the academy). Still, her methodologically most important work is not mentioned in Clemente's recent "survey." For the professional intellectual community in Italy, with very few
exceptions, the work with which our international colleagues engage in
dialogue might as well not exist.[10]

On the other hand, locally as well as internationally, oral history in
Italy exists and thrives: the researchers who collected three hundred life
stories of partisans in Genova may not receive institutional recognition,
but they have done very important work. I would submit that the vitality
of oral history in Italy depends on its background as politically engaged
social practice. It seems to me that whatever methodological insights were
achieved by Italian oral historians, they were generated in the context of
trying to understand not oral history per se, but the history, memory, and
subjectivity of working-class people, of women and the feminist move-

ment, of youth and radical movements. In almost all cases, the people involved in the research were also, at some personal level, involved with the significance of the object of their research.

I would like to conclude with a few remarks on the relationship between this book and my earlier one, *The Death of Luigi Trastulli*. In that book, I quoted my friend and comrade Amerigo Matteucci, construction worker and mayor of the mountain village of Polino, who sang, "Forgive me, friends, if I am wrong, but I am still for the revolution." It seems to me that at times readers forget that these lines were improvised in 1972, and project in the book the nostalgia for a lost vision of a cohesive, politicized, militant, working-class culture. When interviewed again in 1993, Matteucci implied that he did not repent or regret *having been* for the revolution, and *would* still be for it if the occasion arose. But things had changed, and revolution was not on the agenda; he did not even use the word. Twenty years before, his words had been ironically apologetic, but his meaning was defiant. Now, the words were defiant, but the tone was apologetic.

This does not mean that the image projected in that book was false— only that it belongs to another time in history. Unless we recognize this fact, it may be easy to use the book as a focus of nostalgia and of optimistic misrepresentation. *Trastulli* has become a history book in the full sense of the word, valid (I hope) for the reconstruction of a still relevant past and for its methodological suggestions, rather than as a representation of society as it is today. Yet, though much has changed and much has been lost, the questions raised by the culture of the working class are still very much with us; the need to imagine future possible worlds is very much a thing of our present, and of our future. This is why, like Amerigo Matteucci, I do not regret or repent having "been for the revolution," or even having projected on the culture of which Amerigo is a representative some of my political and human dreams and desires. Whatever is valid in the theory and methodology delineated in my earlier and current work is very much a product of those projections, dreams, and desires.

WHAT OTHERS DID FOR ME

Oral history is practice and dialogue, and therefore no oral history work exists without the contribution of many others. This book owes its existence to Rosalie Robertson, my editor at the University of Wisconsin Press, who also helped make *The Death of Luigi Trastulli* possible through SUNY Press. Michael Frisch and Ronald Grele were generous with encouragement and advice as they have been for many years. I don't know what I would do without them.

As the notes to the individual chapters indicate, virtually all of the material in this book first saw the light in performance, as papers presented at conferences and meetings of various sorts. Although I have endeavoured to loosen the texts from their occasional moorings, I have retained the sense of dialogue, of addressing a specific audience. Through the people who made these encounters possible, therefore, I also wish to thank the audiences whose patience allowed me to outline my arguments and whose questions and criticism molded them into shape: Cuautéhmoc Velasco, Gerardo Necoechea, Jorge Aceves Lozano, and INAH (as well as Eugenia Meyer) in Mexico City; Dora Schwarzstein, Hebe Clementi, Liliana Barela, the Instituto Histórico and the oral history community in Buenos Aires; Carlos Sebe, Dea Fenelon, Antonieta Antonacci, Marieta de Morais Ferreira, the History Department at the Catholic University of São Paulo and the CPDOC at the Fundaçao Getulio Vargas in Rio de Janeiro; Leonardo Paggi for making me write about Civitella, and Paul Thompson for providing an opportunity to talk about it; Maria Carmen García-Nieto (for Avila) and José A. González Alcantud (for Granada), Viktor Susak (for L'viv); and, again, Ronald Grele and George Lipsitz (for Birmingham).

In many ways, also, all my work has been shaped and made possible by the international oral history community with which I have been involved. In the first place, I wish to thank Luisa Passerini for being around and providing us with ideas and constructive criticism—and for a conversation in Turin where we finally recognized that though we may think we differ, we don't look so very different when seen from a distance. It was essential for me to maintain a dialogue with the friends on the editorial boards of *História y fuente oral*—Mercedes Vilanova, Pilar Gómez (also for intense conversations in Granada and in New Mexico), Cristina Borderías—and the *International Yearbook of Oral History and Life Stories*—Paul Thompson and Luisa again, and Selma Leydersdorff and Daniel Bertaux. With the student collective with which I worked at Villa Mirafiori—Micaela Arcidiacono, Francesca Battisti, Sonia Di Loreto, Carlo Martinez, and Elena Spandri—I shared years of work, discovery, and growth. The shifting, frustrating, exciting community around the Circolo Gianni Bosio, the Istituto Ernesto de Martino, *I Giorni Cantati*—Alfredo Martini, Susanna Cerboni, Cesare Bermani, and many others—are such an integral part of my life that any word of thanks is ridiculously inadequate. And many ideas and formulations that wound up in these pages first took shape in the conversations and exchanges with Mary Marshall Clarke, Alistair Thomson, and Lutz Niethammer during unforgettable days in Brazil.

As always, all oral history is ultimately authored by the so-called informants, or narrators, or interviewees, or whatever inadequate label we use to define the persons from whom we receive our knowledge. There is less fieldwork and more self-reflexivity in this book; therefore, I will thank all of the people who gave me their time and their words through some of those who made me more conscious of who I was and what I was doing: Ms. Julia Cowans, Lodovica Mutarelli, and Giulio R., the homeless activist on the Esquilino hill so long ago, whose last name I was too inexperienced to even get on the tape.

This book is dedicated to Franco Coggiola and Nicola Gallerano.

In 1979, at the Istituto Ernesto de Martino in Milan, Franco Coggiola gave me my first Uher tape recorder. It was a rite of initiation, the sign that I was going to be serious about fieldwork. That same year, we spent days and nights together working at an anthology of the folk music recordings in the Istituto's archives that later became the prize-winning double album *L'Italia degli anni '70*. During one of those long hours, Franco told me a fantasy of his. "When I grow old," he said, "I want to retire into some mountain valley of the Piedmont Alps, and wait for an ethnomusicologist to discover me. And then, sing to him all the songs I know." A fantastic traditional singer who never cared to be on the stage, Franco knew enough songs to dazzle anyone—from the traditional ballads of his native Piedmont (that he had helped rediscover) to American IWW songs and the repertoire of folk singers throughout Italy. He was one of the comrades who identify entirely with collective projects rather than personal rewards. He was discreetly but importantly active in support of Third World liberation movements, and he was the stable force that kept the Istituto De Martino going in the good and bad years. His work is embedded in all the series of the Dischi del Sole, but his signature rarely appears. Franco Coggiola died, too soon, in May 1996.

In 1978, Nicola Gallerano asked me to give an informal talk at the Rome Institute for the History of the Resistance (of which he was president between the late 1980s and the 1990s) on the work I had been doing on oral history. On that occasion, I presented for the first time the papers on the death of Luigi Trastulli and the battle of Poggio Bustone, and my ideas on narrative and imagination. It was Nicola Gallerano who insisted that I publish the paper on youth culture that has been revised to become chapter 14 in this book. At least three other chapters of this book (8, 9, 13) were either presented at or prepared for conferences conceived and organized by Nicola Gallerano. Because of the alienation of urban and academic life, our friendship never developed very far beyond the reciprocal good vibrations. But Nicola was the only "regular" historian who lent a supportive and critical ear to my oral history work for all of twenty years; it was his presence that has kept me going back to the Institute for the History of the Resistance ever since that first informal gathering. If he meant so much to me, even though I was on the margin of his work and life, I can only imagine what he meant to many others. Nicola Gallerano also died suddenly in April 1996. I wish to dedicate this book to him.

Part I

On the Practice
of Oral History

Chapter One

Oral History as Genre

A CLUSTER OF GENRES: GENRE IN ORAL HISTORY, ORAL HISTORY AS GENRE

As the term itself implies, oral history is a specific form of discourse: history evokes a narrative of the past, and oral indicates a medium of expression. In the development of oral history as a field of study, much attention has been devoted to its linguistic and narrative dimensions.[1] Most of this work, however, has been concerned with the analysis of the source, that is, of the speech and performance of the interviewees. Research, in other words, has focused mostly on genre *in* oral history: the use of folklore and anecdote; the influence of other oral or written forms of discourse such as epic, the novel, or mass media; the analogies and differences between orality and writing, and so on.[2]

On the other hand, oral historians have become increasingly aware that oral history is a dialogic discourse, created not only by what the interviewees say, but also by what we as historians do—by the historian's presence in the field, and by the historian's presentation of the material. The expression *oral history* therefore contains an ambivalence that I will intentionally retain in this paper: it refers both to what the historians *hear* (the oral sources) and to what the historians *say* or *write*. On a more cogent plane, it refers what the source and the historian do *together* at the moment of their encounter in the interview.

The complexity of oral history as a sequence of verbal processes and constructs generated by cultural and personal encounters in the context of fieldwork between the narrator(s) and the historian, derives to a large extent from the rich heteroglossia resulting from a dialogic shaping of discourse.[3] Oral history is therefore a composite genre, which calls for a stratified critical approach: in addition to the uses of genre in the collected discourse of the narrator(s), we need also to recognize genre in the public discourse of the historian, and genre in the space between them. If

3

we define genre as a verbal construct shaped by shared verbal devices—whether conventionally established or not—oral history is then both a genre of narrative and historical discourse, and a cluster of genres, some shared with other types of discourse, some peculiar to itself. In this chapter, therefore, I will begin with a few preliminary comments on aspects of genre *in* oral history, and then go on to oral history *as* genre and to genres *in* oral history.

UNTOLD STORIES, TWICE-TOLD TALES

I remember sitting in Santino Cappanera's parlor in Terni, Italy, taping an interview about his life as a steel worker and political activist.[4] His teenage daughter was in the next room, doing her homework. After about twenty minutes, she had moved her chair to the hall, outside the parlor; a little while later, she was standing by the door; about one hour into the interview, she came and sat next to us, listening.

What is spoken in a typical oral history interview has usually never been told *in that form* before. Most personal or family tales are told in pieces and episodes, when the occasion arises; we learn even the lives of our closest relatives by fragments, repetitions, hearsay. Many stories or anecdotes may have been told many times within a narrator's immediate circle, but the whole story has hardly ever been told in sequence as a coherent and organized whole. The grandparent who takes a grandchild on his or her knee and tells the story of his or her life is a literary fiction.[5] The life story as a full, coherent oral narrative does not exist in nature; it is a synthetic product of social science—but no less precious for that. No wonder Santino Cappanera's daughter listened. Her father's boring anecdotes were becoming "history" before her eyes.

Cappanera's narrative also acquired status and importance, in his own eyes as well as his daughter's, because of the interview itself. In fact, even when stories have been told before, they have never been told to that special listener and questioner who is the oral history interviewer. The interview implicitly enhances the authority and self-awareness of the narrator, and may raise questions about aspects of experience that the speaker has never spoken or even seriously thought about.

Thus, an oral history interview tends to be a story untold, even if largely made up of twice-told tales, and the speaker tends to strive for the best possible diction. The novelty of the situation and the effort at diction accentuate a feature of all oral discourse—that of being a "text"[6] in the making, which includes its own drafts, preparatory materials, and discarded attempts. There will be gradual approaches in search of a theme, not unlike musical glissando; conversational repairs and after-the-fact corrections, for the sake either of accuracy or of pragmatic effectiveness; incremental repetitions for the sake of completeness and accuracy, or of dramatic effect. This personal effort at composition in performance[7] is supported by the use of socialized linguistic matter (clichés, formulas, folklore, frozen anecdotes, commonplaces) and by the example of genres derived from writing (the novel, autobiography, history books) or mass media. These established blocks of discourse define secure paths in the uncharted territory of discourse, much like the invisible but rigid airways that guide airplanes in the fluid territory of the sky: I remember the story (a legend, perhaps) about a dock worker in Civitavecchia (near Rome), who was speechless in front of the intellectuals in his Party meetings until he realized he could speak in rhymes, and found his voice.

Between the fluid textual experiments and the frozen formulaic material, the "achieved" discourse breaks through and floats like a moving island, the tip of an iceberg. In order to understand how the narrative is shaped, we must not limit ourselves to these moments of fulfillment; we need to consider also the formulaic materials, the apparently formless connecting and supporting matter, and the dialogic and directive role of the historian.

Though oral history may avail itself of all other recognized and unrecognized genres of oral discourse, from the proverb to the epic poem, yet it is distinct from them all, both for its composite internal structure (a genre of genres), and for its peculiar cultural positioning. While the genres of oral expression and cultures serve their function within the world of orality, oral history begins in the orality of the narrator but is directed towards (and concluded by) the written text of the historian. Oral narrators are aware of this written destination, and bear it in mind as they shape their performance; on the other hand, the task of the oral historian is to write in such a way that readers are constantly reminded of the oral origins of the text they are reading. In the end, we might define oral history as the genre of discourse which orality and writing have developed jointly in order to speak to each other about the past.

HISTORY-TELLING: WHAT IS ORAL HISTORY ABOUT?

As Jean-Marie Schaeffer notes, the classification of speech acts, and of genres of discourse in particular, depends on a fivefold question: *"Who says what in which channel to whom with what effect?"*[8] Taking this phrase as my pattern, I will begin with *what*.

In theory (and in practice), oral history can be about anything; open-endedness at all levels is one of its distinctive formal characteristics. I believe, however, that at the core of oral history, in epistemological and in practical terms, lies one deep thematic focus, which distinguishes it from other approaches and disciplines also based on interviewing and fieldwork, such as anthropology, sociology, and folklore: the combination of the prevalence of the narrative form on the one hand, and the search for a connection between biography and history, between individual experience and the transformations of society, on the other. Elsewhere, I describe this genre of discourse as *history-telling:* a cousin of storytelling, but distinct from it because of its broader narrative range and dialogic formation.[9]

The questions How historical is private life? and How personal is history? may be asked by the narrator, by the historian, or by both; indeed, the issue of what is private and what is public in a person's narrative is often uncertain, especially if we are after the elusive theme of the history of private life. For instance, listening to Maggiorina Mattioli, an old seamstress in Terni, I realized that there was more history in her personal love story than in her reminiscences about the anti-Fascist underground.[10] However that may be, oral history expresses the awareness of the historicity of personal experience and of the individual's role in the history of society and in public events: wars, revolutions, strikes, floods (as in the work of Selma Leydersdorff), and earthquakes (as in the work of Eugenia Meyer).[11]

A by-product of this generic focus is that oral history is more intrinsically itself when it listens to speakers who are not already recognized protagonists in the public sphere. An interview with a chief of state about her political career is, of course, very legitimate oral history, but verges toward more established genres of historical writing.[12]

Genre, then, depends to a large extent on the shifting balance between the personal and the social, between biography and history. *Life and times* is a cliché definition of biography and autobiography in general (*Life and Times of Frederick Douglass,* for one);[13] according to where the scales tip between the *life* and the *times,* oral history shifts between performance-oriented *narrative* and content-oriented *document,* between subject-oriented *life story* and theme-oriented *testimony.* In practice, oral history stays mostly in between: its role is precisely to connect life to times, uniqueness to representativeness, as well as orality to writing. The key word in *life and times* is the one in the middle.

At the core of the narrative created by the classic oral history interview and by the classic oral history text, therefore, we find motifs and themes that insist on the relationship of the individual and the public. For instance, narrators everywhere relish narratives of "standing up to the big man," theatrical anecdotes of personal confrontations with figures of institutional authority in which workers stand up to bosses (especially in stories of union negotiations), rank and file to leaders, students to teachers, soldiers to officers, in complex representations of personal courage, professional pride, or political resistance.[14]

The most common narrative of this kind, of course, is the war narrative. As we know, it is hard to keep any (male) informant from expounding about what he did in the war (or in the service). War embodies history in the most obvious schoolbook sense of the word; having been in the war is the most immediately tangible claim for having been in history. Even in peacetime, the military is the most immediately accessible experience of the public sphere. As Antonio Gibelli points out, participation in the military institution and in war is a crucial passage in the life of the rural masses, marking their entrance into the public sphere and contact with the organization and technology of the modern state.[15] Since the era of air raids, civilians have their own war tales, too: as an old woman explained to me once, in World War I "they fought among themselves out there," but in World War II "we all were involved."[16]

For these reasons, war stories are a recognized thematic genre, with specific formal characteristics, in literature, history, autobiography, and film.[17] Oral history, however, features other narratives that play a similar role but are less commonly recognized. For instance, while I was working on my oral history of Terni, I realized that there were two types of stories that seemed so commonplace that I did not even bother to transcribe them from the tapes: men's stories about war and military service, and women's stories about health and hospitals. It was only later that I began to wonder whether a functional analogy lay behind this parallel exclusion—if, in other words, the genre of the hospital tale may be for women what the genre of the war story is for men.

Hospital tales—especially about assisting hospitalized family members—are in fact one way for women to talk about their effect on the public sphere. Like men at war, they leave their homes to deal with death (playing the mythic roles, respectively, of healers and warriors); like the draftees, they face the state in its bureaucratic and technological aspects; they deal with hierarchies, machinery, and science; and they "stand up to the big man": to doctors, administrators, and their own relatives—usually, males. As Prue Chamberlaine and Annette King put it, in West German women's narratives, "Hospitals form a politically salient meeting ground of public authority and personal intimacy"; narrators often confront this authority structure: "Here the theme is how, an uneducated nobody, encouraged by women in my neighborhood, I gained the determination and confidence to confront the negligence and high-handedness of the doctors." [18]

Hospital tales, then, constitute a coherent, if largely unrecognized, narrative genre, found with little variation across national, cultural, and linguistic boundaries. While the tellers of military tales relish the use of technical language about weaponry and ranking, women struggle with the esoteric language of the medical environment: Giuseppina Migliosi, a seamstress from Terni, has a hard time articulating *commozione cerebrale* (concussion of the brain); Appalachian women in Eastern Kentucky pronounce *autopsy* as *artòpsy* and naturalize *Alzheimer's disease* as *old timer's disease*. Migliosi hitches a ride to leave home to go see her husband in the hospital after a motorcycle accident; Debbie Spicer, a coal miner's wife in Harlan, Kentucky, hires an ambulance to take her husband to a better hospital in a city where she has never been. Spicer contends with the incompetence and carelessness of the medical staff, and Migliosi fights the bureaucracy in the hospital and in the war office in Rome in order to obtain her husband's X rays, have his disability recognized, and get his pension released. Both graphically represent the ambiguous relationship between the powerlessness of their hospitalized husbands, and their own empowerment. Spicer handles her husband like a baby: "They just had him on the table for a long time, and didn't do anything and he had trouble with his bowels and they didn't know it, so his bowels moved. . . . And I washed him, cleaned him up, and spread some towels over him so he wouldn't get too cold till I came back with his pyjamas, and when I came back I put his pyjamas on." Migliosi is forced, and enabled, to take control after the accident turns her husband from an authoritarian male (a policeman and a militant Fascist) to a vegetating body ("a concussion of the brain, fractured skull, all bandaged over, his arms, his head, everything, only his nose and mouth were [in sight]") and a dependent brain- and speech-impaired invalid. [19]

Perhaps war stories are a universally recognized genre and hospital stories are not because wars are "events," while nurturing in hospitals is a continuing function. This fact tells us, however, a great deal about established and gender-determined definitions of what is history and what is not, who is in it and who is not. By enabling us to hear both genres and to identify their relationship, oral history helps us to overcome these prejudices.

WHO SPEAKS TO WHOM? INTERROGATION AND THICK DIALOGUE

There is no oral history before the encounter of two different subjects, one with a story to tell and the other with a history to reconstruct. We tend to forget, however, that the first person who speaks in an oral history interview is usually not the interviewee, but the interviewer.[20] In a very concrete sense, the source's narrative can be seen always as a response to the historian's initial questions: "When were you born?" "Tell me about your life" "Who was the union secretary at that time?"

By opening the conversation, the interviewer defines the roles and establishes the basis of narrative authority. In fact, although an oral autobiographical narrative may look on the surface very much like any other autobiographical *text,* it constitutes a very different autobiographical *act,* because the basis of authority is different. Autobiography (especially if written for publication) begins with a person's decision to write about herself or himself, but in the interview, the initiative is taken by the interviewer, from whom the legitimacy to speak is ostensibly derived. The right to speak, especially about oneself, is not automatically assumed, especially among the socially disadvantaged groups to which oral historians most frequently address themselves. In folklore, authority is derived mainly from tradition; in literary or historical autobiography, it is derived from the person's sense of her or his own importance or ability, which justifies the implicit breach of modesty. In oral history, however, the process of legitimation is more complex. Typical beginnings, such as "I have nothing to say," or even "What do you want me to say,"[21] may be coy maneuverings, but they may also indicate that the narrator feels entitled to speak only because of a mandate from the interviewer: I only speak because you ask me to (and, often, I will say what you want to hear).

Thus, first-person narratives beginning with "I was born" belong in fact to very different genres, because they are the result of very different processes of authorization.[22] When we compare Benjamin Franklin's "I have ever had a pleasure in obtaining any little anecdotes of my ancestors . . ." with Giuseppina Migliosi's "To begin with everything I know: my folks moved from Cesena to Terni," we cannot ignore that the former is a statesman and scientist who has spoken in public all his life (and coyly pretends to be writing a private letter to his son), while the other is ostensibly speaking, in her private parlor, only because her niece and a polite visitor have insisted that she do so. When we take this aspect into account, we recognize the import of the fact that Franklin begins with "I," while Migliosi begins with "my family": the basis of legitimation is different. Consider the following examples also:

> I was born in the city of Cork, Ireland, in 1830. My people were poor. For generations they had fought for Ireland's freedom. Many of my folks have died in that struggle.

> Let us begin with this business. Well, I was born in Terni. Son of a railroad man; son of a railroad man. And—I lost my father at the age of ten.

In the former example (an as-told-to autobiography), the great radical Irish-American unionist, Mary "Mother" Jones, boldly talks about herself because she feels that her long and brave life entitles her to do so. In the second example, as the deictic expression "this business" suggests, the anarchist factory worker Riziero Manconi is responding to an external stimulus, namely, my request: "We would like you to tell us about your life, your personal and political development, what the environment in which you were born and grew up was like, and then go on to your working life and your political activity."[23]

Requests like these set the agenda for the interview and begin to shape its form: the chronological order, the relevant themes (work, politics), the interaction of individual and society ("the environment in which you . . . grew up"). Of course, a political activist and class-conscious worker like Manconi would have spoken about these things anyway (he also talked about things I had not asked about, such as his literary efforts). But—and this is the point—if a different person had opened the conversation with a different question, Manconi would have spoken different words and in a different order.

Both subjects bring to the interview an agenda of their own, which is constantly renegotiated in the course of the conversation. In the case of Giuseppina Migliosi, for instance, I did not want to hear her hospital story, but she felt that, history or not, it had to be told. Maggiorina Mattioli wanted to talk about her love story and I wanted to hear about anti-Fascism; and, once again, she was right. Of course, interviewees *will* talk about really irrelevant private matters, but we should listen and wait, before we judge. For the oral historian, an interview is always a learning experience.

This negotiation, in turn, generates formal variations. In order to retain the floor and have their say, speakers may (like Migliosi) ignore the interviewers' lack of interest, and launch into a straight monologue,[24] or try to win their listeners' attention by dialogic narrative techniques, as Mattioli did by telling her love story with anxious and skilful incremental repetition.[25]

The exchange of questions and answers defines generic variations in several other ways. An interview can shift from a one-way *questionnaire* to *thick dialogue*, according to how much space questions allow for the answers, and to the way in which the answers act upon the questions. In a judicial interrogation or a sociological questionnaire, the informant's answer to a given question may not influence either the form or the order of the questions to follow, but in a thick dialogue, questions arise dialectically from the answers. Once again, it is important to state that neither form is "better" than the other; rather, they are suited to different ends: comparability and factuality in the questionnaire, individuality and subjectivity in the thick, open-ended dialogue. The point here is that different forms of exchange generate different genres of discourse.[26]

The social and personal relationship between the two speaking subjects also plays a role. While interviewing coal miners in Kentucky, I was a "furriner" from "across the waters"; when interviewing the students of my own department in Rome, I was a part of the environment I was investigating. One consequence is that the Kentucky interviews emphasize storytelling and history-telling, with a great deal of straight information and narrative, while the Rome interviews read like tentative essays, replete with commentary, evaluation, and analysis (one verbal clue of this generic difference is the higher density of deixis and allusion, and the diminished attention to chronology in the student interviews). While this has something to do with intrinsic cultural differences (the Appalachian habit of couching concepts in narrative, versus the abstract training of philosophy majors), it also shows that the form of the interview depends on the extent to which the interviewer belongs to the reality under investigation: narrators will assume that a "native" historian already knows the facts, and will furnish explanations, theories, and judgments instead.

Now, as Dennis Tedlock noted, Franz Boas used to warn his students precisely against this type of interview: beware, he taught, of "intelligent Indians" who may have "formed a theory" about the research in progress. Tedlock juxtaposes this injunction against theorizing informants to Margaret Mead's intimation against interfering researchers: "The fieldworker is not in the field to talk but to listen" and should never "express complicated ideas of his own that will muddle the natives' accounts."[27] A fearful symmetry structures this hierarchic separation between the interviewer's *ideas* and the informant's *account*. The fiction of noninterference turns the dialogue into two monologues: informants supply a monologue of brute facts, while historians and anthropologists will supply—later, from the safety of their desks—a monologue of sophisticated ideas that the informant never hears about.

However, human beings, including "native informants," never speak without attempting to form an idea, a theory, of what they are speaking about, to whom, and why. The stereotype of the "dumb Indian" at least exists in the hegemonic imagination, but the concept of a "dumb philosopher" sounds like a contradiction in terms—if not necessarily in fact. A student reversed the flow of discourse by asking a question: "Can I ask a question, too? How did you become a professor, anyway?"[28] A folk singer near Rome formed an opinion about me by noticing the newspaper I had on the back seat of my car. The less the historians reveal about their identity and thoughts, the more likely informants are to couch their testimony in the broadest and safest terms, and to stick to the more superficial layers of their conscience and the more public and official aspects of their culture.[29]

This, of course, is perfectly legitimate if it is what we are looking for. What a culture will most readily tell about itself, what people feel to be the safest form of self-presentation, can be very revealing. On the other hand, a critical, challenging, even a (respectfully) antagonistic interviewer may induce the narrator to open up and reveal less easily accessible layers of personal knowledge, belief, and experience. An informant's dissent from his or her own culture is more likely to emerge when speaking to a dissenting interviewer. One cannot expect informants to tell the truth about themselves if we start out by deceiving them about ourselves. Fascists and capitalists who knew which side I was on often gave me much more vivid and motivated accounts and explanations than if they had blandly assumed I shared their party or class line. Thus, what the interviewer reveals about him or herself is ultimately relevant in orienting the interview toward monologue or self-reflexive thick dialogue.

The myth of noninterference concerns one of the most delicate turns in the passage from field testimony to published text: transforming the informants' speech from one directed to a *determined* addressee, the fieldworker, to one addressed to an *undetermined* and multiple one, the historian's audience. In the opening page of Zora Neale Hurston's *Mules and Men*, her account of a folklore-gathering expedition to her native village of Eatonville, the narrators ask: "Who you reckon want to hear all them old-time tales about Brer Rabbit and Brer Bear?" While they recognize the person who *is listening* ("Well, if it ain't Zora Hurston!"), they don't know who *will read:* the shift from empirical addressee to un-determined implied audience is underscored by Hurston's vague answer: "Plenty of people."[30]

Hurston chooses to retain the traces of the dialogic experience and the personal addressee by foregrounding her presence throughout the book. In more standard works of folklore, anthropology, sociology, and in much oral history, however, the tendency prevails to efface the historian's presence both from the field situation and from the published text, in the attempt to create the fiction that the informant is speaking directly to the reader, and—just like a book—would have spoken in the same way to anyone. Thus, a *personal exchange* becomes a *public statement,* which may be a perfectly legitimate process when this is the effect both parties are looking for (as in the case of "as-told-to" autobiographies of politicians or movie stars).[31] In this case, the writer acts as hired medium through which the speaker writes; in scholarly work, however, the historian speaks through the sources, quoting their words to make a point, and using their artificial textuality to enhance the authority of historical discourse.

Ultimately, in fact, the shift from determined to undetermined addressee is part of the process by which a *performance* is turned into a *text:* a legitimate, indeed necessary process, which begins when the speaker's ephemeral words are fixed on tape or film, to be later transcribed, edited, and published. This brings us to the next question.

THROUGH WHAT CHANNELS? BIOGRAPHY AND MONTAGE

The most immediate difference between a field interview and any other conversation is that in the interview the voices go through some kind of machine: a tape recorder, a camera, or at least a notebook. This acts as a moderating influence on the narrator's perception of the interviewer: the presence of the machine indicates that these words will be repeated, elsewhere, to an absent undetermined audience (hence the ethical requirement always to display the equipment). Technical aspects—the placing of a microphone, the lighting used for video—may incline the interview toward the genre of personal dialogic exchange or that of monologic public statement; in turn, the channels through which this dialogue is made available to the public (akin to Northrop Frye's "radical of presentation") orient the generic definition of the historians' discourse.

In 1972, during a train trip, I turned my tape recorder on in the midst of informal talk with Amerigo Matteucci, a construction worker, mayor of the village of Polino (near Terni), and extraordinary history-teller. Twenty

years later, a local film group taped a video interview with him. The stories and the words were surprisingly consistent (in part because since our
interview he had repeated them in public many times), but the shift from
personal exchange to public statement was clear.[32] In the videotape, Matteucci wore his best clothes, sat at his mayor's desk, and spoke into the
camera a monologue to an invisible audience. His voice was flatter; his
body language (lost to my audio tape, but vivid in my memory) stiffer. On
the other hand, *some* body language and facial expression were at least
visible. Because he was much more aware of speaking in public, and because the fact of filming implies more preparation, he was more coherent
and clear, and the video was a nearly finished product, while my tape required much editing. Once again, my purpose is not to claim that one
form is better than another. A conscious public presentation of self is as
much a part of a culture as a spontaneous, unguarded utterance, but they
are different genres of discourse, and are better served (or more actively
stimulated) by different channels of collection and transmission.

It is beyond the scope of this paper to delineate a theory of oral history
on video or film.[33] I have neither the data nor the competence; besides, I
feel that, since *oral* history implies a centrality of language and sound,
audio tape is closer to its semantic focus. I would like, however, to make
some tentative remarks for future research, based on the video interviews
I have seen.

- The camera has more impact on the interviewer than on the
  interviewee. While the interviewee may shift genres, the interviewer
  tends to disappear altogether. Audio picks up both voices more or
  less equally, but the camera does not dwell equally on both subjects
  (often, the fiction of noninterference induces the interviewer to stay
  out of range entirely).[34]
- There is less time. The visual forms of publication, cinema or TV
  documentary, are usually more compressed than books. While visual
  information is enhanced, verbal space is reduced. It takes more
  courage on the filmmaker's part to include in the finished product
  what I have called the "preparatory materials" of the oral
  performance and to retain the tempo of the narrators. The
  temptation of selecting the "achieved" conclusions, the brief,
  effective statement—the sound bite—is very strong. This reinforces
  the drift from personal exchange to public statement.
- Rather than through the historian's voice, the meaning is
  transmitted mostly through montage (for some reason, voice-over in
  visual presentations is thought to be more authoritarian than the
  historian's voice in books). The result is both more pluralistic

(sources seem to speak for themselves, and all on the same plane)
and more authoritarian (the hand that coordinates and pieces them
together remains invisible). Which aspect prevails depends, to a great
extent, on the sensitivity and professional skill of the filmmaker.[35]
As Paula Rabinowitz has put it in a different context,
"Documentaries that repress the presence of the documentarian's
voice or body posit a natural truth captured at random in words or
images and seemingly open to direct consumption by the
audience."[36]

Ultimately, as far as I have been able to see, we have failed to consistently develop an *analytical,* let alone a *scholarly* form of video presentation, which would necessarily include such devices as stopped frames, slow
motion, repetition, electronic elaboration of images, and, yes, the historian's taking responsibility to speak and interpret in an open, if not authoritarian, manner, as one voice and presence among others in the visual text. Multimedia approaches are likely to generate the same problems
(and some possible solutions) in the near future.

Oral history, however, circulates most often in writing (an irony which
is not lost on its critics, and on most of its practitioners). There are as
many ways of translating orality into writing—transcribing, editing,
writing, publishing oral history—as there are ways of collecting it, and
their generic variety also shifts from project to project, from one disci-
plinary area to another. There is no all-purpose transcript; rather, there
are many specialized transcripts for different subgenres of oral history
discourse. It is one thing to transcribe for a linguistic study of phonet-
ics, and another to transcribe for a project of narrative history. The
same applies to editing: Is it intended to reproduce as carefully as possible the actual sounds of the spoken word, or to make the spoken word
accessible to readers through the written medium? "Accuracy" is recognized unanimously as the aim of all transcribing and editing, but the
term is not easy to define univocally: a transcript so minutely faithful to
sounds that it turns a beautiful speech into an unreadable page can
hardly be described as "accurate." Perhaps the old pun—*traduttore traditore,* "translator traitor"—also applies to the creative job of translating words from speech through tape to page, by exercising selection,
choice, even artistic judgment, in harmony with our interpretation of
what we hear and with our strategy of presentation. Perhaps nowhere
more than in transcription (and editing) is the correlation of form to
aim and genre so stringent.

I will consider here three major genre-defining parameters in the publication of oral history: (1) the scope of the narrative, (2) the representation and continuation of the dialogic experience and of the oral performance, and (3) the intended audience. One other parameter—the intended effect on the reader—will be considered in the final paragraph.

Although oral history is often associated with "microhistory" because of its focus on individual lives and its mode of transmission,[37] the work of oral historians varies widely. The range of characters may go from an individual's life story to the choral reconstruction of a process involving millions of people;[38] the geographic scope may be a workplace, a neighborhood, a town, an international phenomenon;[39] the time period may vary from thirty minutes to one or two centuries.[40] An in-depth life story, a collection of interviews, an interpretive essay on a historical period[41] are all *oral history,* but they are not the same thing; rather, they represent different genres with very different rhetorical strategies.

The most immediately visible generic consequence of the scope of the research concerns the presentation of voices: Who speaks in these books? How many voices are included, and how are they broken down and put together? A work of oral history may be concerned with one voice (an individual's life story) or with many; in the latter case, these may be presented as a series of monologues, or intertwined into a thematic or chronological montage.[42] The shift between monologue and polyphony also changes the interpretative approach. An individual life story is a different genre from a book in which a number of interviewees are presented one after the other as a series of monologues (with or without a general introduction, or introductory sketches to each piece), and both are different from a chronological or thematic montage of interview excerpts.

Thus, two apparently similar books on the same topic, the Vietnam War, may display very different strategies of presentation and interpretation. Both Mark Baker's *Nam* and Wallace Terry's *Bloods: An Oral History of the Vietnam War by Black Veterans* present the interviews as distinct monologues; however, while *Bloods* retains the integrity of the individual life stories, *Nam* subdivides the narratives into thematic sections. Thus, *Bloods* places the Vietnam experience in each individual's life cycle, while *Nam* attempts the reconstruction of a collective, and therefore anonymous, experience. While both display a strategy of objectivity (the interviewer's voice is silenced), the voices of the sources interact in different ways with that of the historian through the form of the presentation and the paratext.[43]

Which leads us to the second parameter: The relationship of these voices to the voice of the historian. To what extent does the publication continue or represent the dialogue and the performance? What is, in each case, the balance between *oral* and *history*, the mode of transmission and factual reconstruction?

If we take five examples from Italy we can see that, while they are all legitimate forms of historical work, the ways of handling the source's speech and the historian's voice are so different that they define very different genres of oral history. Nuto Revelli's books—*Il mondo dei vinti, L'anello forte*—are based on a rigorous distinction of voices: the historian writes rich, informative, sensitively self-reflexive introductions, after which we read the edited testimony of the informants, one after the other, individually. The narrators are allowed to speak at length about themselves, and the interpretation is left to the reader, within the framework designed in the introduction. Documentary objectivity in the arrangement of voice is displayed in order to enhance the subjective pathos of each narrative.[44]

Luisa Passerini's *Torino operaia e il fascismo* is an example of how oral history can be used to produce excellent history without adjectives.[45] Passerini performs a sophisticated reading of the testimony as well as of written archival sources, framed in a tight historical narrative. The interviews are quoted in the same way as historical documents: as textual verifications of a historical interpretation. The book's approach, however, is specific to oral history because it is centered on the reconstruction of subjectivity. While the orality of the sources is scarcely thematized, and little advantage is taken of the possibilities of narrative and linguistic analysis, the "oral" remains essential to the success of this book as "history," through the category of subjectivity.

In Maurizio Gribaudi's *Mondo operaio e mito operaio*,[46] the opposition between "world" and "myth," the effort to bring out factual reality and dispel ideological delusions, leads to an ancillary use of a limited number of oral sources as repositories of mainly factual information about economic strategies and demographic trajectories. The words of the interviewees are hardly quoted at all, and are interpreted rather cursorily, with scarcely any attention to the language, the narrative form, and their less explicit meanings. The balance between "oral" and "history" leans heavily toward the more established forms of the latter. Indeed, this book has been described as a case of "total devaluation of any significance of oral sources."[47]

My *Biografia di una città* is perhaps at the opposite end of the spectrum. An intense use of montage and bricolage of sources (including archival ones) foregrounds polyphony and dialogue. The historian ostensibly speaks as little as possible—providing connections, briefly suggesting ways of reading—yet is very much in control, and at key moments enters the stage to include the experience of the interview as a key to its meaning.[48] The minute fragmentation and recomposition of the voices (and their interaction with other sources) is recreated to convey the dialogic experience of a town's story told by many voices, less as objective reproduction than as creative representation. The models are derived less from history and sociology than from literature (Dos Passos, Conrad, Faulkner), cinema, music (the alternation of solos, arias, recitativo, choral, and orchestral pieces of the baroque oratory). While factual events of history provide the skeleton of the narrative, its meaning lies almost entirely in the lower frequencies of the oral communication.

The most intense and self-reflexive dialogue between the sources and the historian, finally, is represented in another work by Luisa Passerini, *Autoritratto di gruppo*.[49] Weaving oral histories of the student movement of 1968 with the history of her research and the analysis of the interviews, as well as with her own autobiography and psychoanalysis, Passerini creates an original synthesis of autobiography and historiography, psychoanalysis, social history, and literature, which is a new genre altogether. No wonder that this book has also inspired a form of presentation to which oral history seems to lend itself very successfully: a theater performance.[50]

This raises the final question: to whom do these texts speak? Again, the generic spectrum ranges from collections of interviews intended for a broad audience (such as Studs Terkel's excellent books) to scholarly papers meant for selected groups of colleagues at international conferences, or for publication in academic journals with a specialized audience. Another parameter concerns the question of "restitution": does the intended audience include the social circle of the narrators, and what responsibility does the text take on their behalf?

The latter question has been mostly discussed in ethical terms;[51] however, as in the rest of this paper, I am interested here in the linguistic and formal consequences. Speaking to specialists implies the use of a more rigorously technical language (including bibliographies, footnotes, etc.); speaking to the community or to the general public requires a more pointed effort toward communication; the former will be more interpretative, the latter more narrative. Ironically, the originary orality of the sources tends to be retained much more extensively in works not intended primarily for a scholarly audience.

Speaking to the community, or targeting a broad, nonacademic audience, then, does not necessarily subtract from the quality of the work. One of the things that make oral history different is its democratic potential, which can make an oral history project academically relevant at the same time that it is accessible to the general public, not only through readable books, but also through community projects, exhibits, and—as already noted—film, video, the theater.[52] Rhetorical strategies vary significantly, however. An academic audience is almost a captive one: its attention is assumed for professional reasons. In the case of the community or the general public, attention must be gained and retained—or, if the word does not offend—*entertained*. This opens the question on which I would like to end this discussion: What is the intended effect of oral history on its listeners and readers? In other words, Is there an aesthetics of oral history, and what does it mean?

TO WHAT EFFECT? BEAUTY AND TRUTH

In his autobiography, the American writer Paul Bowles recalls meeting in Tangiers a local person, a guard, with whom he struck up an acquaintance: "A few anecdotes he told about his life impressed me deeply, not with their unusual content, but because of the way in which he recounted them. His rhetorical sense was extraordinary; he knew exactly which nuances and details to include in order to make a tale complete and convincing."[53]

It seems, then, that there are two bases for legitimation in telling a life story: either the life is meaningful, or the story is well told (the ideal, of course, is to combine both). The distinction is recognizable in the field of written autobiography: Mother Jones and Big Bill Haywood, historic leaders of labor, publish the stories of their lives as straight autobiography, based on the importance of their achievements and the documentary truth of their testimony. Jack Conroy and Woody Guthrie, rank-and-file workers, also write the stories of their lives, but publish them as fiction, because the basis of legitimation, their most important achievement, is their ability as storytellers.[54] Paul Bowles planned to publish his friend's stories as oral history, but he found a publisher only when he agreed to let them be labeled as a novel. Though they were true stories, what was valuable in them was less the truth than the beauty.

Genre distinctions, as we know, are often blurred in oral performance: narrators do not always stick to a rigid distinction between a true story or a good story; they may be after narrative pleasure while the historian is after hard facts. What do we, as historians, do with the aesthetic project of many narrators, with the beauty incorporated in so many of the stories we hear? Do we, as purveyors of truth, expunge these features from our work (thus, of course, maiming the authenticity of the document), or do we recognize them as also *facts* in their own right, to be acknowledged and used? The way in which the narrators' voices are included in the historian's book also depends on whether the effect that the book is striving for is one of material factuality, or whether the aesthetic value of a good story, invented or not, is taken as a sign of cultural or individual subjectivity, and whether the historian attempts to convey to the reader also some of the aesthetic revelations or pleasures experienced in listening to oral history. In the apparent opposition of truth and beauty, perhaps beauty can be, rather than superfluous ornament, another—and perhaps the only possible—way of telling other truths.

In his autobiography, narrated through the poet John Neihardt, the Sioux holy man Black Elk makes this point several times: "Whether it happened so or not I do not know; but if you think about it you can see that it is true"; or, "Watanye said the story happened just as he told it, and maybe it did. If it did not, it could have, just as well as not."[55] Just as in many of the stories we hear, Black Elk heard in these tales not the truth of material events, but the truth of religious symbol and the truth of possibility: in other words, the special truth of the work of art. Sometimes, this truth told in beauty can also illuminate through symbol and feeling our understanding of history. I will close with one such example.

Dante Bartolini was a singer, a poet, and a storyteller; his work has been an inspiration to me since our first encounter, and is featured at several points in this book as well as in my other writings. He had been a factory worker and a guerrilla fighter in the anti-Fascist resistance; he was also a herb doctor, a barman, a farmer, a killer and dresser of hogs. The day I first met him, he introduced the singing of his partisan songs with a brief historical narrative. The hieratic tones, the carefully timed pauses, the solemn rhythm, conveyed to the story the quality of epic poetry. The facts, however, were all wrong.

> The eight of September, nineteen hundred and forty-three
> the armistice was announced
> the defeat of Fascism and Nazism.
> The battle of Stalingrad
> was the end for the Germans.
> Von Paulus, the commander of the German army
> surrendered after a month of fighting.
> And the war ended.

However,
[the Fascists] reorganized their little Republic in the North.
And we
anti-Fascists
immediately arranged to take up arms.

The weapons factory in Terni.
We went
thousands of workers
we broke through the gates
thrust them wide open
we seized the weapons
some of them
and then we left
for the mountains.[56]

September 8, 1943, is not the date of the German surrender at Stalingrad, but of Italy's separate peace with the allies and of the dissolution of the Italian army and state. Although the Resistance struggle began immediately after that date, the partisans did not obtain their weapons by breaking into factories. If all we were looking for was factual information, this interview would be useless (it would be so even if it was accurate: we don't need Bartolini's testimony to know about Stalingrad). On the other hand, we stand to learn a great deal if we listen to it as the poetic, ritual representation of the meaning of a historical experience, based on the materialization of two metaphors.

The first metaphor is "taking up arms," repeated as "We seized the weapons" (the two sound the same in Italian). The beginning of the partisan movement after September 8 can indeed be described as an act of *taking up arms:* the scene described by Bartolini substantiates a linguistic formula. Yet, it is not invented outright: Bartolini was one of the workers (a small group, not "thousands") who broke into the guard rooms at the steel works and raided the guns, not in 1943, but in 1949, in the nearly insurrectional mood that followed the attempted murder of Palmiro Togliatti, national secretary of the Communist Party. By merging the two events, the narrator establishes a symbolic but real continuity between the Resistance of 1943–44 and the mass protest of 1949: maybe the Resistance wasn't finished yet, and the wounding of Togliatti demonstrated that armed struggle was still necessary; or, conversely, maybe the Resistance is over, and any episode of armed struggle has to be pushed back in memory to a time when it was legitimate.

In the second place, by setting the beginning of the struggle in the factory, Bartolini underlines the class nature of the anti-Fascist movement in Terni: even if the struggle was fought in the mountains, the partisans derived their "weapons"—especially their conscience and solidarity—from the factory, the space where their class consciousness was formed and the continuity of anti-Fascism secured.

The second metaphor is a complex, two-sided one: "We broke through the gates / Thrust them wide open." Breaking the gates is a standard image of liberation; it is, however, most frequently represented as breaking *out*, from prison to freedom. In this case, instead, Bartolini describes the workers breaking *in* to the factory. In the former sense, then, the metaphor describes the Resistance as liberation from political oppression; in the latter, as economic liberation, the workers repossessing the nation's wealth: the epic of the Bastille (prisoners breaking out) combines with the epic of the Winter Palace (revolutionaries breaking in). Freedom and socialism are but two sides of the same metaphor: this is the poetic/political meaning we can *feel* in Dante Bartolini's narrative, if we only listen.

The way we perceive this passage depends on the way we hear it, and the way we hear it and interpret it shapes the way we represent it on the written page. Following Dennis Tedlock's instructions, I have transcribed it so as to follow the rhythmic quality of the voice: if it looks like a poem on the page, it is because, as Tedlock has shown, there is a close relationship between oral history and poetry.[57] This transcription, then, draws our attention both to the sound quality of the performance, and to its poetic, metaphoric implications.

On the other hand, the deeper theme of the performance is memory: it preserves and conveys an image of the past, and in order to do so, freezes it somewhat by the very solemnity of the words and the tone. At one level, Bartolini declares that the Resistance is unfinished, and suggests we should continue it; at another, he projects it into a special epoch in the past, and suggests we commemorate it. If we wished to underscore the latter aspect, we could do so by transcribing it as follows:

> The eight of September, nineteen hundred and forty-three
> The armistice was announced
> The defeat of Fascism and Nazism.
> The battle of Stalingrad
> Was the end for the Germans . . .

Merely shifting the disposition of the words on the page turns Bartolini's narrative from poem to epigraph: a monument, a verbal icon to the Resistance (I have been tempted to write the date, a typical incipit in commemorative epigraphs, in Roman numerals). The passage hesitates between historical statement, epic poem, and monument; the way readers understand it depends to a large extent on the historian's decision to transcribe it, respectively, as linear prose, verse, or epigraph. That these genres coexist in mutual tension in the same words is a tribute to the creative complexity of oral narrative; that we must choose among them as we transcribe is a sign of the responsibilities we take upon ourselves as historians.

Chapter Two

There's Gonna Always Be a Line
History-Telling as a Multivocal Art

A MULTIVOCAL ART

History-telling is a form of verbal art generated by the cultural and personal encounter in the context of fieldwork.[1] It differs from more traditional forms of storytelling in narrative range, and in the kind and degree of audience involvement. The narrative range is wider: prompted by the interviewer, the history-teller weaves personal recollections into a broader historical background, and is encouraged to expand the tale toward a full-sized oral autobiography, in which the self-contained narrative units of anecdotes or tales are included in a more complex framework. In terms of audience involvement, while all oral speech acts and verbal arts imply a degree of interaction, history-telling differs in the following ways:

1. The interviewer is not usually a member of the speaker's immediate circle. Thus, mutual discovery is intrinsic to history-telling: the interviewer tries to learn the history of the interviewee, while the interviewee tries to figure out who the interviewer is, and how to deal with her or him.

2. The interviewer is an especially active listener, who has not only created the history-telling situation, but shapes it by asking questions that are much more directive than the antiphonal audience reactions of traditional storytelling. Often, in fact, the interviewer will ask unexpected questions, encouraging the history-teller to explore new areas of experience, or to verbalize explicitly what is taken for granted and remains unsaid when speaking to members of the immediate community. A good interviewer facilitates the history-teller's agenda and overall strategy, but a good history-teller subtly shapes the tale according to the presence and manner of the interviewer. To a degree much higher than in other oral verbal arts, history-telling is a multiauthored, multivocal genre.

3. Storytelling is a direct tapping of existing, outcropping memory; history-telling, as a cooperative effort between several narrators or between them and the interviewer, is an attempt to *reconstruct* memory. Thus, in a history-telling situation, participant listeners will prompt the principal narrator's memory ("Tell him about the time when you . . .") or take narrative turns themselves in order to achieve a more complete reconstruction of the group's memory (as in *Black Elk Speaks,* in which the protagonist's narrative is occasionally supplemented by those of his friends).[2] While storytelling is largely an end in itself, history-telling aims at the production of an artifact (a tape) and eventually a text.

These differences result in a different use of space: rather than the single speaker facing a circle of listeners, or a circle of speakers, history-telling is staged face-to-face between narrator and interviewer, or even as a circle of narrators facing a usually lone listener/interviewer, across a space mediated by the strategic placement of a microphone.

"YOU'RE FREE TO TAPE JUS' WHAT YOU WANT"

In this chapter I will use as my text one interview, in which two narrators— a man and a woman, husband and wife—tell about life in the coalfields of Harlan County, Kentucky, from the 1930s to the present, with a wealth of detail and an extraordinary command of style and language. Oral history is usually keen to frame individual stories in the collective discourse which is history. But by concentrating on one interview, I hope to show that an oral personal narrative can achieve levels of structural complexity comparable to those of literary texts, and can therefore stand the close individual analysis we usually devote to written literature, while retaining its cultural and generic difference.

I sought out Reverend Hugh and Mrs. Julia Cowans in Lexington, Kentucky, in September, 1983, because friends at the Highlander Center for Social Research told me they were both very fine speakers, singers, and organizers for the union and the civil rights movement. Rev. Cowans had worked many years in the coal mines of Kentucky and Virginia, until he lost his sight from the consequences of an old war wound; a few years later, he received the call to preach. I went to see them on a Sunday afternoon. They lived in a nice house in a middle-class area (they were the only black family I saw on the block; they have since moved back to the black section downtown). At least three generations of children, grandchildren and great-grandchildren kept coming and going through the living room. Also, my wife and another woman, a graduate student from the University of Rome, were with me. The context was halfway between a formal interview and a social visit, culminating in a dinner of fried chicken.

This was my first interview in the Appalachian project, so I was there to listen, rather than to assert a specific agenda of questions I wanted to ask. In fact, it was Reverend Cowans who asked the first question: "You in the United Mine Workers?" After I explained that I was a union member back home, the history-telling could begin.

> Now, you all. Now you're free to tape jus' what you want. I mean.
> First of all, I mean, you know, I'll just let you know my name.
> My name is Reverend Hugh Cowans, Junior and I reside at 3753
> Marriot Drive. And you have come for information and I'll readily
> give it to you. Now back in the thirties when I started in the coal
> mines, I was nothin' but a boy. I hadn't reached my, I had not
> reached my thirteenth birthday—fourteenth birthday, rather, you
> know, because, at that time, you could go in the mines, they'd
> take you at any age.[3]

Rev. Cowans went on for about forty-five minutes, without pauses or interruptions; the conversation then lasted all afternoon. The monologic form of the first section was shaped by several factors: Rev. Cowans's experience in public speaking as a preacher and organizer; his blindness, which made it easier for him to abstract himself from his listeners; and the fact that we, as interviewers, did not yet ask any interrupting questions. He delivered, then, what was largely a set piece, a public performance, which developed into a more personal dialogue only after his wife entered the conversation.

In his opening monologue, Rev. Cowans told the story of his life not in linear fashion, but cyclically, shuttling twice back and forth from "back in the thirties" to the present, and breaking the second cycle into two distinct parts—before and after he quit work in the mines. His speech may thus be divided in three sections, in which shifts in the handling of time and narrative form designate shifting layers of personal experience, from public history told in the third person to more personal biography in the first person.

HISTORY-TELLING AND NARRATIVE MODES

In earlier articles, I have described three modes of history-telling, that is, three ways of organizing historical narrative in terms of point of view, social, and spatial referents:

1. Institutional
   - Social referent: politics and ideology; government, parties, unions, elections, and so on
   - Spatial referent: the nation, the state
   - Point of view: third person, impersonal
2. Communal
   - Social referent: the community, the neighborhood, the job; strikes, natural catastrophes, rituals; collective participation at the institutional level
   - Spatial referent: the town, the neighborhood, the workplace;
   - Point of view: first person plural
3. Personal
   - Social referent: private and family life; the life cycle: births, marriages, jobs, children, deaths; personal involvement in the two other levels
   - Spatial referent: the home
   - Point of view: first person singular.[4]

These modes are never totally and explicitly separate, or separable, in oral history narrative; in fact, history-telling is precisely the art of combining the modes into meaningful patterns. Also, their characteristics are more a matter of tendency than of norm: each history-telling event is unique and creates its own style and grammar. We may, however, use these categories as a map to orient ourselves in the analysis.

Each of the three sections of Rev. Cowans' opening narrative is controlled by a different mode: first the institutional, then the communal, and finally the personal, with frequent overlappings but with a recognizable overall pattern. As we listen to the first section, we can see that it is dominated by the impersonal pronouns and iterative verbal forms of the institutional mode:

> And you worked under all kinds of, oppressive conditions. I mean,
> no organized labor and they had gun thugs. Now what we mean by
> that, they would go to the high sheriff of the county. He would
> deputize'um, and then the company would pay their salary. That was
> in ordinance to keep United Mine Workers OUT.

The iterative form ("they would go") and the impersonal pronouns ("they," "you") designate a general and lasting condition. First-person pronouns and singulative verbs are introduced in anecdotes intended as examples of this broader situation; the narrator then quickly reverts to the impersonal iterative:

> And if you joined it, they would come in and beat your head and
> throw your family outdoors and throw you off the job and everything.
> I remember once on the job that they had my uncle to pull 'is britches
> down and they whipped'im right before my face. And if you had to lay
> off, you had to lay off in the mines, they didn't allow you to lay off at
> home.

The social referent is the union as political institution, with emphasis on the leadership. Rev. Cowans begins by associating himself to the top leaders—"And we were glad when John L. Lewis came along and God sent the man along in, uh, '37–'38 because I was instrumental in the drive, I was one of the leaders of that organization"—and concludes with a discussion of the current leadership crisis in the union:

> I'm sorry that all o' this corruptness come about in the organization,
> but that happens everywhere, you can look at Washington right now.
> The chief of corruption is right there. And some of it sprung from the
> Oval Office . . . And I feel sorry for our president Rich Trumka . . .
> And I don't know what is going to happen 'cause when Reagan taken
> office, he went in bustin' union . . . I mean, all he cares about is the
> rich, ya' understand? And we are at, roughly, a deep-end. It's just
> about to go over it. If God don't help us, I mean, we're sold out.

Having reached the present, Rev. Cowans goes back to the beginning and tells his story all over again in the very next sentence. But he now shifts to the first-person singular point of view: "I have gone in the mines now, I want you to hear this good." He uses the first person consistently from now on, and soon shifts also from iterative synthesis to linear narrative ("Going on forward, I had many things happen to me") and to singulative verbs: "I had left Harlan County where I was instrumental in organizing . . . Left Harlan in '40, and I went to Gary, West Virginia, June—oh, I don't exactly—June 1940. And I started driving mules in the mine."

This second section is an interesting combination of the communal and personal modes. In fact, while Rev. Cowans uses the first-person pronoun of the personal mode, the spatial and social referents are those of the communal mode: the union local, the workplace. While the first cycle was the story of how the union changed the coal mines, the second section is the story of a representative working life. By combining the two modes, Rev. Cowans manages to project his own image as a representative man. On the one hand, he is a representative worker, who shares the experiences of others like him and knows his job: "I said I could do anything around [a coal mine]—and could. I could help on 'lectricity, I said I could lay track, I can timber, I said I can help on the motor, machine, anything you have to." On the other hand, as an organizer in the union, he is also an institutional "representative" of the collectivity of the miners. This section, in fact, includes a variant of the typical standing-up-to-the-boss story that recurs in stories of organizers and celebrated working men.[5] And again he brings it up to the present by comparing the ethnic composition of the work force in the mines in the '30s and today.

So far, the working life had dominated the narrative. We have seen that he begins the story of his life—as many male working-class narrators do—not with the day he was born, but with his first working day.[6] Symmetrically, the second section ends with "the last shift of work I performed was August 31, 1956." In the third section, although the narrative goes forward in chronological terms, the mode shifts dramatically. As he tells about losing his sight, leaving the mines, haggling with the Veterans Administration, and being called to preach, Rev. Cowans no longer tells a story of political and union struggles, but one of intense personal struggle for identity and survival. Now the story is no longer about John L. Lewis, president Reagan, or the mine management, but about his eyes and his God:

> And from then I kept moving and I had not accepted my callin' in
> the ministry. But eventually the Lord bear down so heavy. And I, just
> one day backed in—that was in '60—I just backed my automobile in
> the driveway. And the doctors always did predict I'd lose my sight.
> I just backed my automobile in the driveway and woke up the next
> morning blind as a bat. But the Lord has been good to me. He brought
> us thus far.

The spatial referents again shift toward the personal mode: the hospital, a very important space in personal narratives; and the home: "We lived in a house in Harlan. It was a rent house." Symmetrically, the stories of confrontation no longer deal with bosses, but with landladies.

"NOW, I DON'T WANT YOU PREACHIN'"

"And this is where we are today," Rev. Cowans concluded for the third time. And he yielded the floor to his wife: "Is that right, baby? That's right. And she know because she was raised up on the coal cabin. She may have something she might wanna add. Do you have something, baby, you might wanna add?"

This, in fact, is where I asked my first question, mentioning that I had heard that they had met for the first time when they stood on opposite sides of a picket line. So Rev. Cowans resumed the floor to tell that story, and again asked, "Do you have, do you wanna say anything?" "Well, not really," Mrs. Cowans replied—and then she took over and spoke for almost thirty minutes.

> I mean, I, I was born and raised by there in Cardinal, Kentucky, down South, up in the mountains there, Bell County. That's the only life, you know, that I knew was coal mining. My father, grandfather, great-grandfather—they were all coal miners. And, as my husband said, when I was growing up, the coal mining was just very bad. You didn't really live, you just existed, just existed.

Mrs. Cowans's time and space referents are different from her husband's. Her life story does not begin with getting a job but with being born, and in her narrative there is no break comparable to the "last shift" of work. In her experience, life and working life are never totally distinct. She was never formally employed outside the home and, symmetrically, she is never unemployed, even in her old age, inside the home. Even in her old age, she is helping to raise more than one generation of grandchildren. Her only outside work was domestic work, a continuation of what she did at home:

> Fourteen years old, I had to come out o' school and take care of my mother, my four sisters and brothers. And you know I wasn't trained for anything, all domestic, you know. I knew how to keep house. And that's how I took care of my mother, my sisters and brothers—on my knees, scrubbing floors, climbing walls, just whatever I could do. And I worked all day long for one dollar. One dollar. I mean I worked all day long.

In this part of her narrative, however, the mode is communal rather than personal, and the spatial referent is the town rather than the home. She did not volunteer (and we did not feel entitled to ask for) much information about children and marriages, partly because we were strangers, but also because of her husband's presence. When interviewed alone, five years later, she was much more forthcoming about these topics. Also, she understood immediately that our approach was social and political, rather than personal, and felt she was giving us what she thought we wanted, as well as staying on safer ground.

The coal camp had been absent from her husband's story: his community was the workplace, not the town. The male-female symmetry of spatial referents in this interview followed the division of experiences in the mining community, where the men spent most of the time underground, while the women had to deal with the surface world:

> My mother would send me to the store, you know, the grocery and I never remember axing for but a dollar. One dollar. I've never gone to the window say two dollars, three, five dollars . . . Whatever you had to have, you go to that company store and buy it. You did not leave off of that company property to go to the next town to buy anything and bring it back in there. No, you didn't do that. And that kept the persons more or less, especially if you had a family of any size, that kept you in debt, all the time, you know, you just stayed in debt. Work a lifetime and be in debt to the company, you know. And some of the old coal camps, they had fences. They had guards to let you in there and guards to let you out . . . Like a concentration camp or something . . . And we grew up under those conditions.

Her description of the coal camp, however, is also a way of explaining why she had been on the other side, throwing rocks at the union pickets, when she met her husband. While Rev. Cowans uses personal stories as examples of a general condition, she uses the communal background to make sense of her personal behavior: she threw rocks at the picket because the employers' power extended to the control of what their workers knew and believed. "Whatever the company officials said, that was the law. . . . And all we knew was they were comin' to stop the men from workin', you know. That's all we knew about it. And so I used to get a bunch of kids and we'd line up and get us a pile o' rocks and we'd see them comin' and we start throwin' rocks at 'em, you know." When she recalled having to seek outside domestic work, she explained that "there were no human resources, no welfare, no nothing in Kentucky, that I know about, at that time." Her tale, indeed, was much closer to the form of history-telling that I was looking for: making politics and social conditions come alive through their impact on individual lives.

From this moment on, Mrs. Cowans was firmly in command of the conversation. She delegated to her husband—to whom she deferred openly and sincerely throughout—all discourse in the institutional mode, either by giving him the floor, or by telling stories in which he played the central role. On the other hand, she successfully resisted her husband's attempt to regain control of the general drift of discourse. Though she allowed him to interrupt her, and frequently invited him to speak, yet she was in control: it was she who prompted his memory, suggested topics and episodes, and managed the timing and form of his contributions:

> *Rev. Cowans:*   Baby, let me say somethin'.
> *Mrs. Cowans:*   Now, I don't want you preachin'; lemme hear.
> *Rev. Cowans:*   I'm not gonna preach. I just wanna tell ya . . .

In this, she was helped by the fact that we as interviewers were much more responsive to her approach, and encouraged it by our occasional questions. The result was a much more multivocal, interactive discourse, in which all participants took an active and explicit role.

PLACES OF MEMORY

In this multivocal discourse, the handling of time becomes more erratic than in the two monologues. Rather than the earlier combination of cyclical and linear structures, we find a free flow of nonchronological associations. This is, in fact, the more frequent form in oral history interviews, determined by the interplay of the structure of memory and the dialogue situation.

In memory, time becomes "place": all the recollected past exists simultaneously in the space of the mind. Speakers therefore may tend to arrange events along paradigmatic lines of similarity rather than along syntagmatic lines of chronological sequence. From the strike of 1939, Mrs. Cowans shifted to the Brookside strike of 1973, and Rev. Cowans associated the 1938 union drive to the national miners' strike of 1978.

A more complex form is the multivocal association generated by the interaction of different speakers in conversation. In a typical sequence, a story told by Rev. Cowans about a speech he made in Detroit prompted me to ask him a question about preaching—which in turn unleashed a reminiscence of childhood on an Alabama plantation: "And you see, to make a good minister, you got to bring things to people's remembrance. I remember that now and then that when we worked on the farm and [were] boys down there—you had to go to the plantation owner . . ." The story thus begun evolved into a sermon fragment, which drifted into a speech on civil rights and then into stories about his work in the movement. At this point, Mrs. Cowans was reminded of other powerful speeches he had made, and she took us all the way back to the Detroit speech we had started out with.

In all this free association, however, an underlying structure remains unchanged: the vision of history as a contrast between a generalized "then" and a generalized "now." The watershed between these two epochs is the rise of the union in the coalfields: the past is "before they became organized." Stories about the rising of the union—the organizing drive of 1938, the dramatic strike of 1939–are, therefore, pivotal to the whole structure of the conversation, and both narrators keep going back to them. We might define these events as "places of memory,"[7] and their significance as such is also revealed by the formal organization of the narrative. In the stories about these watershed events, all modes—institutional, communal, personal—come together, as if all meanings converged there. The first-person point of view, the communal spatial referents of town and workplace, and the institutional social referents of union and government all intermingle in Rev. Cowans's story of the union drive: "They [the union] came and the first mass meeting we had was at Verda, Kentucky. That's where I worked." All three pronominal forms—*they, we, I*—are concentrated in this opening statement. He then goes on:

> It was a fellow called Chester Smith. He had a large pasture out there and he built a flat fo 'em and we had many speeches. And we would go and try to get individuals to sign a check-off slip. That was in ordinance to set up a local. And you'd crawl, and I'd crawl up in men's places [in the mine] on my knees and beg them to sign the cut-off slip. And they would cuss me out. But eventually . . . we were victorious, after I guess you can recall—when Mr. John L. Lewis had gone into Washington, that time.

As Mrs. Cowans tells about those times, she also weaves the personal mode (mother and home) together with the communal (the miners, the town) and the institutional (the National Guard, the governor):

> You jus' certainly wouldn't believe it . . . but before they got organized . . . Harlan County blood ran like water. Many a man lost their lives . . . and, oh, they were slaughtered like hogs. I remember right there in Cardinal, baby, when governor Chandler, Happy Chandler, sent those tin horns [National Guard] in 'ere to guard those, what they call

scabs, in the mine and out. My mother used to take in washings and
ironing. And she did they laundry, you know . . . my mother used to
do the laundry for these soldiers that were there . . .

The pivotal function of this "place of memory" is shown by the fact
that this is where the narrative becomes most movingly bivocal. Both narrators take the floor, swapping back and forth, reinforcing each other's
testimony with converging points of view: "I faced the machine guns that
morning," Rev. Cowans breaks in. "You see, we had a women's local in
Cardinal, Kentucky. And their son was manning the machine guns. And
we sent for them. And they came down the road with clubs in their hands
singing Amazing Grace and all o' these spiritual songs. And one woman
looked up from singin' her songs and she said, 'What you doing up
there?' . . . And she got him off that machine gun . . ." After he has told
this story, he gives the floor back to his wife: "Sorry, I just wanted to . . .
go ahead." As she resumes, the story connects back to her early antiunion
days, and forward to the women's role in the Brookside strike of the 1970s:
"And we had women picket lines. I gone on a picket line after, you know,
growing and knowing what this was all about . . . And we takin' coffee
and doughnuts to the men—you know about this Brookside episode, that
Brookside deal. Well, we were just about three miles above this at that
time."

"THERE'S GONNA ALWAYS BE A LINE"

In many oral history narratives, all modes converge not only on pivotal
events, but also on crucial themes. War, for instance, has such a total impact that it can be narrated in all modes: "Mussolini ruined the country"
(institutional); "Our town was destroyed" (communal); "I lost a son" (personal). In the Cowans's interview, all modes converged on another pervasive theme: race.

In Rev. Cowans's opening monologue, each section contains a reference to racial discrimination. The first occurs when he is describing the
impact of unionism. It is a personal anecdote, told in the framework of
the political, institutional discourse.

My father, he's passed and gone now, he told me, says, uh, "You're
crazy to go on those picket lines. You'll get killed." He said, "It's not
going to benefit anybody but the white man." I says, "Well, I know it
will benefit him more than it benefits me, but I see some good in that
for you and I see some in it for me. In your old age I see, I see medical

benefits, I see retirement, and everything, I says, although, I said I
know that it is discriminatory practice in it, but it's better than what
we have working in those water holes and slave conditions. And, sure
enough, when he reached the age of retirement, he had medical
benefits. He died drawing his pension. Now I've lived up to the age
where I draw my pension. And there's nothin' better than United Mine
Workers.

At the end of the second section, the reconstruction of his working life,
Rev. Cowans takes time for another comparison between then and now.
This time, it has to do with the presence of blacks in the social space of
the workplace:

Now if you were black, back when I went in the mines and there was
stevedore work, you got your job. All the man wanted to know [was]:
if you were black, you get a job. If you were white you probably were
layin' track or you were running a motor. Very few blacks operated the
motors then. They, if you worked on a motor at all, you had to be a
brakeman. And my father, he was a machine operator. And they would
put whites with him to learn 'em how to operate the machines, and
after he learned them, then he was subject to be fired. . . . And, when
the mantrip used to run,[8] y'all believe it or not, the mantrip looked like
a bunch o'blackbirds. But now when it run, it look like a flock of geese,
white. You might see one black in there that looks like a fly.

Rev. Cowans concludes his speech with a final reference to racism, which
stresses again the political approach, and an optimistic view in the then-
and-now framework: "But now although there is prejudice within the ranks
of the United Mine Workers, but here is the best thing for the working
man in the mine because all of these issues can be straightened out, and
it is somewhat better now than it was a long time ago." Throughout his
performance, Rev. Cowans never discusses racism in the personal mode,
its impact of racism on his own life and feelings. Only later, after his wife
has shifted the mode, does he tell a story with a personal spatial referent,
about a white lady who refused to rent to them when she found out they
were black.

When Mrs. Cowans begins to speak, she shifts the discourse on race
from the institutional to the personal mode, from politics to feelings. At
first, she also speaks in rather abstract terms, about the KKK, divisions in
the civil rights movement and in the black community, and the NAACP.
Then there is a sudden change of pace: "And we've been—I'll tell you another thing. We've been—'we' as a race—we been oppressed." The change

is palpable also on the linguistic plane, in the shift from the Standard English "we've been" to the black English "we been." As she goes on to describe the discrimination and exclusion of black people in Harlan County, and her struggle, along with her husband, against these conditions, the communal forms and referents are animated by a deeply personal urgency of feelings, revealed by the gushing of words and the intensity of her tone:

> And I'll be da- . . . And if I have to die for standing up for what I
> believe in, that's just the way it'll be. 'Cause fear if, if—see, that's what
> it's about anyhow, they rule you with fear, that's what they did to us—
> threats and fears . . . 'Cause I, I, I, I would rather be dead than to live
> under the oppressive condi—I don't want my children and
> grandchildren to come under what I did, what I had to come through.

Finally, as if making another conscious decision to escalate, she touches where it hurts most, at the very personal level of sexual politics, of lynching, miscegenation, the white fear of rape. "And I'll tell you anytime . . . anytime that they wanted to have, to have trouble, bring trouble with the minorities, they'd use a black man and a white woman." When a nephew of hers is involved with a white girl, and the family is threatened, she says,

> I told 'em at a meeting, I said, now, I'll tell ya right now, if you think
> you prejudiced, I said, you just meetin' prejudiced. That's 'cause I
> don't want my daughter to marry your son anymore than you want
> your son to marry my daughter . . . I said, that's just the way I'm
> raised. I'm, I'm black. God didn't make no mistake when he made me,
> I said. I didn't make myself. He made me what he wanted me to
> be. . . . But now I'm telling you, I don't want my son to have your
> daughter any more than you want your daughter to have my son. . . . I
> said, ain't nobody gonna drag my son or my daughter out, like they
> have done and, and, and hang them or whatever. I said, have been a
> time that this happened, didn't nobody die but black. I said, but,
> brother, you better believe that if they bury somebody black, they
> gonna bury somebody white. I said, you'd better believe that.

It is a long way from the blandly optimistic view of evolving race relations in the union to a dramatic confrontation with lynching. This progression, from the institutional to the personal mode, is shaped to a large extent by another factor: the interpersonal authorship of history-telling. Race is not only a pervasive element in the black experience, but is also a very touchy subject when black history-tellers are interviewed by white historians. The formulaic "I'll tell you," which marks each new step in Mrs. Cowans' narrative, signals also a new step in the relationship—as if

she had either decided that she could talk to us, or that certain things needed
to be told anyway. In the passage in which Mrs. Cowans confronted the
deepest roots of her feeling toward white people, the historical discourse
mingled with an implicit statement about the interview:

> My grandma they, they—she was a daughter of—s-s-slaves. Her
> parents were slaves. And they used to sit around and tell things, you
> know, that happened when they were children and what they parents
> said. And I'll tell you what that will do for you: although you might
> not have done a thing in this world to me, but because you're white,
> of what my parents said . . . I don't trust you, you know. And so for
> being misused by a white person, I've never been. But I've seen
> conditions of others, you know—[of] blacks as a whole—So I was
> raised; my grandmother always told us I don't care what nobody say, I
> don't care how good they look, how good they talk, you gonna always
> be black. There's gonna always be a line.

In saying, "I don't trust you," she is ostensibly, and perhaps intentionally, speaking in general terms, using the impersonal *you*. But I could not
help feeling that this broad, political mode was indissolubly twined with
a very personal, immediate mode: she was talking in general, but she was
also talking to me.

In several passages later in the conversation, Mrs. Cowans endeavoured
to attenuate the impact of this statement by historicizing it. "So, that's
what I had in mind all of my life. OK, but as you live, time changes, see
. . ." "And so when God changed my heart towards a lot of things, then
I could see better. And learn to just love people because you're you, not
because you black." In my second visit, five years later, she was hospita-
ble, talkative, eloquent. But it was said, it remained said, and it was the
most important lesson I learned that day.

One part of the lesson was political: Why, indeed, should she trust me,
just because I may have acted and spoken nicely and sympathetically? As
a character in Toni Morrison's *Beloved* puts it, "Nothing in the world
more dangerous than a white schoolteacher."9 There's gonna always be
a line, Mrs. Cowans said. It takes more than good will and good manners
to overcome the historical barrier between blacks and whites—and I had
learned from Richard Wright's Mary Dalton that it is not up to me to decide when I can be allowed to step across. Perhaps one reason for her relative openness may have been, indeed, that we showed no inclination to
invade her territory.

Another part of the lesson was methodological. The concept of a "line"
is intimately related to writing, and thus evokes the fact that my own role

in the multiauthored and multivocal enterprise begun with Rev. and Mrs. Cowans's narrative was to write it down, turning history-telling into oral history and literary text, which can be distanced from the original narrators and performers. On the one hand, the line is also a class line (between the coal miner's wife and the intellectual); on the other, it stands as the boundary between orality and writing: a written trace of the absence of the voice. Indeed, the polysemy of *line* roots the very concept of geographical and social boundaries in a primary reference to writing. In an essay on resistance to enclosures in South Africa, Isabel Hofmeyr demonstrates that "fencing . . . has a number of cultural functions that are not unrelated to the preconceptions of literacy":

> Fences, for example, "write" certain forms of authority into the
> countryside, and by representing the thin, fixed line of the boundary in
> the earth, they imprint the textual world of maps, treaties, and
> surveying on the landscape. While oral or, more precisely, paraliterate
> societies obviously recognize and mark boundaries, these are always
> fluid and have none of the fixity of the pencil-thin boundary of the
> sheer, narrow fence. Since boundaries are never rigid and, in any
> event, have to be accommodated to the character of the landscape,
> they are always subject to some form of negotiation.[10]

Thus, the interplay of line as metaphor and line as writing points to a complex question of representation: the braiding of "artificiality" and "reality." Ultimately, the line itself becomes a physical *lieu de mémoire*. On the map, the Kentucky-Tennessee line just southwest of Harlan County across Cumberland Gap looks just like a "pencil-thin" straight line across uncharted territory; on the other side of the county, however, the Kentucky-Virginia border follows the winding, natural outline of the mountain ridges. By now, the "written" Tennessee line is no less real than the physical Virginia line: history has its own way of making the artificial real. This also applies to Mrs. Cowans's line: "You don't even be aware of this prejudice," she said, "'til you become a certain age and the parents go to separatin', you know." But just because the line is artificial is no reason to pretend it isn't there. As W. E. B. DuBois put it long ago, "The problem of the twentieth century is the problem of the color line," and it's still with us.[11]

One of the clichés of field work is that the interviewer must endeavor to win the confidence and trust of the interviewee, and to a certain extent this happened also in our encounter with the Cowans. But the plural authorship of history-telling requires a plurality of subjects, and therefore a degree of difference. Thus, much of the eloquence and drama of the interview was generated precisely by the awareness of the distance and difference that still stood between us. When Mrs. Cowans said, "I don't trust you," in one breath she both drew the line and erased the line; as she declared her inability to ignore the line, by recognizing it openly, she was already speaking across it.

Chapter Three

Memory and Resistance
For a History (and Celebration) of the Circolo Gianni Bosio

This chapter was presented at the opening of the seminar entitled "Memory and Human Resistance: Twenty Years of the Circolo Gianni Bosio," in Rome (Dec. 16–19, 1991). Unfortunately, the seminar was the last project the Circolo (a Rome-based activist cultural collective for research in folklore, oral history, and people's culture, named after the great radical historian and ethnologist who was proud to call himself only a "cultural organizer") was able to carry out.[1] With this speech, I thought I had come to praise the group; instead, I came to bury it. Still, as Huck Finn says, it is mostly a true story.

TRUTH AND STORYTELLING

> You don't have anything
> if you don't have the stories.
> Their evil is mighty
> but it can't stand up to our stories.
> So they try to destroy the stories
> let the stories be confused or forgotten.
> They would like that
> They would be happy
> Because we would be defenseless then.
> —Leslie Marmon Silko, *Ceremony*

Stories, Leslie Marmon Silko explains, are the tools we need not just to survive, but to overcome. They are a protection that allows us to save ourselves, but also active instruments for changing the world—because there is power in words. They are made of air but leave their mark on material reality. I want to talk about the twenty-year history (1972–1992) of the Circolo Gianni Bosio, and I want to begin by telling a story. It is taken from the first issue, November 1993, of *I Giorni Cantati*, which was then our mimeographed bulletin on "worker and peasant culture" and lives today as a magazine of "people's cultures and mass cultures."[2] It was told to me by Leonardo Pulcini, a farmer living in a tiny village near the town of Leonessa, in Northern Lazio, on February 6, 1973.

> Here, everything used to belong to seven barons. Then, after a while, they released all the land because they saw it didn't pay, and left. And the reins of all the seven baronies were taken up by one baron, the one that lived over by Pianezza. He would take advantage of everything, plus he choked all his tenants and peasants. When the 29th of July came around,[3] over at Casanova, they had to bring all their cows, and the baron would pick the best ones for himself, he'd pick the best calves, and if the tenants said anything, it was free blows and beatings for all—he had five or six cut-throats, at his service, with cudgels and staffs and all. Then, the wheat: he had it basketed, weighed, selected. What was good went to him, the rest went to the tenants.
>
> Plus, the prettiest thing he did, was when you got married. He would keep her eight days. And if she was a virgin, it was all right; he'd keep her and then give her back to the one who married her. Else, it was blows. It was a bad life, I mean, in those days.
>
> Well, there was this young man, he lived at Pianezza, too. He was going to get married and he didn't like it for his girl—his wife, for he was going to marry her—to have to sleep with the baron. Each time he saw the baron, he almost felt like shooting him. So they begin to get organized, five or six young men: some who were going to get married; others who had married and the baron had waged this violence on them. And they decided to act on the 29th of July, when he was going to choke all the tenants, when all the cows on the plateau, all the sheep that existed then, and the best goats, you have to give them to the baron. If you had chickens, if you had farm tools, he took it all.
>
> This young man began to incite the other tenants. Four or five were already in league with him; others who were being choked and did not swallow the baron's violence easily, also joined. "If I start something, don't you worry, just give me a hand."
>
> When he began to hit the baron's guards, with his fists, with cudgels they had set aside, there was an explosion from all the tenants, who saw that he was beating up this poor baron and all his servants. Those four or five guards he had, they handled them and tied them up. And the baron jumped on his horse and made for Pianezza.

He stayed in Pianezza, under siege, until Christmas. He couldn't get away, because if they caught him they'd beat him up. And the tenants were running things their way. When Christmas came around, it snowed, heavily. The baron went to the blacksmith at Casanova, and the blacksmith told him, "I can shoe your horse, but you must bring the horse to the bake oven, where they make the bread, at night, so nobody sees you. You come round at nine or ten, and I'll shoe your horse," because there was snow on the ground. But when the blacksmith saw the horse, he put the shoes on it backwards.

There were ten more inches of snow on the ground. He had to wait for the snow storm to be over, then got on his horse and rode. He went across the mountain, and the horse went forward but the tracks were backward. In the morning, they discovered the baron had disappeared—"He's gone! he's gone!" They found the tracks on the side of the mountain, heading down. They said, "Let's just follow the tracks, and we'll find him." And the tracks took them to the bake oven. At the oven, they found that the horse had disappeared. "Damn it, he had his horse shoed backwards and fooled us." And they went back up the mountain after him. Meanwhile, he reached Cantalice, and they never caught up with him. At Cantalice he found the coaches from the Vatican, that had come to get him away. Soon as he arrived, he got on the coaches and left; they had fresh horses, and they couldn't catch up. And a baron was saved. And Leonessa was free.

It may not be a true story, at least as it was told; it contains too many folk motifs and stylemes to be factually credible. Also, I find no documentary confirmation. However, Leonardo Pulcini told it with the same intensity with which he told of when the war and the Resistance came to his village, and he was sheltering the partisans, and the Germans came and burned his house and killed his animals—the cows, the sheep he had, the best goats, chickens, farm tools—and the partisans escaped up the snow-covered mountain, just like the Baron of Pianezza. Indeed, in the lower frequencies (to borrow Ralph Ellison's phrase), it may be the same story.

Throughout its many changes and lives, the work of the Circolo Gianni Bosio consisted of a search for the truth of stories and songs, not in opposition to history, but in search of another kind of history. History, we had been taught, is facts, actual and objective events you can touch and see; stories, in contrast, are the tales, the people who tell them, the words they are made of, the knot of memory and imagination that turns material facts into cultural meanings. Stories, in other words, communicate what history means to human beings.

In this imaginary story, then, what counts is less the event told than the telling of the event. It may not be a true tale, but it was really told by a real person. It was not an anonymous "legend" in an impersonal "tradition" enshrined in a faceless "collective memory." It was, rather, the foundation myth through which Leonardo Pulcini, a big dark man, a farmer, and an oral poet, elaborates the memory of centuries of resistance which culminated in the Resistance of 1943–44 but did not begin and, as long as the story is told, will not end there.

To begin with, the truth of this story lies in its material detail: a specific landscape (the first word is "Here"); the rituals of the sharing of the crops (the tenants are left with the bad wheat, which is why this part of Italy was infamous for pellagra); the guards, who seem to come right out of the pages of Alessandro Manzoni; the poverty of the land, the crops that are scarce even before they are divided up; the economic and personal class violence (symbolized by the *jus primae noctis*); the origin of social rebellion in an individual's anger; and the generational implications, a revolt of young people against a custom their fathers had tolerated.

Next, truth is in the language. Leonardo Pulcini oscillates between *il barone* and *lu barone,* that is, between standard Italian and standard dialect, because this story does not belong to a timeless tradition, but is part of a dialogic discourse that resonates both with dialect roots and with the contemporary articulation of the school, of mass media, of the interviewer's own speech. The linguistic mix is the sign of an ongoing cultural change that is implicit in the very sound of the narrator's voice.

It makes sense, then, that moral judgment should be implicit in a linguistic formula. When the peasants begin to beat up "this poor baron and all his servants," on first hearing I took that adjective—*poor*—to be merely formulaic. Then I thought of a literary parallel. When Huckleberry Finn sees the Duke and the King tarred and feathered and run out of town on a rail, he cannot repress an impulse of pity: "I was sorry for them poor pitiful rascals," victims of the reciprocal cruelty of human beings.[4] The "poor baron" is an ironic oxymoron—how can a landed feudal baron be "poor"?—but the phrase also points to the human nature that the baron shares with the oppressed and persecuted peasants who rebel against him, and that the rebels, even in the act of rebellion, are capable of recognizing—as if they saw themselves, always beaten up by the baron's guards, in the baron now beaten up by them. After all, they know very well how the blows feel.

The reversed horse tracks are an image of the unmaking of power. Alone, in the snow, the defeated baron retreads the road that had turned him from a person to a landlord. He needs the help of a humble blacksmith, as if he were a refugee like the partisans Leonardo Pulcini sheltered. Unfortunately, at the end of his ride, the baron is met by the Vatican's coaches (another historical truth: the alliance of Church and aristocracy in the oppression of the peasants), that will make a courtier of him once more. Yet I love the story's double happy ending: "And a baron was saved. And Leonessa was free." The ending suggests that what counts is not revenge, not the punishment of a villain. What counts is freedom.

THE VOICES THAT COME FROM THE PRESENT

This story represents many of the things we learned and did in the twenty years of the Circolo Gianni Bosio.[5] Another story will help us understand them even better.

Sometime in the mid-1970s I was interviewed by a newspaper about our work on folk music, and I told the journalist about hearing the ancient ballad "Donna Lombarda" sung by an old lady at Rivodutri, a village near Rieti, not far from Leonessa.[6] When the article came out, the emphasis was on the fact that we were discovering these very ancient songs, echoes from the past. It bothered me, because what I had insisted on was not just that "Donna Lombarda" originated perhaps in the eighth century, but that it was being sung in the twentieth.

We began with folk music, but we weren't looking for elusive ur-versions, uncontaminated texts, genuine styles. We were interested in the contemporary life of the music, in the fact that those songs were still part of our own cultural landscape. Though old, though rural and poor, the lady from Rivodutri was my contemporary and, as Ernesto de Martino once put it, a citizen of my own country.[7] We were still free of the arrogance that listens only to what contemporary political newspeak calls "the new," the "emerging social subjects." We were, and are, willing to learn from everyone.

Of course, we weren't so superficial as to think it was irrelevant whether "Donna Lombarda" was an old song or a new one, or whether the story of the baron of Pianezza was fact or imagination. This positive datum, however, was not the goal of our research, but rather one of its terms. Only if we knew the history of our texts would we be able to reconstruct the changes and hybridizations that gave them their present shape. We never thought of memory as an archive, as a freezer that preserves data and meanings, but rather as a processor that transforms and elaborates them in osmotic fashion and yields ever new data and meanings that include the old ones—if only to deny or get rid of them. I would later discover Jurij Lotman's teaching, that forgetting is also part of remembering.[8]

For these reasons, we always worked to reconstruct the dialogue and the conflict between the new and the old, the received and the invented, the individual's word and that of the others. Politically, what counted was not whether the message was revolutionary or not; we believed that there is no revolution, no change, no democracy, without the ability and the effort to remember, to tell, to invent—without the elementary basis that is the exercise of the power of speech. It was not the unifying roots, but the diverging branches and the multiplicity of leaves (we called them "one hundred flowers" then); not—we would later learn—ethnic identity, but the myriad possibilities of diaspora.

This is why we were always attracted to hybrid genres: the *ottava rima* (the improvised poetry in eight-line stanzas, as in the canonical poems of Ludovico Ariosto and Torquato Tasso); parody; protest and topical songs. I remember a shepherd near Palestrina, in 1969, telling me that when he went out with the sheep, he would always "carry a sackful of books." Or Riccardo Colotti, a horse wrangler from Tarquinia, who held forth in the tavern, declaiming and explaining Dante's *Divine Comedy* to an audience of his peers and of students from Rome, and taught us all that the Hound announced by Dante, that shall rid the world of hunger and greed, "is this thing they call Communism."[9]

The *ottava rima* is located at the hinge between orality and writing, memory and invention, conservation and improvisation. It is the terrain where the illiterates lay their hands on the book—on the canonical works of Tasso, Ariosto, Giovanbattista Marino (and reshape Dante and Homer)—to appreciate their figurative "darkness" (Colotti), the difficulty that makes them precious, but also to appropriate them and contaminate them with their own imagination, language, and voice. The stanzas from Tasso and Ariosto, released from individual silent reading, sung and chanted competitively in public, are memorized both to preserve and exhibit them and to mine them as linguistic resources and formal models for improvising new verses.

The case of parody and of political songs is not much different. The work we did in Umbria, especially around Terni, in the 1970s, and which I continued in Kentucky in the 1980s, began with the discovery that in those places new topical songs were being created and performed to traditional tunes and formal modes: *stornello*, *ottava rima*, work song, as well as ballad and hymn. Indeed, the new themes and ideas could be expressed and communicated precisely because there were old forms available to give them shape. With relatively few touches, the traditional rural forms became vehicles for sharp commentaries on contemporary industrial reality.[10]

We were also aware that political songs were often the work of more or less "organic" intellectuals rather than rank-and-file workers, and that they used heterogeneous linguistic and musical materials lifted from mass culture and popular music, rather than traditional forms. Yet, rather than rejecting these impure and often awkward concoctions, we were fascinated by parody, the superimposition of radical words on banal pop tunes, because it displayed the whole range of what we would now call *syncretism*—between oral and literate culture, between melodrama, pop songs, and folk music, between sentimentalism and class consciousness, subliterary ambitions and grassroots poetry, the irony toward mass culture and its redeemingly imperfect imitation. In other words, we were beginning to understand that syncretism and multiculturalism can be expressed both by dialogue and harmony, and by conflict and dissonance.

CROSS WORDS

This was the beginning of a radical broadening of our outlook, reflected in the shift from a "bulletin of workers' and peasants' culture" to a "magazine of people's cultures and mass cultures." Our work on folk music had taught us to listen with a different ear to all the sounds of our times. We began a study of the interplay of rules and improvisation in the *ottava rima* (and the blues), and then extended it to the relationship of time and expression in rock and in youth culture.[11] We then went on to study the cultural ingredients of rock music, the class roots of Elvis Presley and Bruce Springsteen and Prince's amazing syncretistic power, and the mixing, shifting, and merging of ethnic and electric sounds, of roots, imports, recoveries, and discoveries in contemporary African music, in Latin American salsa, in U.S. country music.[12] On a completely different level, Ambrogio Sparagna, who started out teaching the *organetto* in the folk music school we organized to finance ourselves, transformed the *organetto* from a solo to an orchestral instrument and went on to write today's most successful blend of Italy's past musical tradition and musical future, playing with equal ease the streets, the folk clubs, and the Philharmonic.[13]

In other words, we had learned to listen to mass culture not as a solid discourse but as a meeting ground of different discourses—discourse from above encountering discourse from below, discourses from many different directions overlapping, mixing, fragmenting again. We never believed the world was headed for solid monoculturalism. This is why we always spoke of "cultures" in the plural, to refer not only to "subaltern" cultures,[14] but also to what we saw as the many different, shifting, competing, conflicting mass cultures that circulate on our planet.

The cultures of the people, always threatened by destruction and fragmentation, had learned to live with a horizon of disappearance[15] and to use the limited materials at their disposal to create beauty and meanings out of the leftover things the rulers did not want. For many of us, especially those who came from the field of American studies, this process was identified with a symbolic object, the quilt, the expression of a rural, female, folk culture that reacts to fragmentation by obstinately picking up the pieces and putting them back together.

The quilt also teaches that the syncretism and bricolage of folk cultures is not the same as the postmodern euphoria of fragmentation. Folk cultures are aware that, while we endeavor to break the chains of reality, reality is bent on breaking us up. Hence, the effort to create out of these fragments a partial, temporary, hypothetical unity, somewhat like Jesse Jackson's rainbow—where colors can still be distinguished from one another, but are not sharply separated. Much of the best in contemporary mass culture carries this message: a rejection of homogeneity enforced from above (but also from below, as in some versions of essentialism and ethnic purity), but also an awareness that the syncretistic multiplicity of which mass culture is made contains both a multiple liberation and a concentration of violence.

Putting mass culture back together, in some kind of temporary unity, with the remaining fragments of folk cultures, therefore, does not mean going back to the past but going forward to create something new. Yet, without the memory of violence, of dispossession, of displacement, of exploitation—and of resistance to all this—we would be only the unconscious vehicles of someone else's inventions.

PEOPLE AND SOUNDS

In the mid-1970s, Giovanna Marini, Italy's greatest folk singer and an early founder of our group, wrote in a memorable article of *I Giorni Cantati*, "Once I used to look for sounds; now I look for people." In 1990, a reader wrote to the magazine to complain about those contemporary musicians who synthesize ethnic sounds in the studio without ever meeting an "ethnic" musician in the street or field, without any awareness of the worlds from which this "world music" originates. Collective oral tradition is all very well, Marini explained, but it is absurd to disregard the individuals in whose lives traditions are embodied. Postmodern displacement is also all very well, our reader wrote, but it is absurd to displace others to place ourselves in their stead. It is absurd to take the sounds we want and throw away the lives we have no use for.

These are the implications of one of the humblest and most important teachings of Gianni Bosio: Never turn the tape recorder off. What he had in mind was not a fieldwork technique, but a relationship with the people we met. We were not out to extract folk items (songs, folk tales, proverbs) but to learn from them (as "historical persons," Bosio used to say)[16] what they have to tell us. And never stop listening.

Thus, at the time Marini was writing her article, some of us were beginning to realize that the apparently loose talk that accompanied our folk music recordings was at least as important as the music and songs themselves. Singers insisted on placing the songs in historical context, and as we listened to these explanations, oral history gradually became as important as folk music as a focus of our fieldwork. This also came about because most of the musicians who had worked with us in the beginning were gradually drifting off (they couldn't make a living, or have a career, on the shaky and narrow basis of the Circolo Gianni Bosio), while those who stayed were more at ease with history and linguistics than with ethnomusicological analysis.

From oral history we learned to go beyond a positivistic approach to history. We learned the truth of the telling as well as the telling of the truth; the importance of language, symbols, metaphors; the work of imagination, dream, and desire. We have spoken and written a great deal on these subjects. Here, I would like to spend a few words on an aspect that became central to our approach and our theory: the personal dimension of field work—the constant shifting and exchange of roles and information between the subjects involved in the interview, the supposed observer and the supposed observed.

Again, I will try to explain what I mean by telling a story, the episode that perhaps taught me the most about the personal and political interaction in fieldwork and in political activism.

It was 1970, the height of the "squatters" movement, the occupation of empty apartment buildings by homeless or ill-housed people, of whom there were thousands in Rome. In one of these occupied buildings on the Esquilino hill, I interviewed one of the grassroots protagonists of the movement: a highly articulate and class-conscious construction worker who had played an important role in several occupations. I learned much about conditions and about the struggle, but the real lesson came at the end, when this militant comrade asked if, among my acquaintances, I knew anyone who could recommend his young daughter for admission to some boarding school where she could continue her studies.

At first, I thought this touch of clientelism in such a class-conscious worker was jarring and disappointing. Then I realized that this man was only using different, if contradictory, strategies to achieve the same goal: the rights of citizenship and equality that the system denied him, and which were embodied in his daughter's education. His full and dedicated participation in a mass movement represented the struggle for future equality, but immediately underneath was his awareness of present inequality, and of his and his family's need to find ways of surviving now, *before* times changed, if they ever did. Thus, his militant activism existed side by side with the strategies of subalternity, and the two were mediated by the prospect of social mobility across generations. "Even workers want to send their sons to college," says a shocked bourgeois character in a famous movement song by Paolo Pietrangeli,[17] and this particular worker wanted at least to send his daughter to high school. Class-conscious rebellion, subordinate clientelism, social mobility as civil right—all these strategies were part of one person. I soon learned to listen not only for the first one, which most pleased us middle-class revolutionaries, to whom education was a birthright and a home was a class right.

Such experiences taught us to look less at the abstract working class of our desires, and more at the concrete workers of our experience, specific individuals whose social lives, needs, and problems did not begin and end with the eight-hour work day. We needed to understand the deeper layers of their imagination, beliefs, desires, and dreams, unless all we wanted to work with were our conceptual puppets. Thus, it was not a shock for us to discover that the same workers from the Rieti SNIA Viscosa factory whom we had seen at the militant 1975 national union rally in Rome were also in attendance at the pilgrimage to the shrine of the Holy Trinity at Vallepietra six months later.[18]

After all, I too had gone both to the rally and to the pilgrimage, and I had not attended as two separate people, as an activist at the rally and as some kind of ethnologist at the pilgrimage. At the rally, we had marched and shouted the slogans with the others, but we had also taped them, and I had worked on a linguistic and rhetorical analysis, which was one way of understanding their political meaning. Though I was not a believer, I had gone to the Holy Trinity shrine not just to tape hymns and prayers, but also to see who was there. Also, I had already learned from the Esquilino squatter the politics of multiple strategies, and it made sense that the workers whose jobs were in jeopardy relied both on their workers' councils and on the Holy Trinity to protect themselves and make some sense in their lives. The tape I have of "Bandiera Rossa," the song of the red flag, performed by Communist workers in pilgrimage at the Madonna del Canneto in the Abruzzi, shows the other side of this double-sided strategy.

For these reasons, the defeat of the working class in the 1980s and the discovery of its limitations and contradictions had much less traumatic effects on us than on the majority of the movement. We already knew about all that; no idols were broken. We have been able to remain on the same side of the social conflict, to keep reading culture as a terrain of class struggle, without having to imagine a monolithic working class, a guaranteed identity, or a solidified culture. We have been able to remain angry at injustice and oppression without having to attribute to the oppressed the virtues that we didn't have—indeed, often recognizing their very weaknesses as consequences of their oppression. Later, Lodovica Mutarelli, an activist of the 1990 student movement, confirmed the same lesson. In order to be consistent with her political beliefs, she had gone to work in a factory, where she discovered that real workers were very different from the myth she had in mind. "The things I believed in truly collapsed on me. But I realized that the principles that moved me were strong. When the myths fell, I might have said, who cares, I don't give a damn. But I couldn't. I guess I really believed in those things, and I still do."[19]

We also learned to recognize the presence of cultural conflict, the tension of hegemony and subordination, of resistance and repression, in noncanonical areas. In 1977, we began to discuss how the approaches we had developed in our work with working-class culture could be used to understand the new forms of youth-culture behavior, and we tried to read the "politics of private life" as a sign not of the end of politics, but of its transformation. We did oral history not only with the past, but with the present generations. As always, we were not interested just in the contents of memory but in its making as well. It was fascinating to see events become memory under our eyes, to see the movement and its members create memory while all the time they insisted that they were struggling *against* it. We did the same with the student movement of 1990, recognizing that apparently innocuous or evasive forms of behavior—the myth of traveling, the image of the mask—were actually vehicles of an unsuppressible desire for otherness. Through these, an apparently pacified generation had been all the time expressing its disaffiliation from the world as they found it.

It was not a surprise to discover that these highly educated young people used some of the same folk devices to resist and adapt to the hierarchic structure of the university that the traditional nonhegemonic classes had used in their own resistance and adaptation. Like the peasants' rebellion against the baron of Pianezza, the student movement was a generational insurgence, motivated by a sense of personal injury as much as by collective material expropriation (after all, full professors are also called "barons" . . .). Like Leonardo Pulcini's story, the movement told us that, beyond and beneath collective identities and crises, there is a bedrock of humanity that cannot be suppressed.

This applies to us, too. The history of Circolo Gianni Bosio and *I Giorni Cantati* is the history of a shifting, fluid group of people who insist on their personal right to create their own syncretisms, and refuse to let themselves be fragmented and sewn back together, unresistingly, in the hegemonic synthesis of consumer culture and status quo politics.

DOES IT MATTER?

In the spring of 1991 I was invited to a seminar with eminent historians, sociologists, and philosophers. I gave a presentation on the oral history of Kentucky coal miners, trying to tell their stories and interpret their meanings, and to show what our approach to oral history could do. At the end, there were comments such as yes, nice, very interesting—but what difference does it make?

My first reaction was to get mad. Must we always explain ourselves, always justify ourselves, as if after all these years we were still talking for the first time? Then I looked for the most honest, and the most provocative answer I could find. What difference does it make? Well, for one, it made a difference in me. I imagine this made no difference for those colleagues of mine; yet, I am still convinced that the personal changes I, and many others with me, went through thanks to the experiences I have been talking about are one of the most important results of our work.

Let us go back to the interview with the leader of the homeless movement who asked for my help to get his daughter in boarding school. It was at that moment that our gazes crossed and we *viewed* each other: looking at him, I saw how he looked at me. A comrade, of course, who spends his nights in an occupied building rather than in his comfortable home— but then, a comrade who *has* a comfortable home: a member of the middle class and the bourgeoisie,[20] who has contacts and acquaintances, who is at ease in the worlds from which the speaker is excluded (incidentally, I didn't happen to know anyone who could help him).

I could have come out of the conversation scorning the opportunistic worker, or feeling guilty for my bourgeois self. For some reason, I came out with a rich sense of our common complexity. I began to feel that interviewing is about the revelation and confrontation of both differences and common grounds between myself and the people who agreed to talk to me. Dialogue is not made possible by pretense of reciprocal identification, but by the foregrounding of difference in the context of seeking equality. Later, in Kentucky, in 1973, a black lady, Mrs. Julia Cowans, laid it down for me: "There's gonna always be a line" between us, she said. "I don't trust you"—and that's why, she implied, I am talking to you—because the world I'm working for is one in which a black proletarian woman and a middle-class white man might be allowed to trust each other at last, abolishing their hierarchies and keeping their differences.[21]

We had always known that, whether the dialogue succeeds or fails, fieldwork is also a form of political intervention, because it encourages an effort at self-awareness, growth, and change in all those involved. Thus, even in our years of most intense political activism, our desire to change the world hinged on our readiness to change ourselves. We soon realized that this was also a methodological requirement for serious fieldwork: unlike hard data or archives, people will not talk to you unless you talk to them, will not reveal themselves unless you reveal yourself. You teach nothing unless you are also learning, and you learn nothing if you don't listen.

This is the lesson of Bosio's "upside-down intellectual": one who is in full possession of all the tools and knowledge of the profession, but also absorbs the knowledge of the working class, of the nonhegemonic world, of contemporary youth and marginal cultures. For those who came to the Circolo Gianni Bosio through the experience of the Appalachian Project in the university,[22] this was also the lesson of Myles Horton of the Highlander Center (one of our models and inspirations): You don't teach anybody anything new unless you root it in what the learner already knows. And it was the lesson of Domenico Starnone, who crossed our path for a while and did some oral history with us before going on to become one of Italy's most brilliant writers, basing all his books on his dedicated work as a teacher.[23] From him, we learned that even the dumbest kid in the class knows things that the teacher doesn't know about the way the wind blows, about television and soap operas, about motorcycles, about what the school really is. Unless you're ready to put yourself on the line, Domenico Starnone teaches us, unless you're willing to use irony and a sense of humor on yourself, you teach nothing, learn nothing, and change nothing.

The Circolo Gianni Bosio has included different people at different times, but it always included people who knew which side they were on but never knew which party lines they were following, which cards they were carrying—or weren't. We always insisted on a concept that is sheer suicide from an organization's point of view: from each according not to what they can or must give, but according to what they *wish* to give. As a consequence, we never were very efficient. As another consequence, even in the hardest of times, when much better structured organizations were collapsing all around us, we survived. We were saved by our independence and our flexibility, for which we paid the price of many frustrations and a chronic lack of means that, in twenty years, never enabled us to raise the rent for a room of our own. The Left, the unions, the progressive administrations, they all liked us and thought we were very nice; but because we were incapable of belonging to any one organization, they would ultimately pass us by for more immediately usable alternatives. We have been one of the most unexplainable mysteries of opposition culture in Rome, a group that went through all sorts of crises learning the art of changing all the time and all the time remaining itself, flexible and unsinkable, invisible and celebrated, homeless and omnipresent, always defeated and always invincible.

The lack of means, the crisis of activism, the fact that we thought nobody was listening to us, all these things had almost persuaded us to give it up. But the increasing difficulty of the times, the proclaimed dissolution of the working class and the fury of self-effacement that affects the political Left persuaded us to give it another try. When we realized we could not afford to disappear, we also realized that it wasn't true that nobody listened to us. Barred from mass media, we had reached numberless people, in casual and informal ways, often without even knowing it. The experience and the knowledge we have accumulated have seeped into the cultural patrimony of opposition and resistance.

Thus we celebrate our twenty years of optimism of the will and stubbornness of the intelligence, together with comrades, friends, groups, organizations, with whom we share the refusal to erase our past and give up our future. I would like to conclude by quoting a precious political teaching from the pages of *Cuore*, a magazine of humor and satire that has helped us put together this event and has become one of the very few serious political voices still heard:

> Boys, let's not lose our cool. Let's just take a little time (a few minutes
> a day is enough) to think, maybe aloud, maybe in public, alone and

with others, about the lovely future they are preparing for us. . . .
Each of us is a Center of Human Resistance, because each of us is
endowed with the power of speech and the power of work.

Postscript

For all practical purposes, the Circolo Gianni Bosio died after this celebration. *I Giorni Cantati* folded, perhaps for the last time, in 1995, after
twenty-three years, quite a run for an unfunded, volunteer radical cultural publication. None of the collectives, groups, and subgroups that contributed to the experience are still together, except perhaps some of the
musicians. The individuals, though, are still around. As artists, journalists, critics, teachers, workers, and students, we're still trying to do and
say the same things. This book is an example, as is the music of Ambrogio Sparagna and Giovanna Marini; but all those who were involved in
the experience are, in one way or another, carrying the heritage into their
life's work. As Wash told Colonel Sutpen, "They might have killed us, but
they ain't whupped us yet." We still have the stories.

Chapter Four

Tryin' to Gather a Little Knowledge
Some Thoughts on the Ethics
of Oral History

RESPONSIBILITIES

Until I was invited to speak on oral history and ethics at a conference in São Paulo and Rio de Janeiro in the fall of 1995, it had never really occurred to me that there might be any specific ethics involved in oral history, other than those involved in being a citizen and a professional intellectual.[1] It seemed to me that, like all researchers, oral historians have the responsibility to follow reliable procedures in gathering information and to respect that information as they draw conclusions and formulate interpretations, whether or not they correspond to their previous wishes and expectations and that, as active subjects of history and participants in its making, on the other hand, we must place our professional and technical ethics in the framework of broader personal civil and political responsibilities. I knew of efforts to draw ethical guidelines for "the profession," but had never been much interested.

Ultimately, in fact ethical and legal guidelines only make sense if they are the outward manifestation of a broader and deeper sense of personal and political commitment to honesty and to truth. In the context of oral history, by commitment to honesty I mean personal respect for the people we work with and intellectual respect for the material we receive. By commitment to truth, I mean a utopian striving and urge to know "how things really are" balanced by openness to the many variants of "how things may be."

In terms of honesty, sticking close to the letter of professional guidelines may not be incompatible with subtler strategies of manipulation and falsification. Ethical guidelines may be, in this case, less a protection of the interviewee from the manipulation of the interviewer than a protec-

55

tion of the interviewer from the claims of the interviewee. Once we have gone through the prescribed steps, anything goes; they can't sue us. I have myself realized that I take most pains to secure written releases and approvals of transcripts and quotes when I am in political opposition to my interviewees and might therefore use their material in ways they might not appreciate.

In most other cases, my guarantee remains (1) that the commercial rewards of anything I do are so slight that they are unlikely to generate serious controversy, and (2) that I have a commitment *to myself* not to use the material in ways that may hurt or displease the person that gave it to me, and therefore I am unlikely to get any complaints that cannot be cleared in good faith. On those bases, I have felt that a verbal agreement, possibly on tape, is as binding as a notarized contract and sufficient guarantee for both of us. I admit that this may be a cavalier attitude toward serious legal problems (and am not therefore in a position to offer a normative ethics or to moralize about anything), and I do not recommend it. In part, it is the result of the relatively unstructured conditions of my own work.[2]

Indeed, it has often seemed to me that the increasingly complex requirements of professional ethics are designed for institutions or persons who have the resources, time, and help necessary to meet them. Their outcome is to cause activist, volunteer, community researchers, often highly ethically motivated, to feel guilty because they do not return copies of all tapes and transcripts, do not keep in touch with informants, fail to secure legal releases, and so forth. Although we should strive to perform all these duties to the best of our ability, we must not allow them to bureaucratize our attitude. While this is no guarantee of truly ethical behavior, it runs the risk of drying out some of the most vital strains that have kept oral history alive.[3]

As far as truth is concerned, the recognition of multiple narratives that is characteristic of oral history ought to protect us from the totalitarian self-righteous belief that "science" makes us depositories of unique and unquestionable truths. On the other hand, the utopian striving for truth protects us from the irresponsible tenet that all stories are equivalent and interchangeable (and therefore ultimately irrelevant). That possible truths are infinite does not mean that they are all true in the same sense, and that there are no such things as falsehood, manipulation, and error.

INDIVIDUALITY, EQUALITY, DIFFERENCE

> People generally think those memories only worthy to be read or
> remembered which abound in great or striking events. . . . It is,
> therefore, I confess, not a little hazardous in a private and obscure
> individual, and a stranger too, thus to solicit the indulgent attention of
> the public; especially when I own I offer here the history of neither a
> saint, a hero, nor a tyrant.[4]

Oral history is a science and art of the individual. Although it is as concerned as sociology and anthropology with patterns of culture, social structures, and historical processes, yet it seeks to explore them primarily
through their impact on individual lives as transmitted by conversations
with individuals about their personal experience and memory. Therefore,
while fieldwork is important to all social sciences, *oral* history is by definition impossible without it. The meaning and ethics of the person-to-
person encounter in the fieldwork experience are crucial to the meaning
and ethics of our practice.

The centrality of the individual is enhanced by the fact that oral *history* is concerned with versions of the past, that is, with memory. Although
memory is always shaped in many ways by the social environment, yet ultimately the act and art of remembering is always deeply personal. Like
language, memory is social, but it only materializes through the minds
and mouths of individuals. Because this individual process is carried out
in a dynamic social environment and avails itself of socially created and
shared tools, memories may resemble one another, overlap, or contradict
one another. But no two persons' memories, like fingerprints—indeed,
like voices—are exactly alike.

This is why I personally prefer to avoid the term *collective memory*.[5]
Though we are working to construct memories that can be shared and
used collectively, yet we should be wary of locating memory outside the
individual. All other considerations aside, this would be ethically ques-
tionable because it tends to make us see individuals as interchangeable
and indifferent. Too seldom, indeed, are we told *who* told the anthropologist *what* myth, or which informant gave the scholar which information
about which trait of the culture. As a consequence, culture is detached
from the people who create and experience it.

Thus, while other social sciences perform the indispensable task of
abstracting from individual experience and memory the patterns and
models that transcend the individual, oral history combines the effort to
reconstruct patterns and models with attention to concrete individual varia-

tions and transgressions. In this sense, oral history is not unlike literature. While literary theory and criticism do work with such transindividual concepts as genre, style, literary periods, literary schools, and literary influences, yet in the end what makes the resonance of a literary work is the fact that it coalesces, transgresses, transcends, transforms genre, style, period, and school in a unique way. Likewise, precisely because it is concerned with common people, with "private and obscure individuals" who may be "strangers, too," oral history does not cultivate the average, but often perceives the exceptional and the unique to be more *representative*. As I suggest elsewhere in this book,[6] the slave who was whipped one hundred times may illuminate the institution of slavery more than those who where whipped 0.7 times per year; the tiny number of drug victims in an industrial town may give us precious clues to youth experience as a whole. And one creative storyteller, a brilliant verbal artist, is as rich a source of knowledge as any set of statistics.

Respect for the value and importance of individuals is, therefore, one of the most immediate ethical lessons of the fieldwork experience in oral history. It isn't only the saints, the heroes, the tyrants—or the victims, the sinners, the artists—who are uniquely resonant. Each person is a crossroads of many *potential* stories, of possibilities imagined and not taken, of dangers skirted and barely avoided. As Luisa Passerini has pointed out, oral history is the ground where "two trends of the contemporary world, the need for democracy and the shift toward subjectivity" meet to proclaim everybody's "right to autobiography" as the "opportunity to narrate oneself, to give a meaning to one's life and one's narrative."[7]

Our art of listening is based on the awareness that we gain something of importance from virtually every person we meet. Each of my perhaps five hundred interviews—and this is no cliché—was a surprise and a learning experience. Each interview is important, because each interview is *different* from all the others.

Therefore, what our work teaches is not the abstract importance of *the* individual proclaimed by liberal competitive capitalism, but the equal rights and importance of *every individual*. Though it does work with elites, oral history started out primarily because we wanted to listen to those who had gone unheard—common folks, workers, the poor and the marginal, women, gays, black people, or colonial subjects. In our work, all the different voices of these private, obscure, and very special individuals are *equally* important and necessary.

Oral history as an art of the individual, then, directs us both to the recognition of difference and to the recognition of equality. Difference in-

cludes, in the first place, the differences among the many people to whom
we speak, but it also includes their difference *from us*, which is why we
seek them out to begin with. This difference, in turn, draws our attention
to the fact that oral historians are also very different from one another,
and they cherish their difference from, that is, their nonconformity to, the
ruling ideas of their society.

One of the exciting differences of the conference in São Paulo was that,
two days after I opened the proceedings with this discussion of oral history as an art of the individual, Mary Marshall Clark lectured on the fact
that oral history is based on the ethics of collectivity and rooted in collective memory. Listening to her, I thought she was absolutely right.
When I told her what I had said, she thought I had been right, too.

Aside from mutual respect for a colleague's ideas, we finally agreed
that, while all of us work both with individuals and with social dimensions, yet we foregrounded different aspects of our work because we both
wanted to stress our difference from our respective traditions. Clark insisted on the collective because she sees oral history as instrumental in
curbing the competitive individualistic ethos that has prevailed in free-
enterprise liberal capitalism in the United States. I, on the other hand,
stressed the individual because I have become aware that the Marxist tradition from which I come has failed to recognize that masses and classes
are composed of individuals who differ from one another. What we both
had in common was an idea of oral history as difference, as an implicitly
antagonistic practice.

In recent poststructuralist thought and in some strands of feminism,
difference has been posited as the only desirable ideal and as opposite to
and incompatible with equality. I would submit that they are two sides of
one coin, the coin of freedom and justice. Freedom means the possibility
of choosing one's own difference, but this choice of difference is only made
possible in a state of equality. Difference becomes hierarchy and oppression unless justice guarantees that this freedom of choice is shared by all:
universal difference is based on universal equal rights (unless, of course,
we are only speaking of the competitive, individualistic "freedom" to assert one's difference over the rights of others). Just as we cannot assert
our different identities if we are all alike, we cannot pursue our chosen
difference if someone has the power to impose upon us either an enforced
sameness (assimilation) or an enforced difference (racism and sexism). In
the struggle for difference, we cannot forget that we also have a dream of
sharing, of participation, of communication and dialogue.

This is what the dialogic quality of oral history and fieldwork implies:

To be truly different we need to be truly equal, and we cannot be truly equal unless we are truly different. As I have argued elsewhere, fieldwork is by necessity an experiment in equality based on difference. There must always be a line of difference across which the exchange becomes meaningful, but there must also be at least a line along which we can communicate the desire for a common ground and language that make the exchange possible—our deep-rooted common human nature.[8]

MINDING OUR MANNERS: THE ETHICS OF FIELDWORK

> If I should tell thee nothing [about myself] how should I learn from thee what I would know?[9]

In the essentially unequal societies in which we live and work, most of our interviews will not take place with persons who are truly on an equal plane with us. Often we talk to powerful, elite people; more often, we are persons of authority speaking to persons without official authority. Too often, the real or imagined power, status, and prestige we draw from our profession interferes with the performance of our work.[10]

So, if we are committed to truth, how do we get our sources to give us their version of what they actually think the truth is? Perhaps we never do ("Where do you draw the line about what you talk about?" says Mildred Shackleford, poet, activist, and miner, skirting a touchy question).[11] We should, however, make an effort to create a setting where people can draw their own lines and make their own decisions about it. This is not achieved by ignoring the differences that make us unequal, and paternalistically (and dishonestly) feigning an equality that is not there. Rather, we should put difference squarely on the table and see it less as a distortion of communication than as the ground itself of communication, placing the conversation in the framework of the struggle and work to create equality. We have both an ethical and a professional stake in this process. As Gianni Bosio put it, cultural work needs to create the political conditions for its difference and existence:

> In order to protect its non-integration, cultural work is led to create the weapons that ensure its very survival. Cultural work necessarily becomes political struggle: for reasons of self-defence, and because political struggle is the highest form of cultural work.[12]

What does this mean when we go into someone's house and ask permission to turn our tape recorder on (I emphasize, *ask permission!*)? In most cases, one does what comes naturally—because if it does not come naturally, it might as well not come at all. Doing the right thing is not a technique that one may learn in those handbooks that tell you to put the interviewee at ease, offer a cigarette . . . Most people are smart enough to know when one is trying to seduce them and use them.

I will try to explain what I mean with a story. Before I started field-work in Harlan County, I had been repeatedly warned that the people there had been exploited culturally and economically so much (alternative version: they were so backward and uncivilized) that they were suspicious of strangers and anthropologists. There had been instances in which such (supposed) intruders had actually been shot.[13] When I finally got ready for my first trip, I called a woman to whom I had been directed, asked if I could come over and do an interview, and she agreed right away. Six years later, she told me she had consulted with her sister over the phone, and they had concluded, "If he ain't too stuck-up, we'll talk to him." In the first place, this raises the question of who observes whom in an interview situation, but the way they decided I wasn't too stuck-up is also interesting. For a number of reasons that I later learned to appreciate and cherish (including her refusal to give up community work), this woman simply refused to do housework. She has two unmarried daughters, three grandchildren, and a disabled husband, so the house was, to say the least, very unkempt. "The reason I talked to you," she explained when we were friends enough to talk about it, was that "you came in and you sat down. You didn't look around for a clean place to lay your butt on."

What this means is that when one does an interview, one is in someone else's space and in someone else's time, and one behaves oneself. At the onset of the student oral history project in Rome, my student collaborators asked me to teach them how to do interviews. I had never been asked to do that before. Ultimately, all I could teach them, the only technique that came to my mind, was to mind their manners. Good manners do not involve only speaking softly, saying please and thank you, sitting down where they tell you, drinking the coffee they give you or the wine they offer you. Having good manners means that you don't go to somebody's house and take somebody's time and start asking questions. You go to somebody's house and start a conversation. The essential art of the oral historian is the art of listening.

Again, the ethical or polite approach is also scientifically rewarding: good manners and personal respect are a good fieldwork protocol. I walked into my Harlan friend's house because I wanted to hear about the struggles of coal miners from the 1930s to the present. What she wanted to tell me about was how hard it was to raise a daughter with an unemployed husband in a culturally and economically marginal area. Even if I had not been interested—which I was—good manners alone would have required me to listen. And by listening, keeping our agenda flexible to include not only what we think we want to know but also what the other person recognizes as important, we always find more than we're looking for.

Another thing about good manners is exactly the opposite of what one gets from those famous fieldwork handbooks, which always tell you to be neutral, be detached, don't interfere. I would say, be open, tell them about yourself, answer questions (if they ask!). I would not reveal much of importance about my life to someone who talked to me in a neutral, detached, impersonal manner. Why should I expect others to tell me about their lives if I am not willing to tell something of mine? The questions our sources ask us—for example, Rev. Cowans's opener, "You in the United Mine Workers?" or Annamaria Di Marco's working up the courage to ask, "Tell us how you became a professor anyway"[14]—are as necessary to the interview as the ones we ourselves ask. They help define the ground of difference and comparability that makes the interview meaningful: that I grew up in a privately owned industrial village facilitated communication with people who remembered the company towns; that my village was different helped identify the defining, peculiar characteristics of theirs.

Good manners, on the other hand, do not consist in always agreeing with the other person. That is, indeed, the worst form of paternalism. In interviews, as in polite conversation, it is quite all right to say things like, "Are you sure?" "I'm not sure I agree," or "I have heard other people tell this differently." Too often, people feel that it is safest to stick to accepted common sense when talking to a person they have never met before. A well-mannered challenge in an interview may elicit expansions, explanations, or analyses that would remain untold otherwise, or, as I often found, it will make the speaker feel that it is all right to voice less conventional views. That I identified myself as a member of a Left splinter group encouraged Communist Party members in interviews in Terni in the 1970s either to articulate the party line more eloquently and in depth, or to voice their own perplexities about it.

Contrary to what I had been led to expect, I found that most people in Kentucky were friendly, helpful, and open. I soon found myself wondering what I was doing right. I took it up in my conversation with Mildred Shackleford, and was rewarded with a combination of objective and subjective reasons, having to do with power on the one hand and with attitude on the other.

> *Portelli:* When I began to do these interviews I was afraid that people would resent me because I am an outsider, and coming from Italy. I didn't find much negative reaction. I think basically it's been because I didn't know much and wasn't in a position to teach anybody anything.
>
> *Shackleford:* I'll tell you something else that makes a lot of difference too. You are not from the United States. You are not from New York or you are not from Chicago or you are not from Louisville or you are not Lexington or Knoxville.
>
> *Portelli:* I thought about that, too. I am not from where power comes from.[15]
>
> *Shackleford:* Another thing that would probably—If you were from Wales and you were a coal miner and you come to Harlan County and you was talkin' to those people about coal mining, they wouldn't resent you, you know. But you are not trying to influence people or anything. All you're doing is tryin' to gather a little knowledge or find out something or get people to tell you stories and they don't resent that.

There is a double structure of oppositions in Shackleford's comments. The first opposition is between center and peripheries: as opposed to the hierarchic difference that radiates from the centers of economic and cultural power, the nonhierarchic difference of a visitor from another periphery of the empire is an incentive to talk.[16] The second opposition has to do with "telling" and listening. People will *listen* to a Welsh coal miner because, combining national difference and class equality, he does not claim a higher status but can contribute useful knowledge and experiences (e.g., on mine safety). On the other hand, people *talk* to me because I *listen* to them: I don't have much to *tell* them, and therefore I am not trying to "influence" them, but only to "gather a little knowledge" and a few stories.

I concluded this exchange with the comment that my work in Appalachia "has been a great learning experience." Appalachian people are so used to being *studied*,[17] *civilized, saved* by outsiders ("We had missionaries coming out of the ears," Shackleford says, that "come in to save the soul of the savage") that they cannot take it anymore. Whatever the reason for my success, it probably boils down to a formula that I had been using spontaneously: I was not "studying" Appalachia (or preaching to it), but "learning" about it.

The point of this story is not how politically correct I was, but that I was not aware of being correct. Once again, I was just doing what comes naturally. Although we may be academics interviewing illiterates, in the field situation they are the ones who possess the "knowledge" we are "tryin' to gather." We may have status, but they have the information and kindly share it with us. To keep this in mind is to remember that we are speaking to, and being helped by, not "sources," but persons. This is not a matter of what kind of formulaic expressions we use in our approach; good manners are only the outside manifestation of authentic respect. Otherwise, we can say "learn" instead of "study" all we want, but our interlocutors will always know that we're putting them on.

REACHING FOR MEANING: THE ETHICS OF INTERPRETATION

After we gather our little knowledge, the next question is: What does it mean? This is where the concept of truth becomes problematic. Not only do we have the problem of combining our historian's commitment to the objectivity of "what really happened" with our postmodern awareness that we will never really find out; we also know by now that a great deal happened really inside people's minds, in terms of feelings, emotions, beliefs, and interpretation. For this reason, even errors, inventions, or lies are in their own way forms of truth.

The fact that we are no longer dealing only with hard facts but also with the soft facts of subjectivity, memory, and storytelling ought not to lead us, however, into the postmodern euphoria of dissolving the materiality and referentiality of the external world into the dizzying possibilities of immaterial discourse. Just as we work with the interaction between the social and the personal, we also work with the interaction between narrative, imagination, and subjectivity on the one hand, and plausibly ascertained facts on the other. We cannot recognize imagination unless we try to know the facts. When confronted with narratives that contradict plausibly ascertained facts, we could either positivistically reject them as evidence of the unreliability of memory or, in postmodern fashion, conclude that it makes no difference—it's only another set of representations. As oral historians, however, we tend to take seriously both the unreliable oral narratives and the plausible archival record, and look for meaning in both, and in the space in between.

Now, the fact that the multiple truths to which we are committed include the soft facts of subjectivity, dialogic narrativity, and personal memory has been used to claim that oral history is unscientific and unreliable. Oral historians have responded both with a heightened and commendable endeavor to eliminate distortions and interferences, and with an increasing tendency to question the very meaning of objectivity and truth. The supposed interference has become the focus of our work.

On the one hand, this development commits us to a recognition of pluralism, of multiple approaches to truth (subjected, as far as possible, to rigorous and accountable protocols); on the other, its lays upon us the responsibility of choice. Scientific objectivity does not consist in absenting ourselves from the scene of discourse and pretending to a neutrality that is both impossible and undesirable. Rather, it consists in taking up the intellectual's task of interpretation.

In an Italian scholarly history journal, I once read what appeared to be a very objective and scientific transcript of an interview with a factory worker. At one point, the narrator's words were interpolated by a piece of information in italics and brackets: "[*colpo di tosse*]" (cough). As I read, I could not help wondering what it meant. Was the speaker clearing his throat? Was his cough ironic, intentional? Had he swallowed something? Did he have TB? There was no way of knowing, because the "objective" stance of the transcriber prescribed a neutral and (supposedly) "mechanical" transcribing, which precluded the expression of an interpretation. Rather than an objective discourse about the source, this was a subjective discourse about the historian: the only information it conveyed was that the interview was transcribed by a very objective scholar who thought it was scientific to name the data but not to risk telling us what he thought they were.

The responsibility to interpret, of course, does not extend to claiming for our interpretations exhaustive and exclusive access to truth. Since its inception, it has been a practice of oral history to quote the actual words of its sources, to a far greater extent than in other disciplines (even documentary history does not quote its archival documents with the same relish with which oral historians quote interviews). Therefore, whatever our intentions, our work has gained an intrinsic dialogic dimension, in which our (explicit) interpretations and explanations coexist with the interpretations embedded in the quoted words of our sources, as well as with our readers' interpretations of them. Thus, readers of my history of Terni discovered paths of connections between the quoted interviews that I had not seen or intended, and yet were there. So what we create is a dialogic text of multiple voices and multiple interpretations: the many interpretations of the interviewees, our interpretations, and the interpretations of the readers.

Now, different interpretations may be incompatible with one another.

Though the most romantic variants of contemporary multicultural theory find it hard to accept, difference is not a gala dinner. Difference, especially in unequal societies, is also disagreement and conflict; it can be war. Thus, while we are bound to report as faithfully as we can what our interviewees actually said, our responsibility toward them does not extend to always agreeing with them. Sometimes our ethics as citizens, as individuals involved in the struggle for democracy, equality, freedom, and difference, may transcend the limited ethics of our profession in favor of a broader, human, and ultimately political ethics. In other words, an interview with someone who holds power over us or over others may not necessarily be subjected to the same set of ethical considerations as other interviews—whatever we may think of the person.

Sometimes, when we interview poor or marginal people, they suspect that we may be spies for the police. Sometimes, when we interview the rich, the mighty, the generals, it may be highly ethical to act as spies in the enemy camp. On the one hand, being open is always the best policy: they are often so proud, so perversely in good faith, that they will tell us anyway, and more than we even imagine. But sometimes, especially when they have their own misgivings, they may be more wary; then, some "honest dissimulation" may be in order. When I interviewed the parson of the neighborhood where I grew up, he remembered me as a moderately church-going middle-class child, and assumed that my politics and his would be the same. He did not ask, and I did not volunteer to undeceive him. So he had no qualms about telling how he used to filter all applications for jobs at the local factory, and make sure anyone suspected of leftist leanings had no chance of getting a job. This interview became the first direct documentary evidence of what we had always indirectly been aware of: the Church's role in political discrimination in that specific context. Of course, because I knew I would use the material against his intentions, I was scrupulously ethical in professional terms: I submitted my transcript to him and got his written approval of the quotes before I published. What I did not tell him was the context in which I would place them, and the interpretation I would give. A good example, I guess, of "ethical" manipulation—in this case, I hope, for a good cause.

When the narrator of the story of the airplane and the stars, on which our book on the student movement in Rome is based,[18] told us that he disagreed with our interpretation of his story, we did not decide to give up our interpretation in favor of his more "authentic" one. Rather, we did two things. Because oral history is dialogic, we still began the book with the story and our interpretation of it, but we ended it with the narrator's counterinterpretation, and then we inserted our interpretation of his counterinterpretation. As he reads the book, he will probably add another step, and I hope this spiral of interpretations goes on forever (accompanied by those of the readers who may disagree with both of us). But I am glad we did not give up what we thought was a correct and useful interpretation simply because it did not coincide with that of the source. We felt that we had the responsibility to document the existence of other interpretations than ours, and, given the source, rather authoritative ones. Rather than effacing ourselves and giving up our sense of what the material meant, however, we felt that the presence of this powerful other version meant primarily that we needed to verify whether our interpretation really made sense, squared up with the rest of the material, and served a purpose. Once we had reasonably ascertained that it did, we offered it as a usable possibility among others. Only by holding on to our responsibility to interpret, and to the risk of being interpreted, do we contribute to the endless spiral search for unattainable truth to which we are ultimately committed.

THE ETHICS OF RESTITUTION AND AMPLIFICATION

The final question is, What do we do with the knowledge we gather and with our tentative interpretations of it? The question of *restitution* has been very important in discussions of oral history as a political and community enterprise (throughout this book, the word *community* is to be understood as always within quotes). However, before we ask ourselves what to do with it, I think we should ask, What do we do it *for*? My sense is that primarily we do it for ourselves, prompted by desire and the need to "gather a little knowledge" and to "get people to tell [us] stories." By listening and talking in depth to hundreds of different people and different stories, I think I have gained a different perception of myself, for which I am grateful.

Doing it for ourselves may also mean that oral history is a job, a career. This is quite all right (indeed, many un- and under-employed oral historians wish it were always so), as long as we bear in mind that we will not be really successful at this job if we allow considerations of career advancement or the interest of those who may be paying or sponsoring us to take precedence over our inner, personal need to know. In oral history especially, because it is so directly linked with personal contact, the need to know has often gone beyond the intellectual passion of committed academics to include a sense of commitment as citizens who are not only students of history, but also active and responsible historical subjects who may be motivated by something broader than ourselves: a community, an institution, a movement, a place.

This is where the concept of restitution comes in. We receive so much from people and communities that we do not feel that our work is complete unless we have returned its results to those who made it possible in the first place. We should remember, however, that the restitution of artifacts—tapes, transcripts, publications—and their availability at museums and archives does not necessarily mean restitution to the community.

On the one hand, museums and archives are not always accessible and friendly to nonprofessional users; on the other, what do we do with the precious informant who does not know how to read the transcript or does not own a cassette player or VCR to play back the tapes? More important, often we are giving back to the community a knowledge that the community already has. They may be pleased to have the tape or the transcript, but sometimes they are not even interested. We feel better about giving those things to them than they do about getting them, which shows again that "ethical" behavior sometimes works more for the benefit of the researcher than of the informant. As Luisa Passerini has pointed out, this "bureaucratic approach"—"as if the question was that of returning an object to its owner"—ignores the "aspects of gift and teaching" that are often very important for the narrators and the interviewees.

If anything, then, Passerini goes on, "the demand is to extend the life and the circulation of narrative, the formation of a new tradition rather than direct restitution."[19] In these terms, what we really give back is an opportunity for the people to whom we talk to organize their knowledge more articulately: a challenge to increase their awareness, to structure what they already know, which begins at the moment of the interview and continues as they are confronted with our conclusions. Our first responsibility in restitution, then, is to the mutual growth of ourselves and the people with whom we engage in dialogue, and it begins at the same time as the interview. Therefore, restitution means more than returning the raw materials; it is also necessary to offer a tentative discourse, a possible organization, a range of interpretations.

This is why I speak of "challenge." Communities are not romantically homogeneous and cohesive; they are also arenas of tension and conflict. Our work, therefore, necessarily documents these aspects in ways that may gratify some elements in a community but may appear hostile to others.

Also, in parts or as a whole, communities may not appreciate the fact that we do not necessarily see them as they like to see or represent themselves (some middle-class informants in Terni felt that my accurate rendition of their speech was an insult to them personally and to the town as a whole). While accepting criticism, we must take responsibility for the fact that restitution is meaningless unless it changes the previous image of the community. Restitution is not a neutral act, but always an intervention, an interference in a community's cultural history.

On the other hand, to talk of restitution only in terms of bringing the information back to where it came from risks a limited, self-reflexive, narcissistic image of the community, consistent with separatist, essentialist versions of cultural difference—as if communities were only interested in hearing and talking about themselves. The real service I think we provide to communities, movements, or individuals, is to amplify their voices by taking them *outside,* to break their sense of isolation and powerlessness by allowing their discourse to reach other people and communities. The point at which I really felt that I had done something for the people I interviewed in Terni was not when I gave them copies of my book, but when, to my surprise, the historian Claudio Pavone used and quoted their interviews from my book in his definitive history and interpretation of the Resistance.[20] Finding their voices in Pavone's book gave my interviewees a sense that their experience and their version of history were now taken into account not only by an interviewer who knew them personally, but by the historians' community at large, and that they had an impact in the making not only of local but of national history. By making their narratives available to Pavone, my book had made it possible for the community to speak to others who would not have heard its voice before. This amplification is the specific restitution that we can make as professional intellectuals who have access to publications and other media. Rather than merely returning to the community the knowledge it already has, we repay and supplement it with knowledge of our own and share it with the portions of world that we are able to reach.

Finally, I will share one more thought about oral history and community. In 1964, Stokely Carmichael told white liberals in the civil rights movement that, rather than interfere with the black community, they ought to go home and organize their own. After learning so much from Kentucky coal miners and Terni steel workers, I began to wonder how I could take that knowledge back and organize my own community—not my neighborhood, which is so reactionary I hope it stays disorganized forever, but my workplace, the community I sense I have with my colleagues and students in the university. This is one of the reasons why, when the university was occupied in 1990, I got a group of students together to write an oral history of this community.

Then I made an intriguing discovery. In most cases, the guilt feeling of the anthropologist and the impulse for wanting to make restitution derive from the fact that one visits a distant community, gathers knowledge, then goes home and writes a book about it, leaving the community behind. In this case, however, things were the other way around: first I interviewed the community, then the community graduated and went away, and the "anthropologist," that is, myself, remained stranded there without a home to go to, because this was it. This may have been a peculiar situation, but it made me wonder about the other communities I worked with. Were they still there? Oral history takes a long time (my Terni project lasted thirteen years, I am into the tenth year of my work in Kentucky, and even the student oral history took five years), and by the time you feel your work is completed, the community you started out with may no longer even be there.

I started out in 1972 to write the epic of the steelworkers of Terni on their way to proletarian revolution; I wound up writing the eulogy of the deconstruction of the working class by deindustrialization in postmodern capitalism. By the time I had my book, though most of the people were still around, there was very little working-class *community* left to give back to. The people who now read *Biografia di una città* in Terni are very different from those who told the stories in it—just as the new students at Villa Mirafiori who read *L'aeroplano e le stelle* may feel that the book is the story of their place but not the story of their lives: they have no memory of the community that was briefly established there in the time of the movement.

Restitution to an evolving community, then, implies less the restitution of identity than the memory of difference. Memory accompanies change, but also resists the changes we do not choose to make—which goes back to oral history as an art not only of what happened but also of what did not happen, what could or should have happened.[21] It goes back to memory as alternative.

In Rio de Janeiro, when I announced that I would spend a day at the beach at Copacabana, someone said, "Don't expose yourself too much to the sun, it's dangerous." As I admired the Botafogo beach from the windows of the Fundaçao Getulio Vargas, my host warned me that the water was too polluted to swim in. Henry David Thoreau once wrote: "Alert and healthy natures remember that the sun rose clear." Well, I remember a time when the sun was not dangerous, when the beaches were clean. I refuse to take it for granted that we cannot swim in the water, that we cannot lie in the sun, that we must be afraid of the beauty of places like Rio. For my children, it is a fact of life: the sun is dangerous and the air and the water are dirty. My duty is to resist this in memory, and tell them what I remember, so they may resist.

Chapter Five

Deep Exchange
Roles and Gazes in Multivocal and Multilateral Interviewing

INTERVIEWING THE INTERVIEWERS

When a group of students and I started the oral history project on student memory and experience in 1990, we were aware that we were embarking in a highly self-reflexive project, with relevant methodological implications.[1] On the one hand, we were doing an anthropological study of our own daily environment, with a social group that we were part of or involved with daily; on the other, the fact that the group included both students and a professor, five beginners and one seasoned practitioner in the field of oral history, opened a space for a stratified reflection on the varieties of fieldwork experience.

Part of the project, then, was that, while the book was to be written jointly, each of us would contribute a separate chapter on one interview experience (in the end, only three of us did so; this chapter—slightly revised and expanded to clarify context—was my contribution to the book). We also planned that, at some stage, I would interview the student members of the research collective. This was intended, on the one hand, to give expression to their own autobiographical impulse and their sense that they also were sources of knowledge on the themes of our research; on the other hand, it was a way to take advantage of the unusual opportunity to observe the observers, to explore the meaning of oral history for individuals who were just beginning to get involved in it.

> *Francesca Battisti:* For me, this opened up the world of oral history, which is fascinating, which is beautiful. I have a black hole of sorts, I don't remember how I began, who got me involved, and anyway I'm very glad. I was scared, I mean it's great because it was an opportunity

72

to speak and to know the people you live with practically every day. It was a good pretext, this walking up to people, excuse me, I am supposed to interview you. . . . Then another wonderful thing is that when you speak with people, you see things that you had not really understood, I mean comparing yourself with the other, the things that emerge—it's beautiful. Because for me the interview is a deep exchange.

"Deep exchange" is an admirable formulation for an idea I had been working with for a long time: that the interview is an exchange of gazes, a situation in which (at least) two people look at each other. The interview I chose to describe in the book, and that I will analyze here, was selected as an especially articulate and complex example of the multiplicity, doubling, and role reversal between observers and observed, interviewers and interviewees, narrators and narratees, in a multivoiced dialogue.

TELL ME HOW YOU BECAME A PROFESSOR

It began as an ordinary (and therefore interesting) interview. I had asked to talk to Annamaria Di Marco (a senior student; not a member of the oral history collective)[2] because I wanted to hear some of the stories she had mentioned in conversation at different times: about depression ("feeling literally *haunted*,[3] how can I say, persecuted by some thing, an entity, an atmosphere, really the sense that it wasn't something that depended on me, and I truly felt the horror inside me, of being, yes, truly haunted by some force that I couldn't . . ."), magic ("Anyway, he told me he would be able to get the mojo off me; in practice, he used to hypnotize me, reciting litanies in Arabic that of course I couldn't understand, who knows what he was saying, and he would burn some substances, he would steep cotton in them and then burn it . . . every tenth session we would do the tarots . . ."), psychoanalysis ("the Christ syndrome, generous me, good me, open-hearted me, actually he explained that being so good and so generous to those who you know don't deserve it is a way of setting yourself up more sternly as a judge . . ."). I also wanted to ask her about her job as jazz singer and vocalist in a popular TV show ("It was truly a national-popular program in the most derogatory sense of the expression,[4] though I never witnessed anything truly demeaning. The work we did was musically acceptable"). Of course, I also wanted to talk about the themes of our research: the university, the occupation, the movement, and so on. The interview took place in my office, but I did not sit behind my desk. Also present was another student, Federico Pellegrini, whom I wanted to interview about his work as a theater actor.

We began with questions and answers, information and stories. Underneath the surface, however, our respective roles were at stake. Both Di Marco and Pellegrini had actively taken part in my courses and seminars, and were enthusiastically working on dissertations in American literature. Thus, they seized on the interview also as an opportunity to speak in a relatively open manner to the professor, to voice their passions (*Pellegrini:* "and then, it's unbelievable, the way when you read Poe, as I went further into the text, I realized that the teachings of Freud are a living thing, a real thing, that emerged and was extraordinarily tangible in Poe"), and also to convey their judgement on my attitude and my teaching (*Pellegrini:* "I chanced into one of your classes on Poe and Hawthorne, and I remember I liked the way you interpreted, so I asked you if I could join the course and you were very rude").

But there is more. Pellegrini openly confessed that his ideal was to become a university professor. Di Marco spoke of professors as role models ("I need someone I can look up to, I need models") that can also be a burden ("I come from a family of, alas, intellectuals!"). This close encounter, then, was for them also an opportunity to investigate closely one of the persons who embody this role: gazes crossed, and while I interviewed them, they were scrutinizing me.

This "deep exchange" aspect of the interview was reinforced by my dialogic approach. Good interviewers always make information on themselves available on demand in exchange for the information they gather. As a consequence, the roles of questioner and answerer undergo quick reversals:

> *Di Marco:*   Unfortunately, all this [going back to the university] has happened late, it ought to have happened when I was twenty-two rather than twenty-seven.
> *Portelli:*   Well, I enrolled in Foreign Languages at twenty-seven—actually, twenty-eight.
> *Di Marco:*   All right, but then how come at age thirty-two you were already a professor!

WHY DON'T YOU TELL HER . . .

To further complicate the conversation, after a while we were joined by Francesca Battisti, a student and a member of the oral history project. At this point, there were two interviewees—Di Marco and Pellegrini—and two interviewers, Battisti and Portelli; the interviewers, in turn, were different in terms of institutional position, generation, and gender.[5]

This situation immediately generated a tension between ways of interviewing. While mine remained an essentially referential approach based on difference, Battisti immediately established her conversation with Di Marco as an exchange of shared experiences on the basis of identity. Throughout the project, this was one of the major differences between my interviews and those collected by the students.[6]

The situation, then, developed into almost an ideal test, almost a laboratory experiment on the roles and dynamics of interviewing. Contrasting and complementary strains in fieldwork—difference and sharing, participant observation and "native" anthropology—converged in one exchange and one text, and conversed with each other on the basis of mutual self-reflexivity and of the stimulation from a curious and active interviewee.

Thus, on the one hand, the interviewee and the new interviewer immediately discovered common memories and spaces ("Do you really know R.?" "Of course. I have been engaged to him." "I was engaged to M. instead." "The guitar player?" "That's right. That's where I must have met you, then . . ."). On the other, concerned that the interview might slide too far into the idiosyncratic and the private, I made an effort to draw it back to a more traditional format ("About this [TV program]. Why don't you tell me about it?"). Fortunately, I failed.

The exchange of autobiographical information, in fact, had been only the contact that opened an equal plane of two-way communication between the interviewer and the interviewee; when two "natives" talk to each other, it is difficult, in principle, to tell who is observing whom. The blurring and reversal of roles soon became explicit; the interviewee Di Marco began to ask questions of the interviewer Battisti. At first, they were about the university: "Are you scared when you take exams? (May I ask questions, too?) . . . Have you already taken your third exam with Portelli?" (I was already marginal, already third person, and always the professor). Then, as the awareness of shared ground expanded, the dialogue began to explore deeper layers of personal experience, into which I would have felt less free to venture: "I found an old diary of mine, my notebook from high school, where I jotted down all the things, the thoughts, the songs, and every other page it says: I want to go away, I want to go away, I want to go away"; "We should compare our notebooks: mine says, out of here, out of here."

At this point, I stepped in again, radically shifting the strategy and aim of the interview to take advantage of the way in which my cointerviewer was gradually being shifted to the role of interviewee.

> Di Marco: I am always running away from some thing, this idea of
>   going away from Italy, I think it's almost an instinct,
>   because I've felt like this since I was a child, I remember
>   the first moment when I thought I don't want to be here, I
>   want to go away—I must have been five or six.
> Battisti: I always had a sense of guilt about it, though.
> Di Marco: No, no . . .
> Battisti: About this thing, running away, because I have already
>   run and will continue to do it.
> Di Marco: Where did you run away from?
> Portelli: That's right, why don't you tell us?

One of the problems we had encountered with the project of interviewing the interviewers was that, after working together for over two years (at that stage), we knew each other very well, and many things had already been told in meetings or in informal conversations. Thus, there was the risk that our interviews might turn into fictions, the staging for the tape and microphone of already-told dialogues, with no real exchange of knowledge and information. In one case, this is precisely what happened; in other cases, the interviews became less occasions to exchange information and ideas than autobiographical occasions, in which the interviewees really spoke primarily to themselves. In view of these difficulties, even though I knew that it was important that I interview the collective, I had hesitated to begin.

The presence of Di Marco and Pellegrini, and the type of deep exchange that Battisti and Di Marco had established with each other, then, gave me the opportunity to ask Battisti to tell the stories, such her adventures in the South Pacific, that she had already told the collective[7] without feeling she was being repetitive: the stories would sound new because she would be speaking to listeners who had not heard them before.

It was a rather novel interviewing situation, in which I would be asking the questions and the answers would be addressed to Di Marco. This allowed me to perceive a further complication in the interview situation: not only does it involve (at least) two subjects and roles (interviewer and interviewee), but the role of the interviewer is in fact the combination of two roles, that of questioner and that of narratee and listener. Ordinarily, the interviewer and the narratee coincide: the person who asks the questions is also the one to whom the answers are addressed.[8] In this case, however, while the usually distinct roles of interviewer and interviewee where increasingly blurred, the usually compact role of the interviewer was being split in two, because I was the interviewer and Di Marco the narratee (by then, Pellegrini had left). I could ask the right questions because I had already heard most of the answers (and only wanted to get them on tape); and Battisti was able to answer at length and articulately because she was speaking to a new addressee. "Listen, while you've got your mouth open and there's a tape recorder on, why don't you tell her what you went to New Zealand for": my shift from "tell *us*" to "tell *her*" sanctions the substitution of the narratee.[9]

Also, the breakup of the roles among multiple subjects (at this point, nobody knew who was interviewing whom) attenuated power relationships, making the narrator less embarrassed and self-conscious: "That's right, so we avoid interviewing me. . . . I who interview others am the first who doesn't want to be interviewed."

ALAS, INTELLECTUALS!

Roles and functions were gradually pieced back together, but in other forms. After a few minutes, the narratee Di Marco also took on the chores of the questioner. Because she could imagine herself in Battisti's place (rather than the experience of otherness, "native" anthropologists explore a range of their own horizon of possibilities), she performed the task differently from the way I might have. Her questions were more practical, sensitive, and intimate: "Where did you go? . . . Did you have money? . . . Did you feel lonely?" . . . Their function was no longer to extract information, but to compare experiences and feelings on an increasingly participative, personal plane: "All my friends are leaving. . . . you know, a while ago, when you were saying that you wanted to move to America, I thought: perhaps we'll become friends, and then she, too, will leave"; "I instead thought: great, if I go to America I'll invite her over." It was in the course of this conversation that Battisti formulated—in the process of experiencing it—her definition of "deep exchange" quoted above.

Then, suddenly, the phone rang. As I got up to take it, the two women went on in their intense, involved dialogue. Apparently, I was out of the picture. The authority figure—the professor, the male, the outside interviewer—was abolished.

Apparently. Even as I was out of the conversation, my delegate—the tape recorder—remained in the center of the stage and kept working for me. In fact, although I had taken advantage of Di Marco's active presence to set her up as "innocent" narratee, the ultimate purpose of the whole strategy was to collect and use the tale in my own intellectual enterprise (albeit, one that was shared with at least one of the participants). Not only would their words remain in my hands and my archive, but—as these lines witness—I would be the one to interpret and write about them. I was using this equal, spontaneous, empathic exchange between two women who were perhaps becoming friends in order to get their stories on the tape and to make them speak more deeply and intimately than if the roles had been left intact. Ultimately, all their words were answers to questions I had asked, or would have asked had I been in a position to do so, or known how to. Was it, then, only a shrewder, more expertly professional use of power and manipulation?

When I listened to the tape later, however, I discovered that, while I was moving aside, burdened by my outsider's nostalgia of identity, Battisti was explaining to Di Marco her own insider's yearning for difference: "I would like to try, to do, after this project is finished, another kind of interviews, another type of research in which I may be more detached, because this project is too emotionally involving. I would like to do a project where I can be more objective, something that may interest me intellectually, and find out what real oral history fieldwork is."

Perhaps, I thought, my task was not to indulge in the guilt and loneliness of separation, but to recognize that difference and distance are as necessary to research as identity and nearness. Power and hierarchy are real presences in personal relationships, and while they cannot be wished away, they cannot prevent us from doing our work either. Democracy is not to pretend these unequal differences are not there; democracy is to face them squarely and to take responsibility for them in the process of working to deconstruct them. Perhaps this is the burden of being, in Annamaria Di Marco's words, "Alas, intellectuals!"

Pellegrini:	In class, you told us several times: you are, you said, intellectuals. Now, by the time we leave here, we are critics rather than intellectuals.
Portelli:	Still a type of intellectuals.
Pellegrini:	Yes, well, perhaps, it's a big word, for us who are still in the university . . .
Di Marco:	Very big.
Battisti:	It used to frighten me very much when you said so in class . . .
Pellegrini:	Yes, it's a big responsibility for us, very big.

Chapter Six

Philosophy and the Facts
Subjectivity and Narrative Form in Autobiography and Oral History

THE RELUCTANT OVERSEER

Born a slave, Frederick Douglass became after his escape an eloquent orator in the abolitionist movement.[1] In the narrative of his life, the white abolitionists saw a living testimony against slavery and felt that his credibility would be enhanced if he stuck to an objective account: "Let us have the facts," they instructed him, and "we will take care of the philosophy."[2]

This distinction between the *facts*, incorporated in the slave's experience, and the *philosophy* reserved to educated white interpreters and sponsors, is a good example of a misunderstanding that has marred the contemporary social science approach to autobiography, life histories, and oral sources. The division of labor between *informant* and *scholar,* and the division of the scholar's labor between fieldwork (collecting the data) and analysis (conducted in separate spaces and times) contributes to the perception of *testimony* as raw material, on which the social scientist performs a verity check and an exclusive interpretative act.[3] The separation between the materiality of the source and the intellectuality of the interpreter is often wrought with class prejudices and, as in the case of African Americans, with racial ones. The hinge of this division of labor is the ambiguous utopia of objectivity, which connects the supposed factual objectivity of the source with the supposed intellectual objectivity of the scholar.

Between these two types of objectivity, however, in the no-man's-land between facts and philosophy, and in the uncertain borderland where they overlap, lies the territory of subjectivity. In oral history and autobiography, the sources are persons rather than documents or artifacts, and persons have an (un?)fortunate reluctance to reducing their lives to data for someone else's interpretations.[4] Whether they take the initiative of writing their autobiography or whether they are merely responding to an interviewer's questions, most people will insist, like Tristram Shandy, on telling both their *life* and their *opinions*. Philosophy is implicit in the facts— there is no narration without interpretation[5]—and the motivation for telling the facts is in most cases the desire to formulate a philosophy. Autobiographical discourse, whether the narrator takes the initiative of writing or merely responds to an interviewer's question, is always about the construction and expression of one's subjectivity. To ignore and exorcise subjectivity, as if it were only a noxious interference in the pure data, is ultimately to distort and falsify the nature of the data themselves.

Frederick Douglass started out as an "oral source," telling his life story orally in public. Because the achievement and exercise of language had been for him the result of a long and dangerous struggle, he could not conceive of himself as merely a body exhibited as living proof of other people's arguments. Both as speaker and as writer, he insisted on interpreting and judging for himself and by himself, and on extracting from the facts a lesson about the subjectivity of all involved. Describing the slave's most immediate enemies, the plantation overseers, he points out that they were not all the same, and that the difference lay also in their inner feelings: "Mr. Severe was rightly named" because "he seemed to take pleasure" in tormenting the slaves, while Mr. Hopkins "was a very different man" who "whipped, but seemed to take no pleasure in it."[6] The discovery of difference, especially inner difference, is the first step toward recognizing the humanity of one's oppressors and thus affirming their own, which their oppressors deny: "I therefore began to think that they [white people] were not all of the same disposition," writes Olaudah Equiano, after his early experiences in slavery.[7]

The important *fact* about Mr. Hopkins seems to be his disposition: less what he *did* than what he *felt* (or, more exactly, what the slave felt that he felt). One might ask what difference could an overseer's feelings make to the slaves who were whipped in any case; yet, the difference is important enough for Douglass and Equiano to register as children and to remember and comment upon as adults. The strokes of the whip, Douglass suggests, leave a mark on the slave's body according to the physical force with which they are delivered; but they also leave a mark on the soul according to the states of mind they convey. Mr. Hopkins's reluctance to wield the lash becomes to young Frederick Douglass a sign of the contradiction between slavery and human nature: even an overseer must eventually recognize the humanity of his subjects, lest he forget his own.[8]

Though slavery dehumanizes both slaves and masters, a bedrock of resistance remains in the slaves' defense of their own humanity and is reflected in the hierarchy's contradictions and sense of guilt. Mr. Hopkins's subjectivity, as interpreted by Frederick Douglass, becomes a major historical fact, because it contributes both to the making of Douglass's own antagonistic subjectivity and to our understanding of what slavery meant to its administrators.

In Toni Morrison's *Beloved,* a slave-owning schoolteacher with anthropological ambitions wields both the whip and the pen, and beats the slave Sixo to show him that "definitions belong to the definers—not the defined."[9] In this anecdote, Frederick Douglass claims the right to create his own definitions. By reverting the gaze and *seeing* his over*seer,* he subverts the observer/observed relationship and becomes interpreter rather than datum, "philosopher" rather than "fact."

TEXTS AND FACTS

The recognition of subjectivity in autobiographies and oral history[10] has met with two orders of objections. In the first place, subjectivity is immaterial and beyond our control; therefore it cannot be the foundation of a serious analysis: how can we know whether Mr. Hopkins was *really* reluctant? In the second place, subjectivity is individual and idiosyncratic, while history and social science are concerned with shared, public, social facts and cultural traits: Are we authorized to believe that Frederick Douglass and Mr. Hopkins represent anything beyond themselves?

On these grounds, social and historical research has to a large extent limited itself to materially observable and possibly measurable phenomena, data, and events. For instance, Nobel Prize winner Robert Fogel and his colleague Stanley D. Engerman in their classic *Time on the Cross* did not concern themselves with the feelings of those who whipped and were whipped, but concentrated instead on counting the number of lashes. By means of ample documentary sources and sophisticated means of statistical analysis, they reached the conclusion that slaves were likely to be whipped an average of 0.7 times per year.[11]

This is a legitimate, indeed necessary approach, because it guarantees a degree of abstraction that allows us to formulate general hypotheses, rules, and interpretations. On the other hand, while we are thankful for abstraction, we need to remind ourselves that it also involves a great deal of simplification. After all, it is materially impossible to whip anyone 0.7 times.

It is also arbitrary to compare whiplashes to one another, on the un-warranted assumption that they are all the same. They vary according to the circumstances, to the physical power and, ultimately, to the pleasure or reluctance of the person who wields the lash. Measurable or not, sub-jectivity is itself a fact, an essential ingredient of our humanity. Rather than excluding it from our field of observation because it is too difficult to handle, we need to seek methods and guidelines for its use and inter-pretation.

Of course we have no way of making sure that Mr. Hopkins really did not enjoy whipping the slaves. Douglass might have misinterpreted his behavior, or invented the whole thing. There is one thing, however, of which we are objectively sure: Douglass's narrative. We cannot touch the facts, and we cannot touch the subjectivity involved in the fact, but we can touch the texts that narrate the facts, describe the subjectivity of the characters, and express the subjectivity of the narrators. Texts themselves are also facts, and as such they can be analyzed by the appropriate meth-ods and disciplines: in this case, linguistics, narratology, literary theory, folklore—and oral history.

This approach also helps us to deal with the second objection, the bridg-ing of the individual and the social. Texts (by which here I mean also the verbal component of oral narratives and interviews) are both highly indi-vidual expressions and manifestations of social discourse, made up of so-cially defined and shared discursive structures (motifs, formulas, genres). Through these structures, then, we can see how each individual text ne-gotiates the interplay of the personal and the social, of individual expres-sion and social praxis. This negotiation varies with each text and each performance, but is always carried out on the basis of recognizable, so-cially defined "grammars."[12]

Indeed, the construction of a literary canon consists of an attempt to establish that certain texts are representative, that is, that they speak for more than themselves, on the basis of qualitative rather than quantitative standards. This is the problem we face when we discuss the representa-tive value of our sources. In an unpublished essay, Stephen Feuchtwang makes the point that the use of biographic materials in oral history and social anthropology is a form of "canonizing" ordinary lives in terms akin not only to the literary, but also to the religious-history meaning of the term.[13] The question then is, What do we recognize in the stories with which we work that makes them relevant beyond the immediate sphere of their individual narrators, the way a literary work is relevant to litera-ture or a hagiography to church history and religion?

THE SERIOUSNESS OF THE WORKING CLASS

One day in 1942, the public squares of Italy were filled with citizens, more or less willing or compelled, listening to Mussolini's broadcast voice, announcing Italy's entry into the war. In Terni, seventeen-year-old Ferruccio Mauri, an apprentice in the steel works, was among the crowd in the town's new main square. Forty years later, he remembered that day:

> They brought all the hands—that's how they called them then, hands—to piazza Tacito [the main square], where the loudspeakers were, the radio that was to broadcast Mussolini's famous war speech, you know. And what impressed me—some may disagree on this, but the ones near me. . . . I was all excited about the war, a naive young boy. I remember that when I started in the steel works I couldn't wait for war to begin. But—but all around me I saw, while I heard that in Rome they were clapping—those around me I saw were deeply worried. That is, for the first time—this is not poetry I'm making—I saw the seriousness of the working class, the preoccupation. Even though I could not understand why. While I exulted, while in Rome people applauded, around me—others might say, "No, they clapped their hands"—but around me, the workers that were with me showed a deep worry, a deep concern.[14]

Again, this is a story about subjectivity. As Douglass interpreted Mr. Hopkins's disposition, Mauri interprets the workers' feelings and attitude toward the war. As Douglass uses Mr. Hopkins to interpret the meaning of slavery, Mauri reads in the faces of his coworkers the meaning of war and Fascism and the conscience of the working class. As Douglass establishes his own subjectivity through Mr. Hopkins's, Mauri explains that *seeing* the working class for the first time (a boy from a petty bourgeois family, he had only been hired at the steel works four days before the declaration of war) marked a change in his personal growth. Yet, like Douglass, Mauri does not believe that these remarks pertain only to his personal sphere: "this is not poetry I'm making," he says, to underline that he is making history, that he is talking about *facts*.

Mauri's intensely personal narrative is wrought with culturally shared symbolic structures and narrative devices. A significant symbol is the contrast between what was happening in Rome and what he saw in Terni: "while I heard that in Rome they were clapping—those around me I saw were deeply worried." Terni is less than sixty-five miles from Rome, and local people often voice the small town's sense of inferiority toward the metropolis, but also the workers' town resentment toward the bureaucratic capital, the "red" citadel's hostility toward the symbol of the Fascist empire. Incidentally, one might quote as many accounts from Rome, saying that people weren't happy there, either; but Mauri's story deals less with the actual situation in Rome than with its representations. In the first place, the sounds from the capital were filtered by the regime's radio, which enhanced the signs of consent for the benefit of listeners nationwide; in the second place, Mauri uses Rome less referentially than structurally, in order to establish by contrast a continuity between local identity, class identity, and personal identity.

In describing the scene, Mauri uses a device that is widely shared both by oral sources and modern novels: the circumscribed point of view. While it recognizes the limitations of individual perception, the circumscribed point of view founds upon these very limitations the authority of the narrative: in modern literature, as in oral and written autobiography, authority is not vested in the conventional fiction of an omniscient, superior, and external narrator, but lies in the limited yet tangible experience of partial narrators immersed in the stream of the story.

Mauri also insists that his is only one of many possible narratives: "some may disagree . . . others may say . . ." His authority derives from the limitation of his point of view: he does not know the truth, but he knows what he saw. He is a partial narrator, because he was standing in the square among the crowd, and could only see a limited portion of what was happening.[15] In order to take a stance as omniscient narrator in that situation, one would have to be located on top of the prefecture building—indeed, in the turret from which machine guns were aimed at the crowd in case of civil disturbances. The contrast between Mauri's point of view and the global viewpoint from the government and police building reproduces the contrast between personal authority from below and institutional authority from above, between inner experience and outer control.

The disappearance of the omniscient narrator dissolves the possibility of one, authentic, verified version of events. Perhaps the closest literary parallel to Mauri's description is the device of "multiple choice" or "alternative possibilities" used by Nathaniel Hawthorne in *The Scarlet Letter*. The novel opens and closes with a scene not unlike that described by Mauri: a public ceremony in a crowded square, in which different people see, or think they see, different manifestations of the same central symbol, the scarlet letter. Hawthorne suggests that the meaning of the scene lies precisely in the symbol's power to generate multiple perceptions, interpretations, and narratives. The scarlet letter, like the accounts of Ferruccio Mauri and Frederick Douglass, is a matrix of meanings: it is not about the content, but about the fact of *meaning*.

Like all interpretative acts, Mauri's account also relies on socially recognized codes to formulate a plausible hypothesis—the expressions on the workers' faces, the fact that they did not applaud (or, like Mr. Hopkins, did so without taking pleasure in it). More than the interpretation, however, what counts is the interpretative performance: Mauri, like Douglass, may be wrong, but his interpretation founds his personal construction of self. It is no accident that, also in narrative form, Mauri places himself at the center of the scene: "around me I saw . . ." The ultimate protagonist is himself and his growing consciousness, and as is always the case with the circumscribed point of view, the story is less about what is seen than about the act of seeing.

Yet even this personal story is couched in the terms of an established narrative genre: the initiation story: "I had been working at the steel works only four days [and] *for the first time* I saw the seriousness of the working class." This story is about the way in which seventeen-year-old Ferruccio Mauri was transformed from a naive boy excited at the prospect of war into the young partisan who joined the Resistance two years later, and into the class-conscious worker and communist militant he remained for the rest of his life. The process of change, the work of consciousness, is expressed in the interview by the work of language. Mauri's digressions, suspensions, repairs, and repetitions are typical traits of oral discourse as dynamic process and performance rather than static text. The careful difficulty with which Mauri creates his account in the course of performing it is a reflection of the difficult work through which the narrator's consciousness appropriated, in the course of his life, "the seriousness of the working class" he discovered that day.

POSSIBILITIES

Frederick Douglass and Ferruccio Mauri, then, give accounts of the creation of their own subjectivity through the encounter and interpretation of the subjectivity of others, in the context of the subjective dimension of historical realities: the relationship between slaves and the plantation hierarchy, between the working class and the war. Indeed, one aspect they have in common is the careful underlining of the distance between story and discourse, between the time of the events and the time of the telling.[16] The question remains, however, whether their narratives are relevant only from the artistic and linguistic point of view, or whether they are also historical documents from which we can draw some conclusions about the broader context of which they were part. In other words, how *representative* are Frederick Douglass and Ferruccio Mauri or, better, how representative are their narratives?

Texts do not become representative because of their statistically average quality. We do not dismiss Dante Alighieri's *Divine Comedy* from our reconstruction of the Middle Ages in Italy on the ground that he was not representative because the average Florentine citizen of that time would be unlikely to produce that kind of text. Rather, we include it precisely because of its exceptionality: on the one hand, *only* a Florentine citizen of that time could produce such a text; on the other, its uniqueness comprehends and defines the range of possibilities of its time and society.

For much the same reasons, Ralph Waldo Emerson could (should) have included Frederick Douglass in his canon of "representative men." In biographical terms, he was a political representative of African American people before and after the abolition of slavery, and a cultural hero for generations of black people; in textual terms, his *Narrative* is an established part of the American literary canon.[17] Ferruccio Mauri, on the other hand, is less easily canonized. He also was an elected representative of Terni's workers in the city council, but he remains closer to the average, common working man than Frederick Douglass was to the average African American. His representative quality, therefore, is to be sought less in his biography than in his text.

His narrative, in fact, is remarkable for the way in which it gathers socially shared symbols and devices—the sense of local identity, the circumscribed point of view, the initiation story, the distance between the young protagonist and the older narrator, the use of digression, repetition and repair—and organizes them into a coherent whole. Mauri's act of *parole*, in other words, reveals and amplifies the expressive possibilities of the *langue*—which is what we might also say for Douglass and for any literary canonical text.

The key word is *possibility*. On the textual plane, the representative quality of oral sources and life histories is related to the extent to which they open and define the field of expressive possibilities. On the plane of contents, it is measured less by the reconstruction of the average experience, than by the subjective projection of imaginable experience: less by what materially happens to people, than by what people imagine or know *might* happen. This horizon of possibilities defines the range of a socially shared subjectivity. In a discussion of slave autobiographies, Ralph Ellison pointed out that a viable description of "one's sense of group experience" is projected from "a vision of what can happen in terms of what [the reader] accepts as the way things have happened." In different words, this is what Ian McEwan implies when he says that "each grief [is] a particular, intricate, keening love story that might have been otherwise."[18]

Let us go back to the average of 0.7 whiplashes per year per slave established by Fogel and Engerman. Once we have this information, the question is, What does it *mean?* On the statistical plane, the authors suggests that it means that slaves were not whipped very often, and therefore whippings did not make much of a difference in their material condition. Together with other similar data, it suggests that slavery was not much different from other conditions of social exploitation or marginality. After all, the difference between 0 and 0.7 is almost negligible.

On the subjective plane of possibility, however, the difference is incalculable. The difference between free workers and slaves did not lie in how many times the latter were whipped, but in the fact that slaves could be whipped, and free workers could not.[19] What defines the slaves' condition, therefore, is not the whippings they actually received but the ones they knew they might receive. If ninety-nine slaves are never touched, and one receives seventy strokes, the latter's "exceptional" experience determines the ordinary behavior of all the others, because it represents everybody's possible fate, and their behavior will be aimed at avoiding it.

Likewise, the number of Terni workers who were killed in accidents at work is rather negligible as a percentage of those who came out unscathed; yet no narrative omits the theme of accidents and deaths on the job. What is representative, then, is not the relatively few who died, but the fact that all lived with the possibility of death by their side every day: the group experience of Terni's factory workers is projected in terms of what could have happened, and did happen to others like them. As another example, in the 1970s, four young people died of heroin overdose in Terni. Respectable people claimed that these were negligible exceptions, because the majority of young people in town lived normal lives as students and workers. One of these "normal" young people, however, a girl, told me that, although she had had no contact either with drugs or with the counterculture, these deaths affected her personally because she knew that but for circumstances, she could have been in their place.[20] Drugs are a tangible possibility in the life of every young person in contemporary urban environments, just as the whip was on the plantation and accidents are in the factory. Consciously or not, people's lives are regulated by the need to prevent these risks; those few who did not manage to do so are the materialization of everybody else's concerns.

Oral history, then, offers less a grid of standard experiences than a horizon of shared possibilities, real or imagined. The fact that these possibilities are hardly ever organized in tight, coherent patterns indicates that each person entertains, in each moment, multiple possible destinies, perceives different possibilities, and makes different choices from others in the same situation. These myriad individual differences, however, only serve to remind us that, beyond the necessary abstraction of the social science grid, the actual world is more like a mosaic or patchwork of countless different shapes, touching, and overlapping, and sharing, but also cherishing their irreducible individuality. As sciences of the individual, oral history and literature deal with the portions of the mosaic that cannot be subsumed under the grid. They give us unwieldy representations, often harder to handle and work with, but perhaps more consistent not only with the presence of subjectivity but also with the objective reality of things.

Part II

Wars

Chapter Seven

Form and Meaning of Historical Representation
The Battle of Evarts and the Battle of Crummies (Kentucky: 1931, 1941)

And I've got scars all over my body, that I can show you, I've got in Harlan. And on my legs and on my arms, where that the scabs would try to back us off the picket line, and that here place, I don't guess you can see it too good, that they pricked the skin up—like that?—and one man held it and held my hand and had them cut that whole chunk out of my hand. And this right here, the doctors, they were afraid it's cancer, but that right there is where that they held a cigar to my hand till it burned out most through here. [In Harlan], in the early thirties. And, I've got scars all over my legs, you can't see 'em too good, right there's a sunken place, and there's a scar. One of it happened when I was in Evarts.
—Frances "Granny" Hager, Hazard, Kentucky, 1973

Near the scene of a sharp bend in the roadway just west of Evarts, for a long time there stood a native rose. The needless crimes that were committed near this rose have been shocking yet the native rose is nearer an interpretation of the life of the good citizens of Evarts than are the crimes recorded near its base. In many trying circumstances, evil agitators of various sorts have flocked to Evarts [so that it] has borne the stigma of crimes which her citizens did not commit.
—Eugene H. Rainey, Historical Resumé of Evarts, 1942

But, on one side of the portal [of the prison], and rooted almost at the threshold, was a wild rose-bush, covered, in this month of June, with its delicate gems, which might be imagined to offer their fragrance and fragile beauty to the prisoner as he went in, and to the condemned criminal as he came forth to his doom, in token that the deep heart of Nature could pity and be kind to him. This rose-bush, by a strange chance, has been kept alive in history.
—Nathaniel Hawthorne, The Scarlet Letter

TWO BATTLES

This chapter deals with the different ways in which two outwardly similar events are recorded by historians and remembered by oral narrators;
it attempts to explain this discrepancy and the meaning of the events themselves.[1]

The events are two armed conflicts between coal miners on one side
and deputy sheriffs and company guards on the other, which took place
in the United States, in Harlan County, in the coal fields of Eastern Kentucky, respectively at Evarts, on May 5, 1931, and at Crummies on April 2,
1941. They are commonly referred to as the Battle of Evarts and the Battle of Crummies. At Evarts, four men—three deputy sheriffs and one
miner—were killed; at Crummies, four miners are known to have died,
but oral sources claim that many more casualties went unrecorded. The
battles took place, respectively, at the beginning and toward the end of a
dramatic era of class struggles between miners and coal operators. The
label "Bloody Harlan," by which the county is still occasionally referred
to, is partly the result of this history.

While the Battle of Evarts is amply documented by official sources and
widely discussed by historians and memoirists, the Battle of Crummies is
hardly mentioned at all except by oral sources. The only recent written
references I could find are by local memoirists who either describe it as a
one-sided "mass murder," or insist that reports have been largely exag-
gerated.[2]

Oral sources depict the 1941 Battle of Crummies as much more dramatic than the earlier one at Evarts. Frances "Granny" Hager, who took
part in both, recalled in detail the Battle of Evarts, but when asked, "What
was the roughest place over there that you can remember? Roughest time
you had here in organizing?" she replied, "Let's see, I'll think the name
of the place—Crummies Creek." Interestingly, her interviewer, a very com-
petent oral historian and cultural organizer from Eastern Kentucky, was
unable to place her reference.[3]

He was not exceptional. When Florence Reece, also an active union
woman from Harlan, and the author of the well-known song "Which Side
Are You On?" also referred to the Battle of Crummies—"Was it 1938 or
1941 when the sheriff's deputy mounted a machine gun on the counter in
the company store and shot down nine miners as they entered the door?
Oh yeah, 1941"—her editor commented that "even the veterans can't recall which episode" she refers to.[4] The only reason I can place Florence
Reece's reference is that, throughout my fieldwork in Harlan County, I

have stayed with miners' families in areas adjacent to Crummies Creek. Every time we passed the commissary store where the battle took place, whoever I was with would point it out and retell the story.

I will try to interpret the discrepancy between the vivid and concrete oral memory of the Battle of Crummies and its absence from the historical record, as opposed to the Battle of Evarts, starting from a nonessentialist definition of *event* as a cultural construction based on the context created by memory through selection and connection among a multiplicity of happenings and by the form in which the story is told. I will then go on to interpret the "meaning" of these events, that is, what they tell us about the culture that experienced and remembered them. Let us begin, then, with a brief rehearsal of the available sources.

EVARTS, MAY 5, 1931

"Evarts [is] a small, rather tired-looking Harlan County town of 1,800 about eight miles east of Harlan, the county seat. When you drive around Evarts you find it hard to believe that anything important ever happened here. But Evarts has seen more than its share of trouble. In 1931 the Battle of Evarts made national news."[5]

"In the early spring of 1931, the Depression, a mild winter, and the seasonal hiatus in the lake cargo trade combined to severely depress the Harlan coal industry," writes historian John Hevener. "In these straits, on February 16, local coal operators declared a 10 percent wage reduction. Because of irregular employment and reduced wages, many miners and their families began to experience the pinch of abject poverty. . . . On Sunday, March 1, more than two thousand Harlan and Bell county miners attended a rally in a Pineville theater where UMW national vice-president Philip Murray urged reorganization of District 19 [of the union]. . . . The next morning, several Harlan firms, whose spies had reported the names of local miners attending the rally, began discharging and evicting members. . . . Most of the discharged and evicted miners moved with their families to Evarts, one of the county's three incorporated, or noncompany, towns."[6]

"You could tell there was something in the air," recalled union miner Chester Pore, who was to spend ten years in jail for his alleged participation in the battle. "Evidently it had to be—not knowing where the next damn meal was coming from, see . . ."[7]

"On Tuesday, May 5th, 1931," writes Harlan memoirist William D. Forester, "the continued pressure exploded. The expected confrontation between the striking or discharged miners and the deputy sheriffs became a reality. . . . Four men were killed and many others were wounded in this fight that became nationally known as the 'Battle of Evarts.' It was charged that concealed miners and sympathizers ambushed a group of deputies on the out-skirts of Evarts, near the railroad track. . . . The dead were: Jim Daniels, a deputy sheriff, Otto Lee, a deputy sheriff, Howard Jones, store clerk . . . and Carl Richardson, alleged to have been in the mob of attackers."[8]

The miners had congregated at the Evarts L&N depot when they heard that a truck carrying furniture for a nonunion worker was to pass through town, accompanied by deputy sheriffs, on its way to the Black Mountain Corporation coal mine at Verda. According to some stories, rumors had spread that gun thugs were coming to Evarts to raid the town and rape the miner's women. As the motorcade passed a narrow cut near the railroad depot, one shot rang out. Here versions diverge: according to the one later upheld by the Kentucky courts, a barrage of fire hit the cars; two of the guards were killed before the cars stopped and Jim Daniels got out to respond to the fire, only to be killed point blank by a shot in the face. According to the defense, the cars stopped, and Jim Daniels got out after the first, isolated shot; he fired back attempting to shoot the sniper, and only then the other miners opened fire on him. Far from ambushing the cars, it was claimed that the strikers were actually running for cover. Granny Hager recalls: "And now when Jim Daniels was killed at Evarts, I was standing ten foot of him when he was shot down, and the men was runnin' goin' over the river bank going behind the crosstie piles; Bill Worthington [a Black miner and union activist] said, 'Granny, why don't you go somewhere?' I said, 'You men took all the hiding places,' I said, I had no choice, I had to stand there!"[9]

Forty-three miners were indicted after the battle. The rank-and-file strike leaders were accused of conspiring to ambush the guards (which they of course denied); eight men were sentenced to life imprisonment and served from five to ten years in jail before they were pardoned by Kentucky governors. After the Battle, the National Guard was stationed in Harlan until the strike was broken and the UMWA withdrew from the county. A few days later, organizers from a dual union, the Communist-led National Miners Union, entered Harlan County, leading to a second phase of the struggle, to which I will return further on.

CRUMMIES CREEK, APRIL 2, 1941

> *Granny Hager:* Crummies Creek. Now, there was killing there and I
> can't tell you just how many that were killed. You see, I used to have
> all of that down, but it got washed away so many times, and burned
> out. But I can't remember how many were killed, but, I don't know all
> that did happen, but they really had a battle up there. I think there
> was five killed. They wanted the scabs to go on to work and they
> wanted to run the union men away, you see, and just let the scabs go in
> an out when they wanted to. And that is really what started the
> battle.[10]

George Titler, who was responsible for the UMWA organizing drive in
Harlan County, writes in his autobiography, "On April 1, 1941, the nation's mines were shut down when operators, including those in Harlan,
refused to sign a contract with the UMWA. During this short strike, one
of the most vicious mass murders in Harlan County history took place at
Crummies Creek. The murderer was gun thug Bill Lewis, who was killed
four months later, and his victims, all union men, were Virgil Hampton,
Oscar Goodlin, Charles Ruth and Ed Tye." According to Titler, Lewis
"was stationed behind a machine gun 'emplacement' on the meat counter
of a company store at Crummies Creek. Four UMWA pickets, who were
tired and thirsty, walked into the store to buy a coke. Lewis cut loose with
the machine gun and killed four of them."[11] An editorialist for the local
Harlan Daily Enterprise noted, shortly after the fact, "A few days ago a
bunch of men invaded the commissary at Crummies Creek Coal Co., and
four of them were carried out dead, and others, wounded. There were
other dead which have never been admitted. A known leader of the men
said the men were shot down when they entered the store to get a Coca-
Cola apiece. Do I believe that? NO!" According to the writer, the same
group had already raided nearby commissary stores, beating up nonunion
miners and threatening officials. "The only thirst the leaders of these men
had was the thirst for the blood of someone not paying dues to the
union."[12]

Oral narrators tell an altogether different story. Some details stand out—
the machine gun on the meat counter, for instance. Others are amplified
and made more contradictory: Did the machine-gun fire start before or
after the men entered the store? How many men were on the picket? Were
they armed? Was all the shooting only on one side? Were there other casualties? On which side? How many?

Plennie Hall: [It was] the day before the battle, and I went into the office and I told Mr. Johnson, Mr. Johnson I says, won't you sign the union, I says. It would be good for everybody, to be satisfied with everything. And he said, hell no; he said he wouldn't join [sign with] the union under no circumstances. And the next day then, the union come up there to stop them from working.[13]

Hazel Leonard: In the morning when the men got out [on strike], they'd all meet at a certain spot [to organize the pickets]. My husband was a rustler; he just went around through the camps, woked everybody up that morning. And, he was s'posed to, he was scheduled to go to Crummies. And, somewhere along there they changed it. They was having some problems at Highsplint. So they sent him to Highsplint. They picked out the ones who wanted to go to Highsplint, and the ones who wanted to go to Crummies. That's how he missed that; he was sent to Highsplint that morning; or he'd been in that too. And all of them carried guns, the union men carried guns: they had to, because they had to protect themselves, you know. And, well, they, when they got to Crummies, it was just like a army there.[14]

Ben Campagnari: There was about five hundred that was on that march. We was all up there [on the hillside at Crummies Creek], and the cars was parked around the commissary; there's a wide place there, we had cars parked all the way to the wood. Anyhow, the union had this van, with a loudspeaker. Virgil Hampton, he was talking over the loudspeaker; they said, they closed the commissary. He said, let them close that damn scabby commissary, he said, we don't want any of it no way. And part of our men was in there.[15]

Hazel Leonard: And so some of the men went on in the store, not knowing that they had it set up, you know, they'd just start firing on them. And so when they got in[side the store] there, they just started shooting the union men. They killed three, I believe it was.

Ben Campagnari: Then the machine guns started shootin', out from the top, upstairs, and it's cutting streaks of that pavement up, it looked like a big twisted tobacco. And, [it's a] thousand wonders [there have] been [no] more got killed than was, see; and there was four that got killed there, see. And, my brother lay down 'side of a car, and he laid down—they punctured a tire, and when they punctured that tire a little gravel flew all over him, he jumped up, went to flyin', thought he was shot.

Plennie Hall: And there was a Hampton boy; he is related to these Hamptons that lives down here, is my good friends. There was three men that was killed, trying to save his life. He got shot in the leg, up in this thigh here, and shot that jugular vein. He was trying to get a bandage around it, keeping him from bleeding to death, and the machine gun upstairs in the office in the commissary [kept on firing].

Granny Hager: Now that was the roughest place we had in Harlan County. Don't now let nobody tell you that they're a brave man or a woman. You see them shot down all around you, or see somebody shot down right by your side, now if you've got any place to hide you're going to try it. I used to be, I thought, brave, but now in a time like that, you'll go if you've got somewhere to go to.[16]

Annie Napier: Didn't they fire them machine guns as long as they could see anybody moving, Uncle Plennie? Kept them pinned down as long as they could see anybody moving.[17]

Plennie Hall: Yeah. Never did know how many was killed at that time. One of them bullets hit me, and I don't know where it came from. It was a machine gun bullet; it was a .45 machine, upstairs. Were you ever in any kind of battle or anything? Never? If [they] ever begin a machine gun fire, you might as well lay there because if you move, or try to get up or get away, you're hurt, killed or either shot. I had the top of my back skin knocked off several times with bullets. I tried to save someone else, I tried to get to him. It's hard to think about, how times were pretty rough at that time.

Ben Campagnari: Now, we were runnin', and we had a pegleg man. You wouldn't believe it. Goin' down that railroad track, and he's hittin' about four ties at a time; and he outrun half of the people that had good legs, and we was all a-runnin' because they was cuttin' down with the machine gun, or tryin' to. But, the way they had it elevated, it's lucky that a bunch of us didn't get—but, I mean, more than what did get killed, you see. Tye, and Hampton—Virgil Hampton, and Tye, I can't think of the other two names. We had three of our men there, and one of the thugs was killed there, but they would never tell his name. And I said right then, "If I ever go on a picket line, again, I'll go with protection." We died just like ducks. Peaceful picketing! But there's one fellow went back to his car, he had a high-powered rifle, [placed] it over the crossing, and boy when you'd seen that thing fire, when I was running, I looked back, and you could see them bricks a-flyin'out there. You know, he was hittin' that commissary, but he wasn't hittin' that window where the machine gun was set up, you see. They had it set up on meat blocks.

Media Jones: [My husband and his brothers] they was up on the mountain in the road up there, in a ditch. But they was close enough that they could see some of the thugs getting killed, and one of them was begging for help. He was shot and layin' and I guess there was people who would have went and holp him but they was afraid to show theirselves, that if they did they'd get shot or something. Yes, my husband was very upset when he came back that night. He had nightmares, you know, when he came home, to think that things could be that rough.[18]

Hazel Leonard: It was in the store, in the basement; the biggest battle happened in the basement. The store manager or something there, I don't know which, maybe the butcher—but anyway, he had a machine gun on the block where they chop meat. And he's the one turned that gun loose on these men that walked in first. And then when he did that—the rest of them was ready. They knew this battle was coming. They knew it; and they was ready for it. I guess all the union men just went in there too [broke into the commissary store], and they just wiped them [thugs] out. They just started killing—when it cooled down enough they could close the doors, you know, they did. I don't know how many they killed; we'll never know cause they didn't let it out.

Plennie Hall: They [the company men] went across a mountain there, toward [Virginia], they went across that mountain with their [dead men's] feet sticking out their windows. Three weeks later I was over there getting a payday, and there was a drain pipe runs down there, and there was somebody crawled in that drain pipe and that died, and the dogs pulled out some of his bones. There never was no more said about it. I wondered about who that could have been, or where they were from. And there's a dance hall on the mountain there, you come past it but it ain't there now, it was back then. In the evening that that killing and all was done, and all them people was going across the mountain, that building was burnt, and I wondered a lot about that. Whether there was a lot of people put in there and burnt or what happened, I don't know.[19]

Hazel Leonard: And, that night, the thugs that lived, they carried all their dead men out of there and hauled them to the top of the mountain, Crummies mountain, and burned them up. There was a place there, that they called the Halfway House, it was just a dive, you know, just for men to drink and hang out at. And they sold booze and everything, you know what I mean. So they hauled all these people out there, that had got killed that night—the thugs. They hauled them all night long up that mountain to that place and then they burned it. They burned them up. And then some women from out West started investigating or having it done, wanting to know what'd become of their husbands, they didn't come back home and they never got any word, what happened or anything. And they never did get no word. They don't know what happened to this day. Their husbands never made it back home, but they got killed and burned up, up on that mountain. 'Cause they'd hired guns, you know, they told me, from out West, somewhere West to come here to do this. And, they meant to kill all the men that went out that morning on that strike, but they didn't, they just killed—four, I guess. One reason I know so much about this, my aunt's husband was one of the thugs. [He] didn't get it; cause he was a police in Evarts a long time, everybody knew him. They run him out of Harlan. They told him they never wanted to see him here again. And she told me.

Two weeks after the Battle at Crummies, another bloody battle occurred on the Tennessee-Kentucky border, at Fork Ridge, in nearby Bell County, costing four lives—including the top officials of the Fork Ridge Coal Company, and a union miner.[20] Shortly after this, the operators signed the contract.

THE GRAMMAR OF TIME

Let us now examine the ways in which the Battle of Evarts is constructed into a historic event, while the equally dramatic Battle of Crummies remains confined to the memories of the participants and their immediate circle. The cultural construction of the event takes place on four interrelated axes: the grammar of time, the spatial referents, the social paradigm, and the narrative point of view.[21] Let us begin with the grammar of time.

Time, as we know, is a continuum; an event, on the other hand, is conceived as punctual and discrete. Events are identified and located in time in terms of a linear syntagmatic axis (chronology), two vertical paradigms (temporal simultaneity, formal similarity), and their combination in historical discourse. The syntagmatic axis breaks the continuum of time into discrete units (a year, a minute, a decade); the most familiar procedure is periodization. The paradigmatic axes of simultaneity designate, among the many occurrences taking place at any given unit of time, the events that go to form the historical canon and combine them in a coherent sequence with related events taking place at other times.

When we apply this grid to the battles of Evarts and Crummies, the

first thing we note is that Evarts came first on the linear axis. It was therefore perceived as a shocking revelation of bitter class conflict and oppres-
sive social relationships within a supposedly democratic nation. Crummies, on the other hand, was a repetition of things known, a *déjà vu*.
Historiography therefore recognizes the Battle of Evarts as the beginning
of an era that was assumed to be closing by the time the Battle of Crummies took place.

This brings us to the vertical axis of simultaneity. Evarts made national
news because it appeared to be representative of the radicalization of social conflict that accompanied the onset of the Depression. The national
media, and urban intellectuals and writers—from Theodore Dreiser to
John Dos Passos, Sherwood Anderson, Waldo Frank, Reinhold Niebuhr—
flocked to Harlan after the Battle of Evarts, to investigate and spread the
news. To all of them, Evarts and Harlan represented the tragedy of the
Depression and the violence of capitalist society.

The Battle of Crummies, on the other hand, did not harmonize with
its historical context of prewar national unity, and therefore seems meaningless, that is, not typical and representative of anything. By 1941, the
Depression was officially over. Franklin Delano Roosevelt's 1937 curse
on both unions and operators—"a plague on both your houses"—reflected
the country's weariness with a seemingly endless controversy.[22] Attention was now focused on the war in Europe, the possibility of U.S. involvement, and the coming war effort. In this context, a gunfight in re-
mote Kentucky had as much chance of being noticed as did a delayed but
representative text of the Depression—James Agee's *Let Us Now Praise
Famous Men*—which appeared in the same year as the Battle of Crummies, and also went unnoticed. The Thirties were over.

Which takes us to back to the vertical axis of periodization. One reason why the Battle of Crummies is missing from history books is that they
take "the Thirties" too literally. For instance, John Hevener consulted pe-
riodicals from January 1, 1930, to December 31, 1939: no wonder he ex-
cludes Crummies. William D. Forester's local history and memoir, *Harlan County—The Turbulent Thirties*, also stops with the signing of the
contracts in 1939: "Let's stop right here, while it's nice and peaceful," he
concludes.[23] The only book that mentions Crummies is not a history but
a personal memoir: George Titler's recollection of his years in Harlan,
based on a personal rather than historical periodization, recognizes that
for Harlan miners the Thirties did not end until 1941—if they ever did.
After all, men have died in strikes in Harlan in the 1970s, and the county
is almost entirely nonunion today.

The breakdown of time also influences the making of the historical event in another way. Conventional written history, coherent with the discrete nature of writing, tends to break down time into discrete, separate events. Oral sources, relying on limited and holistic personal memory, tend to condense individual events into synthetic representations of a continuum. Written histories tend, therefore, to be syntagmatic (one event after another), while oral narratives often lean toward a paradigmatic structure of analogies.

Thus, written histories and memoirs tell chronological stories of distinct *battles*—Evarts, May 5, 1931; Stanfill, July 12, 1939;[24] Fork Ridge, April 15, 1941—while oral sources represent a continuous state of permanent *war*. Historians line up episodes in linear syntagmatic sequence, while oral narrators move back and forth between them in the form of mental associations, like Walter Benjamin's angel of history who, "where we perceive a chain of events, [. . .] sees one single catastrophe."[25] In a typical sequence, which applies both to Mike Mullins's interviews with Granny Hager and to my own with Ben Campagnari and Hazel Leonard, answers to questions about Evarts include references to Crummies. One effect is that the prominence which Evarts receives from having been first in chronological order is very much attenuated in the shuttlework of oral narratives, where both Evarts and Crummies exist simultaneously in the *gestalt* of memory.[26]

This has a bearing on the selection of the "representative" event. A change-oriented history will naturally focus on the event that marks the beginning and the discovery of a new situation. The synthetic *longue-dureé* of memory overrides chronology, and the more dramatic (and, perhaps, more recent) event has more chances of being selected as representative than one that merely happened to be first. In fact, there is a possibility that, once the event is selected, details from other events and situations may become attached to it in memory. Thus, some of the oral versions of the Battle of Crummies may be influenced by its near simultaneity with the Battle of Trace Fork, as well as by another episode that occurred at Crummies in 1931, a few days after the Battle of Evarts, when a march of three hundred union miners was dispersed by the National Guard.[27]

SOCIAL PARADIGMS AND SPATIAL REFERENTS

Let us now move from the grammar of time to the social paradigm and the related spatial referents. No event is recognized as such in isolation;

it needs to be part of a coherent whole—a history, or a story. Histories
and stories are composed by piecing together events that are felt to be
linked by some paradigmatic relationship. One such paradigm concerns
the thread of social reference to which narrators ascribe the meaning of
their stories. Basically, we can identify three vertical levels:

1. *Institutional:* the sphere of politics, government, parties, unions,
   elections; the national and international historical context; ideology
2. *Communal:* the life of the community, the neighborhood, the
   workplace; strikes, natural catastrophes, rituals; collective
   participation in "institutional" episodes
3. *Personal:* private and family life; the life cycle: births, marriages,
   jobs, children, deaths; personal involvement in the two other levels

Each of these levels is functionally related to a spatial referent: the institutional level to the nation or the world; the collective level to the community, the neighborhood, the workplace; the personal level to the home.
One of the differences between the stories about Evarts and those about
Crummies is that they are connected to different social paradigms and
different spatial referents.

No sooner was the Battle of Evarts over than the removal of discourse
began from the collective to the institutional level, and from the community to the State—in both senses, away from the miners' sphere of influence. As Forester aptly puts it, "The telephone lines between Harlan and
[Kentucky state capital] Frankfort were hot with callers. . . . Two days
later, on Thursday, May 7, the National Guard arrived on the scene in
Harlan County."[28] Political and military control was located in the state's
capital, Frankfort, rather than Harlan. The same applies to judicial control: the trial for the events at Evarts was removed from Harlan to Mt.
Sterling, a farming community in the bluegrass region of Kentucky.

Both moves were strategic. The miners' hope that a more distant authority would be more neutral than the local sheriffs was soon disappointed
when the National Guard assumed that its mission was to break the strike.[29]
The removal of the trial to Mt. Sterling also decreased the miners' chances
to be heard. John M. Robsion, counsel for the defense, wrote, "Scarcely
one of our witnesses had any money with which to make the trip to Mt.
Sterling and had no money to pay board or lodging. . . . Furthermore, we
were projected into a Bourbon community. . . . They know little or nothing about those who toil in the mines . . . little or nothing about organized
labor and on the whole are unfriendly to organized labor."[30]

The same local authorities that had welcomed outside control of law and order, however, raised an outcry when it was the other side's turn to attempt to broaden the social paradigm and the spatial referent. After the UMWA withdrew from Harlan, at the end of May, 1931, the communist-led National Miners Union (NMU) came to the area, established a local, and led a strike that lasted into 1932. The NMU's strength lay less in its organization and numbers than in its ability to stir public opinion by mobilizing left-wing and progressive intellectuals. Its strategy was to link the community level and the miners' discourse to a broader audience and a wider reference. Theodore Dreiser's account of his committee's findings in Harlan and Bell Counties, *Harlan Miners Speak,* together with countless newspaper and magazine articles, helped keep Harlan in the news for several months.[31]

On the one hand, the local power structure attempted to stir resentment against these "meddling" outsiders and "agitators" coming from New York to slander Harlan's name. As John Gaventa notes, they used their "gatekeeping" power to keep the miners from learning about the nationwide solidarity to the strike. Local papers censored the news; and Dreiser, Waldo Frank, and other sympathetic visitors were arrested, violently evicted from the county, and framed under charges ranging from criminal syndicalism to adultery.

The result was another, partial, silencing of the miners. "The northern liberals," writes Gaventa, "sought to allow freedom of expression for the miners by challenging the barriers to the exercise of their civil rights; yet the consequence was the transformation of the substance and arenas of the issues away from those originally expressed and felt by the miners." Thus, the framing of Dreiser "received far more public attention than the original purpose or findings of his investigation."[32]

One effect of the experiences of the Dreiser and Niebuhr committees and others was to turn Harlan into a matter of federal concern, a subject of institutional discourse with national spatial referents. A Subcommittee of the United States Senate, chaired by Senator Edward P. Costigan, investigated "Conditions in Harlan and Bell Counties." Though friendly to the miners, the Costigan Committee conducted its hearings not in Harlan, but in Washington; it heard more outside observers than local miners, and dealt more extensively with the institutional level (the violations of civil rights) than it did with the collective and personal issues of the miners' economic rights.[33]

No such thing took place after the Battle of Crummies, which remains strictly linked to the communal paradigm and the local spatial referent. The episode was not considered to be so serious as to require the return of the National Guard. No judicial investigation seems to have taken place. There were no congressional investigations, no stories on the national media, no committees of urban writers and intellectuals, and certainly no radical ideology was involved.

This, of course, has a bearing on the different impact of the two battles on academic historiography. Because Evarts became an issue for the labor movement and for civil rights nationwide, it is widely documented and reported, and comes naturally to the attention of labor historians and historians of the Left. In fact, if historians have a problem in dealing with Evarts, it is the surfeit of written sources, including thousands of pages of judicial papers and hundreds of newspaper and magazine articles. On the other hand, no written institutional records seem to exist of the Battle of Crummies: an admittedly quick search through the appropriate files in the UMWA archives in Washington failed to turn up a single item about it.

The communal memory of Crummies relies, however, on a very tangible record: the building itself, a visible place of memory that keeps the storytelling alive. Symbolically, Granny Hager points out that, instead, the very space in which the Battle of Evarts took place has disappeared: "You see, the new road was put in after this all happened. When I went back over there, I was lost. I didn't hardly know where I was at."[34] The communal space referent is, to use one of Hager's phrases, "washed away . . . and burned out": the memory of the battle survives in individual memory and in the official and historical record. As she graphically pointed out to me during our interview in 1973, however, her memory of both Harlan and Crummies relies on another, more personal spatial referent: the scars and marks that these battles left upon her own body.

POINT OF VIEW

Spatial referents and social paradigms help shape narrative modes and point of view. The institutional mode, for instance, is functionally interlocked with an outside spatial reference, and an omniscient narrator located outside and above the controversy of events—like a judge and a historian. Thus, judicial and historical discourse, related to such institutions as the courtroom and Congress on one hand, and the university on the other, prevails in the discourse on the Battle of Evarts, while discourse on the Battle of Crummies exists only in the first-person narratives of the personal or communal mode.

This is not to say, of course, that there are no first-person narratives about the Battle of Evarts. Their meaning, however, is shaped by the inevitable relationship with historical and judicial narratives. Thus, Granny Hager describes both battles very much in the same terms: the feeling of danger, the act of seeking shelter. However, while textually similar, the two narratives are related to different discourses and different functions. Her description of the Battle of Evarts is at the margins of an overall framework controlled by other, institutional narratives. She breathes the life of detail into the judicial and historical reconstruction, but her story must find its place within its frame, comparing her versions with the official ones ("The man who went to jail for it," she says, "was not the one who did it"). Other narrators, such as Chester Pore, were involved in the institutional story of the trial, and their recollections reflect this fact.

Granny Hager's or Plennie Hall's descriptions of the events at Crummies, on the other hand, are primary sources: any reconstruction of what happened at Crummies can be pieced together only from narratives of this kind. While the discourse on Evarts is, apparently, dominated by the "objectivity" and "neutrality" of institutional omniscient narrators, the discourse on Crummies is available only in the subjective, circumscribed point of view of direct participants and their circle.

A closer look, however, reveals that the display of factuality that shapes judicial discourse in the trial record, the Dreiser investigation, and the Costigan Committee is to a large extent a fiction. Questions, especially in the two committees, are so specific that no reader can fail to realize that they are asked precisely because the investigators already know the answers, and wish to elicit a public repetition of statements already rehearsed elsewhere. While this is neither legally nor morally wrong, and serves certain useful functions, it does inject an element of theatrical performance into what is displayed as factual objectivity.[35] In a more complex manner, the concept of performance also applies to the trial at Mount Sterling, where both sides presented versions calculated to be most favorable to them, and some witnesses clearly repeated prepared statements, possibly suggested by counsel or prosecution.[36]

Now, these performances of objectivity become the privileged sources for would-be objective historiography: there is an inevitable impact of what is known as the "judicial truth" upon what comes to be accepted as the "historical" truth. In fact, judicial discourse directly enters historical discourse. While studiously neutral, Hevener bases his reconstruction of the Battle of Evarts almost wholly on courtroom testimony, hostile to the miners.[37] Forester, antiunion on principle but related to one of the defense lawyers, prefers to leave conclusions open. Titler, who incorporates a pam-

phlet of the miners' defense committee, contrasts the official story with
what he calls "the real story." None resists the compulsion to repeat the
judicial discourse at a more fundamental level: that is, to use the evidence
to attempt a reconstruction of what "really" happened. Was there a lull
between the first shot and the rest? When did Jim Daniels get off the car?
Did he start shooting back before he was hit? Did the conflagration explode almost accidentally, or was it caused by Daniels's response to the
first shot?

All this of course is important and interesting, but finally self-defeat-
ing: although sources about Evarts abound, we are no more sure about
what happened there than we are about Crummies. In both cases we know
who fired the first shot: the miners at Evarts, the company guards at Crummies. In neither case do we know for sure what the miners' original intentions were: was there a "conspiracy" at Evarts? Did miners carry guns
at Crummies, as Hazel Leonard says, or was it "peaceful picketing," as in
Ben Campagnari's version? In both cases, there are good reasons for be-
lieving and disbelieving either version.

The historiographic continuation of judicial discourse misses the point
also for another reason: the attempt to establish a "thick description" of
events obfuscates the need for a thick description of the cultural factors
involved. Once we do our best, and fail, to ascertain what happened, the
central question is: What do the Battles of Evarts and Crummies *mean*?
And the question of meaning sends us once again from the analysis of
"objective" events, back to the analysis of personal stories.

BODY COUNTS

There is another parallel between Evarts and Crummies. In both cases,
the available written sources specify the number of casualties, with names
and all—as it happens, four in both cases. In both cases, however, oral
sources (direct or indirect), suggest that the dead may have been many
more. In another interview, Florence Reece counts eleven victims at Evarts,
seven guards and four miners.[38] Hazel Leonard claims that at Crummies
the miners "killed more of the thugs than the thugs killed of them"; the
Harlan Daily Enterprise columnist mentions rumors according to which
the casualties at Crummies were many more. According to Forester, Harlan Sheriff J. H. Blair was reported to have claimed that "many more miners were slain or wounded in the Battle [of Evarts] than were reported as
casualties." "Many people," wrote Jim Garland later, "ask me why the
miners didn't kill all the gun thugs, pointing out that the miners held such

a majority. [But] you must remember that those hired men did nothing but gun-thugging and that the miners' hands, stiff from working, were slow and clumsy with a pistol."[39]

While the claim of self-defense is made in both cases, yet it is usually the side that *did not start* the shooting that claims to have killed more of the other side than was reported: the sheriff claims that the miners' death count at Evarts was higher; the miners claim a higher body count of thugs, and are apologetic about not killing more when they had the chance (the *Enterprise* column is ambiguous as to which side the unaccounted dead were on). We are used to the opposite: each side usually tries to appear as victims, not perpetrators, of violence, maximizing their own losses and minimizing those of the others. This, in fact, was the case whenever institutional discourse prevailed—the trial, and the congressional investigations—and whenever the focus of space changed from local to national, as in the appeals to public opinion on behalf of the victimized miners.

The attitude toward violence, then, tends to shift along with levels of discourse and spatial referents. In the institutional paradigm and "national" space, violence is assumed to be an exceptional disruption of ordinary peace, and therefore wrong; and the victim is automatically right. We will refer to this approach as the "ethical" code on violence. Thus, the first episode of violence, Evarts, was received with shock, but attention faded away when it became apparent that violence was not an exceptional outbreak, but a permanent ingredient of "normality." Violence was then perceived as a discontinuity not in time (the discrete, exceptional event) but in space: the separate, mythical "Bloody Harlan," labeled as deviant from the supposedly peaceful national norm. This automatically excluded from the national sphere such events as the Battles of Stanfill, Crummies, and Trace Fork: no longer capitalists and workers shooting it out in the class struggle, but hillbillies killing one other as they just naturally will.

Harlan, however, is not another country, but very much a part of America. Its people shared, or were at least aware of, the institutional interpretation of violence, and resentment of the "Bloody Harlan" image was strong, especially among the elites. They, however, could not escape the fact that in their experience and environment violence was far from exceptional. In 1920–1925, Harlan had the highest homicide rate in the rural South; in 1933, Harlan's most violent year yet, fifty-six people were shot to death, mostly in open gunfights, and only six killers convicted.[40] "Hell yes," said Sheriff Blair, four days before the Battle of Evarts, "I've issued orders to shoot to kill. When ambushers fire on my men, they'll shoot back and shoot to kill. That's what we use guns for here"—and the emphasis is on the spatial referent, *here*. The Sheriff and the coal operators openly employed known and convicted murderers and criminals as guards and deputy sheriffs throughout the decade.[41]

But Harlan's endemic violence was less intrinsic to the deviant character of the local population than a result of how the county represented a concentration and precipitate of many aspects of the national experience: a combination of the frontier experience with untrammeled capitalism and the American political system.

On the one hand, the frontier situation is represented by the weakness at best, and the lawlessness at worst, of the law. In Eastern Kentucky, the word *law* does not mean the rule of legality, but an armed deputy sheriff. The uncertainty of the law made the region a paradise for lawyers and a nest of endless litigation, but it also led into the temptation to take the law into one's own hands and end litigation by shooting it out, with a fair chance of impunity. Thus, one of the codes that shape the stories of Evarts and Crummies is a frontier code of individualistic pride and honor, in which the other side draws first but you beat them to the draw, and "fighting words" call for immediate action. "I lived through the aftermath of the mountain feuds," says Everette Tharp, a former union organizer from Hazard, Kentucky: "I lived in an age when people respected honor and truth."[42] In the South, this "American law of honor" is modified by the what H. C. Brearley called the *"code duello."*[43] Bill Lewis, the guard who manned the machine gun at Crummies, was killed four months later by a young miner named William Deane, in cold blood and without apparent motive. George Titler implies that this was an act of retaliation for his crime.[44]

The untrammeled capitalistic development that followed the opening of the coal mines in Harlan, on the other hand, allowed the miners no rights that the operators and the authorities were bound to respect. They were under the companies' control as workers, citizens, residents, and consumers; an expendable commodity that could be replaced by machinery or allowed to live or starve according to the employers' convenience and benevolence, or lack of it.[45] One form of violence that remains a factor in the miners' lives is violent death in the mines.[46] Armed company guards, often authorized as deputy sheriffs, oversaw company towns that retained many features of concentration camps, and quickly repressed any attempts at unionization.[47] The combination of the lawlessness of the frontier and the lawlessness of capitalism generated what a 1935 official report to the governor of Kentucky characterized as a "reign of terror" and a "monster-like reign of oppression" whose "principal cause" was "the desire of the mine operators to amass for themselves fortunes through the oppression of their laborers, which they do through the Sheriff's office."[48]

Political patterns, finally, highlight the fact that violence was, on both sides, almost entirely nonideological. American institutional politics, based on fundamental consensus on principles, are much less ideological than those of other countries. This pattern is accentuated, sometimes to excess, at the local level. Thus, politics in Harlan never were a confrontation of different ideas and views of society, but essentially a grabbing for power and patronage, which generated as much violence and killing as union struggles or private disputes.[49]

Union politics were inevitably patterned after the same model. The local power elite charged outbreaks of violence, such as the Battle of Evarts, to the infiltration of radical agitators; this charge, however, was basically unfounded. The conservative UMWA was much more violent than the radical NMU, which supposedly advocated revolutionary violence. Both the Battle of Evarts and the Battle of Crummies, as well as those of Stanfill and Fork Ridge, were fought under UMWA auspices; the miners were never as nonviolent as during the NMU period.

The politicization of the strike under the NMU implied the search for political, rather than military solutions; the weakness of the union made an appeal to "right" more practical than an appeal to "might." NMU miners and organizers insisted that they were being victimized by the gun thugs and deputy sheriffs. They made a symbolic martyr of the murdered NMU organizer Harry Simms. His funeral in New York, with two thousand mourners, was the ritual through which the NMU, through a national spatial referent, advocated the ethical code against the operators' violence. Thus, former NMU activist Jim Garland is virtually the only writer who asserts, against all evidence, that the gun thugs rather than the miners fired the first shot at Evarts.

On the other hand, a conservative leader like George Titler consistently uses military language and metaphors: "When Deane was asked why he killed Lewis," he writes, "he said he was trying to win a medal." He also writes that the men who went on trial for murder after the Battle of Fork Ridge were acquitted by a local jury because "many people felt they were entitled to medals for service rendered to the community beyond the call of duty."[50]

Rather than reflecting the extremism of ideology, extreme forms of struggle, at least in this case, seem to compensate the the silencing of ideological conflict. Where no ideological issue is at stake, "might makes right," and politics, including union politics, becomes essentially a confrontation of power. Shooting is but a continuation of politics by other means.

When our sources talk about "battles," they do not mean the term as metaphor or hyperbole, but literally. The very apparatus of war became part of people's daily lives, as Harlan was repeatedly under military occupation and martial law between 1931 and 1939, over both union conflicts and electoral politics. The fact that the miners' lives were at stake reinforced this perception: "It got to the point where I didn't consider it a strike, I considered it a war against starvation," says former NMU activist Tillman Cadle.[51] A front-page headline of the New York Times told the nation the same story: "Harlan Coal Fields Face Civil War; Kentucky County Is an Armed Camp."[52] The description of those years as a permanent state of war rather than a succession of isolated battles is not only a memory construct but also a description of how people actually experienced them.

In a war, violence is not an exception but the rule: what counts is not to convict the others of violence, but to use violence more effectively than they do. In the ethical code, the victim is the moral winner; in the military code and in the honor code of the frontier, the victim is the material loser. This is why both sides swell the body count, and some still complain that it was not higher. In this, Harlan is as American as apple pie: swelling the body count is precisely what American institutions did in the international spatial referent of the Vietnam war (as long as the question was who was winning. In Panama and the Gulf, where military victory was never in question, the issue was moral and legal, and U.S. national discourse did its best to shrink the body count). Only in the context of war can we understand these stories, and face their horrors. Here is a story of ordinary Vietnam routine, told by an officer of the special forces:

> Anyhow, we had these bodies. Of course, right away, my men would chop their ears off. They dry the ears and wear them around their necks. The CBS and UPI guys got there and the bodies don't have any ears . . .[53]

And here is a story from Evarts, 1931:

> Ben Campagnari: And you know this Joe Rossini [not the real name]. . . ? He was the one [who picked up] Mr. Daniels's head, and he picked up pieces of skull, and he showed my daddy in the courthouse, it had blood on it. He said I'm gonna make me a watch from out of this. And he was I-talian, see.

The man Campagnari refers to may be the same "old miner" who told the story to a magazine interviewer, many years later:

> We went over after the fight and we was looking where he [Jim Daniels] fell at, and there was a piece of his skull . . . a kinda oblong piece . . . layin' on the ground. They just shot it loose there and it peeled outa the skin. . . . I picked it up and scraped the meat off of it, made a watch belt out of it. Took it to Middlesboro and sold it to one of them Ball brothers down there, run one of the bars. Took in $50.[54]

VIOLENCE, SOCIAL PARADIGMS, SPATIAL REFERENTS, AND THE CAMERA EYE

As we have seen, it would be misleading to oppose a "national" ethical code and a "local" military and frontier code. Rather, all these codes co-exist and interact *within* the miners' culture, as well as within American culture at large.[55] In Harlan in the 1930s, the balance shifted according to the historical and political context, to the miners' pragmatic choice of strategy (implying selection of social paradigm and space referent) and to the system of communication. We can see this interplay of codes at work in a brief analysis of three more recent strikes.

In the 1970s, Harlan again made national news, when the two-year strike at the Brookside mine was covered by the award-winning documentary movie, Barbara Kopple's *Harlan County, USA*. In 1987, I interviewed one of the leaders of the strike, who was also very close to Kopple's film crew. When asked whether he would do it all over again, he replied—half serious, half mocking: "Next time, no movie, and much more violence." One cannot help being reminded of the Vietnam officer whose only concern about the earless bodies was what CBS and the UPI would show. Clearly, the presence of outside observers tends to shift the social paradigm (from personal/communal to institutional) and the spatial referent (from local to national or international). It therefore defuses the military code in favor of the ethical one. One reason why the battle of Crummies did not enter the historical record is, as Hazel Leonard remembers, that the killing of the thugs was kept secret by the miners' community.

Outside observers always to some extent impose their own, public, agenda. The presence of the Dreiser committee in the 1930s redirected attention from the material plight of the miners to the question of civil rights. The film crew was sent to Brookside, as one of its members told me, precisely to prevent an eruption of violence, and succeeded in tilting the cul-

tural balance toward the ethical code. Rather than matching the operators' violence, the miners chose to expose it and be the moral, rather than
the military, winners: when a striker was killed by a company guard, the
government induced Duke Power Company to sign the contract. The camera close-up on the victim's brain on the asphalt, parallel both to the
pieces of Daniels's skull and the Vietnamese ears on CBS, was a metaphor
of this strategy.

Things were not that simple, however. In a dramatic meeting, the miners debated whether to respond according to the ethical, military, or honor
codes, and the choice was pragmatic rather than moral: the ethical code
prevailed only when the union and the government assured that it would
guarantee the signing of the contract.[56] In fact, one reason why the government intervened was to prevent the implementation of the other codes:
"Some of the miners, the union miners, the first thing that was in their
mind was revenge. And I saw that. I saw fear, in some people; fear that
what had been a very tense confrontation up to that point, fear that that
could become much more tense and that confrontation could escalate into
a little war, on Clover Fork."[57]

In 1978, a new strike occurred at the Jericol mine, in Harlan County.
This time, no film, and more violence, on both sides. The victim this time
was a nonunion man, a scab. Rather than a military victory—which the
presence of state troops made impossible—this contributed to an ethical
defeat. The strike was lost.[58]

Finally, a cultural trace of the perception of strikes as wars appeared in
the use of camouflage in the 1989 Pittston coal strike in Virginia. Although
they described this practice as only a form of identification,[59] the guerrilla implications were very solid in the miner's history and tradition.[60]
Violence at the Pittston strike was eagerly anticipated, and as much as
prompted, by the media.[61] The media combined their "gatekeeping"
power, keeping the strike away from national scene (a striker stated that
"if this had happened in Poland, it would be front page news every day"),
and "mobilization of bias" by focusing discourse almost exclusively on
"violence." By excluding the strike from the broader spatial referent, and
thus favoring the military code linked to the restricted spatial referent,
the media helped make violence more likely; by focusing on violence as
an issue, they prepared to defeat the strike on the ethical plane.[62]

The union successfully countered this strategy by broadening the space
referent through the rank-and-file grapevine, which made the miners' Camp
Solidarity a meeting-ground of workers and sympathizers from all over
the United States. Shifting the spatial reference from local to national helped

prevent the shift of the code from ethical to military. In their statements and interviews, the miners stressed their victimization by company guards and state troops, and the Virginia governor's impending threat of militarization of the struggle. Finally, even the media had to admit that, while acts of sabotage against things and equipment occurred, the only violence on persons was perpetrated against the miners, not by them. The strike finally had to be mediated at the federal level, and ended in a compromise.

CONCLUSIONS

This chapter has asked two questions:

1. Why is the Battle of Evarts a recognized historical event, while the Battle of Crummies is excluded from standard historical memory?
2. What is the cultural meaning of these two events?

The first question was answered in terms of time, space, social paradigm, and narrative mode. In terms of time, the Battle of Evarts, as opposed to the Battle of Crummies, was perceived as the beginning of a historical period, harmonizing with coeval events, and falling within the time span of conventional periodization. None of this applied to the Battle of Crummies. In terms of space and social paradigms, the Battle of Evarts became national news and a symbol of a national situation. It was dealt with by agencies, institutions, and intellectuals whose sphere of action was outside the local environment, while the Battle of Crummies remained in the communal and personal sphere. In terms of narrative modes, the Battle of Evarts has been told by omniscient outside narrators, in the authoritative judicial and historical mode, while the Battle of Crummies remained the property of folk historians and oral narrators. Thus, while the Battle of Evarts fit a chronological narrative of distinct events (battles), the Battle of Crummies became the symbol of a whole period represented as permanent war.

The second question, cultural meaning, recognized the presence of three overlapping codes concerning violence, which interact in American culture at large, as well as in the specific culture of Harlan coal miners: an ethical code, tied to institutional discourse and national space, which condemns violence as a disruption of supposedly ordinary peace; a frontier honor code, which commands violent response to violent aggression; and a military code, which accepts violence as the norm in a state of war. The shifting balance of these codes has been shown to be a factor in the evolution of specific strikes, as workers endeavored to apply the code that would pragmatically assure the success of their struggle.

Chapter Eight

Absolutely Nothing
Wartime Refugees

EXODUS: BACK TO NATURE

Santino Cappanera:[1] In early July, late May or early July [1944], the raid came at night. This night raid, we had never seen an air raid at night in Terni. So we thought we were safe, at night. But that night the planes came, lighting up the sky, like it was day, the light was dazzling, truly dazzling. And this air raid lasted one hour and fifteen minutes. The morning after, when it was over, and day came, we were all crazed, like, understand? all the people were out of their heads . . . it was terror, they were terrified.

So we made up our minds: all to the mountains, toward the mountains. And, as far as possible from the town. We started off, children, women, old men: because men, say, from sixteen to fifty, there were none left around. They had all either taken to the hills with the partisans, or were in the war, or something. And all this mass of people streamed toward, toward the mountain.

When we reached the last houses beneath the hills, there was a lot of us. But we had nothing to eat; nothing. I mean, nothing, in the true meaning of the word, because no stores were open; nothing, absolutely. Those who might have had something were the farm families; they might have had a little wheat or flour, or something like that. Anyway, out there, thirty or forty of us, a whole group of people, we fed for several days on a pig, torn to pieces and cooked in a barrel, understand; with no bread or anything, and not even forks—we didn't even have those, so we used sticks, pieces of wood.

Anyway, I leave it to your imagination how people can live, you know, ten days or so, with nothing; absolutely nothing. Water—that was all. And at night we slept under the railroad tunnels; on top of the tracks, because there was no other, no other choice, I mean. I think this lasted twelve, thirteen days, or so. We were on the Terni-Sulmona railroad; it wasn't running because the bridges were down, so we

114

knew the train wasn't coming through. So we all slept in this tunnel, in conditions that were indescribable, I mean when you think about it today it seems impossible that we could live, you know, like that, and yet it is possible. And I think some had it even worse. As for me, I had it hard, those fifteen days, because, I was a boy, there was nothing to eat; there was nothing. I mean, this pig which, someone found it, I don't know who or how, I don't know who it belonged to, they killed it, they tore it to pieces, like that.

The twelve days between June 4 and 16, 1944 (when the town was liberated by the partisans and the Allies) were the culmination of the destruction of Terni, which had begun with the Allied air raids of August, 1943.[2] Terni had remained under German and Fascist occupation, and in those months it was hit by more than one hundred raids, always aimed at the civilian population, at the historical center and the railroad system, rather than at the factories and industrial facilities. The number of victims is still unknown; the majority of the population was left homeless.[3]

Thus began the exodus of a whole town, on foot, on bicycles, on carts, from the factories and the working-class neighborhoods toward the hills and the countryside.

> *Antonina Colombi:*[4] Along the road, our mattresses [loaded on a cart] hit a low branch and tore open. Father began to cry: we have nothing left, home is destroyed, we have nothing, even the mattresses for our beds. . . . All that wool. . . . We had to sleep on the floor, I was in labor, and above us lived a teacher; he raised pigeons and kept telling me, "Don't hurt my pigeons, they're hatching." Lice, all down on top of me. Those were old houses, bug-ridden, lousy, dirty. He kept saying, you can stay here three or four days, but don't ruin my pigeon brood. I lay right under the hatching pigeons, covered with lice. We left soon after the Germans came through; in fact I delivered there.

If the purpose of the air raids was to annihilate the structure of civil society, the stories of the refugees show that it was achieved with a vengeance. Many symbols represent the refugees' sense of being bombed out of civilization, almost back to a state of nature. Colombi's labor ranks lower than the pigeons' brood; she finally gave birth "without a midwife, just an expert woman . . . one of those who . . . peasant women, I mean. She collected my child." Nights are spent on the floor, on the ground, in stables and chicken coops (Alvaro Valsenti: "My brother and I pitched a tent outside; my father and mother slept in a little room with a manger—

I mean, it had been used as a stable before."[5] People are associated with animals, lice and bugs, excrement (Antonina Colombi: "When we came home afterwards, the Germans had stolen all the beds, we didn't find a thing. Then—should I say this?—they, the Germans, had crapped all over the place. On the cupboard, on the dinner table, on a big piece of paper, on a dish"). Families are stripped of essential property: the loss of symbolic objects (the bed, the mattresses), the violation and fouling of the home, the sense of having "absolutely nothing," all concur to make the refugees feel that they have been pushed outside the pale of human society.

Return to nature is, however, an ambivalent experience. The probably stolen pig is torn to pieces in almost barbaric fashion, and eaten with bare hands, symbolizing a step back to the savage state, from the cooked to the raw. It is a common symbol in narratives of exposure to the wilderness. In her Indian captivity narrative, for instance, Mary Rowlandson dwells on how she eagerly ate horse liver, which she had previously thought inedible, half raw "with the blood about my mouth."[6] But, just as the Indians' "filthy trash" becomes "sweet and savory" to Rowlandson's taste, so the pig becomes a symbol of new-found community, eaten communally in the hunters' solidarity of the ritual sharing of the prey.[7]

Thus, while some describe the refugee experience as total privation, others remember it as a return to a golden age of primordial abundance, a great rural feast. The theme of rural abundance is found both in oral narratives and literary representations. In Alberto Moravia's *La Ciociara* (translated in English as *Two Women*), the scenery of festive abundance, fine air, and plenty of food in the first section sets out the tragic conclusion of the story: "You'll see, you'll both come back fat and sleek, and this will be the war's only effect on you. . . . Out there in the country you'll find cheese, you'll find eggs, you'll find lambs . . . you will eat and be all right."[8]

The fact that for many of these narrators the refugee experience is also a turning point in the history of their childhood contributes to this attitude. I must have been less than three years old when my family was evacuated to Moricone, near Rome, so it's hard to tell whether my associations are actual recollections or echoes of family talk; but what the place evokes for me is a dark, makeshift dwelling space, the extended family, and lots of food. "Every day was Sunday for us," says Rita Luciani, who was twelve, recalling the rural games, the practical jokes, the pancakes, the vintage season ("You'd take those bunches of grapes and just rub them on your face"), "and I lived like a peasant, almost like a pasha, I mean, I got fat because every morning we'd eat broad-beans, broad-beans with maggots in them, and they tasted good."[9] Maggots are just as disgusting as the lice in Antonina Colombi's shelter, but here they represent, rather than the fall into uncivilized conditions, the shedding of civilized daintiness and disgust.

On the other hand, the promise of rural happiness also smacks ironically of Fascist propaganda: "Mussolini always said, go to the country! Don't you like the country? He wanted us to go live in the country" (Antonina Colombi). However, the peace of the country is one thing, and war is another. Moravia's *Two Women* begins with a rural feast, and ends in rape. Though I did not come across equally tragic stories, yet the possibility of violence—of which rape is the ultimate symbol—looms large in these stories of brutalization and social dissolution. Just as her delivery takes place beneath the lice and pigeons, the attempted rape of Antonina Colombi takes place in a chicken coop: *signorine* and chickens seem to be equally on the Germans' mind.

> *Antonina Colombi:* Later, when I was getting ready to deliver, I was the only young woman in that place, the Germans came by, in retreat, and wanted to carry me away with them because I was the youngest. And I was lucky. I sent them over to Casciano—those two Germans, one was from Ukraine and one from Germany, must have been two meters tall. And I told them, "Go over there, the schoolteacher lives there, and she speaks German, she understands you, she has chickens, go, go." And they: "Be signorine?" "Oh yes," I said. And they said they wanted some nooky nooky. They wanted to break our door; they had their guns in their hands, we were all in there, my husband, too; and this man says, "Vincenzo, he's taking your wife, have you lost your mind, for goodness' sake? Let's kill that German." I said, "Don't kill anyone. I'll take care of it." They took me by the hand and went where the chickens were; they wanted to open the coop and carry me inside. At that point Pietro came by, a man whose wife was at Casciano. He was running, because he had seen what was going on. "Pietro! Pietro Pietro Pietro Pietro!" He says my mouth was all crooked, from fear, from the fright I had taken. I said, "Pietro, listen, they want the schoolteacher, they want the chickens, they want . . ." I was making it all up. He says, "All right." So they [the Germans] took him by the hand: "Be signorine?" He had a young wife; he didn't know what to say. They go to take my hand and take me along, and I say, "Let me go, there's plenty of signorine over there." Later, Pietro told me, "You put me in a lot of trouble," he says; "I had a young wife, too." And the teacher's daughter, she was young. And all escaped from the back [of the house], with ropes, with bedsheets. Some took the animals, some took their possessions . . .

The polarities of brutality and abundance are related to a polarity of interpersonal relations. Some narrators remember a "war" of all against all
(Arnaldo Lippi):[10] Antonina Colombi does not hesitate to send the Germans to the schoolteacher to save herself. Others, on the other hand, recall a heightened sense of solidarity (Anna Santini: "We were good to each
other, in fact, we loved each other more"). Pietro risked his wife to save
Antonina Colombi.[11] Lippi is a factory worker and a political activist;
Santini is a small merchant. Often, the distinction between nature as chaos
and nature as community corresponds to the difference between political
activists, whose ideal of solidarity is identified with the proletarian community of the factory and who see the migration as a dissolution of social ties, and those whose urban experience or ideology had been more individualistic or private, who rediscover a more communal way of life.
Taken together, these stories are not unlike the memories of the Great Depression collected by Studs Terkel, in which a generalized state of individualistic war coexists with the discovery of shared humanity in a time
of crisis. Like Depression stories in the United States, Italian wartime and
refugee tales are used by the older generations as cautionary tales, to tell
their children to be grateful for the good things they have and to stop com-
plaining so much.[12]

STEALING: THE LAW AND THE FAMILY

In all these narratives, the protagonist is the family, especially the extended
family before the urban nuclear model prevailed: "All refugees together,
brothers and sisters and parents, all together" *(Celsa Paganelli).*[13] The family mediates between individualism and solidarity, nature and society: it
is both an extension and an overcoming of the individual self (caring for
others than oneself, and yet one's *own*); it is both a natural and social institution. Thus, in the archetypal refugee and Depression novel—John
Steinbeck's *Grapes of Wrath*—Mama Joad's mission of "keeping the fam-
bly together" legitimates the use of all means necessary, including violence. In *Gone with the Wind,* written during the Depression and dealing
with a war and the dissolution of a society, Scarlet O'Hara, with her face
against the earth, feels authorized to ignore all the laws of society in the
name of the family and the land, sources of *natural* law: "I'm going to
live through this, and when it's over I'm never going to be hungry again.
No, nor any of my folks. If I have to steal and kill—as God is my witness,
I'm never going to be hungry again."[14]

As far as we know, the refugees of Terni never had to kill to survive.

But they did not hesitate to steal, for the sake of the family. A story told by Anna Santini concentrates much of the ambivalence of the refugee experience: laws are suspended, and families that rob together survive and stay together. She dwells on the contact of bare hands with the earth when stealing potatoes to represent the stripping away of all but essential survival, and uses motifs of masking and sudden spurts of abundance to evoke the sense of a feast and, again, a ritual (the time, aptly, is Easter, and the anecdote begins and ends on this note).

> Once, I remember, it was Easter. And in the house we were hungry, I remember, seven or eight of us. So our daddy, he's dead now, he up and said: look, there's this farmer lives down the road, he's full of God's plenty; he sells it all on the black market to the stinking rich— you know, they'd go to him, hand him a lot of money, and buy. So daddy found a machine gun, dirty, old, out of order. And he says, "Look here, listen to what I say: we'll wait until dark, and then, we'll all go down there with this gun, and pretend we're the police, the ration card squad."
>
> So we got organized, seven or eight boys and girls and dad leading the way, with this gun, rusted and unloaded; all disguised with handkerchiefs on our mouths, big woollen caps on our heads. Well, when this man sees us—"What's the matter? what's going on?" Daddy walks up to him and says, look here, somebody spilled the beans on you, you're selling everything on the black market and you don't give anything to the poor people. There are families here that have small children, hungry, you won't even let them have a little cheese". . . . "No, no, it isn't true". . . . "Watch out, we're going to arrest you." "Please, please don't, don't hurt me, I'll do anything just you drop the charges . . ."
>
> Well, to make a long story short, he gave us a lamb, two or three cheeses, and, what made us happiest, two big bottles of olive oil. Oh yes, and two fresh ricotta cheeses, just made, because he kept sheep. A nice hen. Flour. And we celebrated Easter.
>
> Afterwards, when all this food was eaten, hunger came back. And then, there was no getting out of it, we had to go out and steal—in the fields. And, stealing in the fields was dangerous, because if the farmers got you they'd stone you, and some of them kept rifles handy. In fact, at night, we got organized, around one or two a.m., on moonless nights, off we'd go—stealing. I mean, stealing potatoes is hard work, because you have to dig them out with your hands. And then again, around dawn, we'd go home with five or six backpacks full of food, vegetables, potatoes, and it would keep us for two or three days. And then, after three days or so, we'd do it again. So we lived.

The prepolitical suspension of ordinary laws often extends into politically motivated acts of sabotage against the German forces and the Fascist collaborationists. Even when they stayed away from direct involvement, refugees were also one aspect of the resistance: their noncollaboration with the Fascists and the Germans was a factor in the collapse of the system. Survival, the dissolution of law and order, and resistance—the refrains "So we lived," "That's how we lived"—are linked together in a number of stories:

> *Alberto Petrini:*[15] My luck was that, after he was disabled, daddy had
> started a business selling firewood. So my brother and I would go to
> the woods, cut down a couple of trees—it was all right, there was
> nothing, no one to stop us, law and order were gone. We'd get a
> cartful of firewood, and sell it. Or—I'm telling you the whole truth—
> when this wasn't enough, we'd take our umbrellas and go rake olive
> trees. I mean—to scrape us some oil. And, often we'd steal grapes.
> That's how we lived. We'd take our dogs and hunt for hedgehogs—if
> we found a chicken or two, we didn't mind. There was no way to earn
> any money, other than working for the Germans. You ask me, how did
> I survive? Well, look, they said I was crazy. They said I was crazy,
> because I would go down by the station, hide in a creek bed, and wait
> for the alarm to go off. As soon as the alarm rang, the German
> sentries ran into the shelter and left the wagons, full of supplies for the
> troops. And then you'd get up, jump, run to the wagon, open it,
> grab—like, four or five pairs of shoes, and then run. If the German
> had stayed out of the shelter, he'd have shot you down. But they were
> more scared than we were. . . . Good shoes, boots and all: I didn't sell
> them, I bartered. A farmer, you offered him a pair of boots, it was like
> you had saved his life, because there were no shoes to be found
> anywhere. So I'd say, you give me two kilos of flour, or something. I
> didn't want money. Give me a couple of rabbits. . . . Payment in
> nature.

EXCHANGES: THE COUNTRY AND THE CITY

"We exchanged goods, as it were. Barter" (Gino Brunelli).[16] The plunge out of monetary economy, back to barter, is also part of the process of return to a precivilized state of nature. Petrini's story, however, also draws attention to the wartime interaction between the country and the city, farmers and factory workers. Heavy industry was established in Terni in the 1880s almost entirely by outside decisions, and was dropped upon a territory that depended to a large extent on agriculture and on rural culture. While they reshaped the town's identity, industry and the working class remained to some extent an extraneous, artificial presence. The country and the town engaged in a complex tension and interchange. Resident urban factory workers resented the "unfair" competition of rural commuters, who seemed to them politically backward, obedient to factory brass, and less willing to struggle because they had supplementary sources of income and alternative means of support. The rural workers, on the other hand, brought into the factory elements of cultural resistance to industrial space and time, adapting to industrial conditions the traditional peasant forms of self-protection and defense. In turn, the factory had an impact on the countryside, injecting traits of proletarian and industrial culture into a relatively well-preserved, rural sociocultural context.[17]

This background articulates the country-city interaction during the influx of wartime refugees seeking shelter and survival in the hills and valleys around the town. "A conflict developed, which impoverished city people even more, because, even if peasants did help the refugees that camped out under their trees or in the woods, the city folk were forced to sell everything they had, they had to eat out of their own fat" (Arnaldo Lippi). What developed was an exchange between the necessary (food), held by the rural population, and the superfluous, brought by the city refugees: shoes (Alvaro Valsenti: "The peasants, in deep country, when it comes to clothes, shoes, this kind of things, were poorer than city residents"), tobacco, salt (Alfeo Paganelli and Antonina Colombi's families survived by setting up a trade route for salt and tobacco, bought in places away from the war theater, and brought back in with periodical and adventurous bicycle journeys), or soap.

> *Anna Santini:* I began to work the black market for shoe polish. Soap was getting scarce; I still had some left in the store, so we held on to it until there was none to be found, and then I jumped into the black market. There was no soap anywhere, so it was like gold, like gold. We would sell these things that they lacked; all these young wives, young girls, they'd see a cake of soap, a bottle of perfume that they didn't have, and with those little nothings I would fetch home a chicken, a piece of bread, three or four kilos of flour.

It was also an exchange of cultural models. For the price of a chicken, the young rural generations had access to elements of urban life style; for the price of a cake of soap, city folks rediscovered the centrality of a natural act they had been taking for granted: eating.[18] Urban refugees brought to the exchange other cultural prerogatives. Mobility had always been a part of urban, rather than rural life styles, and now that they were compelled to move, they managed to turn themselves into peddlers and black market operators on the road. Technical knowledge acquired in the factory allowed them to exchange skilled work for food: "We went around fixing all the agricultural machines and equipment, whatever we found. When they'd ask, 'How much do you want?' 'Nothing.' 'What do you mean, nothing?' 'Whatever you've got; a peck of beans. Give me some beans. You want to, give me a drop of oil, a piece of lard'" (Arnaldo Lippi).

Just as in the factory, the refugee experience articulated the polarity of egotism and reciprocal solidarity according to the existing relationship between each family or individual and the rural background. Many urban families had country relatives; for a number of them, the exodus meant going back to the home village. In Greccio, "most [of the refugees] were people who had relatives, who had acquaintances" (Luigi Menichelli).[19] Family relationships were supplemented by networks of friendships, neighborhood, workplace. Sante Carboni was boarding with a family in Terni, and when they went to stay with friends in Stroncone they found a place for him to stay too.[20] Alvaro Valsenti found temporary shelter through his brother's coworkers; however, since he occupied a more peripheral place in the network, his family had to settle in "a barn, abandoned rooms where they kept corn to dry," while his brother's family found a regular house.

NEUTRALS AND RESISTERS: PARTISANS AND REFUGEES

Toward the end of the war, the country-city relationship was shaped also by another experience: the partisan movement. One of the earliest and most active partisan brigades in Central Italy, the Brigata Gramsci, was formed in Terni mainly by factory workers. The brigade, however, operated in the hills and the countryside around town, and its effectiveness and survival depended on its relationship with this territory and its population. Therefore, the "intermediate" workers—industrial workers with a rural background, especially those who lived in the villages of the Valnerina—became the backbone of the partisan leadership.

"Pure" urban industrial workers—especially recent immigrants, who had no roots in the territory—were limited by their continuing dependence on the factory for survival: "All tried to find a place in a range of thirty, forty kilometres, so they could keep their jobs" (Fabio Fiorelli).[21] This link was retained until October, 1943, when the air raids closed the factories down: "I did go out as a refugee, but not very far from town, I kept going to and fro. I went to work until [the air raid of] October 14; remember that I gave it up after October 14" (Alfio Paccara).[22]

The loss of contact with the workplace reinforced the priority of survival, by any means necessary. In a way, the sense of having dropped out of history, out of organized society, is expressed also by a neutral, spectatorial attitude toward the historical events that took place on the edge of the refugees' daily life. The emphasis on *seeing* and the balance of killings in Rita Luciani's narrative and the insistence on his personal friendship with both sides in Alfeo Paganelli's combine the refugee's neutral estrangement—the ideology of noninvolvement of those who do not "meddle with politics" and step aside to wait out the war—with a sense that the partisans are, ultimately, their natural allies.

> *Rita Luciani:* When I was staying in this village, Lugnola, one night, I was staying with this lady who had little children; one of them woke up. And from outside we kept hearing—it was night, deep, dark—we kept hearing outside some strange noises, sort of hushed. In those days one didn't have a sense of what could be happening, because it was wartime, and. . . . So we peeked out of the window without turning on the light, to see what was happening, and the Fascists had the whole village surrounded. Because the partisans had a camp up high on a mountain, nearby. Which partisans after dinner toward dawn, toward midnight, used to come down to the village, make the round of people's houses, and some would give them one thing and some would give them another, I mean, we all tried to help them. So one fine day the Fascists and the Germans got together and surrounded the village. Hunting for these people, these partisans, and also to mop up all the men who were maybe dodging the draft or who had gone AWOL on September 8.[23] Afterwards, listen, first thing they mopped up all the able-bodied men, and then we saw up the side of this mountain the Fascists climbing along with the Germans, and meanwhile we saw the partisans getting ready to face them. . . . You'd see all those little clouds of gunfire, of shots, until at one point the Fascists came back down because the partisans, who knows, maybe they had a drop on them, they were well entrenched, what can I say?
>
> Another episode I remember of the war, all these actions, they call them reprisals. There was this mailman from Configni who also carried the mail to this village, called Lugnola. And the partisans told him, go ahead and carry the mail, we don't care if you're a Fascist, as long as you don't wear the [post office] uniform. But this man still had Fascist ideas. So they told him, look, we're warning you once, we're warning you twice, but if you're not careful you'll come to a bad end. So one fine morning we saw him coming to bring the mail, and then

start walking to another village nearby. We were young kids, with
nothing to do, so we just looked; and we saw the partisans come
down, catch this man, drag him behind a bush, we heard two or three
rifle shots, and they killed him. Because it wasn't only the Fascists that
did such things. Partisans made reprisals, too, understand?

Alfeo Paganelli: You'd make shift now with one thing and now with
another, selling, mostly selling, to these country folks who had a
surplus of food, wine, oil, everything. So we would sell these things
that they needed, salt, matches, and also we sold cigarettes. [The
partisans] would come to where we were staying, to buy cigarettes,
too. The partisans came, and the Fascists also.

At the time of partisans and Fascists, maybe the column of the
partisans would arrive today. They come down—they knew me, they
were all friends of mine, the partisans and the Fascists: they were all
from Terni, I knew them well. "Say, you got cigarettes?" I say, "Yes, I
do." They say, "How much?" So and so. He'd give me the money, and
then ask, "Have you seen the others?" "Well, not today."

Maybe the Fascists would arrive next—"You got cigarettes?" "Yes."
They'd come over, all the platoon. After, they'd say, "Have you seen
the partisans?" "Well, they came by yesterday; be careful, you take
this other road." I mean, I was sorry for them, they were all my
friends, all my friends, because, even if he thinks different from you,
getting killed. . . . Why don't you kill the big men, the big men who
wanted these things to happen, not us workers who have to kill one
another for their sake!

COMING HOME

Most narrators describe the refugee experience as a parenthesis, but it also
left permanent marks. Just before the native population began its exodus
from town, Terni had received an influx of immigrant labor force attracted
by the expansion of war production. These newcomers were also involved
in the refugee exodus, but didn't go very far, and were the first to return,
because they had no roots in the country. Some of the native refugees—
especially those with deeper roots in the local traditional culture, and those
who had lost their possessions and homes in the air raids—chose instead
not to return. "Many never returned, they had no contacts left in town,
they stayed where they were. It is important also in terms of identity. A
number of Terni natives remained in the country, out of town, while the
newcomers who had come to work in the factories during the war moved

into the old working-class neighborhoods that had been bombed and emptied. The identity, the roots, changed" (Fabio Fiorelli).

Those who returned and found their houses devastated and destroyed, had a hard task before them: finding the strength to begin all over again.

Celsa Paganelli: When we came home, my dad had a stroke; he was paralyzed from his throat down. Because he said, the house, the October air raid when the alarms didn't go off, it tore it down. And we weren't finished paying for it yet. I was fixing it, adding a floor, and I didn't have a cent. So dad began to have trouble speaking, and the paralysis grew on him, after that. He said, "The house is gone; even the beds to sleep on are gone." So mother hugged him: "We'll start all over again." He says, "I don't want to die a refugee." And as soon as we came back he died. He was beginning to sort the rubble, he was brave, he was making order in the ruins, to begin again.

Chapter Nine

The Battle of Poggio Bustone
Violence, Memory, and Imagination
in the Partisan War

THEY'RE AFTER US

Vero Zagaglioni, partisan commander of the Brigata Gramsci, operating near Terni (Umbria) in 1943–44, recalls,

> The night of the ninth of March [1944], when we reached [the mountain hamlet of] Cepparo, this man came over to us. Says, "Look, the Fascists are in Poggio Bustone, and they're looking for you. They say," he says, "'Ah, where are the partisans? They're hiding from us'" . . .[1]

On March 10, 1944, the Fascists of Rieti (a province seat in Lazio, near the Umbria border) came to Poggio Bustone, a small town in the Sabine hills, to mop up draft resistors for the Fascist army and to arrest political dissenters. At their head were Captain Tandurri of the Fascist militia, and the *questore* (chief of police) of Rieti, Panaria. A song written by partisan Dante Bartolini imagines them, strutting into town as if they owned it: "With all your arrogance \ And the way you acted \ You seemed to be the master \ Of the whole human kind."[2] Vero Zagaglioni goes on:

> At this point, I began to wake up those who were already lying down, tired from the action we had carried out that night. Yet, when I told them, "Look, the Fascists are at Poggio Bustone and they're looking for us," when they heard the word "Fascists," their spirits picked up. Once they're awake, I said, "Now let's have a serious talk."

The Fascists surrounded the town with armored trucks, and killed a young man who they thought was going to warn the partisans. "Thus began the tragic manhunt, from house to house, in barns, in stables, and in haystacks. Young people were dragged away violently, and then others, too—fathers, older men. Those who resisted were beaten savagely."[3] When Vero Zagaglioni's partisan detail reached the town, partisans and Fascists engaged in one of the fiercest battles of the partisan war in Central Italy.

THREE WARS

In this chapter I analyze the narratives of the battle of Poggio Bustone as examples of the meaning and memory of the anti-Fascist Resistance in Italy.[4] The Resistance has been recognized until recently as the foundation of the Italian republican democracy. This principle, however, has been increasingly questioned, in political and historical terms, from many points of view. While the Right questioned the identification of the Resistance with national identity, the Left was increasingly embarrassed by the rediscovery of the violence inherent in the partisan struggle.

For a long time, official interpretations represented the Resistance as a united movement of the Italian people against the Fascist dictatorship and Nazi occupation. The central role of the communist partisans in this struggle was the foundation of the legitimacy of the Communist Party as a democratic force in the national anti-Fascist covenant. Today, this covenant no longer seems to hold. Now that the Communist Party has disappeared as a major political presence, anti-Fascism no longer seems to be the force that holds the country together (nor is any other alternative in sight).[5]

Under the domesticated anti-Fascist consensus, the fact that the Resistance had actually been a war, fought by a diverse and militant movement, was somewhat hushed in favor of more acceptable features, such as patriotism and heroism. Today, the discovery that partisans not only died, but also killed is used, at best, to equate partisans and Fascists (in the name of common pity for the dead, or of their symmetrical extremism) or, at worst, to represent the Resistance as an explosion of extremist Bolshevik violence. Rather than patriotic Italians, the partisans are murderous communists.

The Left, which had adopted the pacified image of the Resistance in order to reinforce its democratic credentials, has always been ambivalent toward the fact that the Resistance was a war. Not only did the revisionist use of partisan violence seem to atone for the much worse violence waged by Fascists and Nazis, it also seemed to stain the immaculate image of a people's patriotic movement. Since the immediate postwar years, in fact, the Fascists had claimed that the Resistance had been a *civil war,* in order both to denigrate the partisan movement and to claim their place as a legitimate part of the Italian people. Some progressive historians, including the ex-partisan Claudio Pavone, also subscribed to the civil war description as a more realistic representation not only of historical events, but of the actual nature of Italian society; until very recently, the Left strenuously rejected these theories. In his recent, definitive history, Claudio Pavone shows that—without in the least diminishing its political and moral value—the Resistance must be seen as the intricate knot of three different, though overlapping wars: a patriotic war, a class war, and a civil war.[6]

This chapter explores some of the ways in which the nature of the Resistance and of the role of violence in it have been elaborated by the partisans themselves, ranging from denial that any violence occurred to the claiming of violence as part of their own experience and identity. The battle of Poggio Bustone lends itself to this analysis because it is the subject of a number of narratives that represent the events in contradictory, distorted, sometimes invented ways. Rather than dismissing them as historically unreliable, however, we may find in their distortion of facts and in their mutual contradictions precious hints of the work of memory, imagination, and interpretation.

WE WANTED THE SKIN OF THE FASCISTS

I will begin with Dante Bartolini's song, both to underscore the creative dimension of the narratives discussed here, and because it is the most formalized reconstruction of the events at Poggio Bustone. Though a member of the Gramsci Brigade, Dante Bartolini did not take part in the battle of Poggio Bustone; he was, however, the Brigade's recognized poet and song maker, and composed the song on the basis of the stories he heard from and shared with his comrades. The song, therefore, is not merely a story, but already a story made of stories.

Non ti ricordi più del dieci marzo	Have you forgotten the tenth of March
quello che facesti a Poggio tu?	and what you did in Poggio?
volevi a noi tutti fucilare,	You wanted to kill us all,
mentre questo non accadde più.	But this never took place.
Vile Tanturi	Coward Tanturi,
la condanna si avvicina	Your sentence is near,
e la tua carneficina	And for the massacre you did
la dovrai presto scontar.	You shall soon pay the price.

IL TRADITORE TANTURI

Or chiuso te ne stai nella prigione
un rimorso ti sta a lacera'
certo ti pentirai quello che hai fatto
ma il pentimento più non gioverà.
O scellerato
traditor degli italiani
hai difeso i pescicani
pe' aumentar la schiavitù.

Now you are locked in prison
Torn by remorse.
You repent of what you did,
But repentance will not help.
You rascal,
Traitor of Italians,
You protected the sharks
To make our slavery worse.

Mentre passeggiavi per le strade
il mattin del dieci marzo tu

un intimo compagno ci ammazzasti

o vigliacco che facesti tu.
Tre nostri cari
in quel giorno so' scomparsi
anche lor dalle lor tombe
griderà vendetta a te.

While you walked the streets
On the morning of the tenth
    of March
You killed a close comrade of
    ours.
You coward, what did you do?
Three of our dear ones
Passed away on that day.
They too, from their graves,
Shall cry vengeance on you.

Era le dieci e venti del mattino
di partigiani si stava a parla'

tu coraggiosamente sei partito
a chiedere rinforzo alla città.

Al tuo partire
al comando fu il questore
quel vigliacco e senza cuore
in quel giorno ebbe a mori'.

At ten-twenty in the morning
There was talk about
    partisans.
Bravely you ran
To get reinforcements from the
    town.
After you left
The *questore* was in charge.
That heartless coward
Also had to die that day.

In piazza principale del paese	In the town square
i rastrellati conducesti tu	You gathered the prisoners.
tra questi altrettanti ne chiamasti	You took a number of them
ed al supplizio li portasti tu.	And brought them to torture.
Quanta importanza	With all your arrogance
con quel tuo modo di agire	And the way you acted,
ci sembravi il padrone	You seemed to us the boss
dell'intera umanità.	Of the whole human kind.
Per fortuna qualcuno del paese	Fortunately someone from the town
andiede ad avvertire i partigiani	Ran out to warn the partisans
che in brutto stato si trova il paese	That the town was in danger
e presto lo venissero a salvar.	And please come save it soon.
I partigiani	The partisans
come lupi so' arrivati	Descended like wolves,
tanto rapidi e assetati	Quick and thirsty
di quel sangue traditor.	For that treacherous blood.
Un'ora di terribile bufera	An hour of terrible storm
diede la vittoria ai partigiani	Yielded victory to the partisans
dieciotto so' i Fascisti che ammazzati	Eighteen are the Fascists that were killed
tra questi anche il questore a comanda'.	Among them the chief of police.
Dei Fascisti	Those Fascists
superavano i duecento	Were more than two hundred
sol dieciotto partigiani	Just eighteen partisans
glielo misero spavento.	Scared them away.
C'erano tre famosi comandanti	There were three famous chiefs
fra i Fascisti e i questurini	Of the Fascists and the police
che fecero succede'l gran macello	Who caused that terrible slaughter,
al tribunale dovrà compari'.	And they shall face the court.
Mi scuserete	Please forgive me,
io non son compositore	I am not a composer
figlio di un lavoratore	A worker's son,
meglio non vi posso dir.	Better than this I cannot say.

Mario Sabatini, who fought at Poggio Bustone, relates,

And then we started down the hill. We were twenty-six, with twenty-six rifles. We came down, and we found this crowd of Fascists, maybe more than a hundred and eighty or two hundred. So they say, "Look, we'll give you anything you want, just don't attack us." Instead, I mean—we wanted the skin of the Fascists! We wanted the skin of the Fascists. There's no backing out now: I mean, you're killing our comrades, how can we stop? So we didn't heed them, and attacked. And then a woman, an old woman—"Look, the trees are moving, the woods, with all these partisans coming down, must be two hundred." Must have been twenty-two, rather. I remember [a Fascist], he was singing, "I won't give up my machine gun," that famous Fascist song. He had his finger on the trigger, aiming toward where we stood. So I took a walk around the village, a blow in the pumpkin, and he was gone.[7]

Vero Zagaglioni: And then it began, inside the town. At one point, I came back to the upper square, and I saw this stream of Fascist militia going down toward [the village of] San Pietro. Then with my rifle, I lowered my sight, and fired. I guess the bullets, when they fell down there [must have hurt]. After that, we came into the town, and we were telling them to surrender because we were fighting for free Italy, the usual talk, I mean. But they wouldn't listen.

Bartolini's song and the narratives of Sabatini and Zagaglioni are good examples of Claudio Pavone's "three wars." The patriotic war is implied in linguistic formulas: Tandurri is a "traitor of Italians," and Zagaglioni tells the Fascists that "we were fighting for free Italy" (but he adds that it was "the usual talk," as if to suggest that it was only a cliché). Class war is implied in the identity of the narrators, all factory workers; Bartolini underlines it when he signs himself as "a worker's son," and pictures it in the image of the arrogant Fascist "boss of the whole human kind." The civil war, finally, is represented by the vivid descriptions of hatred and violence: Zagaglioni's pleasure over the effect of his bullets, Sabatini's crude blow to the Fascist's "pumpkin." Generations of nice patriotic feelings about the Resistance are exploded when Bartolini describes the partisans as bloodthirsty wolves, or when Sabatini insists that "we wanted the skin of the Fascists." These witnesses have no doubts: the Resistance was not a gala dinner. It was a war, with all that war entails, objectively and subjectively.

These narratives, then, offer an interpretation of the battle which is in line with the most advanced contemporary historiography. Their historical accuracy, however, is accompanied by an imaginative dimension that expands the performance toward epic and myth. The old woman's image of the partisans' descent in the form of a moving forest in Sabatini's account reminds us of the final battle in *Macbeth*, when Birnam wood comes to Dunsinane (Act V, sc. 7), as prophesied by the witches. A story I heard in a bar in Poggio Bustone in 1982 evoked another mythological precedent: in order to seem more numerous than they were, the partisans supposedly mixed with a herd of sheep coming down the side of the mountain—like Ulysses and his comrades hiding underneath the sheep in order to escape from Polifemo's cave in the *Odyssey*.

It is not necessary to claim that these stories descend from these literary parallels (although, unlike Shakespeare, Homer is familiar to the oral improviser poets of Sabina). What is important in the parallel is that it draws our attention to the use of symbols. On the one hand, these mythic narratives underline the cunning with which the partisans disguise the inferiority of their forces to frighten the Fascists. On a deeper level, both images show the partisans literally merged with the land where they were born and for which they are fighting, while the Fascists are regularly described as outsiders in league with the foreign invaders, even though they, too, may have been local natives.

As we will see, the presence of imaginary tales and motifs does not contradict the accuracy of the historical interpretation. Indeed, it is through such imaginary motifs that we may glimpse the work of memory and interpretation, and the traces of the narrator's subjectivity at the time of the events.

THE PRIMAL SCENE

Once the partisans arrive in town, the stories begin to fragment and contradict one another, and become increasingly confused as we approach the climax of the event: the killing of the Fascist commanders. Let us take two written testimonies, gathered in the same book, which describe the event very differently. Ezio Ottaviani writes,

> The questore was invited to surrender, in order to avoid unnecessary bloodshed. His men, however, answered by firing on the partisans. Then the partisans hurled some hand grenades down from the chimney. After this eloquent warning, the chief decided to surrender. But he came out of the house shooting, and the partisans killed him.[8]

Let us now compare it with the version written by Silvio Micheli:

> The [Fascist] commando was barricaded in a house. Some partisans, among them Enzo Battisti, a student from Poggio Bustone, and Uragano [Hurricane, battle name of Enzo Cerroni], climbed the roof and exploded hand grenades down the chimney to persuade the Fascists to surrender. But it was not enough. Captain Tandurri and the questore Pannaria fired back with their machine guns. The struggle went on. Suddenly, the partisans dropped in through the chimney and ordered the Fascist officials to drop their arms. The chief of police tried to mow them down by turning around and firing, but the partisans' volley was faster.[9]

These two versions contain the most important contradictions: whether the Fascists were killed inside the house or in the square, and whether or not they had surrendered before they were killed. Most versions corroborate Ottaviani's account, according to which the Fascists died in a desperate sally out of the house. Vero Zagaglioni says that the Fascists were barricaded inside and were offered a chance to surrender ("Come on out with your hands up, and we won't do anything to you"); someone dropped a grenade through the chimney to drive them out, but "they didn't come out with their hands up, they rushed out with machine guns and hand grenades," and died in the square: "Then somebody among us, he was faster with his gun, and got them."

There is also a version by Fascist historian Giorgio Pisanò, who denies that the Fascists surrendered, yet describes the same sequence of events:

> The more numerous nucleus [of Fascists], including the questore, barricaded themselves in Mrs. Cecilia Desideri's house, and kept on fighting bravely until they ran out of ammunition. When the Fascist fire slowed down, some partisans climbed the roof and dropped hand grenades through the chimney, shouting to those inside to surrender. The Fascists, however, refused, and attempted a desperate sally but were mowed down as they came out of the house.[10]

Micheli's version, according to which the Fascists were killed *inside* the house, is corroborated by another partisan's account. According to Mario Filipponi, who also fought in the battle, one of the partisans "hurled a bomb inside; then he came in through the roof and killed six or seven of the big shots." These versions, however, are probably contaminated by the memory of another episode in the battle, which Mario Filipponi also remembers. In this case, the partisan Enzo Cerroni ("Uragano") heard that some wounded Fascists were inside a house: "He goes, finds a Fascist, and—tac!—he up and shoots him cold. Because the Fascist had his machine gun in his hand. Meanwhile, [Cerroni] hears a noise behind him. He was quick—'Come on out, all of you!' There were about eight, ten, of those big chiefs; he drew them out, and then he executed them on the spot."[11]

The double contradiction (the place of the death and the question of surrender) is underscored by the presence, in practically all the narratives of Poggio Bustone, of an apparently superfluous motif, which can also be traced to parallels in literature and mass culture: the Fascists always attempt to shoot first, but the partisans beat them to the draw. When Enzo Cerroni drops into the house where the wounded Fascists are hiding, a man aims a machine gun at him, but he is faster and kills him; he repeats the feat a moment later, when he turns upon hearing a noise and mows down a number of Fascists that were getting ready to shoot. It is a very cinematic account, paralleled by the episodes in the narratives of Zagaglioni and Filipponi, in which the Fascists reach for their guns but the partisans are "faster" or "smarter." This motif has been described as a "primal scene" in Western films and novels: the gunfight between the hero and the outlaw or the Indian.[12]

In this archetypal scene, the hero never draws first: he shoots only in legitimate defense, beating the bad guy to the draw, proving his prowess and, in the process, legitimizing the conquest of the West. Though the partisans are struggling to liberate their own land rather than to conquer somebody else's, yet this justification for killing occurs regularly in Resistance narratives.

For instance, the killing of three German soldiers in a bar at Civitella della Chiana (Tuscany), which precipitated a German reprisal and the killing of more than two hundred civilians, is justified by the partisans in self-defense terms that are outwardly very much like those of the narratives of Poggio Bustone. The difference, however, is that—but for self-defense—the episode of Civitella would be a cold-blooded killing, and has been described as such in alternative local memories.[13] At Poggio Bustone, on the other hand, there was a war on, and weapons were being fired at large on both sides. In such a context, it makes very little sense to invoke self-defense and insist that the Fascists tried to shoot first—unless the narrators are obscurely trying to justify something, which may be, ultimately, that the state of war made it necessary to perform an act that they still have trouble dealing with: to kill. Perhaps the whole Resistance was one huge act of self-defense.

THEY HAD TO DIE WITH THE OTHERS

These implications of the contradictions *between* the stories are reinforced by the contradiction *within* them. For instance, Ottaviani writes that the *questore* "decided to surrender" but then says that he "came out shooting." Zagaglioni underlines that "he came out, but not with his hands up as we had ordered." Sabatini incongruously mentions a Fascist offer to surrender, rejected by the partisans ("We'll give you anything you want, just don't attack us"). Bartolini's song says that Tandurri and Pannaria shall "stand in judgment" (more literally: face the court), although he knows that they are already dead.

On the one hand, the theme of self-defense points to an unease concerning the way in which the Fascists were killed; on the other, all this wavering about the surrender suggests some kind of unclear exchange. Was there, rather than an open fight, a negotiation, a "trial," an execution?

The facts are not easy to ascertain. It must be noted, however, that the Fascist version also denies that the killings were done in cold blood: according to Pisanò, the Fascists came out of the house with guns in hands, shooting, and were killed in battle. Of course, it is possible that he denies that the Fascists surrendered in order to throw a heroic light on their deaths. He does claim that a Fascist prisoner was executed summarily in the square. But his description of the officials' death confirms Ottaviani and Zagaglioni. We may take as the most probable hypothesis that the Fascists were killed in action, attempting to leave the house in which they were surrounded. But in that case, why all this ambiguity? Perhaps what the contradictions and the symbols in the stories point to is less the obscurity of the events than the darkness of subjectivity: not what the partisans did, but what they felt.

I will try to explain this by discussing a clearly invented tale. It was improvised by Dante Bartolini in a performance for a young radical Left audience at the Circolo Gianni Bosio in Rome, in the 1970s. It is not a true account; but, like many of Bartolini's invented tales, it points to another level of truth.

> Then the prefect, the questore and all the brass, and the ones in charge, they hid inside a room. And a woman who saw them says, "They're in there, the rascals!" There was a partisan near me; he heard this drama, and told them from outside: "Come out! If you come out peacefully—maybe—you will be spared. Else, I'll burn you all in there." They opened the door, raised their hands, and came

forward. They came out, in the square, where all the other corpses
were. As they were standing in front of them—drrrrrr! all mowed
down to the ground. They had to die with the others.

Let me repeat: this is not a true account. But let me also repeat: this is
why it is important. Why, among all the possible versions, does Bartolini
select one that is the least honorable for the partisans, turning an open
fight into a summary execution after an ambiguous ("maybe") offer to
save the lives of those who surrendered? By subverting the self-defense
narratives, Bartolini illuminates some of the reasons for their existence.
  "They had to die with the others," Bartolini says. In his song, he declares that they will have to face the court. In both texts, he describes the
death of the Fascist chiefs as an act of justice. To invent a summary execution on the public square means, then, to suggest that no matter how
the Fascists had acted, the partisans—"wolves thirsting for traitor blood"
—would have killed them anyway. Surrender or no surrender, as Sabatini
says, "We wanted the skins of the Fascists." What these contradictory and
symbolic narratives may be covering up is less what the partisans *did* than
what they *felt:* they need to justify not the killing of the Fascists in battle,
but the rage, the hatred, the desire to kill them that they carried inside
them, and apparently shared with the population. One only has to listen
to some of the accounts of what happened afterward:

> *Mario Filipponi:* But the population, soon as the Fascists began to
> run, the population stepped in. All—with pitchforks, it was a sight
> that can't be described. I remember that while my men and I were
> marching into the town, I saw the people carrying the Fascists' bodies
> stuck on pitchforks; and they lined them up on the trees, one for each
> tree. At the entrance of the village; and they had them in a row, like
> hay. Savage; a scary sight.

> *Mario Sabatini:* Ah, this is very important, because if you're putting it
> on tape . . . When the town's children saw the Fascists on the ground
> like that, they'd go with sticks, pop their eyes out after they were
> dead. Brazen, an incredible show. Boys, children, who know nothing
> about Fascism, about partisans, nothing, you know. Well, it really was
> a battle that can go down in history along with the others.

The death of Tandurri, Pannaria, and the other Fascists, then, may have
been both necessary for self-defense and deserved as an act of justice. But
it was accompanied by dark feelings (and, in some cases, dark actions)
that are both hard to admit and hard to deny. We *had* to kill them, and
this may be all right; but we also *wanted* to kill them (some may have *en-*

joyed the killing), and this is harder to recognize. This double reluctance generates the distortions, the contradictions, the symbols, the inventions: the unnecessary denials are the vehicle of the revelation.

JUSTICE AND VIOLENCE

Describing the scene at Poggio Bustone, Bartolini used a revelatory word: *drama*. His account of the battle, in fact, has a theatrical dimension, almost like a pageant: his is less a historical account than a dramatized interpretation of history. Though there was no public execution of the Fascist officials that day at Poggio Bustone (the Fascist historian mentions another execution, but the partisan sources are silent about it), such scenes did happen during the partisan war. One episode which Bartolini did witness took place at Polino, a mountain village where, on December 4, 1943, the local Fascist officials were executed—as the Communist underground newspaper then put it—"in full daylight, in the town square."[14]

As he does in other contexts, Bartolini conflates two episodes, placing the Polino execution at the culmination of the battle of Poggio Bustone to create a unified symbol in which both events are enriched by being placed in reciprocal context (while, incidentally, shifting the episode in which he participated to the center of the whole experience).[15] Polino and Poggio Bustone were the partisans' closest confrontations with death as perpetrators rather than victims. It was then that these young people who were ready to die for country and freedom discovered that they were also ready to kill.

Seen in this context, then, the narratives of Poggio Bustone also concern the difficult question of partisan justice: the death sentences on Fascist "criminals," spies, traitors carried out during the period of the occupation. Once again, in these episodes, the question of self-defense and the question of legitimacy were tightly woven together.

Legitimacy is the theme of the newspaper's account of the Polino execution as a formal, public act, which proved that the partisans exercised legitimate, if provisional, state power over a territory they had rid of traitors and invaders. As the war went on, however, the partisans lost control of the territory, and the legitimacy they derived from it became more difficult to assert. Political power was, therefore, overshadowed by self-defense.

Especially after the battle of Poggio Bustone, Fascist and Nazi reaction and widespread mopping up operations pushed the partisans back into the mountains and into the underground. Partisan justice became much more difficult, and urgent: on the one hand, formalities could be observed even less than before; on the other, dispatching spies and informers became a matter of self-protection. In those emergency situations, Comunardo Tobia explains, "there was no such thing as an eight-month sentence. It was either acquittal, or death."[16] In the performance in Rome where he told the story of Poggio Bustone, Bartolini also gave a dramatic rendition of such executions done at knife point at night. Zenoni, a Gramsci Brigade official, explained, "Well, sentences were executed according to the situation you were in, it's not as if you had the possibility of arresting someone and put him in jail; it depended on what you could do. Any means was good. Make as little noise as you can. You couldn't shoot them, you know."[17] During the postwar antipartisan reaction, it was Zenoni who had to "stand in judgment," before civilian courts that equated the partisan sentences to war crimes:

> During the trials, when they accused us of these things, that it had been done in a somewhat barbaric manner, I told the judge: "You should have been there with us, defending Italy; if you had been, we would have let you be the judge, we would have kept records, things would have been done more correctly."

The problem of justice, however, is only one part of the problem of violence. Even when the war is a "just" one, the memory of violence, and of what its perpetrator has become, is hard to countenance in the time of peace. The partisans also find it difficult, in the time of memory and recollection, to reconcile the immediate necessity and the state of mind of that time with their present values and feelings, to reconcile the memory of violence, hatred, and excess with the ideals of democracy and civilized society (which, to further complicate things, are the ideals they were fighting for in the first place).

It must be said that, "first strike" or not, much of this violence and hatred was a reaction to the Fascist atrocities: "And this poor man, Mario Magrelli, was caught by the Fascists. He was riddled with knife wounds, his eyes gouged, his face cut, that's what the Fascists used to do" (Dante Bartolini). "You understand that partisans became like animals in the mountains: one had his father executed, another something else . . ." (Bruno Zenoni). "We, after that thing [the killing of a partisan], became even more evil than we already were . . . I mean, already . . . But after that, we became evil" (Mario Sabatini). But what turns human beings animated by feelings of solidarity and equality into "evil" "animals" is, ultimately, war itself:

Mario Filipponi: When you've been eight, nine months, a year up in the mountains, you come down, you're a half beast. There's no two ways about it. You're not a normal man. Today, I say, I was a beast. I realize that in those times I had lost my reason. You've come down the mountain with that constant hatred, constant war, weapons, always expecting to be shot in the back, always expecting a bullet, you've become so charged that before you get back in line with the idea of . . . society, it wasn't easy, it took a long time.

Poggio Bustone, the deadliest event of the Resistance on the Umbria-Lazio border, is the memory that compels narrators to deal with the fact that theirs was a war, and that a war, even a war of liberation, is made not only of cruel actions that can be understood in historical context, but of subjective conditions, feelings, states of mind that are a constituent part of those actions, but that are difficult to countenance afterward. It is one thing to remember what the fighters *did;* it is quite another to remember what they *were.* "Evil" "half beasts," "wolves," "savage": the narrators use these words to distance the memory of what they had become, but also to retain it. Claudio Pavone speaks of the "disgust for the violence in which one was immersed," but along with this disgust remains the need to preserve the wholeness of one's experience and identity.

The cleansing of violence from the official discourse on the Resistance was perceived by a number of those who fought in it as a denial of their role, an expropriation of memory. As they tried to make a space for violence in their narratives—to justify it as a necessity of the times, sometimes to redeem it as revolutionary value (as in Bartolini's speech to the young radicals in Rome)—they also tried to rescue the memory of the Resistance as class war and civil war from under the suffocating whitewash of the exclusively patriotic war.

This makes them, if we listen and try to understand, more articulate and credible historians than those professional writers and administrators of history who constructed the myth of a domesticated, pacified, almost nonviolent Resistance and who, when war and violence came out of the closet, albeit through the distortions of right-wing revisionism, were unable to face it as other than an incomprehensible specter from which they could extract no meaning and knowledge, but only horror, broken apologies, and silence.

Chapter Ten

The Massacre at Civitella Val di Chiana (Tuscany, June 29, 1944)

Myth and Politics, Mourning and Common Sense

MOURNING AND COMMON SENSE

*I begin to work on the draft of this essay on August 21, 1995.
Yesterday, for the second time in a month, an unknown hand has
painted a black swastika over the stone that commemorates the
place, around the corner from where I live, where in June, 1944, the
Germans in retreat from Rome killed thirteen prisoners, military and
civilians (among them, Bruno Buozzi, a founder of the Italian union
movement). A few weeks later, the Germans set up their defense line
near Arezzo, in Tuscany.*

On June 29, the German occupying troops executed 115 civilians, all
men, at Civitella Val di Chiana, a small hill town near Arezzo, in Tuscany.[1] The same day, 58 people, including women and children, were
killed at the nearby hamlet of La Cornia, and 39 at the village of San Pan-
crazio. Ostensibly, these actions were retaliations for the killing of three
German soldiers by partisans in Civitella, on June 18.

I heard loud gunfire, banging on doors with muskets and rough
orders. Suddenly our door was shaken by violent banging. I went to
open and two Germans came into the house pointing their rifles at
us; they inspected each room and ordered us out. Accompanied by
gunfire and shouts, I started walking out of the town, followed by my
children. What a shocking spectacle appeared before my eyes! Many
men were already corpses, soaked in their own blood; the houses were
on fire, half naked women and children came out of the houses pushed

by the Germans. We took refuge in a wood, with other women whose husbands, brothers, or fathers had been killed. (Anna Cetoloni, widow Caldelli)[2]

When we reached the square by the church, what we saw chilled us. What a heart break! From the open doors of the houses came rows of massacred men! Pieces of brain were everywhere and the blood flowed all over, a true slaughter. The burned houses began to collapse, the dust and smoke were unbearable. One of my husband's brothers and an uncle had also been killed. (Rina Caldelli, RB, 256–7)

[The next day], with other women, we returned to the town to look for our husbands. As we reached the square where all the hats and the blood were, among cries and screams, we found our beloveds inside the houses, in terrible state, all hit on the head, and someone had had his head blown off. Us women, I don't know who gave us the courage to do all this, we carried the dead to the church, all together and helping one another. After doing this we didn't know where to stay because the town was in a terrible state. We went back to the wood. The next day we took heart once more and went back to town where all together, still helping one another, we built coffins and put the dead inside and carted them to the graveyard. There we dug the graves, lowered the coffins, and laid the earth over them. (Lucia Tippi, widow Falsetti, RB 286)

These events have generated what Giovanni Contini aptly described as a "divided memory."[3] Contini identifies, on the one hand, an "official" memory that commemorates the massacre as an episode of the Resistance and assimilates the victims to fallen martyrs for freedom; and on the other hand, a memory created and preserved by the survivors, widows and children, that focuses almost exclusively on their personal and collective mourning and loss. Not only does this memory deny any connection with the Resistance, but it blames the partisans for causing, with an irresponsible attack, the Germans' retaliation: "Now it is all blamed on the Germans. . . . But us, we blame the partisans because if they hadn't done what they did it wouldn't have happened. They killed for retaliation" (M.C.).[4]

The present parson of Civitella, and survivor of the massacre, father Daniele Tiezzi, is probably correct in his judgment that the partisan action was conducted with "extreme irresponsibility."[5] The partisans around Civitella were not highly organized and politically aware; the usefulness of their action is at best uncertain. It is not clear whether they intended to kill the Germans or only to disarm them, nor whether they shot them in cold blood or in self-defense. They made things worse by acting inside the town walls and failing to remove the bodies and other traces of their action, thus inevitably involving the population. Later, they were unable to defend or help the town in any way. However, those who pulled the trigger in the slaughter were the Germans. The probable irresponsibility of the partisans cannot in any way overshadow or justify their calculated responsibility.

These two memories—that of the institutions and the celebrations inspired by the Resistance, and that of the community—have clashed several times in the past, even physically, as the local population perceived the official celebrations in the name of the Resistance as a violation of their memory and loss. The international conference "In Memory: For a European Memory of Nazi Crimes after the End of the Cold War" (Arezzo, June 22–24, 1994), from which this chapter originates, was intended also as a restitution, by scholars close to the Left, to Civitella's disregarded and violated memory.

This restitution, however, took place in an ambiguous historical context. At the time of the conference, for the first time in Europe, a party directly derived from Fascism, Alleanza Nazionale, was part of the Italian government. The Left, uncertain of its reasons, wary of all ideology, and shocked by defeat, too often uncritically adopts the reasons and ideologies of others, including some of its former adversaries. Such an outcome was very much a possibility in the case of Civitella, if only because of the dramatic nature of the events, the gravity of the errors of the past, and the fierce resentment of the survivors.

The narratives of Civitella leave one breathless. It is the scholar's task, however, after accepting the impact, the step back, breathe deeply, and start thinking again. With due respect for the people involved, the authenticity of their sorrow, and the seriousness of their reasons, our task is still to interpret critically all documents and narratives, including theirs. As I will try to show, in fact, when we speak of a divided memory, we must not imagine only an opposition between a spontaneous and pure communal memory versus an official and ideological one, so that once we deconstruct the latter we can implicitly take for granted the unmediated authenticity of the former. We are dealing rather with a multiplicity of fragmented and internally divided memories, all one way or the other ideologically and culturally mediated.

In many of the papers presented at the conference, however, reverent contemplation—no doubt justified by the dramatic quality of the events and the emotion and pain of the witnesses—prevailed over analysis and interpretation. Thus, while Giovanni Contini analyzed the contradictions in the partisans' testimony,[6] no one did the same with the testimony of the survivors—if not to question their credibility, at least to investigate the structure and meaning of their narrative construction of the events. Thus, Valeria Di Piazza identifies entirely with the survivors' reluctance and need to speak, and dedicates her paper to the dilemma of the "expressible/inexpressible" and the difficulty of communicating and sharing mourning and loss: "What all the 'civitellini' tell is true: you cannot tell, you cannot explain, you cannot let the other understand. A person who has never experienced this kind of events would never be able to feel what the people of Civitella have inside."[7] As Pietro Clemente describes it, "It is as though the researchers who join in dialogue with a mourning that thought cannot control became infected with it and needed to begin their own elaboration of this loss."[8]

Clemente agrees with the historical evaluation, according to which the partisan's error does not remove the Germans' guilt; he points out, however, that the anthropological point of view is concerned "with a community's representations, rather than with the truth of facts or the trend of values." The self-enclosed communal mourning of Civitella, he goes on, is an act of resistance against the atomized individualism of modern thought and, as such, a "scandal" against "the inability of lay and Resistance thought to understand experiences other than their own model."

I am not sure that this inability to understand experiences and modes of thought other than its own is a prerogative of lay and progressive thought (which, on other hand, is quite aware of the problem).[9] Perhaps religious, especially Catholic, thought is not entirely immune either. Also, encountering and understanding experiences other than its own ought to constitute the very essence of the anthropological experience. Thus, it is true, indeed, that death, mourning, and loss are unspeakable experiences, both in themselves and because of the intrinsic limitations of language: it is uncertain whether *any* experience can be truly *told;* it is a commonplace that no one can share another's experience, painful or not. Yet, the fact remains that, at Civitella as elsewhere, the unspeakable *is* spoken. The effort to speak the unspeakable results in interpretable narratives, cultural constructs of words and ideas. Thus, Francesca Cappelletto and Paola Calamandrei find at Civitella a "group memory . . . moulded in the course of numberless narrative occasions," formalized in narratives endowed with "a highly cohesive form, structured and focalized around a political theme":

> There are recognized narrators, and even some "thematic" specialists,
> experts of specific portions or episodes of the story. Also, one can
> clearly perceive, in the narrative situations, an element of social
> control upon the way in which the events are told.[10]

The contradiction between these structured and socially controlled narratives, and the "inexpressible" described by Valeria Di Piazza is strident,
but superficial. Precisely because the experiences are unspeakable, and
yet must be spoken, the speakers are sustained by the mediating structures of language, narrative, social environment, religion, politics. The
resulting narratives—not the pain they describe, but the words and ideologies through which they represent it—not only can, but must be critically understood.

As Pietro Clemente writes, "The initial scandal . . . was the discovery
that the collective memory of the survivors not only refused to consider
itself a part of the Resistance movement, but took an open stand against
it, blaming the local partisans as circumstantial cause of the massacres."
It seems to me, however, that in this case the "scandal" is translated in
a political and narrative construct that participates fully in the common
sense of the "grey zone" of Italian ideology—the area of "normality," of
"nonresponsibility and innocence" between the victim and the execu-
tioner.[11] For instance, only two days after the Fosse Ardeatine massacre
in Rome, in which 335 civilians were exterminated in retaliation for the
killing of 32 German soldiers, the *Osservatore Romano,* official newspaper of the Vatican, described the partisans as "guilty," the Germans as
"victims," the victims as "sacrificed persons."[12] Perhaps the "scandal"
begins at this point.

The fact that it is translated into a conservative cliché does not detract
from the dignity and pain of the survivors of Civitella. Indeed, it is a
weakness of Resistance historiography that it never took this common
sense seriously enough; finding it in so "pure" and largely justified a form
ought to constitute an opportunity to understand the ethical limitations
of the Resistance and the power of the ideological constructs that contribute to its desecration in the contemporary political arena.

Indeed, mourning, like memory, is not a compact nucleus impenetrable to thought and language, but a process shaped ("elaborated") in historical time. For instance, like the testimony of the partisans, that of the
survivors also changes with time. In the testimonies given to the British
inquest in 1945 and those collected by the writer Romano Bilenchi in
1946, the theme of the partisans' guilt surfaces occasionally and indirectly, but it is not the dominant structuring element that it becomes in

the narratives collected half a century later. As Contini writes, "The conflict with the partisans is less a point of departure than a point of arrival." What prevailed openly in 1946 was the resentment toward the Germans: "And there we wept all together, thinking of the sorrow that had struck us, and cursing the Germans" (Ada Sestini, widow Caldelli, RB, 55). Many narrators insist on the inhumanity and cruelty of the Germans: "It was ten o'clock, the machine guns were almost stilled, but we heard the voices of those beasts thirsty for innocent blood singing, laughing, playing their instruments"; "the slaughter over, the Germans, their hands and clothes still stained with the blood of our dead, while the town was collapsing, ate with good appetite bread and cheese" (Rina Caldelli, Zaira Tiezzi, RB, 256, 280). These images all but disappear in later testimony, overwhelmed by antipartisan resentment; the very tone of the narratives evolves from the material details of 1946 to the pathetic accents and occasional clichés of 1993–94.

Several factors may account for these changes. Witnesses might have been reluctant to criticize the partisans in the immediate postwar period, when the latter enjoyed high prestige and some political power; abuses perpetrated by the partisans after the war, to "punish" people who were respected by the community and had not been more Fascist than the rest, accentuated the hostility among the people of Civitella. The wave of antipartisan trials, the controversies over the responsibility for the Fosse Ardeatine massacre, and the consolidation of the common sense mentioned above may have supplied the survivors' resentment with a narrative and ideological apparatus that had not yet taken shape at the time of the earlier testimony. The fact remains that this supposedly impenetrable memory and loss are in fact intensely related to history and time.

What applies to time also applies to space. At Vallucciole, only a few miles from Civitella, on April 15, 1944, the Germans murdered 108 men, women, and children, again in ostensible retaliation. Yet in the interviews gathered at Vallucciole, "the theme of [the partisans'] guilt . . . appears to be attenuated, or even entirely absent. . . . The central theme and reference for the interviewees is the responsibility of the Nazis and Fascists" (Cappelletto/Calamandrei). Beyond the two historians' explanations (different social and demographic structure, different structure of the event), this discrepancy confirms that the "scandal" of Civitella is not eternal and universal, but rather historical and specific. This does not detract from its impact, but rather focuses and specifies it, subtracting it from generic universalism to endow it with the conflictual power of a narrative opposed to other narratives.

Clemente's distinction between the historian's "facts" and the anthropologist's "representations" is entirely correct. However, it is only by considering them jointly that we are able to distinguish them.[13] Representations and facts do not exist in separate spheres. Representations work on facts and claim to *be* facts; facts are recognized and organized according to representations; facts and representations both converge in the subjectivity of human beings and are dressed in their language. Creating this interaction is the task of oral history, which is charged as *history* with reconstructing facts, but also learns, in its practice of dialogic field work and critical confrontation with the otherness of narrators, to understand representations.

INNOCENCE

August 22. By the monument, only three or four volunteers, local mechanics and artisans, with sandpaper and sponges, discuss with professional competence the tools needed to restore the names of the victims. Grey-haired remnants of the old neighborhood before gentrification, perhaps they remember.

> M.C.:   There! That was the beginning of the sorrowful history!
> Interv.:   What had happened?
> M.C.:   The partisans had killed the Germans.

Almost all the narratives of the massacre of Civitella begin with the killing of the Germans: "On June 18 . . . by the hand of the partisans two German soldiers were killed. That was the beginning of my agony and that of all the people of my town"; "At dusk on June 18, I don't recall exactly at what time, the relative calm that reigned in town, in spite of the approaching of the front, was suddenly shattered by the sound of gunfire."[14]

In narratological terms, the *incipit,* the beginning of the tale, marks the passage from balance, stillness, and order to disorder, conflict, and motion. Before the tale begins, by definition, nothing happens, or at least, nothing worth telling. This standard opening of the narratives of Civitella suggests that, before the partisan action of June 18, 1944, nothing was happening there: "We at Civitella [were] at ease . . . because until June 18 we had felt the war only to a certain extent" (M.C.); "at Civitella we lived easy and happy" (P.F.).[15] Civitella was a town "framed by the green of sweet-scented woods," a "small ancient world full of subdued and mysterious charm" where "the extreme political factionalism, that divides the souls and fuels hatred, had never existed." Neither the Fascists nor the Germans had bothered anybody: "Those who in good faith had believed in those [Fascist] politics had not committed any heinous action." As for the Germans, "Trouble, they gave none" (M.C.)[16]: "Sometimes they would actually come into the house asking for a drink or something, but they never bothered us." Calamandrei and Cappelletto describe these representations as images of "paradise lost" and an age of "innocence."

> I was eight years old and I suppose I was a happy child.
> For the duration of the war, we lived all together in the family house in town, with my parents, grandparents, my two sisters, my brothers and many other people who were close to us. (Maria Teresa Paggi Massi, *CR*, 303)

"Paradise" and "innocence" are strange images for a town that had lived through Fascism and war and was now under Nazi occupation. While we must accept them as representations, we need, however, to interrogate ourselves about their relationship with "facts."

Let us take the testimony of Alberto Rossi, who was fifteen then. He describes that time as one "of war and sadness" but also, understandably, of adolescent enjoyment and play. Surprisingly, however, he finds the motives of enjoyment precisely in the presence of war:

> The occasion to satisfy some of our desires presented itself to us in the early months of the year when, near the town, the Germans installed a depot of fuel and one of ammunition. We then began to raid those places and, avoiding the close surveillance of the Germans, often managed to take a few things that filled us with enthusiasm. (*CR*, 229)

Of course, there is nothing wrong with this Tom Sawyerish childhood reminiscence; indeed, it reminds us that most recollections by today's survivors are memories of men and women who were children or adolescents at the time, and who see the massacre as the end of their childhood and youth. The problem arises, however, when this childhood memory is repeated intact by the adult narrator, and contributes to the shaping of contemporary memory. Thus, Alberto Rossi does not recall that in April, 1944, because of a raid in that same ammunition depot, the Germans had killed a seventeen-year old boy, Giulio Cagnacci. Rossi has every right to forget; we, as historians and anthropologists, have the duty to consider both Cagnacci's death as a fact, its omission from Rossi's testimony as a representation, and how one evolves into the other.[17]

The same applies to broader representations of prewar Civitella. The town was no stranger to territorial and class articulation and tension. The ancient walls separated hierarchically the population of the town (land owners, artisans, professional people) from the countryside and the outlying hamlets: "This town was much envied by nearby towns . . . because it was a well-to-do place" (V.L.); "We were castle-born! We didn't get along with the peasants. . . . We tended to be city folks! We thought we were a little better than them," says M.C. More crudely, S.M. speaks of "hatred" between Civitella and the county-seat, Badia al Pino. He adds that, when the road was opened between Civitella and the hamlet of Cornia, "a mass of workers began to come into town, and this mass of workers were truly a mass of shit. [Edoardo] Succhielli [the partisan chief] lives there."[18]

With this final clause, S.M. frames the conflict between survivors and partisans in the context of preexisting tensions between the "castle-born" and the "peasants," the "artisans" and the "workers." The anger at the partisans for irresponsibly killing the Germans inside the walls also includes the sense of an invasion of the town's space by the lower classes of the countryside. This invasion continued after the war, when the "young Communists" of the countryside came to boss around people in town (Duilio Fattori, CR, 448)—in part, perhaps, to make up for past humiliations.

There is, then, a double displacement, in time and space. In space, the invaders are the partisans, rather than the Germans. In time, history does not begin with war, or even with the first local victim of the Germans, but only with the first reaction of the partisans.

To me, this seems to be the basic and radical meaning of the "scandal" of Civitella. It is the Left that causes "scandal" because it insists in going against the inevitable order of things—nature, human inequality, the market. The very existence of the Left is an invasion, an interference, injecting strife and history into quiet and nature.[19] Of course, since the natural order coincides with the power of the strong over the weak, the Left's guilt is also that of being weak and part of the weak (the narratives of Civitella underline this point systematically: "I mean, when you do not have the strength, how dare you go and kill a German?" [P.C.])—always taking up arms against heaven and never conquering it.

The narratives of Civitella, instead, do not intend to question any order. Their fierce attacks on the partisans are never placed in the context of an explicit antipartisan ideological option. The narrators do not bother to oppose the general ideology of Italy as a "republic born of Resistance" (as the phrase goes, or used to go), but modulate it with their resentment against the specific Resistance near them: "There was hatred toward the partisans—not for those in the North, but for the pseudo-partisans, for the locals" (V.C.);[20] "I would save as partisans those in the North, who protected the factories, not these ones!" (P.F.); "I admire the Northern partisans, who may have done some good things. But these— these in our area, no!" (B.B.).[21]

This is a variant of the "not-in-my-backyard" syndrome: for the "grey zone," all acts of Resistance are all right in the abstract and in the distance, never in the concrete and near home. Like all common sense, of course, this discourse can stand only because it contains a dose of truth: if only because they had less time to organize, the partisans in Central Italy often had less sense of direction and strategy than their brothers in the North. The ideological meaning of this discourse, however, is distinct from the referential function that supports it: parallel antipartisan narratives, praising the Resistance broadly and blaming it in the specific, are found all over Italy, including the North. Some of the assumptions of this discourse, therefore, deserve a closer look.

In the first place, the immediate usefulness of partisan action is a controversial and yet only a partial question. In guerrilla warfare, no single action can be considered decisive; yet the partisan war of attrition caused enough trouble in the rear of the German lines to deflect significant forces for a constant "cleansing" of the territory.[22] Though motivated as retaliation and reprisal for individual partisan actions, the numberless German massacres in the Tuscan Apennine region served mainly to protect the battlefront from this disturbance, which included the noncollaboration of large sectors of the general population. In their early testimony, the women of Civitella pointed out that the Germans allowed eleven days to go by before they retaliated. "Life had become calm like before." "Meanwhile the Germans perfectly played their shameful deception" (Corinna Stopponi, widow Caldelli; Elda Morfini, widow Paggi, RB, 260, 278). The implication seems to be that the link between the partisan action and the massacre may be less direct than it is purported to be: three days after the massacres, Civitella was selected as a defense bulwark for the retreating German line. By July 2, when the Germans moved in, the territory had been effectively cleansed.

In the second place, the importance of the partisans is less military than moral. The Axis would have lost the war even without their intervention, but it is because the partisans existed that Italians can claim to have been actors and not merely objects in their own liberation. The usefulness of the partisans, like that of the African American regiments in the Civil War, lies where others see their guilt: in the fact that they existed. If we keep this in mind, perhaps we may understand the psychological need behind the ill-conceived attack at Civitella: aside from many other occasional and possibly less noble motives, the partisans needed to prove that they existed, because in their existence lay the redemption of the whole country.[23]

The historical presence of the partisans illuminates by contrast the narrators' tendency to belittle their own. V.C., for instance, praises the "martyrs [of Civitella], who had done nothing against the Fascists, who had fought in the First World War, who had given their country what they were supposed to give." In this way, he claims for the victims of Civitella the great Christian and subaltern virtues of docility and obedience. By describing them as "martyrs" he includes them in the great narrative of Christianity, but violates the meaning of their death precisely as do the partisans who claim them as "martyrs" of the Resistance. Martyrs are always "guilty" of a militant disobedience and fully aware of its consequences; the victims of Civitella, instead, "died innocent": "We hadn't done anything wrong; we were only concerned with work, with the family." The dead of Civitella had not done anything that might explain their deaths. Victims, not martyrs, their loss is even more difficult to elaborate and understand.

The inexplicability of these deaths also depends on the purely negative definition given of innocence, in its etymological sense of harmlessness (non nocere). Being without guilt, however, does not mean being without responsibilities: having done nothing wrong is one thing, but having done nothing against wrong is another. In these narratives, instead, having done nothing against Fascism and the German occupation becomes almost a virtue: it is the innocence of the "grey zone," of the so-called attesismo (waiting out), of those who "do not meddle with politics" and try to stay outside of history—only to have it suddenly and brutally thrown at them.[24]

The dehistoricizing approach also shapes the judgment on the Germans. In Moby Dick, when Captain Ahab announces his intention to chase and punish the white whale, his first mate Starbuck objects that it is blasphemous to seek punishment upon a "dumb brute" that "smote thee from blindest instinct."[25] As a natural being, the whale is not morally responsible. If it dismasted Ahab, if it sinks the ship and drowns the crew, the fault is only Ahab's for assaulting it.

> M.C.: Everyone knows that the Germans are a bad race . . . that they
> are cruel. . . . Why did you have to mess up with them? Listen—there's
> a lion, and he's savage, but he has already eaten; why do you mess up
> with him? He'll eat even if he's not hungry! He's savage!

V.C. also makes the same point: the partisans knew that the Germans
were savage and cruel *(feroci)*, and should not have provoked them. The
more the narrators of Civitella speak of the Germans as "savage beasts"
(bestie, belve), the more it seems to me that these terms, originally introduced to denounce the German's evil cruelty, have evolved into a way of
absolving them by removing them from the sphere of moral judgment:
the ferociousness of this "bad race" has all the inevitability of a natural
fact.[26] Not once in the contemporary written and oral testimony does
anyone question the "law" that exacted a number of civilian Italian lives
for each German soldier killed.

> They had it posted up at the town hall: For each German killed there
> will be fifteen civilians killed. So they had even warned the population.
> So if they came to take this retaliation—I mean, somebody pushed
> them to it![27]

The partisans "knew that the ten-for-one rule was in force" (V.C.). "They
knew that, for each German, ten civilians would be killed" (P.C.). The
passive impersonal form ("civilians would be killed") removes the Germans from the position of grammatical and moral subjects. The law exists, and that is all. Nobody asks who established it, with what legitimacy
and consent; nobody asks whether its enforcement is always inevitable or
whether it involves each time a moral choice by human beings.

The only laws that apply without the consent of the ruled and that are
in force inevitably and with no mediation are the laws of nature. If one sticks
an arm into the cage, the lion bites; if one hunts Moby Dick, the whale de-
stroys the boat; if one attacks the Germans, the Germans retaliate. The lion,
the whale, the Germans are not responsible. Responsibility can only be attached to those who, being human, attempt to interfere with nature and its
laws. Perhaps this is why no one asks why, if the "law" required fifteen Italians for one German, the ratio at Civitella was forty to one.

MYTH AND POLITICS

*August 23. The monument is clean, the names restored. In thanks to
those who did the job, rather than to commemorate the dead, slightly*

embarrassed and hoping nobody sees me, I buy some flowers and put them by the stone.

The most moving moment of the Arezzo conference took place on the square of Civitella, where the slaughter had begun. Ida Balò, acknowledged voice of the community and its memory, retold the story, splicing into a dramatic patchwork the narratives of her neighbors and friends, and pointing out the places in which each scene had taken place. Later, a moving performance in the church ("Voices of Memory," by Paola Balò) gave to the same stories the form of a sacred play.

Both the narrative in the square and the play in the church highlighted three episodes that I had not heard about before, and that had all the power and prominence of myth: the parson Father Alcide Lazzeri begs the Germans to kill him and save his flock, and is then killed with the rest; a German soldier refuses to fire on the victims and is executed by his officers; years later, two Germans, one a veteran of Civitella, come to town and ask the parson for a forgiveness that is freely granted.

The story of Father Lazzeri's sacrificial offer appears in one narrative of 1946, and is contradicted by others. According to Maria Assunta Menchetti, he told the Germans, "Take me, and spare my people." Corinna Stopponi and Gino Bartolucci, who was closest to the scene (he was one of the hostages, and saw the priest being killed), only say that he "died a hero, after blessing his people" (RB, 268, 261, 277). The more recent narratives, however, only credit the former version, which casts the priest in a role sanctioned by Christian martyrology (CR, 95, 285, 211). There is little doubt, however, that the priest refused to save himself and willingly died with his flock.[28]

The other two episodes are also attested by only one witness each:

> Suddenly I saw a sergeant beckon as if giving an order. Five men were then pushed toward the nursery school, among them the priest with a young seminarian beside him. . . . The sergeant seemed to order an armed soldier to shoot. But an unusual thing happened: the soldier who had received the order stared at the prisoners and did not move. The officer scolded him, we could tell from his gestures and tone of voice, and again ordered him to fire. But he hung undecided. The sergeant then pushed him aside and with a weapon which I think was a machine gun he himself fired upon the five men.
>
> [Then the sergeant] pushed the "traitor" aside and, uttering loud and angry words that I could not understand, made him turn around and shot him in the head. (Luigi Bigiarini, CR, 259–60)

One sweet morning of July, 1983, two rather elderly men visited me in the vicarage of Civitella della Chiana. They asked to see the parson. They said they were Germans, one of whom had been a member of the armed detachment that on the morning of June 29, 1944, sowed death and ruin in Civitella.

[He told me:] "I am one of the Germans who were here for the retaliation that day. Tell the people of this town, Father, that I had much sorrow in my life, that we were very young, and that Hitler had poisoned our youth. I ask forgiveness for all." (Father Enrico Biagini, CR, 453)

There is no reason to question the credibility of these narratives in order to identify their mythic dimension: a myth is not necessarily a false or invented tale; rather, it is a story that becomes significant as it amplifies the meaning of an individual event (factual or not) into a symbolic and narrative formalization of a culture's shared self-representations. In this case, through the narratives of sacrifice, mercy, and forgiveness, the community of Civitella formalizes its relationship to the most dramatic event in its history and defines its own identity as a Christian community. This explains why the priest could assume the authority to pardon on behalf of all and without consulting anyone.

What remains striking is that the German visitor insisted on belittling his own responsibility, blaming all on youth and Hitler, and that the priest did not think of asking even his name and address or military unit (unidentified at that time). The more directly mythical aspect of the tale, however, consists in its classic function as of reconciling opposites: the image of Civitella as a Christian and forgiving community with the unforgiving attitude toward the partisans.

> V.L. We still bear, even fifty years later, this hostility, don't we, toward the partisans; we still feel that way, don't we? . . . in spite of our religious faith.
>
> I. Because they once in a while should have come, should have said: "We were wrong!"[29]
>
> V.L. We still do not have this attitude of forgiveness . . .
>
> I. . . . we go to church . . .
>
> V.L. But we should. We ought to change . . .
>
> M.C. Believing in God as we do, we ought to forgive . . .
>
> V.L. Forgive because they, too, made a mistake, they were only boys, they saw the weapons, they did what came easiest . . .
>
> I. Without thinking of the consequences . . . they were young . . .
>
> V.L. We ought to see things differently after fifty years . . .

> *I.* We should ask the Lord, we do not have the strength . . .
> *M.C.* It's not something we can control. We have it inside us!

The crucial factor is in I.'s statement: at least one German asked for pardon for all, but the partisans never did (V.L. returns to this point later: "In all these years, not once, did the partisans say, like, 'This action of ours was a mistake'"). By pardoning the German, Civitella allays its doubts about not forgiving the partisans: the German repented, the partisans didn't. In this way, Civitella can retain both its image as a Christian community, and its resentment toward the partisans.[30]

The story of the reluctant soldier, on the other hand, is part of a mythic narrative found all over Europe, including the Fosse Ardeatine massacre, known as the story of the "good German." This myth, frequently associated with episodes of World War II (including the Fosse Ardeatine),[31] is in turn a variant of a broader narrative, found also in other contexts. For instance, both oral sources and the congressional record carry a version concerning the death of the worker Luigi Trastulli, killed by the police in Terni: "Luigi Trastulli was climbing a wall and a machine gun volley froze him dead. And we see Luigi Trastulli lose his grip on the wall's edge while another policeman, maybe more human, lowered his gun."[32]

Actually, Luigi Trastulli was killed in the middle of the street. Placing the scene over and by the wall connects it to the iconography of Resistance (the images of executed partisans) and, most importantly, of Crucifixion. The roots of the myth, in fact, are probably to be found in the folk tales inspired by the apocryphal gospels, in which a Roman centurion stops his comrade from piercing Jesus with his spear.

Like all mythic narratives, this is not a univocal narrative, but a matrix of meanings, a grid of oppositions: it depends, ultimately, on whether the person who stands out is perceived as a representative of, or as an alternative to all the rest. The "good German" and the merciful centurion may either confirm our faith in the remnant of humanity that survives even in the most cruel torturers, or highlight through the humanity of one the inhumanity of all; it may mean that the soldiers were forced to fire or lose their lives,[33] or that resistance was possible, and that if more than one had resisted, perhaps the tragedy might have been avoided. As Primo Levi says about an incident at Auschwitz, "If anomalous Germans, capable of this modest courage, had been more numerous, the history of the past and the geography of the present would be different."[34]

The central statement of the myth, in all cases, is that when collective violence causes innocent victims (Christ, the Ardeatine, Trastulli, Civitella), there is always in the murderers something or someone that resists. It may be so, or it may be only that we need to believe it. In his intriguing *Il disperso di Marburg* ("The Missing Soldier of Marburg"), the historian and partisan leader Nuto Revelli inquires into stories of a possible "good German" who used to ride in the countryside of Cuneo during the war, and into his own irresistible impulse to believe in this image and to know more about it. In the end, Revelli and his helpers succeed in attaching a name and a biography to that image, but not in confirming the man's innocence and noninvolvement in the Nazi massacres in their area. One of Revelli's young German correspondents writes,

> The image of the "lone rider" who caresses children and plays Bach in his leisure hours is dissolving. It seems to me more likely that he was scouting the territory. Better to face reality, rather than the images generated in our heads. But what shall we do without those images?[35]

The image of the music-loving Nazi, familiar to the iconography of the concentration camps, as well as the classic image of the occupying soldier who gives candy to the children (repeated in so many American movies), are both projected by Revelli's correspondent. On the other hand, they have a factual basis in Civitella: Father Tiezzi remembers four Catholic Austrian soldiers who came to help sing the Mass in the church, before the massacre; and the candy givers were the very same soldiers who walked the streets of Civitella surrounded by the local children, on their way to being killed by the partisans (Alberto Rossi, *CR*, 231). They are the first "good Germans" in the story. The 1946 narratives, in turn, remember them only as "drunken" and "full of wine," while the only musical Nazis mentioned are the ones who sang and played their instruments while Civitella burned (*RB*, 272, 278, 256).

That these images have a factual foundation does not detract from their mythical status: in fact, the main myth-making process at work in the memory of Civitella seems to be less downright invention than the amplification of the meaning of individual events. What really counts is not so much whether the good Germans existed and gave candy, but the deep-rooted need, even in their victims or enemies, to believe in their existence. "What shall we do without those images?"

I had been so much impressed by Ida Balò's public narrative that the next day I took the opportunity of the lunch break in the conference to ask her to tell me again the stories of the pardon and of the good German, and to answer a few questions. The most surprising thing she told

me was that, for a long time, the people of Civitella had not believed the
story of the good German, because the sole witness was not a native of
Civitella: evidently, his story could not be assumed in the town's narrative.[36] People either did not believe it, or did not think it was important.
Only "about ten years ago," Ida Balò explained, had the story become
part of town's collective memory, and of her own communal narrative.[37]

Balò also repeated the story of the German who asked to be forgiven,
much as it appears in the parson's written testimony, with only two variants: she thought that the visit had happened at night, and that the event
had taken place "about ten years ago."[38] Our conversation took place in
1994, at the time of the fiftieth anniversary of the massacre; evidently,
"about ten years ago," Civitella was getting ready to celebrate another
decennial anniversary, and these two mythic narratives became functional in that process.

Civitella always protested the anniversary celebrations performed in
the name of the Resistance. For a long time, the opposition took place between the civil celebrations in the square and the religious ceremonies in
the church and the cemetery: "We never, in these fifty years, spent the
29th of June without commemorating that day. . . . I'm talking of the religious celebration, understand? Because we never took part in any other
ceremony" (V.L.). Gradually, however, protest developed into the creation of alternative public celebrations built around an official narrative
based on the survivors' own myths and values, and entrusted to their own
institutions. Significantly, V.C. describes the celebration of 1984 as "the
first," not because it was, but because it was the first time he felt publicly
represented:

> P.C.   The first commemoration was when they inaugurated the chapel
>   down at the cemetery, and Fanfani came.
> V.L.   In '84 . . .[39]

Amintore Fanfani, a conservative Catholic politician who held every office in Italy's government for almost half a century (including the pre-
miership several times), had his electoral base in the province of Arezzo.
His name is frequently evoked in the narratives of Civitella as the "providential" benefactor who helped the town's postwar "resurrect[ion]."[40]
This, of course, does not detract from the authenticity and power of the
narrators' stories and feelings: it may very well be that, for once, Fanfani
was truly closer than others to the material and emotional needs of the
people. His visible presence, however, especially in connection with the
intriguingly crucial celebration of 1984, confirms that memory is "di-

vided" not just between an "official" and a "communal" memory, but also between *two official memories* and two alternative ceremonial series administered by opposite political and institutional camps. The history of Civitella's memory is incomplete unless it includes the history of its public manifestations.

This public memory, embodied in its own narratives and recognized narrators, books of testimonies, sacred plays, and political representatives, is not only fully legitimate, but also replete with important values, such as innocence, meekness, obedience, mercy, forgiveness, and family and group solidarity. It is based on lived experience and deeply felt emotions. It remains, however, a highly ideological and institutional construction, distinct from the personal memories on which it is based.

Pietro Clemente speaks of Civitella's "collective memory"; Giovanni Contini of "the town's" memory; Cappelletto and Calamandrei of "group memory." These are all legitimate terms of historical discourse, at least since the work of Maurice Halbwachs. We must not forget, however, that the elaboration of memory and the act of remembering are always individual: persons, not groups, remember. Even when Maurice Halbwachs claims that individual memory does not exist, yet he always writes, "*I* remember." On the other hand, Halbwachs describes as an individual, even lonesome, process what is an essential activity of memory: forgetting.[41]

If all memory were collective, one witness could serve for an entire culture—but we know that it is not so. Each individual, especially in modern times and societies, derives memories from a variety of groups, and organizes them in idiosyncratic fashion. Like all human activities, memory is *social* and may be *shared* (which is why each individual has something to contribute to "social" history"); however, like *langue* as opposed to *parole*, it only materializes in individual recollections and speech acts. It becomes *collective* memory only when it is abstracted and detached from the individual: in myth and folklore (one story for many people: the "good German"), in delegation (one person for many stories: Ida Balò), in institutions (abstract subjects—school, Church, State, party—that organize memories and rituals in a whole other than the sum of its separate parts). These three types of memory are all found at Civitella; the pressure to *not forget* and to derive memories from *only one group* (the tight-knit circle of the survivors) materializes the "social control" described by Cappelletto and Calamandrei as the pressure of "collective" upon "individual" memory.

Once we realize that "collective" memory is other than the memories

of individuals, we can no longer describe it as the direct and spontaneous
expression of pain, mourning, or scandal, but as an equally legitimate
and meaningful formalization mediated by ideologies, languages, common sense, and institutions. We must no longer look for oppositions only
between fields of memories, but also *within* them. The brilliant definition, "divided memory," must be enlarged and radicalized to define not
simply the dichotomy (and implied hierarchy) between the institutional
memory of the Resistance and the collective memory of the community,
but also a fragmented plurality of different memories.

The "town's memory" itself is not a solid whole. The unspeakable
memories withheld even in the family circle coexist with the equally authentic and moving memories publicly displayed in the square and the
church. Memory, then, is divided by generations; more dramatically, even
individuals are internally divided between the desire to be silent and forget and the need to speak: "*I did not want* to write anything, because it
is a painful toil for me, and because I had promised my brother I would
not do it, and for this I am sorry. But *I had to* because our mother would
have been pleased" (Giuliana Sabatini Migliorini, *CR,* 322; my italics).

The *town's* memory is also socially divided—at least if by "town" we
mean Civitella as it is today and the people who live in it, rather than a
frozen image of 1944. Many of the contemporary inhabitants moved in
after the war; among them are the descendants of the "peasants" and the
"mass of shit" kept once outside the walls and today outside the narrative: "With the other people who did not live at Civitella, with them, we
don't talk about it. They were all peasants" (S.M.). These new people,
however, also have memories of their own, which ought perhaps to be
recognized as part of the memory of what is now their town.

The memory of institutions and the memory of the Resistance are also
divided. A paradox in the Arezzo conference was that it looked at times
as if the only "official memory" were that of the Resistance, and the only
"ideology" that of the Left. It is a fact that we are living at a time in which
opinion-makers and politicians are able to claim that a "Marxist hegemony" and even a "Communist government" have ruled Italy in the last
fifty years, turning this ridiculous lie into common sense with hardly any
opposition from those who ought to know better. It is also true that the
province of Arezzo has had a leftist administration since the war. But anyone who has worked in Arezzo recognizes even in the controversy over
the celebrations at Civitella the historical tension between the local institutions held by the Left and the presence of the central institutions of the
state controlled by a powerful figure like Amintore Fanfani.[42] Even in

"Red" Tuscany, after all, prefects are appointed by the Ministry of the Interior, the banks are controlled by capital, the air-waves are dominated by the national networks, and the major paper is the conservative *La Nazione*.

Partisan memory never coincided with the deep discourse of the state. The Resistance became "official" memory very late, and at the price of being turned into a ritual of commemorative stones and wreaths, a reconciled and innocuous ceremony belonging to a political sphere from which common people feel increasingly estranged. Even then, the official memory of the Resistance is one thing if it is celebrated by a president like former partisan Sandro Pertini, or by a reactionary and corrupt one like Giovanni Leone. In fact, V.C. suggests that the current president, Catholic Oscar Luigi Scalfaro, ought to attend the celebrations in Civitella, but claims that if Pertini had shown his face he would have been jeered out of town.

Finally, even individual local partisan memories are multiple and divided: the contradictory versions given by the partisans of the action of June 18 are also an effect of the fragmented perception and evaluation of that crucial event. One such divided memory is that of the partisan leader Edoardo Succhielli, who defended his version in public with court suits and books, but probably knew all along what he admitted—maybe too late—to historian Giovanni Contini: the action was a mistake and brought ruin to the town and its people.[43] Another divided memory is that of Dr. Gambassini, the town's physician, who helped the partisans and left Civitella after the war. It is said that he carried deep feelings of guilt inside him all his life, but he apparently represses them in his published autobiography.[44]

The Arezzo conference was important because it listened to some of these other memories, respected their bearers, and entertained a dialogue with them (I hope they also listened to us), and it placed the events of Civitella in the perspective of a history that involves an entire continent. It would be a mistake, however, to take the memories of Civitella for a solid nucleus, impenetrable to thought, immune to history and politics, and inaccessible to critical analysis. Confronting other people's memories and being changed by the encounter is dialogue; uncritically giving up our own is surrender.

August 24. It rains, but my flowers are still there. Today's paper says that "for at least two months, swastikas have stained the monument to the martyrs of the Resistance at Ostia, while the borough does

*nothing about it." The borough of Ostia (Rome's seaside suburb) is
chaired by the (ex?) Fascists of Alleanza Nazionale. The national
news in the same paper informs us that a judge in Argentina denied
extradition for Eric Priebke, Nazi torturer and an officer at the Fosse
Ardeatine massacre. He never had to ask for anybody's forgiveness.*[45]

Postscript

As I prepare this book for the press, Eric Priebke has been extradited and
is on trial for the Fosse Ardeatine massacre. He has offered his "condo-
lences" to the families of the victims. During the trial, a German military
historian has testified that there were cases in which Nazi soldiers and officers asked to be exempted from participating in massacres, and suffered
no consequences. According to another former Nazi witness, who was
Priebke's second in command in Rome at the time, Priebke was also responsible for the massacre of the hostages commemorated by the stone in
my neighborhood. "He was in charge," this witness said; "he wasn't following any orders."[46]

Chapter Eleven

As Though It Were a Story
Versions of Vietnam

> I'm telling history as if it were biography, they way we used to. Always in relation with politics, with the life of society. (Alvaro Valsenti, steel worker)[1]

"Look," says Valtèro Peppoloni, worker and activist from Terni, Italy, "I was a young Fascist—I won't hide it. If this is history, we must tell it like it was."[2] Rather than factual objectivity, however, what he had in mind was personal subjectivity: "like it was" does not refer to historical events but to personal growth, not to history but to his place in it. After this methodological premise, he began his narrative of the Spanish Civil War, which he fought on the wrong side.[3]

Peppoloni feels that in telling his own story, he must be responsible to "history." On the other hand, a Vietnam war veteran tells the history of that war "as though it were a story." War is the ground where *history* and *story*, two directly related words, overlap and coalesce. War as event and oral history as discourse, therefore, share the fact of being the grounds of encounters between personal experience and history, the spaces where the individual narrative of biography meets the collective narrative of history. In oral history, history is represented through the personal experience of specific individuals, while biography is sustained by the accent on individual participation in historic events. Narrators articulate memory, evaluation, and anecdote in the dialogues with interviewers who are trying to reconstruct a broader framework and therefore invite them to highlight the encounter between history and their lives, private worlds and events of general interest. Also, oral history is an opportunity for relatively obscure narrators to be canonized in public discourse, a public speech act by people who rarely have the opportunity to speak publicly.

161

In this essay I investigate the ways in which the interaction between biography and history, between individual and institutional identities, operates in some narratives of Vietnam war veterans. I will refer to two published collections of interviews: *Nam: The Vietnam War in the Words of the Men and Women Who Fought There,* by Mark Baker (1982), and *Bloods: An Oral History of the Vietnam War by Black Veterans,* edited by Wallace Terry (1984). Both books take a basically journalistic approach; they listen to oral sources with a sympathetic sensitivity but do not concern themselves with the methodological and interpretative problems raised by oral history. In both texts, the dialogic form of the interview is reduced to monologues, as if the interviewees were addressing directly an impersonal reader rather than their empirical interviewer and narratee.

The two books, however, take very different approaches to the presentation of their materials. While *Bloods* presents individual narratives separately and designates the narrators by name and rank, *Nam* chooses to keep narrators anonymous and to break and reassemble their narratives in thematic sections (through which, however, some personal stories can be identified and followed). Thus, *Bloods* presents the Vietnam experience within the frame of each individual life, while *Nam* attempts to reconstruct a shared, collective, and therefore anonymous history. We might say that the former is biography-oriented, and the latter is history-oriented. Overall, *Nam* as a book describes a general flow of events that drags along fragments of individual experience, while *Bloods* stages the repetition and variation, similarity and difference, of individual experiences.

Both, however, convey the sense that oral history is less the "testimony" of events than a "construction" made of words through the cooperation of editors, interviewers, witnesses, and narrators, all of whom endeavour to shape in language the form and meaning of experience and memory. In this chapter, therefore, I deal less with events per se than with the subjective relationship between individuals and history as expressed by the formal implications of language and narrative.

This implies a final preliminary consideration. What follows is not an interpretation of the Vietnam war, but an interpretation of two interpretations, founded in turn upon the cluster of the narrators' implicit or implicit interpretations. This is not to say that it makes no sense, but that its sense lies less in a history of facts that in a history of their meanings for those who lived through them and came back to tell the tale, and for those who listened to the tale and spread it around.

PRONOUNS: CITIZENS AND CONSCRIPTS

> I just say I don't want some government telling me what to do.
> (a customer in the Wagon Wheel Cafe, Strong City, Kansas)[4]

> As long as the white man sent you to Korea, you bled. He sent you to
> Germany, you bled. He sent you to the South Pacific, to fight the
> Japanese, you bled. (Malcolm X)[5]

"With the creation of the nation state, the establishment of compulsory military service, and the formation of mass armies," writes historian Antonio Gibelli, "access to the military institution and participation in wars became an essential ingredient in the life of the peasant masses, a crucial passage in the relationship between peasants and the state, the country and the city." In World War I, Gibelli goes on, "the subordinate classes experience for the first time to such a wide and pervasive extent the presence of the extraneous power of the state." World War I, he concludes, "coincides with the first generally shared experience of modernity," inclusive of its organizational and technological aspects.[6]

Unlike Italy, the United States never had a large "peasant class," yet to many of its citizens the American state remained an extraneous presence, not downright hostile but often distantly neutral. The aphorism "That government is best which governs least" opens Henry David Thoreau's essay on "Resistance to Civil Government" and speaks equally for the libertarian Left, the business center, and the radical Right.[7] As the proudly independent Kansas cafe customer formulates it, "I" is on one side, "the government" on the other. Malcolm X plays upon this attitude in his speech: beyond his direct address to African Americans, who have not had full access to citizenship but have been involved in all of America's wars, his words also bear a message for all those proud American individualists who will not allow the government to tell them what to do, except (unlike Thoreau) when it tells them to shed blood and go to war.

This contradiction is usually resolved rhetorically, by replacing the state with the nation: wars are fought for America, not for the government. Yet, in the relative ideological homogeneity that characterizes American politics with respect to other Western democracies, the distinction between America and government (both embodied by the president) can at times be blurred. Also, it is the government that decides when America needs to fight a war, and wars are waged by huge governmental machines. The antibureaucratic attitude, the irony and resentment toward the brass, and the sense of loss of identity that is widespread in war narratives are an expression of this contradiction. One narrator in *Nam* describes his induction in the terms of a negative initiation:

> We're there for a couple of hours. You're in your civilian clothes and you've been in them for a couple of days. You feel like shit. When they march you out, all of a sudden it's by the numbers. All your hair's gone. You don't even know who you are.[8]

The deeper implications of this transition are couched in the grammar of the passage. "*We're* in there. . . . *You're* in your civilian clothes . . .": the shift from the first person plural *we* to the second person impersonal *you* bridges a traumatic change in self-perception. This is a rather unusual narrative form, in which the autobiographical narrator refers to himself in the second rather than in the first person. As Philippe Lejeune has shown, autobiography is defined as such by the correspondence of the first person singular with the name of author, narrator, protagonist.[9] When, in an autobiographical narrative, pronouns and verbs begin to fragment and multiply, it means that identity is questioned: in this case, from being a person among persons (*we*), the narrator becomes an impersonal entity, shorn of clothes, hair, and personal pronouns.

A song from the Vietnam war also begins in the first person, expressing the memory of a personal and civil identity at risk: "*I* walked away from freedom and the life that *I* had known" Induction consists of the encounter with an impersonal entity that manipulates the subject's consciousness and is designated in the third person: "*they* set my mind for war." At the end of the process, the subject is assimilated and repeats the slogans of the institution as if they were his own: "freedom is *our* mission." But how can freedom be one's mission, if the speaker has walked away from freedom in the first place? This contradiction is mediated by the initiation process: *I* goes through *they* and comes out *we*.[10]

The narrators in *Nam* and *Bloods* systematically use the first person singular to speak of their lives before induction and war. It is the natural autobiographical *I* of the independent citizen and the first-person narrator. For instance, Haywood T. Kirkland says, in *Bloods:* "*I* was basically a C-type student in high school. I guess *I* didn't care much about anything except pool. By the time *I* was sixteen *I* had won a lot of championships at the Boy's Club."[11] The first word in *Nam* is *I;* nine out of the first ten sections of testimony in the first chapter begin with the first person singular.

The decision to enlist is generally presented as a personal choice and told in the first person. But as the process unfolds, the narrative shifts gradually toward the plural: the narrator is injected into a collective process and joins a shared identity. The opposition tends to be between *we*, the army as community of men, and *they*, the army as impersonal organization and branch of the government: "I don't feel like *we* got beat in Vietnam. . . . America should have won the war. But *they* wouldn't free *us* to fight" (Harold Bryant, *B*, 35). In this case, "America" is the element that bridges the contradiction between *we* and *they*.

Nam stresses the initiation theme, contrasting the experience of the war with the expectations of the young soldiers: "I was young and innocent and I was under the impression that enlisting was the All-American thing to do"; "[the Marine Corps] helped me grow up. I grew up in Vietnam." Recruits expect that the war will make men out of them: "One way or another in every generation when there was a war, some male in the family on my father's side went to it. I never had it drilled into me, but there was a lot of attention paid to the past, a lot of not-so-subtle 'This is what a man does with his life' when I was growing up" (*N*, 12–13). At the end of the process, however, rather than finding themselves, they often feel they have lost something: "But by the time you get to the end of that whole process, you feel you're the badassest thing that ever walked the earth. When they call you Marine in the graduation ceremony, there's tears in your eyes. You are thoroughly indoctrinated" (*N*, 17). The sharp shift from the tearful emotion of the narrated subject to the pitiless self-judgment of the present-time narrator is not unlike the memorable hair-conking scene in the autobiography of Malcolm X.

In the passage above, the crisis of identity is expressed by the irruption of the second person *you*: "*They* have *you* jump. *You* never get up in the morning like normal folks" (*N*, 15, 16); "As soon as *I* hit boot camp in Fort Jackson, South Carolina, *they* tried to change *your* total personality. Transform *you* out of that civilian mentality to a military mind" (Haywood T. Kirkland, *B*, 109). This narrator is an *I* when he hits boot camp, but becomes a *you* by the time the sentence is finished and *they* are through with him.

Second-person narration is a figure of ambiguity: *you* is both a dialogic personal pronoun that evokes the empirical situation of the interview, and an impersonal pronoun that designates the crisis of identity in a collective process and a repetitive routine.[12] Thus, a novel told entirely in the second person, like Jay McInerney's *Bright Lights, Big City* comes across as a pathetic monologue that invites readers to put themselves in the narrator's place: it could happen to *you*; or, what would *you* do if you were in *my* place? But even when the second person is ostensibly a way of addressing the interviewer, the combination of the dialogic and the impersonal *you* suggests that the experience cannot be told but only felt. Only by sharing the narrator's point of view can the narratee grasp the meaning of the experience.

The second person, however, is less important in itself than in its shifting interplay with other pronominal forms. In these autobiographical narratives, *you* has a strong impact because it replaces and abolishes the *I* with which the story had begun. In the narratives of Italian student activists, as Elena Spandri has noted, the "objectifying *you*" functions as a symbolic extension of autobiographic discourse "toward a range of collective possibilities": it is both a way of "relating to the world" and "a sort of personal displacement, a difficulty in keeping together the interior and exterior aspects of identity."[13] In most of these narratives of Vietnam, instead, the shift from *I* and *we* to the pathetic/impersonal *you* takes place at the time when the citizen loses his identity and is turned into a soldier: the accent is on the displacement rather than on the extension of the self.

In his "Message to the Grassroots," Malcolm X uses the second person both as dialogic appeal to the audience, and as narrative persona to articulate a metaphor of loss of selfhood under external control:

> It's like when you go to the dentist and the man's going to take your tooth. You're going to fight him when he starts pulling. So he squirts some stuff in your jaw called novocaine, to make you think they're not doing anything to you. So you sit there and because you've got all that novocaine in your jaw, you suffer—peacefully.[14]

Once the narrators begin to describe their experiences in Vietnam and recount combat situations, the use of pronouns tends to fragment, following the individual and shifting patterns of relationship to the events. But the first person tends to become dominant again as soon as the narrative begins to describe the return home. At this point, however, it articulates less the citizen's individualistic pride than the veteran's solitude and loss of communication: "*I* looked at *them*, and *they* weren't even listening" (*N*, 201).

A very articulate example of this use of pronouns is the narrative of Harold Bryant (*B*, 22–4). He begins, as usual, in the first person, emphasizing his affirmations of identity: "*My* left ear was pierced when *I* was nine. You can imagine the teasing *I* got in high school for wearing an earring. But *I* felt in this small way *I* carry on the African tradition. *I* would

go into the Army wearing the mark of the African warriors *I* descend from."
Bryant's narrative skips the phase of induction, and he continues in the
first person singular until he reaches Vietnam. He achieves, however, an
effect of estrangement by shifting from active to passive verb forms, from
"*I did* my basic and my AIT at Fort Leonardwood [*sic*], Missouri" to "*I
was sent* to An Khe." He locates his initiation directly on the battle field,
and consequently this is where he makes the canonical transition from *I*
to *we* to *you:*

> I was one of those replacements.
>   We probed for mines, blew up mines, disarmed and blew up booby
> traps. If *you* saw a trip wire, you could take a look at what was
> happening. *You* could see where the booby trap was.

The description of the handling of booby traps continues in the second
person: it is a moment of shared danger, and, more importantly, a routine in which saving one's life depends less on personal initiative than on
following standard routines ("if *you* don't crimp right . . . it will blow *you*
up"). In fact, the first person returns soon after, in the plural, both to express collective solidarity and to deprecate a failure to follow correct procedure: "*We* lost three guys from rushing or crimping wrong."
   In such moments of crisis, the individual becomes relevant again, and
Bryant is once more a first-person protagonist: "One time *I* had to get a
guy off a mine," he begins, and the *I* dominates the anecdote for two pages:
"*I* dug all around the mine with my bayonet. *I* told him *I* was gonna try
to diffuse [*sic*] it. . . . *I* thought *I* was seein' the plunger rise, so *I* told him
to stop."
   The first person also prevails in the section about his return (which is
told out of chronological sequence). Rather than the pride of the resource-
ful ghetto boy and of the war hero, however, this is the *I* of a person who
has no *you* to speak to, nor a *we* to speak for and from: "Finally, *I* got
guys that asked me what it was really like. And when *I* was trying to explain it, after a while, *I* saw *they* got disinterested. So *I* just didn't talk
about it anymore."

POSSESSIVE ADJECTIVES: BLACKS AND AMERICANS

> Imagine a Negro: "*Our* government"! I even heard one say "*our*
> astronauts." They won't even let him near the plant—and "*our*
> astronauts"! "*Our* Navy"—that's a Negro that is out of his mind, a
> Negro that is out of his mind. (Malcolm X)[15]

> We had a new Navy. The first ships were named after black heroes.
> The first black was promoted to admiral. Ten percent of our NROTC
> units were set aside for predominantly black colleges. (Lieutenant
> Commander William S. Norman, *B*, 237)

The relationship between war and citizenship becomes even more complicated in the case of African Americans. On the one hand, as Malcolm X
points out, the exclusion from full citizenship makes "access to the military"
either impossible or absurd. On the other hand, participation in wars—
from the black regiments in the Civil War to General Colin Powell in the
Gulf War—has been a channel that African Americans have used to claim
their citizenship rights. It was Olaudah Equiano, the first major Anglo-
African autobiographer, who first used the expression "our land forces"
and "our ships" to refer to the British Navy on which he was embarked.[16]

Early in the Civil War, Frederick Douglass insisted on the recruitment
of black troops as evidence of his people's patriotism and "manhood":
"Let the slaves and free colored people be called into service and formed
into a liberating army, to march into the South and raise the banner of
Emancipation."[17] Later, W. E. B. Du Bois championed black participation in World War I as a sanction of citizenship, while denouncing discrimination and segregation in the armed forces: "We gained the right to
fight for civilization at the cost of being 'Jim-Crowed' and insulted."[18]

It would be easy to read the testimony of black veterans in *Bloods* and
in *Nam* for expressions of dissatisfaction and protest. Some of the veterans became radicalized, if often temporarily, through their experience in
the war and their impact with the military (see for instance Reginald Edwards, *B*, 14–15). But this way of reading would only serve to confirm
the preconceived expectations of a progressive, liberal, radical imagination, and to miss a part of the complex truth of African American experience. The function of historical research and of literature, however, is
not to confirm what we already know, but to question our assumptions,
not necessarily in order to renounce our principles but to stand by them
in more articulate, realistic, effective fashion. Otherwise, we would be interrogating the text with the same naiveté of the Vietnamese officer who
interrogated Colonel Fred V. Cherry, black POW:

> He was a very good interrogator. He read a lot of novels, and he knew
> black literature. He had read *Raisin in the Sun* and *Invisible Man*. He
> knew more about Malcolm X than I did. And he was versed in Stokely
> Carmichael's philosophy. Absolutely. Stokely was helping them with
> broadcasts from Hanoi. (*B*, 340)

On the strength of this knowledge, the Vietnamese interrogators "couldn't understand why I couldn't be on their side, on the side of another colored race." But Cherry explained that "I'm still an officer of the United States. . . . I always kept in mind that I was representing twenty-four million black Americans. . . . I'm just not going to denounce my government or shame my people" (B, 41). "*My government*": should we say, with Malcolm X, that Cherry is "a Negro that is out of his mind"? Perhaps. On the other hand, perhaps Cherry is a black man who has more than one thing on his mind, and is not the only one.

A narrator in *Nam* is a member of the Nation of Islam, who remembers thinking, "Why should I go out and fight for the system when my people are catching a lot of chaos from being under it? . . . If I had to pick up a gun, let me pick it up and turn it on the system" (N, 18, 20). As he becomes involved in the war and faces death together with the rest of his company, he begins to feel that "I was no longer the Black Muslim revolutionary. I was one of the boys" (N, 49); "I had pride in being black. But I also had pride in being a Marine" (N, 166). He is thus caught in a contradiction that renders him speechless when a Vietnamese girl, whom he rapes and kills, asks him: "Hey, you're black, why are you doing this to me?" (N, 149).

"Let's face it," says Lieutenant Joe Biggers, "we are part of America. . . . I don't feel because my grandfather or grandmother was a slave that I should not lift arms up to support those things that are stated in the Constitution of the United States" (B, 135). "I am a black American," says Robert L. Mountain. "If I'm going to say I'm a black American, then I must be ready to defend my country when her shores are invaded. I can't enjoy all the liberties that we have rights to in America and call myself a black American and say this is my land and not be willing to support her in war or time of need" (B, 373).

African American soldiers claim their American identity and citizenship precisely in the standard terms of American ideology (which is the most convincing proof of their American-ness): rights, freedom, standard of living ("Economically, black folks in America have more money than [in] Canada or Mexico," Reginald Edwards, B, 17). It does not matter that no one is invading America's shores, that Canadian citizens are on the average much better off than U.S. blacks, or that democratic rights are not an exclusive property of the United States. Ideology is not *about* fact: it *is* a fact, and as such we need to confront it.

If we put Malcolm X's speech side by side with these narratives that apply unproblematically the problematic *my* and *our* to the speakers' relationship with America, we recognize a paradox: America does not fully belong to black people, but black people belong to America. In a passage fascinating for the ideological dislocation it contains, Robert L. Mountain defines himself as an American citizen at first in opposition to reactionary racist discrimination, but ultimately in opposition to radical antiwar protest: racists tell him that "this is still not my country. . . . But my flag flies outside my door. . . . I tell my wife, I wish someone would come and burn my flag!" (B, 373).

The first-person identification with America that allows Mountain to speak of "*my* flag" is involved with contradictions. First of all, his shared American identity is acquired, in part, at the price of personal disidentification. After the war, Robert L. Mountain proudly waves "his" flag; but he remembers very well the alienation he felt upon his first experience of the army. This feeling is rendered in the narrative by a startling shift between past tense and historical present, between past emotions and present judgment, and with the ironic detachment of free indirect speech, a symptom of a divided self:[19]

> And it was strange because I want to go to Vietnam now, because I want to shoot just one Communist to see how he looks when he falls. That's stupid as hell, but this is the way they had me programmed. . . . I'm an American fighting man. I serve the forces which guard democracy, my country. Gung ho. All the way. Not from enthusiasm, but from training. This is my profession. (B, 211)

Mountain had been taught that "the Vietnamese were killers. Once in a while, black veterans remember feeling that they were fighting another colored people; on the other hand, they often refer to the Vietnamese with the same racist or paternalist terms (*gooks, dinks, papa san, mama san*) as their white comrades (B, 54, 59, 31; N, 48–49). Doubts about the war tend to emerge the moment the narrators realize that "gooks" are people. While dragging a Viet Cong's body that came apart in his hands, Reginald Edwards "started thinking . . . All of a sudden I realize this guy is a person, has got a family. All of a sudden it wasn't like I was carrying a gook. I was actually carrying a human being. I started feeling guilty. I just started feeling really badly" (B, 13). Those African American veterans who see the Vietnamese as persons are more likely to distance themselves from "we Americans" and speak of "white Americans" or just "Americans" in the third person, even in opposition to "blacks": "Poor Vietnamese. So many times Americans would degrade them" (Dwyte A. Brown, B, 319); "I think *blacks* got along better with the Vietnamese people, because they knew the hardships the Vietnamese went through. . . . But *Americans* had a different idea" (Emmanuel J. Holloman, *B*, 101).[20]

The most critical factor is the discovery that wearing a uniform does not guarantee recognition of citizenship. Edgar A. Huff was one of the first blacks accepted into the Marine Corps, in 1942, but as he went home on leave with his uniform on, the Atlanta police arrested him, claiming that "There ain't no damn nigger Marines" (*B*, 177). He fought in Vietnam, retired with honors, and was congratulated by the president and even by the governor of Alabama on his retirement. But the war was not over for him. Three weeks after his retirement party, he was dining with friends and neighbors on his front lawn, in the shadow of his flag:

> At this time, a car drove up. And four white marines started throwing
> hand grenades. They were white phosphorus. Threw one right
> through my station wagon. Threw another at this lady's Cadillac.
> Guess they thought it was my Cadillac. And they threw another one
> into my house. And another one hit the Marine emblem on my gate.
> (*B*, 184)

Malcolm X once told a debate antagonist that the word used by racists to described black Ph.D.s is still *"Nigger!"*[21] Ultimately, this applies also to black Marine sergeant majors: Huff's aggressors explained that they "didn't understand how a nigger could be living that way, sitting out there eating on a nice lawn, under that American flag I fly every day." The Marine Corps, Huff comments, "never did nothin' to them at all" (*B*, 184–85).

"I fought for thirty years for the Marine Corps," Huff comments, "And I feel like I own part of this ground that I walk on every day, especially this that I own." But his right to say "this land is my land" and to call the American flag "my" flag is still in doubt.

Sergeant Robert L. Daniels, who lost an arm in Vietnam, sums up the contradiction with an ironic juxtaposition between the estranging second person of official ideology and the paradox of a denied possessive pronoun: "*you* s'posed to fight for *your* country. And *you* come home. But where is *my* country when *I* come home?" (*B*, 282). And Harold Bryant—who, like the Vietnamese interrogator, is aware of Ralph Ellison—concludes, "No. America has not yet welcomed me home. Not me as a black man. . . . We're still invisible men" (Harold Bryant, *B*, 364).

POINTS OF VIEW: MEMORY AND JUDGMENT

> You want to hear a gen-u-ine war story? I only understand Vietnam as
> though it were a story. It's not like it happened to me. (Epigraph in
> *Nam*, 1)

> When you've been eight, nine month, a year up in the mountains, you
> come down, you're a half beast. There's no two ways about it. You're
> not a normal man. Today, I say, I was a beast. I realize that in those
> times I had lost my reason. You've come down the mountain with that
> constant hatred, constant war, weapons, always expecting to be shot
> in the back, always expecting a bullet, you've become so charged that
> before you get back in line with the idea of . . . society, it wasn't easy,
> it took a long time. (Mario Filipponi, partisan)[22]

"Davis would do little crazy things. If they had gold in their mouth, he'd
knock the gold out 'cause he saved gold. He saved a little collection of
gold teeth. Maybe fifty or sixty in a little box. And he went and had about
100 pictures made of himself. And he used to leave one in the field. Where
he got the gook. . . . Wherever he would see a gook, he would go after
them. He was good" (*B*, 54). "Armstrong was ruthless, man, really ruthless. . . . One night [after we killed two Viet Cong] Armstrong immediately started cutting ears off and put them in his rucksack. Then he cut
one man's neck off, and stuck the whole head inside" (*B*, 116). "Then
Emo took out the little bag again. He fumbled with the yellow pull-strings
and opened it. He poured the human teeth on the table. . . . They were
his war souvenirs."[23] The first two passages are from the narratives of
Vietnam veterans; the third comes from a novel, Leslie Marmon Silko's
Ceremony, which refers to World War I but was published in 1977, immediately after the Vietnam war. Together, they draw our attention to a
pervasive metaphor for the horrors of war in general, and Vietnam in particular: the fragmentation and dismembering of bodies.

Mark Baker, perhaps intentionally, places a story that foreshadows this
theme immediately after the opening of *Nam*. A medical student finds
that someone has cut off a cadaver's finger; to carry the prank further, he
saws off the whole arm, takes it along in his car, and sticks it in the hand
of a tollbooth attendant. He is invited to leave the school, and a week later,
receives his draft notice (*N*, 6). Symmetrically, *Ceremony* ends with the
veterans' bloody repetition of the scenes of dismemberment they had witnessed in the war: "Pinkie held his leg, and Leroy cut the whorl from the
bottom of his big toe. . . . They had a paper bag they had emptied of wine

bottles. Emo was holding it with the palm of his hand supporting the bottom of the bag because it was soaked with blood, and the brown paper was beginning to dissolve around the bleeding chunks of human skin."[24]

In war, human beings are authorized, indeed compelled, to commit inhuman deeds that are hard to countenance in retrospect: the recurrent shift we have noticed, between the remembered thrill and the present disgust is the most visible narrative representation of this contradiction. The usual autobiographical distance between the narrating and the narrated self becomes dramatic when the subject must reconstruct his wartime experience and subjectivity in peace time. This is why the gaze, the point of view, becomes so crucial in these narratives.

> So at that time they had this game called Guts. Guts was where they gave the prisoner to a company and everybody would get in line and do something to him.
> We had a lot of new guys in the company that had never seen a dead NVA. And the officer was telling them to get in line. If they didn't do anything, he wanted them to go past and *look* anyway.
> That's how you do this game called Guts.
> So they took the NVA's clothes off and tied him to a tree. Everybody in the unit got in line. At least 200 guys.
> The first guy took a bayonet and plucked his *eye* out. Put the bayonet at the corner of the eye and popped it. And I was amazed how large your *eyeball* was. . . . (Richard J. Ford, *B*, 55–6)

The prisoner is literally cut to pieces, his tongue sliced, his teeth pulled out. But it makes sense for the torture to begin with the eye, because the whole episode is about seeing: by forcing the reluctant recruits to witness the scene, the officers force them to acknowledge their complicity. There are also narratives about being seen: on the one hand, the soldier Davis leaves his photograph as signature on the corpses of his dismembered victims; on the other, an officer is embarrassed when he realizes that the CBS and UPI crews will see that his men have cut off the ears of dead Vietnamese (*N*, 140). What the men do as a matter of course in the space of war becomes inconceivable when looked at from the space of peace, by the viewers at home.

Eyes, mirrors, cameras occur often in *Nam*, representing the doubling of point of view between looking at the horror and the horror of looking at themselves or being looked at. After a massacre in a village, "all these Instamatic cameras began to appear and flashbulbs began to pop simultaneously. I had a very strange feeling, as if I was projected somewhere outside of it. Pop. Pop. Pop. I saw it as if it were in a pantomime, slow motion."[25] Photography estranges the massacre with "the strobe light effect of the flashcubes"; it objectifies the horror turning the perpetrator into a spectator; and accomplishes a ritual appropriation of the deed: "They're smiling these big smiles of great joy, like something wonderful had just happened" (N, 113).[26] As he looks at his comrades looking through the cameras, he experiences the doubling of point of view and anticipates the autobiographical split between the narrated self in the past and the narrating self in the present. When he adds, "I don't want to give the sense that I wasn't elated by the whole operation," the very involved syntax of the phrase declares the distance between the narrator's elation then and his embarrassment now.

The splitting of the gaze has also more disturbing forms. Looking at his own eyes in the mirror, a soldier feels that war has turned him into someone else: "There's another person in the room. . . . Then I realised I was looking in a mirror and hadn't recognised my own reflection. Was that me? . . . I'd become one of those guys I'd seen when I first arrived in-country. Now I had that look in my eyes" (N, 81). For one returned veteran, looking at his photo album has the same shocking mirror effect. In them, he sees the person he had become during the war, and does not recognize it: "We started looking at the album and I just flipped out. I started throwing shit everywhere. I beat my wife over the head with a full quart bottle of beer. . . . I just flipped when I saw those pictures in the book. My head just went away" (N, 222–23). Another veteran remembers how he and his comrades "posed and snapped pictures" while a prisoner slowly died at their feet: "In retrospect," he concludes, "I'm ashamed of it. I'm glad I don't have any of the pictures: I'm a lot more ashamed now than I was then" (N, 139).

One can get rid of the prints, but not of the memory. Thus, the veterans' narratives use a number of devices, formulas, and metaphors to deal with those images, mark their difference from what they had become, and try to absolve themselves from what they did. "You're a half beast," says an Italian partisan; animal imagery is a pervasive metaphor of total difference, representing the loss of humanity caused by the war: "I went to Vietnam as a basic naive young man of eighteen. Before I reached my nineteenth birthday, I was a animal. When I went home three months later, even my mother was scared of me" (Arthur E. Woodley, B, 283).

Being an animal also means being beyond the pale of free will and moral responsibility. One narrator used the zombie as an image that links loss of humanity with subordination to outside control, underscored by the second-person narrative and the geometrical perception of space:

> Every day you're out on patrol. Intelligence says they're out there, so here you go walking around in little geometric triangles. Go to this checkpoint, go to that checkpoint, go here, go there. Day in, day out, day in, day out. You get into a mind-numbing routine and before long you're a fucking zombie. (*N*, 65)

The easiest way of absolving themselves is to lay responsibility on the context: everybody did it, they forced us to do it, we were carrying out orders. "It was encouraged to cut ears off, to cut the nose off, to cut the guy's penis off. A female, you cut her breast off. It was encouraged to do these things. The officers expected you to do it or something was wrong with you. I was in another environment where I had to act according to them" (*N*, 50–51). The animal imagery suggests that what they did was somehow "natural," in that environment.

Losing one's will to the environment is often represented by the metaphor of being turned into a machine by "training," "setting," or "programming." In this case, the idea of "automatic" behavior supplements that of "natural" reaction to environment: "Automatically in a combat-like situation you feel that your life is threatened, so you open fire on anything and everything that moved. It was like instantaneous. You couldn't stop it. That's how you're trained" (Arthur E. Woodley, *B*, 299). The machine with which he becomes identified is probably his "automatic" weapon: "training" may mean both the making of a soldier, and the aiming of a gun.

The ex-Muslim in *Nam* combines the metaphor of the machine with that of the animal. About his baptism of fire, he says, "It was automatic. I didn't think. It was spontaneous"; about a rape in which he participated: "After we raped her, took her cherry from her, after we shot her in the head, you understand what I'm saying, we literally start stomping on her body. And everybody was laughing about it. It's like seeing the lions around a just-killed zebra" (*N*, 147–48). In both cases, turning himself into a machine and an animal was the passport to become "one of the guys" and participate in a collective *we*.

Sharing the horror, in fact, becomes a way of initiation into the community of war. Environmental pressure, personal horror, and military training converge in the narrative of a veteran who learned to overcome his disgust and horror when his comrades forced him to kick the brains out of a dead man's skull: "I'm kicking and I'm kicking and all of a sudden, the brains start coming out on the other side. Oh shit. I thought I was going to die when I saw what I was actually doing" (*N, 46*). The first-person narration in the historical present tense is a vivid rendition of the excitement he felt then. Though he represents himself as already divided at the time, he narrates the anecdote without any apparent detachment. Moral judgment must be looked for, if at all, in the folds of the language, in the shifts of pronouns and verbs. He praises his comrades who induced him to do what he did, and with whom he is now joined: "They were serious men, dedicated to what they were doing"; their ability to overcome horror is the only guarantee of survival. But he also hints that they secured survival at the price of their humanity: "I'm saying to myself, these guys are professionals, but they're crazy. How could you remember these things they did?" Once more, the play of pronouns is the axis of meaning: he says *they* and *you* as if he could not bring himself to ask the real question—"How can *I* remember these things *I* did?"

Just as pronominal shifts represented the transition from citizen to soldier, they also shape the uneasy continuity or difference between personal and shared responsibilities. For instance, Arthur E. Woodley oscillates between *we* and *you* in the description of a rape, on the one hand sharing guilt with the others, and on the other distancing it into a routine act, even more horrible for that, but less personal. If all did it, if it happened all the time, than one cannot be singled out for blame.

> We thought, Why kill a woman and you had no play in a couple
> weeks? We didn't tie her up, because you can't seduce a woman too
> well when she's tied up. So we held her down. They didn't wear what
> we call underclothes. So there was nothing when you tear off her
> pajama pants. She was totally nude 'cept for the top part of her body.
> But you wasn't after the top part of the body anyway. We found out
> she was pregnant. Then we raped her. (*B,* 297–98)

He uses the same device to describe a massacre: "One time *we* went into a village," and then "*you* feel that your life is threatened, so *you* open fire." (*B,* 299). His reaction to the rape episode, however, is interesting and complex. After abusing the woman for five days, the platoon decides to kill her lest she spy on them: "I don't think we murdered her out of malice. I think we murdered her because we didn't want to be captured." The difference between the time of narration and the time of the deed is marked by the shift between plural and singular pronouns and between past and present tenses: "I think" versus "We thought," "We raped," "We killed" of historical time. This transition indicates that the narrator now no longer submerges his responsibility in the actions and practices of the group.

We understand better the development of Woodley's conscience if we compare it with a canonical literary text. In *Moby Dick*, Ishmael experiences the same immersion in an impersonal mass identity and the same submission to authority: "I, Ishmael, was one of that crew; my shouts had gone up with the rest; my oath had been welded with theirs." It takes a long time for Ishmael to shift from collective emotion to personal judgment, to separate his voice from that of the crowd, and say, "I was fatally conscious of something fatally wrong."[27]

It takes Woodley even longer, but his narrative compresses the transition in a very brief space. When he says "I think" in the present tense, he suggests that he is changed, and is not even sure how the person he was then really thought. At this point the narrative, *I* breaks through, and Woodley also becomes conscious of something horribly wrong:

> After a while, it really bothered me. I started saying to myself, What would I do if someone would do something like this to my child? To my mother? I would kill 'im. Or I would say, Why in the hell did I take this? Why in the hell did I do that? Because I basically became a animal. (*B*, 298)

Though he now claims he did not participate directly in the rape, he takes personal responsibility for letting it happen: "Cause I was in charge. I was in charge of a group of animals, and I had to be the biggest animal there. . . . When I seen women put to torture as having Coca-Cola bottles run up into their womb, I did nothing. . . . What could I do? I was some gross animal" (*B*, 298).

MADNESS AND POWER

> I remember thinking this insane thought, that I'm God and retribution is here, in the form of my machine gun. . . . You begin at that point to understand how genocide takes place. . . . But I could appreciate in a black way that you can take anybody given the right circumstances and turn him into a wholesale killer. That's what I was. I did it. Bizarre. That's what it was. It was very bizarre. (*N*, 105)

Madness is the ultimate alibi for loss of responsibility and humanity, a radicalization of the metaphors of the animal and the machine. While these images imply that the narrator has become somewhat *less* than human, however, the discourse of madness may suggest that men became irresponsible because war made them *more* than human with its godlike power: "I have to admit I enjoyed killing. It gave me a great thrill when I was there. . . . There was a certain joy you had in killing, an exhilaration that is hard to explain" (*N*, 144).

> But in the Nam you realised that you had the power to take a life. You had the power to rape a woman and nobody could say nothing to you. That godlike feeling you had was in the field. It was like I was a god. I could take a life, I could screw a woman. I can beat somebody up and get away with it. It was a godlike feeling that a guy could express in the Nam. (*N*, 134)

> Basically I enjoyed Vietnam. It was the most vivid part of my life. I enjoyed the anarchy of it. You know, self-law. No one ever bothered you. You know what it's like to walk down the road with twelve guys armed to the teeth and anybody who shoots at you is in trouble? You're living every minute . . .
>   When I came back to America, I'll tell you a little secret, I was doing a lot of stick-ups. Because I wanted that *thing*. (*N*, 217)

This is what *Ceremony* is about: the difficulty, for those who have been animal, machine, zombie, and God, to become again mere human beings. The veterans in the novel get drunk on beer and war stories, trying to perpetuate the time when they could kill yellow men and possess white women. Rather than exploring the distance and the change, then, recollection becomes a continuation of war with other means, a way of perpetuating the excitement that was the most unforgettable part of the experience.

But there is a difference: Tayo, the half-breed protagonist of *Ceremony*, is outside the circle of war stories and watches the ritual of death and dismemberment from a distance. He has shared the same experiences, but now he looks on the scene with the eyes of one who has seen the horror and refuses to perpetuate it. Though tempted to kill the murderers to save their victim, he holds himself back in order to break the spiral of witchery and death. The difference, then, is between those who try to hold on to their war-created self, and those who recognize the fragmentation of identity and attempt to heal it, in themselves and in their society and culture.[28] I *was* an animal, says Woodley, as if to say, now I am a person again, like Tayo, unlike Emo. "I changed. I stopped wearing the ears and fingers. . . . I started disliking myself for what America, the war, and bein' in the Army had caused me to become" (*B*, 300–301).

"There were all kinds of sexual overtones to [torturing women]," a veteran recalls: "Domination. The misogyny of war" (*N*, 152–53). And, looking back, he concludes:

I turned the crank a couple a times myself. I feel bad about that. The thing I feel the worst about was that my own humanity was called into question, my own values, my own sense of myself as a moral, righteous person . . .

The war took my measure. Not just me, but me and my culture. (*N*, 153)

Part III

Movements

Chapter Twelve

I'm Going to Say It Now
Interviewing the Movement

A PARADOX: THE MISSING ORAL HISTORY OF 1968

When the student movement broke out, between the end of 1967 and the beginning of 1968, I was not around.[1] I had just completed my law degree and was serving my stint in the Air Force. But precisely because I was in the service through the first few months, I could identify with the anti-authoritarian spirit of the movement, and even through the biased reports of a generally hostile press, I could tell that its essential meaning was a huge battle for free speech. Young people were tired of being talked about; they were determined to speak for themselves.

The movement spoke to itself in countless meetings, great and small, and addressed the outside world mainly by means of the megaphone and the mimeograph. These forms of communication suggest that the speakers were many, perhaps as many as the listeners; and that their acts of speech were intended to be quick and ephemeral: a leaflet and a speech in a meeting are easily made, and easily discarded and forgotten. The movement's words were meant to be accessible now, not to last forever. When Phil Ochs sang, "I've got something to say, sir, and I'm going to say it now," the key word was *now*.[2] And although Ochs referred to the Berkeley Free Speech Movement, his song also applies to the Italian situation.

This has important consequences for the historical perspective on the movement, and especially for its oral history. Much has been written about the student movements of the 1960s and 1970s, especially around the twentieth anniversary year, 1988, and much is expected to be said as the thirtieth anniversary approaches in 1998. There has been, however, little serious historical research, and hardly any oral history. The bulk of this literature was composed of ambiguous reminiscences: leaders' autobiographies, a few controversial pamphlets, a great deal of discussion on whether the student movement was the breeding ground of terrorism, or whether terrorism was a betrayal of the movement. The exceptions were few[3] and hardly any used oral sources. Luisa Passerini wrote a fascinating book, combining autobiography, oral history, and the history of her own historical research, in a path of self-discovery through the critical rethinking of those years (*Autobiografia di gruppo,* 1989). Her work was part of the international project which resulted in the excellent book *1968: A Student Generation in Revolt,* edited by Ronald Fraser (which failed to find an Italian publisher). I had included some interviews with student activists in my oral history of Terni, which was, however, as peripheral to the movement as those interviews were peripheral to the book.[4] Cesare Bermani, and the radical history journal *Primo Maggio* regularly published interviews and conversations with members of the New Left, but concentrated mostly on the working class and on the 1970s. Autobiographies and books of interviews by and with former terrorists also included reminiscences of 1968, but always in the perspective of what came later. The archival situation is also disappointing, and while this is true for the whole oral history situation in Italy, the history of the 1960s is especially scattered and undocumented.[5]

Now, this is a serious paradox. Oral history, at least in the shape it has taken in Italy, can be considered in many important respects a product of 1968. Of course, it existed before: Gianni Bosio, Danilo Montaldi, and Rocco Scotellaro had been aware of oral sources and used them, in different forms, since the late 1950s.[6] After 1968 both Bosio and Montaldi joined (again in different and almost antagonistic forms) the broad New Left originated by the student movement (Scotellaro had died years before). The political tension and the focus on subjectivity that have characterized most of Italian oral history in the 1970s and even in the relatively quiescent 1980s, both in and out of the academic field, can be traced back to these origins.

I will try to discuss the paradox of the missing oral history of the movement with reference to two aspects: the formation of sources (the expression of 1968), and the collection of sources (research about 1968). The following are the most important factors influencing the formation of sources:

- The technology of the word
- The social composition of the movement
- The movement's forms of discourse

The most important factors concerning the collection of sources in historical perspective are those which make up the classic parallelogram of forces of all interview situations:

- The relationship between observer and observed
- The relationship between narrated self and narrating self

THE FORMATION OF SOURCES

Let us begin with what I have called (lifting a phrase from W. J. Ong) the technologies of the word.[7] The student movement of the 1960s is the first mass movement entirely originated in the electronic age. It is also the first mass movement whose entire membership is highly literate, by definition the most highly educated portion of the population. Therefore, the student movement did not entrust its collective memory to the individual memories of its members, or, at least, did so to a much lesser extent than earlier mass movements. Oral narration and memory, storytelling and reminiscence were, rather, restructured within a general reorganization of the technologies of the word. This process runs through the modern age, at least as far back as the invention of printing; but it undergoes a sudden acceleration in the years of the movement. I would describe this process as one of focalization and intensification of certain forms of orality. The very presence of printing and writing encourages alternative uses of the word, and therefore (as all literate cultures do), the movement reads and writes obsessively but also speaks a great deal, and is both unconcerned and confident about saving its words for the future.

Since other ways of preserving words are now available, the voice is no longer needed to perpetuate identity and memory. Voice rides time rather than resisting it; orality is freed to improvise, to converse, to interact loosely on the spot, reacting to the immediate situation. Liberated from the burden of public memory functions, orality is made available for the expressive functions of the individual. For the first time, the speech of a mass movement reserves a great deal of room for informal, ephemeral, personal expressions of subjectivity.

Hence, a problem for coeval fieldworkers. A movement was being created under our own eyes, and we had the machinery to record it (the 1960s were also the age of the relatively inexpensive portable tape recorder) but didn't know *what* to record. Like Bob Dylan's Mr. Jones, we knew that "something is happening here," but we didn't know what it was. Unlike

Mr. Jones, we reacted by listening, and keeping all our organs and instruments indiscriminately open.[8]

One of the effects of 1968 on me was the decision to go back to school (to study literature, this time); the other, to buy a tape recorder and join the Istituto Ernesto de Martino, a Milan-based group of independent radical historians, folklorists, and musicians. On purchasing the tape recorder, I received from my two Istituto de Martino mentors, Franco Coggiola and Gianni Bosio, the two pieces of advice that were to be all my training previous to undertaking fieldwork: Don't place it on the table unless you want to pick up the engine's hum, and never turn it off. I sometimes forgot the former; the latter, never.

The rule of keeping the tape running at all times descended from the political nature of the Istituto's origins and work: it was interested in people's lives, rather than in their folklore, and by keeping the machine open it signified to them that we were interested in all of what they had to say, that we would not break the contact when their agenda differed from ours. But in the context of 1968 this approach had an additional reason: We did not discriminate because we had no framework for discrimination. The recording of the movement was linked to what, at that time, we referred to as the question of "urban research." The Istituto de Martino took its name and impulse from the work of the historian and ethnologist Ernesto de Martino, who had been the first to tie ethnological research with the advent of popular movements in the rural south of Italy and in the Third World. Bosio's idea was to carry de Martino's insights to the industrial North.[9] The methodological background of the Istituto's work, therefore, came from the experience of ethnological and folklore research in the rural South, but there was very little folklore visible in the urban industrial environment. Therefore, although we did collect and store everything (including scores of personal narratives, anecdotes, and oral histories), what we knew to look for and to work with were the formalized structures of expression we had found in rural contexts: folk tales, rituals, songs, proverbs, and so on.

This emphasis on form was also related to our unconventional reliance on sound rather than writing as our prime form of communication. The Istituto de Martino was one of the driving forces of the Italian folk revival, through the Nuovo Canzoniere group of musicians and songwriters. Much of Bosio's own historical research was published in the form of long-playing records rather than books (I followed his lead: my work with the homeless people's movement in Rome produced a record of songs, sounds, and sayings, rather than a documentary book).[10] In spite of our extremist austerity, by adopting concerts, rallies, and records as our prime form of communication, we had to make allowance, if not for entertainment values, at least for aesthetic ones, and for forms that could retain the attention of an audience.

None of these were forthcoming at our first approach to urban situations. The homeless people's movement, in which I was active, was an exception, since it was made up mostly of rural southern immigrants, who still used the traditional folk forms on occasions. But the city itself was something else, and the industrial city par excellence, Milan—which is where our ultimate target, the working class, was more concentrated— was much harder to crack than a basically southern metropolis like Rome. I recall a tape in the Istituto de Martino archives, in which someone in Milan had simply stepped down to the corner and turned the tape recorder on: we don't know what to look for, so let us just start listening to whatever sounds the city makes. This was quite something else from going to some rural person and asking them to sing "Lord Randal" (a version of which, *"Il testamento dell'avvelenato,"* I did collect in Rome from a Calabrian immigrant woman).[11] We were moving from the full formalization of folk culture toward the apparent formlessness of the urban environment, and were not yet ready to distinguish among noises, sounds, words, speech, discourse, and form.

Thus, we used the tape recorder much like a candid camera. We would just automatically shoulder it and turn it on wherever we went. Gianni Bosio taped the incidents in Milan in 1969, in which a policeman was killed and the student movement was blamed. His tapes confirmed the students' version of the episode, but they were not admitted as evidence in court, and no one bought the long-playing record of noises, police whistles, screams, and snatches of conversation that he put together from those tapes.[12] I hid my machine under a loose overcoat and taped the policemen as they evicted squatters in Rome; the record had some songs in it—one was later a folk hit of sorts—so it found a few buyers. We were recording events and participating in them, but we were not participant observers—the two roles, that of participant and that of observer, were still distinctly separate within each of us. Contrary to positivistic myths, the interaction of these is what makes research meaningful, because it implies a project, a perspective, and interpretation—flexible, replaceable, open, but always there. The paradox is that, since we *were* helping to organize the squatters or demonstrate against the police, we were in fact "interfering" as activists, but our mixture of positivistic ideology and radical criticism of the division of roles and labor induced us to step back and disappear as researchers. In Bosio's phrase, we were creating the sources for future history. But we were not doing historians' work yet.

Thus, we recorded movement situations, collective and public events: demonstrations, meetings, sit-ins, and dozens of long, drawn-out, free-form conversations, in which there was no distinction between the person behind the tape recorder and those in front. The political, social, personal homogeneity of the fieldworkers with the movement prevailed over the distance which is as necessary to fieldwork as empathy is. We were not participant observers, because our participation overcame our observation. Moreover, our observation was obfuscated to begin with by our lack of a clear idea of what we were supposed to observe (one consequence is that the mass of taped documents we collected became very hard to index or describe, and has, therefore, been used much below its potential). I did dozens of interviews with squatters (and Bosio and Cesare Bermani interviewed radical working-class activists and leaders), but no one thought of doing *interviews* with movement people: the sense of otherness, which is inherent to the interview approach, and which we felt in terms of class and/or generation with labor or homeless people, was missing in our relationship with the student movement (even though all of us, including myself, were at least slightly older). It would have been like interviewing ourselves. I might add that in later oral history work on the movement, the ethnographic attitude is still underdeveloped: unlike working-class oral histories, the extant work on the student movement still relies mainly on "elite" interviews with leaders and protagonists rather than with the rank-and-file (this is the case also with Luisa Passerini's interviews on 1968, as opposed to her work on the Turin working class).

The magmatic shape of the movement's urban discourse was not, however, totally without form. Some of these forms were precisely the ones we had always looked for—songs, for instance. On March 1, 1968, the students in Rome, for the first time, fought back the police in front of the School of Architecture at Valle Giulia; when Paolo Pietrangeli (a member of the Nuovo Canzoniere) wrote a song about it, it did not merely glorify the event but also expressed very vividly the subjective changes which had made it possible:

> E mi guardavi tu con occhi stanchi
> ma c'eran cose certo più importanti
> No alla scuola dei padroni
> via il governo, dimissioni.

> And your eyes looking at me seemed tired
> But more important things were going on:
> Down with the bosses' schools,
> Out with the government, resignation now![13]

The song voiced the collective discovery of the *personal* meaning of politics (the reverse of the political meaning of the personal, which characterized the 1970s): a tired love relationship was less important than an incipient revolution (I'm afraid at the time I had misgivings about the song because it was too "subjective," not political enough). We had been looking for folk songs, however, and "Valle Giulia" clearly was not one. It had not been created by the working classes or the rural proletariat—conspicuously absent at Valle Giulia—but composed by an educated, middle-class individual. It had not gone through the oral tradition: as soon as Paolo composed it, it was printed on vinyl and distributed in record stores. There were long discussions on the nature of these new protest songs and their relationship to the tradition of radical folk music, and we were gratified when another of Pietrangeli's songs, "Contessa," spread orally through the movement and became a collective property. But we were not prepared to analyze the relationship of vinyl to folklore and mass movements, or to think of these songs as an expression *of* the movement rather than a commentary *about* it. Again, something was happening, but we didn't know what it was. On other hand, let it be said in fairness, whatever it was, we helped create, sing, print, and distribute it.

Slogans are another example. In all respects, a slogan is a "folk" expression. It is created, transmitted and modified orally; it is based on formalized rhetoric and metrics resembling the proverb and the *stornello*, and its composition is perhaps the closest thing that ever existed to Gummere's communal creation (by the "demonstrating throng," as it were). Yet, we never took them seriously. I remember some desultory conversations in the late 1960s, and then I never thought about slogans again until ten years later, when I wrote an essay and tried to make a record of workers' (not students') slogans.[14]

The most collective form, however, was the movement's speech itself. The discovery of the so-called Left-ese speech and its representation as a truculent and abstract jargon by the conservative media in the 1970s was one of the most effective tools of the deconstruction of the movement: the first step in our defeat was the ridiculing, travestying, and stereotyping of the way we spoke. This was made possible by the fact that the movement itself had never seriously thought about its own linguistic creativity. When this cultural aggression came, it found us unprepared, without data, and without a theory (besides, we had just discovered irony, and thought it was a good and healthy way of laughing at ourselves), and it literally silenced us.

THE COLLECTION OF SOURCES

I had never done any systematic interviewing about the student movement. But when I finally did, I could immediately perceive that the very cornerstones of the interview experience were very different from my previous or current fieldwork with Italian steelworkers and Kentucky coal miners.

Let us begin with the interviewer-interviewee relationship. I said that oral history, in Italy, is to a large extent a result of 1968. This means that whenever oral historians tackle 1968 they are involved in something akin to autobiography—maybe not personally, but scientifically, inasmuch as we are dealing with the roots of our scientific identity and method. Even though I was not present at the "battle" of Valle Giulia, I am doing autobiography when I interview people about it, because it was one of the events which molded the very tools I am using, my very approach to reality (as people remember where they were when they heard of Kennedy's assassination, I remember very clearly the scene when I first heard about it). Since so much of the political debate about 1968 has to do with its legitimacy (Was it terroristic? Was it totalitarian? Was it anticultural?), by exploring 1968 I am exploring the legitimacy of my own work. This is why Luisa Passerini was so right in her *Autobiografia di gruppo*, twining together her own autobiography, the history of 1968, and her own collecting of that history.

The other difference of which I am acutely conscious concerns generational distance. The longer I work with oral history, the more I realize that something has changed. For one thing, I am getting older. When I began, there used to be from thirty to fifty years between myself and the narrators; now, the average distance is about ten or fifteen. When I interview movement people, the distance gradually flattens and tends to disappear; in some cases, it is reversed. My whole relationship to this history changes: I am no longer collecting memories of events that happened before I was born, but versions of events that I am old enough to remember. I compare my sources' narratives to my own as a potential source. I have less a sense of the past, more a sense of contemporaneity.

Even with miners or steelworkers, I found that being of the same generation means sharing many experiences and memories. Not only did we listen to the same records, but we belong to the first generation that made listening to records a form of collective identification. The dialogic nature of all interviews is made even more tangible when there is so much in common. Interviewing the movement belies the theater of abstraction and detachment, the "playing dumb" which is so often exchanged for a good objective interviewing technique. It may make sense for me to ask a Kentucky coal miner "What happened in Evarts on May 5, 1931?," or a Terni steelworker "Who won the local elections in 1920?" (a battle between miners and gun-thugs; the Socialist Party)—the narrators can assume that I don't know the answers because I am a foreigner or so much younger. But when a movement activist says, "My initiation was Paolo Rossi" (a student killed by the Fascists at the University of Rome in 1966), it makes absolutely no sense for me to ask "Who was Paolo Rossi?" The inevitable reply would be, "Who are you trying to kid? You were there, or you should have been." I was at the office, less than a mile away, and never found out until I read the papers the next day.[15]

The fact that these are educated individuals, literate in much the same way as we are, means that the types of discourse they possess are the same types that we use; it is very easy for them to detect our little interviewing techniques. On the other hand, we also know very well their countermanipulative maneuvring, because we use these same methods too. These two factors—shared experience, shared types of discourse—create the interview as a much more fragmented, less continuous text than when there is more distance between the two interacting subjects. There is more allusion and less enunciation; more exchange, counterinterrogation and comparing of notes, and less narrative monologue.

The interviewees' relationship between narrating and narrated self is also different. The activists of 1968 have gone through a very peculiar phase of history. In these twenty years, history has been much faster than at other times, the pace of change much quicker. Can we really remember ourselves before women's liberation, before the environmental movement, before color TV?[16] These twenty years have also generated deep changes in the way people look at themselves. The "me decade" was not as intense in Italy as in the United States, but the politics of private life, the autoanalysis approach learned from the women's movement, the role of imagination and subjectivity, and the new legitimacy of mass culture have all given us a different outlook on ourselves. Many of the people we talk to have gone through traumatic experiences and radical personal changes: "yuppie-ism" and success have created as many fragmented identities as jail, terrorism, and the crumbling of many pillars of our faith and actions. To some, 1968 is a faded memory; to others, it is a gnawing guilt.

Finally, the very process of remembering has come under attack in these years. On the one hand, the "now" culture of the mass media has combined with the political propaganda which depicted 1968 as a big mistake that was best forgotten. On the other, certain influential thinkers and groups on the extreme Left actively fought against memory as a piled up, ossified burden of tradition hindering the revolutionary new.[17] The two approaches were not as separate as they might seem; they often overlapped, and communicated, and fused in the name of "modernity": the only "good" 1968 was the "modernizing" one, especially with reference to life styles—the one that gave us divorce and rock, abortion, and a new style of dress.

Thus, the distance between narrating and narrated self is, for comparatively young people, immense. A miner or steelworker in his seventies has less difficulty in remembering the 1920s than many a forty-year-old ex-activist has in remembering the 1960s—not because the change has been less wide (steelworkers have color TV, too), but because it has been more gradual and, most important, because the change took place at a different time in the personal life cycle.

The student movement was a movement of adolescents; its members were between eighteen and twenty years old, and they were in a personal state of flux while all these social changes were happening around them. Besides, it all took place at a time in history when the definition and duration of adolescence were being stretched to unprecedented limits. Again, old steelworkers or miners can remember what they were doing at the age of seventeen, because in most cases they were already engaged in their adult occupation, working at the mill or the mine. But for student activists, the combination of osmotic but constant biological change with dramatic historical change makes it difficult to stabilize in memory the forms and times, the very terms of the change that has occurred.

THE BATTLE OF VALLE GIULIA

Different personal histories influence the recollection of the same event, and the internal difference between narrating and narrated self generates narrative forms and a set of shared motifs. The battle of Valle Giulia, on March 1, 1968, was a traumatic experience, almost an initiation, for a generation of students. For many, it was the first confrontation with the police; for all, it was the first time that the students fought back. As Paolo Pietrangeli sang, "Suddenly, a new thing happened: we didn't run, this time we didn't run" ("*non siam scappati più*"). Later, Pietrangeli recalled: "It was a mixed feeling, the feeling that something had happened, that the student movement was becoming something else, something bigger, there were slogans that before had belonged only to the workers."[18] All narrators focus on the moment they first saw the police, but their perceptions and memories diverge sharply:

> *Massimo Pieri:* And then we reach via Gramsci, in front of the School of Architecture, and we see the police and the carabinieri—more numerous than we expected, ready for war, organized.[19]

> *Lucio Castellano:* They were few, and not very warlike. Indeed, what really struck me was that they were old, or at least that is how I remember them. Old, and few, and relaxed, too, like us. We stepped on to the gate as if it were the most natural thing in the world, and suddenly they attacked us.[20]

> *Raul Mordenti:* I mean, they were really no good—they were funny, they were ugly—they looked like they had their asses on backwards . . . they wore those heavy overcoats that hindered them running . . .[21]

The recollection is influenced, first of all, by the subjective state of mind at the time of the events. According to Massimo Pieri, as the students walked toward the School of Architecture, "it was a demonstration without slogans, tense and silent." "The demonstration," says another narrator, "was like a holiday, relaxed . . ." Everybody remembers the slogans; a verse of Pietrangeli's song repeats them. Pieri, apparently, came prepared to find a state of war (and comparatively prepared to fight back: "It's not as though we hadn't foreseen violence—but throwing eggs or something. I mean, that was the level of violence then"); Lucio Castellano was taken by surprise. Thus, Massimo Pieri was tense, while most of the others were in a mood of celebration. Paolo Pietrangeli speaks of the demonstrators' "total naiveté," and recalls that a friend marching beside him said, "Nothing can happen today: the Socialists are in the government." This confirms a finding of all oral history work on collective events: masses of people may be involved, but individuals always come with different reasons, expectations, states of mind.

The other influence is later personal history and subjectivity at the time of the telling (as hinted by the opposition between Pieri's historical present and the others' past tense). It would be silly to attempt deterministic interpretations of these contrasting recollections; it strikes me, however, that of the four witnesses, Pieri was the one who had changed least since then. He has always been associated with the most "unruly" ultraleft element, which tended to have a rather military view of political struggle. Valle Giulia is a historical event but also a founding myth, and it sustains this militant identity.

Lucio Castellano, on the other hand, was active in the same groups as Pieri for a few years; he was later arrested and tried (some of us say, framed) for terrorism, and found innocent after spending a couple of years in jail awaiting trial. He saw Valle Giulia in the perspective of the violence and repression that came later; perhaps he also tried to project an "innocent" image of 1968, as opposed to those who see it as the seedbed of political violence and terrorism. Certainly, he had given the question of violence more thought than all the others. Raul Mordenti, finally, was always identified with the moderate wing of the student movement; he plays down the role of physical repression in order to emphasize the cultural and political struggle. A final paradox: according to Sandro Medici, an expert journalist who has studied the police records for that day, the police force at Valle Giulia was "a small but powerful and well-trained army. . . . It was a true military operation."[22] It seems that Pieri is right after all. Paolo Pietrangeli also remembers the awkward, heavy overcoats worn by the police; but he also remembers "the cops on those jeeps, down below Valle Giulia, who drove in circles and hit us with their sticks. It was frightening because they were very good drivers but there was always a chance someone might wind up beneath the wheels because they were reckless."

While these versions are, at least partly, a matter of opinion and judgment, two other testimonies differ in terms of facts:

> *Roberto De Angelis:* I can still feel the impact of the tear gas cans they shot, way up in the air, very naively, in a curve. This was the first and last time I saw tear gas that didn't go further than fifteen or twenty feet. By 1977, they were shooting straight at face level.[23]

> *Maria Rossi:* [At Valle Giulia] It was bad, because they were shooting straight and low. I had never seen tear gas cans, and they were deadly.[24]

Quite possibly, the police did both: they sent the cans up in the air to spread the tear gas, *and* shot them straight and low to hurt the demonstrators (at least one student demonstrator was killed in this way in the

1970s). The difference between the testimonies of Roberto De Angelis and Maria Rossi may simply be one of point of view, of where they were in the battle. According to Paolo Pietrangeli, tear gas was shot "not so high, not very high. Sort of halfway, a middle sort of thing." But the recollection is also influenced by their subjectivity, then and now. De Angelis instinctively compares Valle Giulia with 1977 ("In memory," he says, "all these things overlap. Things don't come out unless you compare them and bounce them with each other"), a year in which shooting, on both sides, was definitely at face level. He was active in the movement then, and, like Lucio Castellano, sees Valle Giulia as a rather tame affair when compared with the battles of nine years later: "It was a violent morning, but not one of those days when you expect to be shot." On the other hand, Maria Rossi's subsequent political history is much less militant, though her ideas may be as radical; to her, Valle Giulia stands as the primal encounter with violence. In fact, while both Roberto De Angelis and Lucio Castellano had some small political experience before Valle Giulia (they had been in the Communist youth movement), this was Maria Rossi's first demonstration; she still identified with her middle-class student status, and recalls being shocked at the sight of policemen beating up members of her own class as they did workers. Ironically, though they stand at opposite ends of the political spectrum of the Left, Maria Rossi's state of mind while walking to Valle Giulia was similar to Massimo Pieri's: she was in the process of breaking with her own class, and sees tension in what others see as a holiday ("In those days, demonstrations were all very tense, nervous.") Narrators seem to have a hard time separating their state of mind from objective events—perhaps because the real events and changes were taking place in the mind.

Thus, the stage of the personal life cycle at which crucial events take place influences recollection and representation. In another article, I have commented on how working-class activists in Terni often thought of working-class history as a series of missed opportunities, but each set *the* turning point at the time of his own most intense involvement in historical events.[25] The battle of Valle Giulia stands, clearly, as a beginning ("*un fatto nuovo,*" "a new thing," sings Pietrangeli), a sort of collective initiation. At the individual level, however, its image depends on whether the encounter with political violence and the question of responding to it were being raised for the first time or had been faced before. Thus, Raul Mordenti's rather ironic view of the events at Valle Giulia must be seen not only in the context of his later political history, but also of what came before:

My initiation, I mean the shock, was not in '68, but [the death of]
Paolo Rossi. This is what turned me into a comrade, because I saw the
Fascists, I got beat up, I first thought about fighting back, because they
were professionals, some of them would hold you and the others beat
you up, a very scientific and shocking thing. And much more shocking
to me, who after all was nothing but a democratic young man, was
turning to the police for help and discovering that they were in league
with the Fascists.

The tendency of many narrators to represent the battle as less dramatic
than it really was introduces the question of narrative forms. There is an
implicit relationship between autobiography and irony: in both cases, the
speakers step outside and look at themselves as if at another person. In
the narratives of 1968 this ironic element is accentuated, symmetrically
with the greater distance we have described between narrating and narrated selves. Thus, many narratives are couched in irony and mock-heroic
style:

> *Paolo Pietrangeli:* I was there with [the girl] who later became my wife.
> First thing, she sprained her ankle, so when we had to leave, to run, I
> had to carry her on my shoulder. And I tore my pants on a piece of
> wire. It was grotesque, me carrying this small girl on my back, my
> pants all. . . . That morning I had put red underpants on, and it was a
> total embarrassment, I didn't know what to do. Luck was that I had a
> sweater and sort of draped it around me.

The following is the history of the occupation of a high school in Terni in
1968:

> *Walter Mazzilli:* In this first phase of the student movement, our
> demand was freedom of assembly. We wanted the students to have a
> room in which to meet, in every school. And, and we carried out one
> of those actions—heroic, in quotes—which led to the occupation of a
> wing of the Technical Industrial School. I mean—to give you an idea
> of the conspiratory style of those days, we, the leaders, initially
> planned to occupy the building by climbing the outside wall with
> ropes at night, and barring the gates in the morning. And I remember
> that the expert was supposed to be comrade Sandro Berarducci,
> because he was a member of the Alpine Club or something, so he was
> supposed to be an expert in knots, ropes, and all. Then, fortunately,
> rationality prevailed, and we followed another strategy. We were going
> to wait for the bell to ring the end of classes, and then the comrades
> who were in school would have chains, nails, wrenches, and hammers
> in their bags, and they would hide in the toilets, and after everybody

had left they'd come out and bar the gates. We had to give up this solution, too, because our strategy was so secret that everybody knew about it, so our comrades were watched. In conclusion, at 3 P.M. we finally invaded the Technical Industrial School by walking in through the main gate, which had been closed earlier, very wisely, because everybody knew there was going to be an occupation; but we were able to sneak in, because a truck arrived carrying fuel for the heating system or something—so the gate was opened and we, thirty bold and daring young men, we walked in and barricaded ourselves inside. And we declared a meeting of struggle and protest. And the whole thing was, under certain aspects, comic. Under others, I don't want to exaggerate, not tragic, but dramatic.[26]

As we already noted, this is an educated movement. Its rank and file came from the best schools; so the mock-heroic mood is often heightened by parodic references to heroic examples drawn from classical history.[27] When the police broke into the first sit-in at the School of Humanities in Rome, Raul Mordenti was reminded of the first barbaric invasion of the republican Roman Capitol—"We waited for them like Roman senators, all seated, very decorous"—and the humorous contrast is enhanced by the fact that the police, possibily not educated to recognize historical precedent, did not treat them "decorously" at all. Another mythical episode from ancient Roman history (the battle between two sets of brothers which settled the account after the rape of the Sabines) shapes Massimo Pieri's recollection of a scene at Valle Giulia: "It was getting hot, and the *carabinieri* were getting tired. I was running with three or four other comrades, and we stopped and turned, and there was only one of them left behind us. So I shouted, 'One of you against one of us, let's take off our coats and fight like men.' He thinks it over for a second, and then starts taking his coat off to play the Curiatius."

But they were also young people of the 1960s, shaped by mass culture as well. They played soccer and read sports papers, and they had grown up on a fare of Western movies. They thought that rules and fair play still applied, as in a game. "At the beginning, the two lines were facing each other. It was a Trojan war situation. One side hurled stones, the other tear gas. A boy was left on the ground, maybe wounded. And [one of the demonstrators], making wide gestures with his hand, as if he were the Red Cross, went out to help him. He was beat up mercilessly, because rules don't hold anymore, this is not a sport" (Paolo Pietrangeli). They were also fresh out of childhood, too. The "conquest" of the School of Architecture was both a rude awakening to some, and the crowning of the formative experiences of junior-high-school classics, football, hide-and-seek, Cowboys and Indians.

> *Paolo Pietrangeli:* At first the police charged, then it looked like they were withdrawing, so we all walked into the building. And they locked us in—like so many chickens. The fighting was tough, I got hold of a piece of marble, or plaster, and dropped it on a cop's head. For two days after that I was in turmoil, I kept asking whether anyone had been seriously wounded. . . . Anyway, we took—the police let us walk in. But when it came to getting out . . .

> *Raul Mordenti:* At last we entered the School of Architecture. There were a few policemen in the hall, and Oreste [Scalzone, one of the leaders] made a very amusing speech—amusing, to think about now. That is, he granted them immunity if they went out with their hands up.[28] Literally. "Don't be afraid," he said; "You shall not be hurt, just raise your hands and go." The cops were kind of surprised, too. It was fun. And it wasn't militaristic; it was the power of politics against the power of weapons; because we were completely unarmed but—the feeling was, we had scored, we had made fools of them, we were home free.

Chapter Thirteen

It Was Supposed to Be Happening in Berkeley
The 1960s Meet Eastern Kentucky

> *There are no guarantees, of course.*
> *There are no guarantees.*
> *But if it could work.*
> *If it looks like it's worth the risk.*
> —Gurney Norman, Divine Right's Trip

A LONG WAY TO HAZARD

David Walls: I think my first awareness of the Appalachian area really developed while I was a student at the University of California at Berkeley.[1]

Gurney Norman: I got a creative writing fellowship. . . . It carried me from Kentucky . . . to California and Stanford.[2]

This chapter is not about the 1960s in Appalachia—a dramatic period, from coal strikes to the War on Poverty, from the struggles against strip mining, unemployment, and black lung to the Miners for Democracy movement—but rather about the geography of the youth movements of that time. In a nutshell, it is about how the paths of David Walls and Gurney Norman crossed on the way from Kentucky to California and vice versa.

Histories of the movements of the 1960s have focused primarily on the most visible centers of irradiation—Paris, Berkeley, Rome. The geography of the decade, however, was much broader and deeper. Movements reached also into supposedly isolated and "invisible" peripheries with no university population, such as Hazard and Harlan in Kentucky (or, as I will discuss in chapter 14, Giulianello and Guardavalle in Italy).

199

Johnny Woodward: Yeah, when I was a high school kid, I was a
radical. I joined the Vistas,[3] which I guess for that time was a radical
bunch; we decided that when the Kennedys came down the path of
their trek across Appalachia and its poverty-ridden communities, we
were gonna go over and protest. Which we did. And I was standing
there with a little brown bag over my head, I had a couple of little
eyeholes cut in it, and we had our little signs, you know, protesting
our economic conditions and our educational systems. And Robert
Kennedy walked up and stuck his hand to me, said, "Son, tell me your
problem." It took everybody by surprise at first. And I finally, I guess,
collected myself and we sat down in the lobby and talked. And he
wanted to know what the problems were, how he could help, where
we were from, and we had a long talk, good long talk.[4]

The major issues in Appalachia (poverty, labor, environment, local
politics, community organizing) did not concern youth per se. Yet young
Appalachians had grievances of their own, related in their own ways to
broader issues, and showed more acceptance or at least curiosity for the
mostly young volunteers who flocked to the region in the time of the War
on Poverty.

It was not a one-way exchange. Appalachia did not just absorb influences from the center; it taught the generation of the 1960s such oft-
forgotten issues as class, poverty, and memory. As Merle Travis sang,
"It's a long way to Harlan, it's a long way to Hazard."[5] "It was a long
way from California way back to Hazard," repeats former Appalachian
volunteer David Walls. Those who traveled this road had much to learn
and much to gain.

David Walls: I was active with the student political party at Berkeley
called Slate and I had been a Slate representative at the associated
students and had been involved with the student movement at Berkeley
and the movement against Atmosphere and Nuclear Weapons Testing
and the beginnings of the Civil Rights Movement in the San Francisco
Bay area. I think, in 1962, I read two books that were very important
to me: one was Michael Harrington's book *The Other America,* which
was a general introduction to poverty in America. [It] made clear that
there were many poor, rural, white Americans, including a brief
discussion at least of the Appalachian region. And, secondly, and
maybe more powerfully, Henry Caudill's book *Night Comes to the
Cumberlands,* published in 1962, and it was a selection of a book club
that I belonged to, and I read that book and was very interested in the
region. And over Easter, in 1963, SDS held an Easter conference in
[Hazard], Kentucky, in support of the [coal miners' strike]. Well, we

couldn't figure out a way to get there; it was a long way from California way back to Hazard just to do over the one-week Easter break, but I was aware of the conference, and thought about it and read something about it and reports that came out, so it was on my mind.

A few months after the SDS gathering in Hazard, twenty-two-year-old Liz Blum, just out of college in Vermont, with a family and personal background of union and civil rights struggles, drove up to visit a friend who was living with a miner's family as a summer volunteer.

> I had heard about Harlan County, and I heard in the songs the word "holler." And when I got there I realized what a holler meant. It made such an impression on me. I remember driving up that holler, I had never seen any hillsides that were as steep as in Kentucky, that had actual plants growing on them. It just made an incredible impression on me. And I can still remember the corn growing there, and I remember that gardens were growing on these hillsides that seemed to be straight up, and they had a lot of vegetables growing. But, the people were so sympathetic, and they were so warm and friendly and they cooked—it must have been a Sunday afternoon—they cooked a meal for us, I don't think I've ever eaten such a big meal. I think we spent two nights in Hazard, and then we went to Lexington for a night, I remember, for the trial of these miners. And I remember the big contrast between Hazard and Lexington. Driving into Lexington I remember seeing a lot of horse farms, these beautiful Kentucky bluegrass, and, I mean, it was so obviously poor in Hazard. And in a way it was like, you know, there were two different Americas. It seems they [the miners] were kind of out of their culture and out of their element. They did not have a chance in the trial.[6]

In the summer of 1964, Walls went to Washington to work for the Department of Health, Education and Welfare, and for the Office of Economic Opportunity. "I met some of the people who were running the Appalachian Volunteers,[7] and they urged me when I was tired of being a Washington bureaucrat to come see what it was like to work directly in the field with them." He joined the organization, and was sent "to Harlan County, Kentucky, to work with the Vista volunteers and to prepare for the summer volunteer program which used large numbers of college student volunteers for an eight week period in the summer."

Meanwhile, while California was coming to Harlan and Hazard, Hazard and Harlan were going to California, and back. The Appalachian writer Gurney Norman had been a student at Stanford in the early sixties. "In January of '64," he recalls, "I returned to my hometown of Hazard,

Kentucky, and took a job with the newspaper . . . little knowing that major events—of world significance—were about to happen right in my hometown. And what this was about was the whole attention that was just being thrust suddenly upon Appalachia."

Years later, Gurney Norman told a class in Rome that he belonged to two countercultures: the psychedelic culture of California, and the folk culture of Appalachia.[8] The last chapter of his novel, *Divine Right's Trip*, is a visionary reconciliation of these countercultures: a joyous wedding scene in which a Zen priest and a Baptist country preacher officiate together and exchange texts, while a Berkeley hippie girl and an old mountain lady discover that they have much in common—hand-weaving and midwifery, a cosmic attachment to the land and the extended family.[9] It was an avowedly fantastic and utopian scene. Encounters between hippies and mountain people tended to develop along less idyllic lines. Yet it was a powerful vision, and many on both sides tried to make it come true.

CHANGES

"Hazard became the center of attention in Appalachia's troubles because of a wildcat strike of coal-miners that erupted throughout the Appalachian fields at the end of the summer in 1962." In September, the miners of Eastern Kentucky struck to protest the loss of jobs, the loss of hospital cards, and widespread anti-union practices.[10] These were some of the consequences of a 1950 agreement between the United Mine Workers and the Bituminous Coal Operators Association on mechanization, reduction of the work-force, and union-management cooperation.

> *Johnny Woodward*: There was an agreement, but there was little pockets of localized union activities that just refused to go along with the sweetheart contract, as they called it—they really called it the yellow dog. They felt like they'd been sold out. There was a lot of resistance, a lot of resistance to that. My dad had a lot of union activity, and he was on a blackball list for a long time; he couldn't buy a job. And that, that hurt us a lot. Most of the people who resisted have left, they didn't have any choices. The sweetheart contract, or the yellow dog contract, lasted here until the early nineteen-seventies.[11]

"The issue," explains Norman, "was total disenfranchisement of all these middle-aged miners." Though expelled from the labor force, they had survived, thanks to the union's pensions and medical benefits for which they had fought and paid all their lives. Now they stood to lose this as well: "In about '62, Tony Boyle of the United Mine Workers, his administration, they canceled the medical cards of just hundreds and thousands of loyal union men. And so suddenly these guys were just totally pissed at the union, at the coal industry, at everybody. And they began, in effect, to riot." "Roving pickets" roamed through the region shutting down one mine after another; "There was a lot of violence that came out of that; you didn't always know who did it, burned tipples down, blew up cars and railroad bridges and that kind of thing." In an autobiographical essay, a young woman from Hazard who signs herself "Peg" describes what it meant to grow up under these conditions:

> I would be asleep at night and wake up to the sound of dynamite charges
> blowing dozers and trucks half way to heaven. Sometimes we would
> count four or five separate charges going off in one night. [One night]
> as we got to the point in the road where the creek bottom widened
> and the L and N trestle crossed the creek, a volley of gun shots barked
> from ahead of us at the trestle. Bullets flew all around us, screaming
> into the pavement at our feet, both sides and over our heads.[12]

Journalist Dan Wakefield wrote, "Unemployment is ordinarily a dull subject, but violence titillates everyone, and I imagine it was this aspect of the Hazard situation that drew so many of us reporters—like vultures circling in on the wounded town—to what had previously been an unknown place."[13] History seemed to be repeating itself: thirty years before, journalists and reporters had been attracted to adjoining Harlan County by the news of the battle of Evarts.[14] As in the 1930s, while physical violence attracted the attention of the media, economic violence drew the support of young progressives and radicals. Unlike those of the 1930s, however, these were less the members of an organized, class-conscious Left than the members of a protean, idealistic youth culture that rallied around civil rights, pacifism, student movements, and the broad hopes of the Kennedy era—which, as all know but few remember, all but begins in Appalachia, with the rediscovery of poverty and class struggle in the midst of the affluent society.

> *Gurney Norman:* The Appalachia angle begins in the Kennedy
> campaign in 1960 when Hubert Humphrey is the favorite, Lyndon
> Johnson is the next favorite, and Kennedy is just this kind of dark
> horse, but Kennedy picks up steam, and he defeats Hubert Humphrey
> and LBJ in the West Virginia primary. And Robert Kennedy was his
> campaign manager and spent a lot of time in West Virginia and met
> these coal miners, these old UMW guys, and these people turned it

around, and that's where Kennedy picked up his momentum that took him all the way.

With the start of the War on Poverty, the roving pickets movement was invited by government to reorganize as the Appalachian Committee for full Employment. "One of the first things that it did, was to host a national meeting of SDS students at Hazard to investigate the conditions that prevailed and which were causing a lot of human suffering" (Norman). David Walls could not come, but Norman was there, and he said it was a turning point: "Here is where my real political consciousness began." As the editor of the local paper, he met journalists and media people "from the major cities of the world [who came] to this little town. . . . This stuff . . . was supposed to be happening in Berkeley and Boston and New York, and here it was happening right in Hazard, and that was incredibly exciting to me."

These visitors were one more link to the world for an Appalachia that was already going through changes on its own. While it suffered from the crisis of its major industry, coal mining, which brought unemployment and increased poverty,[15] the region also felt the impact of the relative economic prosperity and the expansion of mass communications and culture that characterized the decade. Appalachians had fewer jobs and more TV sets. As they became aware of the affluent society around them, they (and the younger generations especially) also became increasingly aware of their exclusion from it.

An example of this ambivalence is the demise of the company-town system. In the model town of Benham, "the company [International Harvester] sold the town. They sold all the buildings and all the houses to the people. In other words they got out of the rent business; they got out of the store business; they got out of the post office business" (James Goode).[16] While this development was a sign of modernization, an emancipation from paternalistic relationships (company employees became home-owning citizens),[17] it also marked the decline of the coal-mining culture and way of life that had sustained the coal towns as communities. Thus, going from the relatively well-endowed company school to the poverty-ridden public schools was, for James Goode, "like going from daylight to the dark."[18]

For generations, coal mining had been the unquestioned end of Appalachian adolescence. Now, mining jobs became both less available and less desirable, and the younger generations were forced to consider alternative routes.

TALES OF TWO WORLDS

> *Bobby told Lucy, "The world ain't round*
> *Drops off sharp at the edge of town*
> *Lucy, you know the world must be flat*
> *'Cause when people leave town, they never come back."*
> —Hal Ketchum, "Small Town Saturday Night"[19]

When you got close to the Harlan County line, you were close to the Virginia line. And when you were in Virginia, you were in a state that ended at the ocean. Think of that. The Atlantic Ocean, just beyond those hills there. For that matter, think of the ocean in this very valley here, a million years ago. (Gurney Norman, "Night Ride")[20]

"We didn't know what the rest of the world was like. We didn't have anything to compare ourselves to" (Johnny Woodward). "I didn't know the sea had no bottom at all. You know when they let on they'd gone to the moon, I began to wonder wouldn't it be amazing if there was another world underneath us just as there's one above? See, the sun sets on one side of the sky and then comes up on the other side in the morning. Wouldn't it be possible that there is another world underneath us?" (Lydia Surgener, preacher).[21]

Time and space often seem different in Appalachia. Space is perceived as more enclosed, both claustrophobic and protective; time seems deeper, with generations following one another and passing memories on in an interrupted chain that reinforces the sense of place. Appalachia was never entirely isolated, yet there was always a cultivated sense of distance. Suddenly in the 1960s space opened and time accelerated. There were other worlds beyond the edge, and they were both accessible and more encroaching.

> *Mildred Shackleford:* A lot of the stuff pioneer people [did] we were still doing in the '50s: we made our own bread; we made our own soaps; sewed our own clothes. We made our own bed covers. And it was almost like growing up in two worlds, you know, one world you would go to school and there was all this modern-day stuff like television and telephones, people talking about rocket ships, and we would come home from school—and here our grandparents, both of 'em, my grandfather had been born in a one-room cabin with a dirt floor, and it was just like living a hundred years in the past and like living in the future too.[22]

On the surface, there are few signs of generational conflict in the narratives of Harlan and Hazard. Many stories stress parental support for the struggles of the younger generation; others connect young people's actions with the awareness of the injustices suffered by their parents. Always, the link with the past and the family is very strong.

> *George Ella Lyon:* One time I was sitting down to write and I couldn't get started, so I looked at my hands. I noticed my rings—these are my grandmothers' wedding rings—and I got to thinking about how I was married to my grandmothers. A poem came from this, because it was so powerful to me to think of having wore rings and these rings having gone through their lives. . . . And I feel very much a part of them, I feel that their stories and their voices are part of what informs my writing. As I grow older I feel less and less of an individual in a way; I feel more connected and that the stories I have to tell are themes I know in ways other than experience, my own thirty-nine years' experience. I have been told these things, some of them, but I also feel there's a deeper knowledge which we share somewhere beneath our own consciousness . . . maybe this is similar to what Jung called the collective unconscious.[23]

Yet tension and difference surface from time to time. In Gurney Norman's story "Home for the Weekend," when the extended family converges toward a free-for-all fight, the author's alter ego, Wilgus, "was the only one in the family who felt any impulse to go the other way,"[24] symbolizing the conflict between loyalties to family and place, and the impulse to take off in new directions. Harlan-born writer George Ella Lyon derives her stories and her sense for them from the family's oral tradition, but her work also embodies conflict and tension. Her play *Braids* (1984) is based on the twined monologues of three generations of women, with sometimes irreconcilable points of view:

> *Emma:*   Then why didn't you hear me when I cried for help?
> *Glenna:* You never cried help!
> *Emma:*   I never cried!
> *Glenna:* You had everything! A good home, parents who loved you—
>   why would you do such a thing?
> *Emma:*   I don't know.[25]

Gurney Norman's Wilgus "was a college student," and college was "a gateway to the world" both for the character and for the author, Gurney Norman. Raised in a working-class family, he had been enabled by a scholarship to attend the University of Kentucky and then Stanford. He studied with Malcolm Cowley and Frank O'Connor at Stanford and became a core participant in the countercultural community that gathered around Ken Kesey (to which he returned for a time in the late 1960s). George Ella Lyon, from a middle-class family, went to college because her parents expected her to, but it was a journey of discovery for her as well: "Within two weeks I was totally in love with it. It was wonderful, I just couldn't believe that." Places like Center College, in Danville, Kentucky, or Ohio University in Athens can open up space and speed up time as dramatically as Berkeley:

> *George Ella Lyon:* I went to college and it was wonderful. I found friends, and people interested in writing, and teachers I could really talk to. There was a march after the invasion of Cambodia, there was a moratorium where we read the names of everybody killed in the war and stopped classes. There was a group of us who picketed barbershops because they wouldn't cut black people's hair in Danville.[26]

> *James Goode:* [The University of Kentucky at Lexington] was full of unrest, full of drugs. . . . It was a typical university, a typical American university in that period. I remember Timothy Leary coming, and the police had the house surrounded; they were doing LSD. I remember at UK they burned the ROTC building down. The governor brought the national guard down, they brought in anti-aircraft guns, anti-tank guns. And we couldn't reconcile that—what were they gonna shoot? I remember participating in occupying the administration building at UK. That was a period of a lot of anxiety and unrest. The students had an agenda other than the classroom that I don't see much anymore.

For others, however, especially those who came from a different class and educational background, the impact was more traumatic. "Athens was quite a shock for me," writes "Peg" from Perry County:

> It seemed that everything ran faster than our creek ever did. There were so many things to experience. I didn't hardly know where to start; movies, plays, playing frisbee on the green, dope, new books. A thousand and one enticements. For two months I felt like I was one huge, human sponge, soaking up everything I could get myself into. I was feeling good, knowing that I was on my way from being just another poor, dumb hillbilly from Perry County.[27]

"Peg" had grown up listening to her family's stories of strikes, broadform deeds, bulldozers and strip mines, amid sounds of struggle, the fear of unemployment, and the nightmare of losing her father to death in the mine. She sums it all up as the "curse" of the mountains. In order to get away from it, she accepts a nursing scholarship in Ohio, thinking she will never return home "except to visit." "But on November 1, at midnight, everything came crashing down around my feet": the nonacademic employees go on strike and throw a picket line around the cafeteria. "It was like a flashback, a lightning bolt from the past into my new world," she writes. The "new world" is as strife-ridden as the old: "'The curse' again. It had no right to follow me this far from Perry County."

Unlike other students, she cannot afford to buy food elsewhere; unlike them, this "poor, dumb hillbilly" knows "the first commandment of the coalfields—*Thou Shalt Not Cross A Picket Line!*" Finding herself for the first time on the other side of the line, she guiltily crosses at lunchtime; but cannot bring herself to do it again at supper. After eight days of hunger and mental confusion, eight nights of dreaming of her father and uncle on that same picket line, she collapses and has to go home—"If for no other reason than to sort all this craziness out."

Home closes upon her like a "womb": "I could tell from everyone's face they were glad that I was all right. That same warm, loving feeling I had always remembered from my early years." As she walks the hills and tries to make sense of the past, she renews ties with her family and tries to prepare for another birth.

> As things loosened up more and more between us, I was finally able to tell them about "the curse." I told them . . . about what I was learning all that spring, that you just couldn't escape, and at least for this hillbilly, there had been none.

SWAPPING SONGS

> *Sidney Douglass:* I was a high school student in the fifties and I graduated in '61. High school students were interested in rock and roll, Elvis, and Chuck Berry, but the predominant music that you heard on the radio was country music. At the time there was only one station, and they played country music most of the time, till I think after three o'clock the radios were playing rock and roll, 'cause that's what the children, the teenagers, liked.[28]

"I grew up listening to the Grand Ole Opry," says Douglass; today, however, "It's funny, with our children who are going to high school, it's not the thing to particularly like country music." Country music had no generational identity: both children and adults used to huddle around the radio to listen to the Grand Ole Opry. Moreover, country music had a local connotation: it was often about themselves, and came from back-grounds very much like their own (the popular Osborne Brothers were from Hyden, just across the mountain; Loretta Lynn boasted of being a "Coal Miner's Daughter" from Butcher Holler, Johnson County, in East-ern Kentucky).

Rock and roll and television brought Harlan closer to national styles of consumption, but also divided it internally along generational lines. Once the local radio realized that the music had to change when the kids got out of school, youth culture had come to Harlan.

The process continued through the 1960s. Tommy Sweatt returned to Lynch from the University of Kentucky, where he had been a disc jockey on the campus radio station, and helped revolutionize music consump-tion in the black youth community. Connecting with national musical trends was another way to open up space, but it was also another blow to the community's own cultural expression:

> *Tommy Sweatt:* That was about the end of the local band era, because you go and you get you a band, and you play the best you can, and we'll say, at our best we might know fifteen songs. So if we sing five at all pretty well, every time a record changes on the charts, people want to hear it, what they hear on the radio. So, that's how the disco era actually started. High-tech music, played over a sound system; then people got to where they liked that better than they liked having a live band.[29]

Of course, people had been young before in Harlan as everywhere, and there had been specific forms of youth behavior. There was, however, no glamour associated with being young, nor any pressure to *stay* so. Young people wanted to grow up, and certain rituals (guns, cars, alcohol, sex) marked stages in becoming an adult. Youth behavior was associated with a broad rowdiness that prepared people for the rough life of Harlan but was also supposed to be left behind as they grew up. Tommy Sweatt, who later became a coal miner and Methodist preacher, recalls,

> I was young and crazy. I mean I used to carry my gun with me everywhere I went. I was known to carry one. People were leery of me. And the things that you do, they may be nothing in your eyes; between Saturday night and Sunday morning, what you said and what you did may not have been too much at all, but in somebody else's eyes, after that story has been retold a few times, then all of a sudden you're either a maniac or Superman. [Stories were told] mostly about how I could drink, how much I did; and about me and my .45; or driving

backwards down the street in my car. You know, I said why the heck
turn it around, it goes backwards too.

The 1960s made a difference: youth became a distinct culture and
market, a group of consumers with styles that had to be catered to. Youth
culture, however, is both international and very local. Just as it made
Harlan less distinctive, youth culture was shaped also by such cultural
forces as religion, family structure, and emigration. Walking into the
record store in the Harlan mall in the late 1980s, I could see at a glance
the peculiar shape of the generational split in music consumption. As a
saying goes in Harlan, there are "two sides to everything,"[30] and there
were also two sides to the store: one wall blue with sing-along gospel cas-
settes for church use, and the other black with T-shirts and record covers
of heavy-metal music. The struggle between God and the devil over the
souls of men goes on in generational and musical terms in the Harlan
mall record store.

On the other hand, as a corollary to the same saying goes, there are
also "two sides to everyone." Many people grew up in two worlds at the
same time and had both a blue and a black wall inside them; the split occurred not only *between* generations but also *within* individuals. In 1988,
a twenty-year-old, illiterate girl who talked about going to discos on Saturday nights and handling snakes in church on Sunday morning, and
wanted to learn the alphabet to read both the Bible and love stories in
magazines, told me about how her life was divided between the splinters
of her family in Chicago and in Harlan, between the impulse to leave and
the nostalgia to come back. And she concluded: "Here [in Harlan] I like
rock music; there [in Chicago] I like country." It's like living with a permanent sense of lack, always listening for the music of another place.
Young people with a deep-rooted sense of place seem sometimes to feel
out of place everywhere.[31]

The 1960s also brought other sounds to Harlan—and another puz-
zling question of identity.

> *George Ella Lyon:* I listened to the radio a lot. Simon and Garfunkel
> was [popular] then, and that was related to what was at the time being
> called folk music. And so I started getting *Sing Out!*—even published
> a column there—and through *Sing Out!* I started writing to people in
> Ireland and England and Switzerland and, and I found out partly from
> them that I was a folk . . .[32]

"This was in the 1960s when war on poverty started, and Appalachia
began getting a lot of attention; however bad the press was, we was still

on the news and on the magazine covers and on T.V. and so forth," and she could not recognize herself in the images she saw on the media. "I was neither the poor miner's kid nor the rich mine owner. And I remember being embarrassed and also thinking I wasn't really, I wasn't really an Appalachian. Not so much thinking to separate myself but thinking I don't fit any of these definitions." So she sought another, urban role model:

> *George Ella Lyon:* I wanted to be a folksinger in Greenwich Village, and I wrote songs, every political thing that happened I had a song, and I sang a lot of different things. . . . I listened to Bob Dylan and wrote songs about the Peace Corps and the War and so forth. I wanted to live on Bleecker Street and sing at the Purple Onion.[33]

Ironically, everybody on Bleecker Street wanted to be from Harlan County and sing songs by Harlan's Aunt Molly Jackson, Sara Ogan Gunning, Jim Garland, and Florence Reece. In the folk music revival, Lyon had an image of her own hometown and culture reflected back at her, with a new twist: not the shame of poverty but the proud history (and mythology) of resistance.[34] "My daddy sang to me, we had seven radios in the house, my grandmother played and taught to play the piano. But it was a long time before I saw or realized that music and literature could come from the mountains." Appalachian music, however, was familiar to the revival's collectors and musicians, from the work of Alan Lomax and Mary Elizabeth Barnicle in the 1930s to that of Perry County's Jean Ritchie in New York in the 1950s.[35] Thus, while George Ella Lyon was planning to go to New York and seek out Bob Dylan, she didn't know that Bob Dylan had already come into Hazard, in that crucial winter of 1964.

It was not a memorable visit. "The car was filled with used clothing that Dylan had collected for the striking miners in Kentucky," his biographer writes, but the encounter was shaped by Dylan's self-centered phase and cultural stereotypes. In Hazard, he resented that the organizers, while thankful for the material help, were too busy to pay much attention to him. Later, he picked up a man walking down the road, gave him a ride, and bought him a drink: "'This guy's groovy,' Dylan said. 'Real miner.' . . . They threw questions at him . . . stereotyping him as The Miner, grooving on him being a real miner, not seeing him as a man with a wife and kids, struggling to get along."[36]

Dylan was only one of the young urban folk singers who, like the writers in the 1930s, were drawn to Kentucky during the coal miners' strike. Other encounters were less superficial, and while the miners may not have gained much, at least the visitors learned something and helped spread the news. Tom Paxton reported, "Saturday night [in Hazard], we had the first honest-to-goodness Hootenanny I was ever in. We sang union songs, mostly, and they never sounded like that in Washington Square. I could go on, but what mattered was here was a grass-roots, feet-on-the-ground movement moving toward real goals."[37] The miners' example of organizing led Paxton and others to attempt to create a New York Council of Performing Artists. The group did not last long, but some of the songs that resulted from the Hazard experience were among the best creations of the urban folk revival: Phil Ochs's "Hazard, Kentucky" ("Well, minin' is a hazard in Hazard, Kentucky"), Eric Andersen's "The Blind Fiddler" ("I lost my eyes in the Harlan pits in the year of '56"), or Tom Paxton's "High Sheriff of Hazard" ("He's a mine owner too, you know which side *he's* on . . .").[38]

The folk revival's most important song about Appalachia, however, was the result of another Hazard-Berkeley short-circuit, the collaboration between two women who never met each other. In 1963, Mrs. Clara Sullivan, of Hazard, wrote a letter to the *Progressive Labor,* the newspaper of a Communist splinter group that had intervened in the Hazard strike. She described the struggle, the betrayal of the leaders, and the contrast between the wealth of the operators and the hunger of the miners:

> The operators have beautiful homes, Cadillacs and aeroplanes to enjoy, and our homes (camp houses, by the way) look like barns. . . . The operators wouldn't go in a mine for fifty dollars a day. I've seen my husband come home from work with his clothes frozen to his body from working in the water. I have sat down at a table where we didn't have anything to eat but wild greens picked from the mountain side. There are three families around me; that each family of seven only had plain white gravy and bread for a week is true. Is this progress or what? I just can't understand it.[39]

In Berkeley, the radical singer-songwriter Malvina Reynolds read the letter and turned each paragraph into the verse of a song:

> What operator would go dig coal
> For even fifty a day on the mine pay-roll!
> Why, after work my man comes in
> With his wet clothes frozen to his skin,
> Been digging coal so the world can run
> And operators can have their fun
> In Perry County.[40]

The young people who left the mountains renewed Appalachian literature and music, placing their awareness of their native roots in a broader
perspective. Gurney Norman developed his writing skills in the creative
writing workshops and the counterculture of Stanford—but labeled his
novel "a folk tale." George Ella Lyon recognized "exactly the world as I
experience it" both in her matrilineal ascent and in Virginia Woolf's *To
the Lighthouse;* James Goode writes poetry influenced by T. S. Eliot, e. e.
cummings, and Robert Frost—"I'm of the generation of Lawrence Fer-
linghetti, Allen Ginsberg, people like that"—and composes country-style
ballads about local events and situations.

Appalachian music in the 1960s was also a combination of the folk revival with the native musical resources. Guy Carawan at the Highlander
Center in Tennessee had set the example in the late 1950s by rediscover-
ing the contribution of music to social struggles, from civil rights to Appalachian movements. In the 1960s and after, a number of activist musicians—Tom Bledsoe, Si Kahn, Rich Kirby, Mike Kline, Billy Ed Wheeler,
Randy Wilson, and many others—collected and composed the new songs
for the movements to save the land and the people. The Appalshop media
cooperative in Whitesburg recorded and filmed the history and music of
the region. By the mid-1970s, George Ella Lyon "was going back to
singing and playing the guitar and all. Not singing so much Bob Dylan,
Janis Ian, and so forth, but singing Jean Ritchie, songs that sounded like
home."

That Mrs. Clara Sullivan's letter was addressed to the *Progressive
Labor News* indicates that not everybody in Hazard eschewed the "Bol-
sheviks" who at least took an interest. Yet journalist Dan Wakefield, in
his "In Hazard" essay (see note 13), found it ludicrous that the same
paper reprinted a song from the 1930s, Florence Reece's "Which Side Are
You On," about such long-ago local characters as 1930s Sheriff John H.
Blair.

A true anthem of the Left since the 1930s, this was indeed "a big song"
for visitors like Liz Blum, but what Wakefield did not know is that also
many local people in Harlan remember both the song and J. H. Blair. In
1974, Florence Reece was singing "Which Side Are You On" again in
Harlan during another miners' strike, and in 1981 she sang it in Washington on the unions' Solidarity Day march. During the miners' strike,
the media took pride in their well-balanced reporting that granted equal
space to the unequal voices of the miners and of the operators, and neu-
trally annotated violence on both sides. Perhaps this is why Dan Wakefield particularly objected to the verse that Liz Blum still remembers:

"they say in Harlan County there are no neutrals there: you'll either be a
union man or a thug for J. H. Blair."

WHO ARE "YOU PEOPLE"?

> *Linda Hairston:* I was young. But I have protested, I like to protest.
> And anything they had at school, anything that was racial and I didn't
> like it, I was the one that protested. And there was a [teacher] that
> knows me very well, he says that he was glad when I, you know,
> graduated from Lynch high school, because I was the only person that
> would stand up—for anything that I felt that was right. He said that I
> had the guts of a hog, 'cause I was just stubborn.[41]

In spite of the relative "invisibility" of black people in Appalachia,[42]
of the absence of a significant history of slavery and of the plantation system, and of the relatively integrated policies of the miners' union, Appalachia was no racial paradise. Even in a model company town, children
grew up with discrimination: "Lynch was very, a very prejudiced town. I
was twelve, I got slapped at a drugstore downtown—I forgot the name of
the drugstore, but I was slapped, and my father almost went to jail for
that, 'cause this white man slapped me because I went and sat on the
barstool, and blacks weren't supposed to sit on the barstool. And I never
forgot it. I could remember times when my mother said, "You can't go in
that bathroom, you've got to go around here and use it on the ground,
'cause you know you don't go in there," and I was determined that I was
going" (Linda Hairston).[43]

Young people were on the front line of the civil rights struggle, because
its primary testing ground was the school system. The autonomous
school system was crucial to the life of the black communities in Harlan
County, and not everyone welcomed an integration that meant its demise.
"When this, uh, integration started, well you better believe [there] was
just as many blacks against integration as whites," says Mrs. Julia Cowans, who was then living on Clover Fork, on the other side of Black
Mountain. "'Cause I didn't wanna go to school with'em, didn't want my
children goin' to school with'em. Let them go to they school and they go
to theirs, see." Integration was accompanied by a sense of loss: "We lost
everything down on this end, you see, we lost it all. Our teachers and
everything else we had" (Earl Turner).[44]

Lynch-born sociologist William Turner wrote, "In the Septembers of
1960 through 1963, all of the 'colored schools' that dotted the coal
camps of Middlesboro, Lynch, Benham, Jenkins, Hazard, Harlan, Pine-

ville, and throughout Eastern Kentucky were closed as the "dual" systems were abolished. . . . Ironically, the college-going rate of blacks (especially males) in the region dropped PRECIPITOUSLY after 'integration.' . . . Today there are fewer than 20 African-American teachers in the school systems in Bell, Harlan, Perry, Floyd, and Knox counties in Eastern Kentucky. Makes one wonder if change is always progress!"[45]

One thing that Appalachia does, indeed, is to question the meaning of progress. On the one hand, school integration eroded the self-sufficiency of the community by taking "knowledgeable people out of the community" (Dallas Blue) and replacing them with white teachers who were not interested in stimulating and challenging their black pupils.[46] On the other hand, integration and the civil rights struggle enhanced the sense of personal worth and autonomy by promoting full citizenship and making new roles available. Though critical of school integration, Mrs. Cowans was also proud that her daughter "was the first black girl that ever made the sorority. She was the first black girl ever to be a cheerleader."[47] Through the media and individual contacts, the civil rights movement linked the community to a broader framework and gave it a sense of sharing in the making of history.

> *Tommy Sweatt:* We had our own sit-ins, demonstrations, yeah, things like that. We had a minister come in, named Matthew Peckway. Matthew Peckway came to Lynch in the fall of 1963. I was a freshman in high school. He actually came from down in Florida, Alabama; he had been in marches, rubbed elbows and talked with the late Dr. Martin Luther King, Dr. Ralph Abernathy, a group like that. When he came here, all the civil rights struggle, with sit-ins, bus boycotts, hoses, and police dogs, and all that kind of stuff, Lester Maddox with his ax handle down in Georgia and George Wallace and that kind of stuff, it was all over the news; and most of the black people here, we had a few establishments where we'd go if we wanted to go out, you know, and stuff; but there was segregation. We still had segregated schools; they never integrated the schools until that same year, by the fall of '64.[48]

Harlan County contributed to the civil rights movement the experience of the union movement, through people like Rev. Hugh Cowans, an active union man since the 1930s, his wife Mrs. Julia Cowans, and Bill Worthington, a veteran of the struggles in the 1930s and a leader in the black lung movement in the 1960s. The spirit of the civil rights movement continued in the 1970s. When the black community of Sanctified Hill was threatened by a landslide, the people got together, contacted lawyers and government agencies, and obtained government funding to build a new community, aptly named Pride Terrace.[49] Earl Turner talked about becoming the first black mine foreman in Lynch: "They had a problem where all the mine foremen in the mines were white, and they didn't have any black foremen. They passed a few discrimination suits, United States Steel was running the corporation in here, and when I got out of the service—I was black, I was young, I was a veteran—they hired me, they hired two people."

Ironically, however, as Turner points out, this process came late: just as they began to make gains, black people started "phasing out of coal mining" because of the "erosion of the base of the population" due to emigration and failed turnover. Turner also sees school integration as partly a result of the general decline of the area's population: "When we got ready to integrate, one [reason] we integrated so easy here [in Lynch]: in '62 and '63 this place was gettin' smaller. And you had to maintain a class A school, you had to have so many pupils. Black schools get smaller and the white school was gettin' smaller. So, in a way, the black school's the one lost."

"Most of the kids were all poor, and together anyway. They play together in the evenings and everything. So just going to school together was no factor" (Dallas Blue). For the young people who faced one another across race lines in the classroom, however, things were not so easy: "We were like sittin' on the side, blacks were sittin' on one side, whites on the other side. We didn't like white people, I guess white people didn't like me" (Linda Hairston).

Mildred Shackleford: I can remember when the first day that black kids came there and all white kids came in, we were already there, I don't know if it was because they had to bus them so far to get the black kids there, but all the white kids was already seated in the classroom. There was four rows of seats, and the white kids were in the first three rows and there was one row of seats left, and all these black kids come in and they just went down that row there and sit just one right after another. And every white kid in there was just a-staring as they went by trying to figure out what it was, you know, that made 'em so different from everybody else—what the big deal was, you know. Why was everybody sittin' there with abated breath to see what was going to happen when the black kids come into that classroom with all these white kids. Of course, nothin' happened, you know. Sit there and looked at each other and looked at each other and after two or three weeks, the ones that was aimin' to make friends, made

friends, the ones that had picked up too much of the hate and stuff
that they couldn't tolerate it, just stayed away from 'em. And things
worked out fairly good. They got along. Some of us did. And the ones
that couldn't or wouldn't, didn't. They left each other alone and I'd
say the black kids'd probably felt better to a certain extent staying in
their own school. They was shy. They wasn't too much in the way of
gettin' out there and takin' a baseball bat and beatin' people over the
head and saying, 'I want my liberties. Give me my rights' and stuff.
No, they were more along the line of sittin' back and makin' sure
somebody didn't hurt 'em. Because it was dangerous to be doin' any of
that—even in Harlan County.

Black kids didn't always sit back defensively, however. "I was put out
of school because I beat this white girl up, because she called me a nigger," recalls Linda Hairston. To some, racial insurgency was also the continuation of youthful unruliness by other means:

Linda Hairston: I was driving at thirteen without any license. Very
spoilt, too, my mother always spoiled. . . . I've done these things, I
outran the cops. And my mother always thought I followed the crowd,
but gist of it was, truth, the crowd always did what I did. I was the
peer—you know, they say peer pressure? I was pressure on everybody
else. I had no peer pressure because they either did what I said or I'd
say forget it. I'll put it that way. I'm very outspoken. My mother, for a
while, she used to tell me, "You're not ready for this place," and I've
grown up where I'm not ready for this place, the reason I say it,
because I'm very outspoken. If there's something that I don't like, I'll
tell you.

Mildred Shackleford: Our senior year in high school we had this
teacher who was supposed to be teaching a class called the History of
the Colored Man—now it couldn't be the history of Blacks, it had to
be the History of the Colored Man. And he lived in Cumberland,
which if you know anything about Harlan politics, you know that
Harlan is a dry county, Cumberland is a city that's wet. And he would
bring us a bottle of liquor to school every day or every other day,
whenever we would rake up enough money to get it, he would bring
us a fifth of bourbon back to class. And we was sittin' in there one
day. The boys was in the back havin' a card game, gambling for
money. We were sittin' up front talkin' to the teacher, and there was
two or three black kids sittin' up there with us and we was all drinkin'
a bourbon and havin' a good ole time and these three black kids got
up and left. And I reached over and got one of 'em's glass and said,
"Pour me a shot of that." And [the teacher] grabbed it up and he

wiped it out, and he said, "You don't want to drink after them niggers." And it just hit me. I said, "I didn't know you was prejudiced. Don't you find it slightly ironic that you feel the way you do and you are teaching this class?"[50]

Linda Hairston: And we had a big fat principal over at the Lynch high school that hated black kids. He really hated black kids, and created a lot of problems. I think that was the year of '70 . . . no, '69. I think it was '68 or '69. He hated blacks. And there was no way you could really tell your parents this man really hated blacks because he would get in front of them and . . . but then behind their backs he would do other things to black kids. "Why don't you mop that thing? Why don't you do this? . . . You're dumb. . . . You people!" I hate that. That's an expression, don't ever say that to me because I hate it. "You people!" Why, who you people? Who are "you people?" Why are you talking about you people like—"You colored people," I hate "you colored people" because I told the principal one time, "colored?" I had done something, he said "Colored people, if they just don't do this . . ." I said, "Colored people? When I was born I was black," I said, "and my mother raised me, I was black; when I go out in the sun, I'm black," I said, "When I die I'm gon' be black. You white: you born red, when you're in the sun you turn pink, when you die you gonna be grey. . . . What do you mean colored? I'm black! But you change colors, you know . . ."

Young people were on the line for the whole community, literally redefining what it meant to be black: "Every child that could sponsor himself with fifty cents for registration as a child proudly wore his NAACP lapel button" (Tommy Sweatt). The awareness that everybody's rights were at stake in the classrooms contributed to the parental support that characterizes these narratives. The children were acting after their parents' teachings. "My father and mother would say, we're all alike, you don't have any prejudice, they taught me how to be this way" (Linda Hairston). Parents were fiercely supportive of their children's rights.

Earl Turner: You remember them two black boys at the Olympics in Mexico when they held that black gloved fist up? Well, that was the same year, playin' a football game right in November. Tony, my son, was class president; he was smart. And it was real cold that night; it was cold as a whiz. Lot o' people, I guess a couple thousand people over 'ere. And they played the national anthem. Everybody didn't get up and stand. Everybody didn't. And Tony didn't. And [the school superintendent] called him in his office the next day. He said, "You bein' the class president you supposed to stood up." He claimed Tony stood up with his fist like this. He told Tony, "I'll tell you where you oughta be; you oughta be in Mississippi, goddammit, in a cotton patch picking cotton." And [Tony] told him, he said, "No, you ought to be in Vietnam with a bullet up your ass." [My wife] had to pick up Tony at school afterwards that one morning. She woulda killed him [the superintendent], too, with a .38 special. She said, "You don't run on my child like this."

"And I'll tell you, anytime—anytime that they wanted to have trouble, with the minorities, they'd use a black man and a white woman" (Mrs. Cowans). School integration, with the increased contact between young people of both races, made interracial dating or the possibility of interracial sex an arena of struggle.

Mildred Shackleford: I went to a football game one night and I was seen with this black boy and we were drinkin', which was the biggest form of entertainment in Harlan County, is get out and see how drunk you can get or how much you can drink. And the next day the principal calls me to the office and he says, "I saw you out with that nigger last night. I'm goin' to call your daddy up and tell him about it." I said, "Okay, call him and tell him." I gave him dad's telephone number and I said, "call him up and tell him whatever it is you want to tell him." And he said, "You mean to tell me your father knows you are out runnin' around with niggers and he don't care?" And I said, "Well, my father knows I have black friends cause I take 'em home with me, you know, there have been times when they've come in the house and eat supper. So if you want to call him up and tell him that, do it."

Julia Cowans: I lived kind of down the hill, and it was a man, some families, lived kind [of] up the hill. They didn't have no mother, but they had a father, these boys. And every day at noon them kids would come out from over at that school, right up that hill, up to this house, white and black, girls and boys. You'd see 'em sneakin', goin' up 'ere, to this house. Well some of the parents, the white parents, got ahold to it, and they started raisin' a whole lot of Cain. In fact, the daddy of two of the girls, he got the police. This man told [the sheriff], "My girl's up here, in this house with these black boys. I want you to put them in jail." [The sheriff] said, "Now wait a minute. Have your girls said, cried rape? Was anybody raped? I sat and watched them come and you watched them come up to that hill and go to that house. I can't put anybody in jail."[51]

The tragedy that might have followed was prevented also by the changed attitude of black people. Mrs. Cowans made it clear that the past was over: "I said, 'Ain't nobody gonna drag my son or my daughter out, like they have done and, and, and hang them or whatever.' I said, 'Have been a time that this happened, didn't nobody die but black.' I said, 'But, brother, you better believe that if they bury somebody black, they gonna bury somebody white.' I said, 'You'd better believe that.'"[52]

> *Mildred Shackleford:* When the union was at its height in Harlan County, they had a lot of interrelationship between the blacks and the whites because you couldn't be accepted into the union if you were not willing to accept everybody. And Bill Worthington used to tell me about softball games and stuff that he had with people down there.[53] Thirty years ago, these black people, these white people were playing with each other and they were eatin' together and sittin' around together. They should keep that in mind and not forget it, because that is one of the things that, it makes people stronger—to remember what they've had and hang on to it and don't turn it loose. It will make you a better, decent human bein'. Don't ever turn it loose and don't ever forget about it. Because when you do, you lose somethin' and Harlan County has lost a lot of it. So we are havin' to do it all over again.

FACING THE FACELESS

> *Johnny Woodward:* There's a friend of mine who has a very profound statement about growing up in a coal camp and being a poor kid. He says he was happy as he could be when he was a kid growing up. Didn't have any worry, didn't have any problems—he was poor; didn't know he was poor. And he said that all his life he would overhear conversations, from his own cousins, talking about "them poor sons-of-a-bitches down there." And didn't know until he was sixteen years old that he was the poor sons-of-a-bitches they was talkin' about. And he said that just depressed him beyond no means, and that he really didn't know it was a bad shape he was in until somebody told him. I resent the fact that I had to find out the fact that I *was* poor and that I was, I guess, underprivileged. In the truest sense of the word.

There were a number of reasons why poor people in Appalachia would not perceive themselves as such: the quasi-Calvinistic moral stigma on poverty and the traditional independence and pride associated with mountain culture; the relative homogeneity of rural society; and the relative isolation of the region. The stark contrast between the way the min-

ers lived, the relative comfort of the middle classes, and the wealth ex-
tracted from the land, however, were immediately visible both to the
young volunteers from outside and to less underprivileged Kentuckians:

> *David Walls:* I hadn't seen poverty at that level, the level of poverty, of
> poor housing, of ramshackle housing, of the lack of sanitation in
> communities, a bad water system, of non-existing sewer systems.[54]
> That was a shock to me: to see that much poverty in an industrial
> community that had been functioning at a high level, that had a few
> [model] towns that were like the U.S. Steel community at Lynch, or at
> Benham, but to see the rest of Harlan County outside of the cities of
> Harlan in such a dismal shape, with such a poor educational system
> and poor health care for people, was shocking to me.[55]

> *George Ella Lyon:* I saw this at school, very clearly, as well as driving
> up and down the road. I remember one time at my church—I belonged
> to the Disciples of Christ—some very poor kids came to our Sunday
> school and were not treated well at all. They were clearly not
> welcome; the Sunday school teacher didn't like having them there.
> This bothered me a lot and I asked my mother about it. The next
> week, when the kids didn't come back, I mentioned them to the
> teacher. She said, "Well, it's really for the best. They wouldn't have
> been happy here. They're more the Church of God type."

"We knew that we were sort of shunned or looked [down] upon, but
we didn't know the magnitude of it; we didn't realize we were the object
of the War on Poverty," says Johnny Woodward. As he stood in line for
commodity groceries, people stared and he could not figure out why. It
was only through the eyes of others that the poor in Harlan had a new
look at themselves. The Vista volunteers in Evarts, Woodward goes on,
"had these kids down here starting to think. Starting to read material
other than what we had been handed in the classroom. And once these
kids began to see really what life was here and then the big picture, they
started asking questions."

> *Mildred Shackleford:* I never had too much respect for the social
> system because I had always figured it was just so unfair that these
> little kids, sittin' here just as sweet as they could be, everybody was
> makin' fun of 'em because they was eatin' buttermilk and cornbread;
> and all these other kids who didn't really have all this much, had just a
> little bit. But I never did have too much respect for a kind of system
> that always picked out weaker people or people they think is just a
> little bit different.

Johnny Woodward: I was enlightened to the point I realized I was a
poor kid, and there was no reason for it. I shouldn't have to grow
up that way; I very much resented that. If our political and social
structure was balanced out, my dad could find work, not be blackballed
and, you know, so could my mother. I also recognized the fact that not
only were we deprived of, I guess, just a living, or a normal life, but we
were denied an education. They didn't want us to have an education.
They did not provide us with an equal opportunity to be educated. And
I guess the Vistas were a chance to vent all of that, in a positive manner.

Mildred Shackleford: I got involved with [the Vista volunteers] because
I thought they had somethin' different to offer and I wasn't too
sophisticated at that time. I was about sixteen or seventeen years old
when I got involved with them. I was readin' a lot. I was finding out
different things. The involvement in Vietnam—I was findin' out a little
bit of it and I found out that what the United States was doin' at that
time in that country wasn't somethin' that I could respect. And I was
doin' it on a national level and the Vistas was doin' it on a local level,
and I found out that the two related to each other a lot, but I hadn't
really met it before because I hadn't thought of lookin' at Harlan
County in the same way that I looked at Vietnam, but that's one thing
I did learn from those people pretty quickly is that was one way of
lookin' at it. In a way, we were more like the people in Vietnam than
we were [like] the people in the rest of the country.[56]

Loyal Wagner, a native Appalachian from Virginia, served in Harlan
as an Appalachian Volunteer in 1968, and discovered there both a "great
[cultural] kinship" and political similarities to what he had experienced
earlier with the Peace Corps in Bolivia: "If you look at it politically from
the colonial standpoint, you have those huge mines there, you had the
huge logging operations. They were entities that were controlled from
outside; I think they were colonial in that local people had no control and
no say over it. These organizations didn't just run their companies, they
ran the schools, the government, and everything. So in that way I would
think of it as a Third World state."[58]

Although they were mainly young themselves, the Appalachian and
Vista Volunteers did not address themselves specifically to youth. Their
primary concerns were strip mining,[57] the reform of community action
programs, the struggle against black lung and for the rights of disabled
miners and widows. But they soon discovered that one of their immediate antagonists was the school system, its bureaucracy, and its power
structure, and that students were among their primary allies.

"Harlan County at that time," says Mildred Shackleford, "the school board was the political power, they were the ones that had the most pull, they had everything under their thumb."[59] Volunteers and students jointly challenged the system in terms of both ideology ("We were very limited in what our study material were; we were pretty much told to study this and not this," Johnny Woodward) and services ("They wanted to know why we had the sorriest school in the county system, and why our teachers most of them didn't even have bachelor's degrees when the rest of the schools in the county had Ph.D.'s").

> *David Walls:* It was clear that the local political machine, which we learned had come in as a sort of reform democrats around 1936 during the New Deal, was now an entrenched political machine that was very corrupted, and it really controlled people through the distribution of jobs, not only general public jobs but particularly through the school system. When I saw my first election, which was not long after I arrived in Harlan County—I got there in October and it must [have been] November 1966—to see people openly buying votes, openly passing out money, behind the polling places, to see schoolteachers passing out money was a shock to me. They managed to have an elaborate system of patronage, not just with teachers, but more importantly with the jobs for bus drivers and cooks and janitors in the school, all the jobs that required less formal education, and this was probably, given the decline of the coal industry, maybe the major single employer in Harlan County.

> *Mildred Shackleford:* One of the first things that I can remember we got involved in was tryin' to get the principal to close up a hole in one of the bathrooms. It was an old building and it had never been maintained very well, and the seventh and eighth grade building had already been condemned two of three years in a row and was considered unsafe. So they was tryin' to get the principal to patch a hole that was lettin' raw sewage leak out in the school yard. And they had this little paper, *Clover Fork Newsletter* I think it was, and they published an article about the bathroom, pictures of it, and the principal was threatenin' to expel them; of course they didn't care whether they got expelled or not. And I got into it, we got into things that was just a little bit more along the lines of what kind of teachers we had, or the teachers that were worth havin'.

"The A[ppalachian] V[olunteers]," David Walls recalls, "started as this very do-good, simple program of college students working weekends," based on a "consensus model of community development." Gradually, the volunteers became aware that this approach might not be enough. As the programs began to attract staff and volunteers who came from the movements of the 1960s, "a more radical notion of what was involved in social change" developed. Once again, this was the result of the encounter of the external and the local: "the combination of the external environment nationally with the Civil Rights Movement, and people's local experience, quickly radicalized, at least in American terms" many of the volunteers and a number of local young people.

When Robert Kennedy's senate committee on hunger and malnutrition came to Kentucky in 1968, it was this group of young people who confronted him. "At the Neon gymnasium in Letcher County, a group of teenagers from Harlan County went and demonstrated, and they put paper bags over their heads because they said they were the faceless people in the county—that they had no voice, they had no face, they were not represented in local politics, and they saw no future for themselves there. Also they were somewhat afraid about recrimination from their schools if they presented themselves more openly" (David Walls).

Kennedy asked them to come forward and testify. *The Mountain Eagle*, out of Whitesburg, Ky., reported, "Tommy Duff, a student at Evarts High School in Harlan County, said he had been expelled because he had taken pictures of conditions in the school restrooms and had them printed in a community newsletter. He and a large number of students asked for better schools," for jobs, and for changes in the school system. "Many of the group wore paper bags over their heads—this, they said, was to show that they were the faceless people in the eyes of the school board—and carried signs saying 'We can't eat your fancy promises.'"[60]

CULTURE WARS

> *Gurney Norman:* [When the SDS came to Hazard in 1963], the town
> filled up with these radical-looking kind of kids. Part of the style in
> those days was the women would wear jeans with these big boots up
> to the knee almost, and then some of them had fur hats and, you
> know, the style was that you didn't bother to try to ingratiate yourself
> with anybody; you held yourself aloof. . . . There was one time when
> everybody was eating in this one restaurant, it was like the whole
> bunch of kids over here, and some of the businessmen were over there,
> and they were outraged that these people were over here not knowing
> their place, you see. . . . And I was eating with these people and this
> businessman was very worried about me and he—he remembered me
> from my crewcut days and he had no idea how much fun I was having.

He called me aside as we were going out and he says, "Watch 'em,
Gurney, watch 'em," he says, "be careful," he says. "I know who those
people are in college," he says, "they're *art* majors."

It was the styles of the newcomers, even more than their ideas, that
shocked traditional Appalachians—and exhilarated and attracted many
local young people. "They were different" (Johnny Woodward); "They
had something different to offer" (Mildred Shackleford). They represented an open space of imagination and new life styles for young people
who saw no future and found little to please them in the present. "The
only thing here was the coal mines. You graduated on Thursday, and
Monday you went into the coal mines" (Curtis Snow).[61] "The biggest
form of entertainment in Harlan County, is get out and see how drunk
you can get or how much you can drink" (Mildred Shackleford). "Back
up in the hollows, some of them get married young, twelve, thirteen. But
it's really nothing else for them to do around here besides getting married
and working in the coal mines" (Wylletta Lee).

> *George Ella Lyon:* There were kids who were almost doomed from the
> ou:set because the social system was such that they were on the
> outside. The only way these boys could make a name for themselves
> was to steal something or punch each other out. The girls could act
> out sexually. For poor kids who were trying not to be invisible in that
> setting, these were the options.

"I got into trouble the whole time I was goin' to school. I got into a
fight with some guy when I was in the seventh grade. He called my sister
a name and I pulled a knife on him. I was never much to respect authority" (Mildred Shackleford). To some extent, then, latching on to the volunteers was a translation (and continuation) of the traditional youthful
unruliness and rowdiness into a social and political action that also included having a good time and going places.

> *Mildred Shackleford.* Most of the kids that got involved with the
> Vistas at that time, or a lot of 'em, were kids that were homeless, so to
> speak, didn't have much in the way of family life; some of the black
> kids got involved because they were lookin' for a little bit more, but a
> lot of the kids [that] were what would be considered drifters, losers,
> got involved with the Vistas; a lot of those kids that was involved with
> the Vista wasn't interested in goin' on to school or anything. They was
> mostly interested in havin' a good time, get out and sneak off and get
> drunk, just carry on like that. I was too responsible and straight-laced.
> [But] we had time, you know. I mean seriously we did. We went

places. We went to West Virginia. I remember one time goin' to the
SCLC conference in South Carolina and I had a wonderful time. I got
to stay over to the beach and goin' swimmin' and played tennis and
stayed in some ole southern mansion down there that had those trees
with all that moss growin' on it, three meals a day served to you, you
didn't have to do any cookin' or anything . . .

The different life styles of the volunteers, however, damaged their
credibility. Don West, a minister, poet, cultural organizer, and a veteran
of the struggles of the 1930s, compared the dangers of organizing then
with the relative safety and decent pay of the "transient" poverty workers. They came, he wrote, to sow their "radical wild oats" and then go
home to their middle-class lives. "The southern mountains," he wrote,
"have been missionarized, researched, studied, surveyed, romanticized,
dramatized, hillbillyized, Dogpatched and povertyized again," and this
looked like just another of those cycles.[62] Harlan County, Shackleford
recalls, used to be a missionary destination: the urban churches "were
sending missionaries to the deepest, darkest Africa to save the savages.
They also sent them to Appalachia to save the little hillbilly kids. They
came in to save the soul of the savage." For both missionaries and
"poverty warriors," West says, the basic concern "was not how they
related to the mountains but how the mountains related to them and their
notions." This "'superior' approach" often resulted in blaming the victim rather than the economic system—and, occasionally, in colonial,
exploitative attitudes. "I resented some young man coming here to tell
me that Mr. John Doe up in the holler needs to get out and get in touch
with the real world. I said, young man, Mr. John Doe up in the holler
just might know a whole lot more about the real world than you do."
says Ms. Gladys Hoskins, secretary of the Harlan Chamber of Com-
merce."[63] Loyal Wagner explains: "They were a lot of people with pretty
good intentions, but they were sort of living out their dream of what the
world oughta be, and they might have been using local people to carry
out their mission of change. I agreed with their criticism of what was
going on here, but I wasn't sure that that was the proper way to do it"
(Loyal Wagner).

> *Mildred Shackleford:* We had kids from California, and they would
> come and they would have dope or whatever, you know, and they
> would have a good time and they would get out and buy quilts off of
> old ladies for $2 a piece or $5, and they would take them back home
> and they'd laugh about what a good deal they got, you know. I

remember this one kid was after guitars. And there is a famous brand name of guitar that people like Hank Snow and a lot of other people used, and there were people in Harlan that had that sort of thing because they had got it years before when the price had not been too awful high. And this guy ran around and I bet he bought five or six of those guitars and he was gettin' them for $30 or $40 a piece. And they were really worth $5, 6, 700. He just laughed about it, you know, because he was gettin' these guitars at such a good price. And he was running around driving a little MG and he was gettin' two, three hundred dollars a week from his folks in California and he was gettin' pay salary by the AVs. And one of the guys that he bought one of those guitars from was living in a three-room shack and he had a little ole $130 pension from Social Security. And I asked that boy one day, I said, "Don't you feel the least bit guilty about doin' that, don't you feel guilty for hurtin' them? You are supposed to be helping those poor people." "Oh, but that is different," he said.

In 1932, Theodore Dreiser was expelled from Harlan County for having allegedly spent the night in his hotel room with his secretary. In the 1960s, sexuality was still on the agenda. Outside Appalachia, the sexual revolution was in full swing. Many volunteers were young people away from home for whom, says David Walls, "this was, after college, their first significant life experience, and it was very intense. The emotional and sexual relationships among the staff and the volunteers and the Vistas were very intense." Inevitably, "some of the uncomprehending outside summer volunteers would do outrageous things" that estranged them from the communities they were supposed to help. The volunteers responded by trying to learn the culture and participate in the religion.

David Walls: [Joining the church] was a wonderful experience. I was both partly in my mind standing back from it, but also very moved by the intensity of people, the sincerity and depth of their experience, and the way in which their songs and their feelings obviously involved the many sorrows and hardships of their lives and their ability to deal with those. Though they may not have accepted us as saved, yet by and large they appreciated our efforts, our willingness to attend their church. Isn't that respect for their religion? On the other hand, many of them, most of them, were themselves people who had returned to the church as older people, after leading lives that could have been much wilder than ours, in some respects, at least, more dissolute, after drinking wildly and carrying on and breaking the law and so far and so on. None of them were saints, and their religion recognized that they were not, and they had repented and I think they had some knowledge that while very different, we may not have been unlike them as young sinners either.

"They tried hard to fit in; they tried to adapt to us, instead of changing us until we fit their mode of doing things," says Johnny Woodward: "They weren't very successful at it, because you don't become, you know, an Appalachian overnight. But no, they didn't try and change us into their mode." Though she ultimately judges that "Vistas and those people of that sort really didn't do all that much for Harlan County," Shackleford recognizes that "a few learned a little bit from it." And they were not entirely safe from political repression and physical violence.[64]

> *Johnny Woodward:* Well they were considered to be Communists.
> Radicals, trying to overthrow the status quo. They came to Evarts and
> signed up a little place, and—they weren't accepted at all. They were
> threatened, they were physically abused, their houses where shot into,
> the windows were broken out. . . . A lot of them would be caught out
> driving and they would run them off the road into the ditches. The
> reason they did that was because they had these kids here starting to
> think.

By urban radicals educated with memories of the 1930s, Eastern Kentucky "was seen as a very militant place—I guess there was some romanticism attached to it, too. A lot of people knew that there was work to be done among the whites, too, you couldn't have a revolution of just blacks" (Liz Blum).

At the time of the roving pickets, groups like Progressive Labor thought that "the revolution has broken out. Because you've got armed guys going around and it's civil rights time"; so "they came down into Kentucky to bring arms to the miners. And they immediately ran into the contradictions of the place, which is that even though these people were dispossessed and disenfranchised and are in a local uprising, they're totally loyal Americans" (Norman). A number of narrators—obliquely and off the record—suggest that a handful of local individuals in and around Harlan County might have covertly retained radical and revolutionary allegiances formed during the 1930s. The Appalachian and Vista Volunteers, however, did not cultivate such illusions. This, however, did not spare them from Red-baiting.

There is a stubborn political and religious identification between outsiders and Communists in Harlan County. Once in the Cranks Creek Holiness Church an old lady, hearing that I was from "across the waters," asked me, "Are you a Russian?" I explained that I was not, and that "anyway, the Russians are people, too." To which she replied, "Then why do they want to come in here and kill us?" By the very token of being outsiders, the volunteers were almost automatically Communists—and one could tell by the way they looked.

> *James Goode:* My dad was respected as being an intelligent man; and
> yet my daddy was a bigot—in a lot of ways, too. I was brought up to
> hate Catholics and to hate Communists. And that more than likely
> Catholics *were* Communists. And until I left home I always believed
> that; I always was suspicious of Catholics. And my dad kept a library
> of very right-wing material, anti-Communist material. We was gonna
> be taken over by these—people. It was about as conservative and
> Reaganite a view of Communism as you can get. And my daddy
> preached that to me: "We gotta fight those people, these people, you
> know, they don't shave their legs, and they've got furry hats on . . ."[65]

However, as David Walls remembers, "Younger people had a considerably different outlook," thanks in part to a sense of generational and cultural distance from their elders and kinship with the young volunteers: "They knew their lives were going to be different, and they were being influenced to some extent by television, by movies, by rock music" (Walls). "My parents," remembers George Ella Lyon, "projected a lot of suspicion about these outside radicals who might be 'coming in to stir things up.' You have to see this in the light of past violence. I was not encouraged to be too friendly with these people. I remember a group at Cumberland; I went to do an interview for the local paper, and then we sat down and played and sang and had a good time. There was a Community Action group there who had set up a community center. They had a nutrition class and a crafts class. These were the things I'd been sent to interview them about."

> *Johnny Woodward:* When we were first told that these people were
> Communists trying to come in here and overthrow the government,
> we had a meeting with 'em and said, "Look, if you're Communists,
> you know, tell us now. We've come this far with you, but if you're
> Communists, that's not the direction we're headed. If that's your bag,
> your thing, then you'll have to go in that direction without us." And
> they emphatically denied anything having to do with any Communism
> whatsoever. And we stayed a pretty close-knit bunch, until they were
> really forced to leave.

When the high school students in Evarts tried to present their grievances to a school board meeting, they were refused the floor and ejected
from the building by the police. Johnny Woodward recalls,

> The following night a group of parents got together and called a
> meeting with the Vistas and all the students who were there, and one
> of the Vista leaders said, "Now, Johnny, don't say anything out of the
> way, because if you do these parents will just get up and leave and
> we'll lose all communication with 'em. All they want to do is find out
> what you guys are doing, what you wanted, and what the Vistas have
> to do with it." I promised I'd be a good boy. We had the meeting and
> one parent, in particular, was on the school board, and he began
> making a lot of very very strong and negative comments about the
> group and the Vistas and our purposes—"a bunch of long-haired,
> dope-smoking Communists." I made a few irrational statements; the
> parents simply got up and walked out. And then things deteriorated
> and those folks had to leave.
>   *Portelli:*   They left *you* behind.
>   *Woodward:*   Yeah, they left a bunch of us.[66]

EPILOGUES

James Goode: One of the things that I said in 1970 in the preface to
my first book was that I felt like not only were we mining the natural
resources of our area, but we were also exporting our talent. That all
the people who were products of this educational system, who were
intelligent at all, got the hell out, and they went somewhere else, and
they spent their talent. And that we were losing a great resource, in
that we didn't try to keep people here. And so I decided, I suppose
I decided this in the 1960s when I was in college, being a liberal
democrat at that point in my life, I decided that I was gonna come
back. And that whatever talent I had, no matter how limited it might
be, whatever talent I had I was gonna try to invest it back in the
culture from which I came. I like this place: I like the geography, I like
the people, I like the food. I feel comfortable here. I think we have an
immense number of problems that need to be solved. How are they
going to be solved if all of the people who can solve them leave?

Johnny Woodward: We had a couple of fellows in our group who had
to leave Harlan—just high school kids, local kids. They had to leave
because of—we started our own press, we had a little press that we,
we'd write our own articles, we'd go and take pictures of all the things
we wanted to improve.

Portelli: I wonder if any of that stuff is . . .
Woodward: I seriously doubt it.
Portelli: . . . preserved somewhere.
Woodward: I seriously doubt it. It was probably burned when the Vistas left.
Portelli: See what happens to opposition culture—it gets burned.
Woodward: Yeah. But there was one fellow whose name was Tommy Duff; he was very, very active; very radical. He believed very strongly in whatever we did. And he had to leave Harlan County. He ended up committing suicide. He realized he couldn't come back and—he was a very highstrung fellow—he had to commit suicide. I think it was probably related to him having to leave and not being able to come back. We had an interesting 1960s and '70s, we sure did.

Chapter Fourteen

Luigi's Socks and Rita's Makeup
Youth Culture, the Politics of Private Life, and the Culture of the Working Classes

The revival of radical student movements in 1977 created a serious problem for the Circolo Gianni Bosio. Could we, as a collective of Marxist-oriented cultural researchers and organizers, identify a continuity between our work on the history and culture of the working classes, our participation in contemporary movements, and the need to study the culture of these movements? This chapter is a reworking of a document for internal discussion that was written in 1978. It was also the beginning of an ongoing effort to establish a critical connection between working-class cultures and mass cultures. Though thoroughly rewritten, it is therefore to be read not only as a description, but also as a representation of the time, not just *about* the movement, but an expression of it. In fact, after it was first published in a history journal, excerpts from it appeared also in New Left papers.[1] Subsequent developments in social history, women's studies, and cultural studies (still, however, a relatively obscure entity in Italy in the 1990s) make parts of it seem dated. To my knowledge, however, this was the first paper that mentioned the Beatles in an Italian scholarly history journal—and linked them with Calabrian picture brides.

In this adaptation, I have revised some of the language, cut sections that would now appear redundant or more hopelessly dated, revised the footnotes, clarified the allusions, and added a few examples from later work conducted in the spirit of this paper. I have, however, kept the present tense of 1977–79.

NEW SUBJECTS, NEW QUESTIONS

The radical youth movements of 1977 and after have changed our perception of working-class history and culture. They have defined memory

232

as the paralyzing weight of the past and the bureaucratic compulsion to repeat its empty practices, and they have rejected an identification with the working class, its organizations, and its leadership. In this way, they challenge the meaning of the work we have been doing to research and organize working-class culture, history, and expression.

On the other hand, most of us are involved in those movements, which directly concern our generation and (or) our workplace as students or teachers in the school system and the university. Unless we want to accept a split, which we always rejected, between our political and our cultural work (and relegate our cultural work to the sphere of archaeology or nostalgia), we must try to come to terms with the new issues, not because they are fashionable, but because they concern us.

This may be hard to do, because the so-called new subjects (socially or subjectively marginal youth) raise issues that affect our lives but seem unrelated to the world of the urban and rural working classes, or to include them only as individuals rather than social forces. Rather than with strikes and economics, the movement is primarily concerned with personal development, lifestyles, forms of community, the politics of private life, gender, and generational identities.[2]

"Youth" as an identity is by definition a temporary one, yet a wide area of social dissent and disaffiliation prefers it to class as a ground of self-recognition; not only in the university, but also in leftist and union clubs and locals, often "young proletarians . . . choose . . . to meet as 'young people' rather than as 'workers.'"[3] This is not merely an effect of what Pier Paolo Pasolini lamented as the "assimilation" of younger generations into an undifferentiated consumer culture,[4] or even of the increasing distance of the reformist Left from the experience of the younger generation. It is, rather, an effect of the shift and extension of capitalistic domination from the sphere of work and economics to that of consumption and private life. "The 'private' spheres in which feelings used to be exchanged and individual rewards were dealt out," writes sociologist Alberto Melucci, "are invaded by media manipulation and become places of mobilization of resistance and conflict." Therefore, "in a society that locates production increasingly in the control of feelings and personal relationships, class conflict and collective subjects are transformed, and the traditional categories become inadequate. . . . New class demands . . . are raised by new collective subjects representing the social groups more directly affected by the transformation of the forms of social production and domination."[5]

On the other hand, the invasion of private life and what Pasolini called the modernizing "homologation" of consumer culture do not take place in forms entirely indifferent to class and social stratification. On the one

hand, Pier Paolo Pasolini points out that the dress codes and body language of the younger generations have become totally assimilated: "In a
square full of young people, you could no longer tell, from their bodies,
the workers from the students, the fascists from the antifascists."[6] On the
other, folksinger Giovanna Marini sings about working people whose
"assimilation" is but another form of subordination:

> con le case a imitazione di quella del padrone
> e figli a imitazione del padrone
> ma quella vostra crolla e i figli ve li hanno rubati
> la sua è di roccia e i suoi figli abbronzati.

> (with homes that imitate / the boss's home / and children that imitate /
> the boss / but his house is made of rock and his children are tanned /
> yours is crumbling and your children were stolen.)[7]

Precisely in order to resist the homogenization that Pasolini denounces
and the invasion of private life that Melucci describes, we need to identify the class differences beneath the veneer of assimilation, and enhance
the material resistance of class facts to immaterial capitalistic domination.
Marini's ballad recognizes both the immaterial manipulation of desire
(workers *want* their children to look like the boss) and the material difference that frustrates it. For both Pasolini and Marini, the blurring of
class barriers has eroded the class identity of the workers but not the class
power of the bourgeoisie. The promised access of the masses to the master's forms of consumption has been traded for the master's access to the
minds of the workers; but the promise has remained elusive, and its achievements only superficial (lifestyles rather than standard of living; appear-
ance rather than property). Pasolini writes that a "classless hedonism"
induces young people to imitate the models they see in advertising, but recognizes that "a poor young man in Rome is not yet able to reproduce those
models, which causes in him anxieties and frustrations on the edge of neu-
rosis."[8] To identify the class-defined nature both of the enforced models
and of the obstacles that frustrate their achievement—in other words, to
retain class as one of our interpretative tools in the new context of mass
society—means both to reconstruct the autonomy of identities against
assimilation and manipulation, and to continue the struggle over material conditions and property—and perhaps to help bridge the gap between
those who see themselves as "youth" and those who see themselves as
"workers" (as well as the gap within those who are both).

Our contribution can also consist in holding on to the historical approach. While we are now more keenly aware that "the personal is polit-

ical," yet the personal did not *become* political in the 1970s. Let us take a lesson from the feminist movement and the youth movement, and reread working-class history for the traces of political struggle in the personal sphere. In this way, we can help contemporary movements connect to a broader history and gain a clearer perception of both continuities and differences, while painting a more accurate and comprehensive picture of the history of the nonhegemonic classes.

THE SKIPPED GENERATION

On Good Friday, 1977, a few months after the occupation of the university in Rome, I drove to Giulianello, a village about fifty miles south of Rome, to record folk songs. A young local comrade, Raffaele Marchetti, was my guide.

Until recently, Giulianello had been part of a landed estate, and the village retains its feudal structure, as hardly more than the courtyard of the landlord's mansion proudly standing in its middle. Even after the occupation of the lands, land reform, and the breakup of the landed estates in the 1950s, social relationships remained dominated by the feudal paternalistic benevolence of the landlord toward his tenants and farm hands.

We recorded an extremely beautiful version of the Passion song, performed by the village women in a procession from which the priests were excluded. We also collected satirical and topical songs from the late 1940s: "Stalin, my angel, we were expecting you at the railroad station" (after the Left's defeat in the 1948 elections, the author sang it to the landlord, who praised him for his wit). The real epiphany, however, was the conversation with Raffaele Marchetti, while driving around from one singer's house to another. Of course, I didn't tape it: it did not occur to me that a twenty-year-old law student might be a "historical source" and a "bearer of folk culture." Thus, I reconstruct what he said on the basis of the notes I jotted down later, faithful to content but shorn of his remarkable style of folk storyteller cum political activist.

"If you live in a village," he began, "you have a great sense of community, of belonging, of togetherness. But you also feel the weight of social control, of unwritten rules and sanctions. News travels fast, which is an element of sociability but also means that you can't escape and have a private space of your own. This is the way things are—or at least, the way they were until people said it was enough." It all began when a junior high school (sixth to eighth grade) opened in the village: "Out of about seventy children who went into the sixth grade, only six made it to high school in Velletri, and all failed the first year. I am the only one who remained in school." The impact of Velletri—a small town, but the gateway to the larger world—was a trauma. "We boys from Giulianello went through all sorts of humiliations. From our teachers, because we wrote in dialect and didn't know there was another way to express ourselves. I quarreled with a teacher because I had written *formicola* instead of *formica* [ant], and couldn't see what was wrong: I had always called it that way. And humiliations from our peers: we didn't know the fashions, we had never heard of the Beatles."

From this difficult initiation, however, the boys from Giulianello (they *were* all boys) brought back to the village all the emancipating power of consumer culture: small towns or near-villages like Velletri, Cori, and Artena play in this story the role of Paris in the novels of Balzac. In other words: the most important social struggle in Giulianello after the occupation of the land and the breakup of the estates was the young people's long war of attrition to abolish feudal relationships in their personal and cultural lives. Young people began to skip Mass on Sundays and to show up late for family meals. Raffaele remembered the turning points the way other people remember standard historical events, with dates and names:

"The first was Luigi, who came to town without his socks on. People said it was to be expected, because years ago his mother had also gone around with no stockings on, and he had taken after her. Then came Rita, who went to a dance in Artena and would let no one stop her. Again, people said it was because she had no father to control her." Nonconformity began to surface where the chain of control was weaker, but these leaders were only the tips of a slower and deeper iceberg. "I waged a two-year battle," Raffaele recalls, "to grow my hair over my ears. There were two barbers in town, one from Giulianello and another who was more broadminded because he was from Cori. So us boys, we would go to him, and he would cut our hair imperceptibly longer each time. My father saw my hair getting longer but couldn't say anything because there never was a visible difference. At the end of two years, my ears were covered."[9]

This, then, is the social history of a village beyond the Roman Hills, from the breakup of the landed estates to the present. I said to Raffaele that it seemed to me that there was a generation that "did" Fascism, the war, the struggle for the land, and then a generation that "did" the Beatles, long hair, student movements. What happened in between? What about those who were adolescents between 1955 and 1960 (incidentally: my generation), who no longer learned the folk songs but had no access to the new cultural developments? I always felt that this was a "skipped generation," at least culturally. Raffaele agreed.

"You're right," he said. "Here at Giulianello there are about thirty or forty males of that generation, in their thirties now, who never got married. They could no longer accept arranged marriages—'You go see such and such person, we're already agreed.' But they had no way to make their own contacts with girls. There were no parties, no opportunities to meet. So they stayed single."

Thirty or forty bachelors in one generation in such a tiny village is a major historical and anthropological fact. In the first place, it links the breakup of the landed estate with the crisis of the family patterns that went with it: the collapse of the landlord's feudal power entailed the crisis of parental authority in the family, but did not replace it with alternative means of gender communication. Stranded in the midst of change, the "skipped generation" of Giulianello paid for economic emancipation with sexual solitude, and both aspects are inextricable parts of working-class history. Indeed, arranged marriages are still a fact in the rural provinces south of Rome in the 1970s.[10] But there is more.

The end of feudal relationships, in fact, took place in the context of the collapse of rural society as a whole. The young rural generations had access to the land at the time when Italy was changing, economically and culturally, from a rural agricultural nation to an urban industrial one, and lifestyles and patterns of behavior and consumption were changing accordingly. This is a major irony in recent Italian history: the rural generation that gained access to the land was also the generation that no longer wanted to live on it. The land might give them a living, but did not promise a life—at least not when compared with the promise of the cities and the factories. Perhaps for these reasons, had the Giulianello bachelors been able to meet the girls, the girls might not have wanted to marry them anyway.

In fact, Raffaele Marchetti's story has two heroes, the boy Luigi and the girl Rita, as if to remind us that we need to look at this history from the point of view of both women and men. Women were also bent on gaining their freedom of choice, and the men did not like it one bit. Just a few years earlier, in the Red citadel of Genzano, a few miles from Giulianello, the Communist farm worker Silvano Spinetti wrote a number of protest songs. One of them had a verse against American imperialism, one against the Church's political interference, and one against women who (like Rita) danced and wore makeup. Interestingly, the anti-imperialist verse sang about "*la signorina America*," projecting America as the symbolic prototype of those modern young women with makeup on their faces. There is a remarkable contradiction between this vision of modernity as political and sexual marginalization, and history's progress toward liberation, which he celebrates in another song.[11]

This universal theme takes on specific historical overtones in the perspective of the "skipped generation" and the transition from traditional rural to urban consumer culture. By "painting" their faces, women proclaimed that they *had* a face, and impinged on the traditionally male preserve of sexual aggressiveness and choice. But while in songs like Blind Alfred Reed's "Why Do You Bob Your Hair, Girls" the condemnation is moral and religious, in Silvano Spinetti's it had class overtones: "They're putting on a lot of style, they won't accept a worker anymore."[12]

Just as rural working-class men have trouble finding girls who will marry them, women have trouble finding in their own environment husbands who will not chain them down to traditional hierarchies and lifestyles. Some get away by finding jobs and moving to town (Rita's history of leisure-time mobility is a hint in this direction). Others escape by another form of arranged marriage.

A brisk trade in "picture brides" links rural areas in the North and Center (the poor mountain provinces of Western Piedmont and the rural background of wealthy Arezzo in Tuscany) with the deep-South hill villages of Calabria: "Some girls get engaged on a photograph. They send a photograph North, and a friend or a cousin send them back a man's picture—You like him? come on over."[13]

There is an extraordinary combination of women's oppression and women's emancipation in these stories. The emancipated northern girls who refuse to marry rural men are replaced by southern women who may still be traditional enough to adapt to farm life, like the girls from Calabria who married rural mountain men in the Alpine province of Cuneo, Piedmont.[14] For these southern women, the North may appear as a step on their way out of their environment and families, toward personal emancipation. Often, these marriages do work—and, for some, they are only a beginning. When an interdisciplinary seminar on women's history at the Arezzo campus of the university of Siena in 1977 "discovered" this subject and got excited about it, a slightly older southern student quietly wept by the window. She had been one of those brides, too, we later learned. She eventually earned her degree in foreign languages and got a job in a travel agency; her arranged marriage turned out to have been a step in her history of emancipation.

Just as in the picture marriages of earlier emigrant generations, this aspect of the politics of private life does not concern the upper and middle class, but belongs to the history of peripheral, rural working classes: an exchange between deep-South Calabria and deep-North Cuneo that does not go through Rome, Milan, or Turin is bound to remain invisible to centralist, institutional historiography. On the other hand, because it concerns "backward" parts of the country and does not involve the sphere of production, it has also escaped the attention of progressive and radical historians.[15]

In the past, we have contributed to proving that history is not only kings, generals, and leaders, but also workers and common people; we must now show that the history of workers and common people is also the history of Raffaele's hair, Luigi's socks, Rita's makeup, the bachelors of Giulianello, and the picture brides of Guardavalle, and that it continues and extends in the youth movements struggling to expand their freedom and to save their souls.

One of the embarrassments of field work has been the fact of always looking for the "old folks"; we need not reverse this approach to start looking only for young people, but it is important to be aware that the young also are bearers of class culture and memory, and may suggest reinterpretations of the past. This approach helps also to bridge the gap between interviewers and interviewees, who turn out to have similar or comparable problems and experiences. When we realize that the history of peasant leagues and workers' unions, of anti-Fascism and of the struggles for the land, does not end suddenly two generations ago, but evolves and changes and continues today in other forms, then we may find it easier to understand that the past history of the working classes is also ours.

WHAT ABOUT US?

We talked about these things, starting with Raffaele Marchetti's story, in a seminar at a public library in Modena, about a month later. Modena is a far cry from Giulianello: a large industrial town in Emilia, it was (and is) a showcase of the Left. One of the wealthiest and better-run cities in the country, universally praised for the quality of its social services, it has elected Communist mayors since the end of World War II. Yet, somehow, the stories from Giulianello also resonated there for people like Bruno Andreoli, a factory worker who was active as a researcher and cultural organizer with the Istituto Ernesto de Martino on folklore and oral history.[16]

I have done some field research, and it began precisely because I am a member of the so-called skipped generation. There were things I needed to rediscover, and which I did not recognize in rock and roll or in a whole lot of other phenomena that were happening around 1956–57. Let me say immediately that I did find these things: I found them in the culture of the rural lower classes and of the labor movement, and this we must remember. Yet, from a certain moment on, what I found there no longer helped me. It was part of my history but did not relate dynamically to my situation.[17]

So the problem was, What were we supposed to look for, after we found the history of the farm-workers' leagues, the history of the folk songs, the history of village solidarity, all these very important things? All I did was look back, at what my father had done, or those who lived in my father's time, and they were great, they had made the leagues, the parties, and so on. What about us? What about us? What had *we* done?

That was another question I asked myself. I started another project in a village, Novi, and I found the usual things you always find: forms of expression, communication, songs, and so on. These are the first things you find. But the most recent local folk songs we found [were] parodies of popular music about events of '48, '53. After that, everything disappears.[18] And this corresponds with the release of [the] Fiat 500,[19] the CGIL's [Left union's] defeat in the elections at Fiat [in 1956], the Communist locals [were] abandoned, and for years there was silence.

If one has a background in the labor movement and in the Left, one knows very well that '52–'53 was one thing, and '57–'58 was another. Things were much harder. I was working in a factory then, and all those things had disappeared. Why? Because, on the one hand, the culture of the working-class movement, as expressed by its organizations, was being integrated in the changes of the social system. The reasons may seem trivial now, elementary: eating. It made a difference, whether you ate one meal a day or two. What was the image of socialism then? It was, Everybody eats. Food for all. At the time, that was the most urgent problem, rather than alienation, say, or man-machine relationships.

This is what working-class culture is made of in and around Modena. It originated in a rural situation and is still functional today, because today's high standard of living, ironically, seems to correspond to what these people imagined then. Yet, contradictions arise. We have made a lot of progress, but we have huge problems because our consciousness, our awareness, may not be ready for the new realities.

Consider our social services: they are always praised in quantitative terms, but we never seriously discuss what they really are, and why we had to expand them so much in the '60s. I think that if the proletarians stopped for a moment to think about their daily lives, they would realize that they are in a mess, because their lives are locked inside the workplace. Outside, and I am talking about Modena, they are totally expropriated. In order to imagine taking back our lives, in order to say "That's not what I want to become," we need to renew our research tools, renew our historical consciousness, renew the conscience that workers have of their situation.

For instance: they may want to be involved in their children's education, but they can't, because from 7 A.M. to 7 P.M. they are locked inside the factory. How can they discuss pedagogy? We complain that kindergartens, which are a social service, are children's dumps: they could be no other way. People delegate, not because they trust, but because the division of labor separates the tasks, and so I must leave the whole thing up to the teacher.

Should I want to question this setup, I find a void before me. I think we all agree that the family is in trouble, that it has no meaning anymore. But where is the alternative? This is why fieldwork in urban environments is political: because it seeks ways in which we may organize our daily lives on the basis of our own needs. As we begin to organize, we concern ourselves with private life as well as with politics, with all the elements of our lives. Until yesterday, we were only concerned with the politics of government, elections, laws, and so on; we took it for granted that a whole area of our lives was all right the way it was. Now this is crumbling. We must get organized and see how things connect, from the smallest detail to the broadest problems. In order to do research, we must change our politics and begin to study, in practice, the relationship of individuals with collective movements. Now I am working in a factory, and I want to start a factory paper. We will write about history told by the people versus history told by the bosses; and we will talk about jobs and seniority; and about the family, racism, about how we feel.

Bruno Andreoli's question, "What have we done," is a way of claiming history for ourselves, rather than just looking back to our parents' generation. Older generations, those that went through Fascism, war, Resistance, hard times in the factories, poverty, and the Depression, often think they have a monopoly on history, and blackmail the younger generations with it. A young woman in Studs Terkel's *Hard Times* complains,

> Every time I've encountered the Depression, it has been used as a barrier and a club. It's been a counter-communication. Older people use it to explain to me that I can't understand *anything:* I didn't live

through the Depression. They never say to me: We can't understand
you because we didn't live through the leisure society.[20]

The use of history and memory as generational countercommunication
is one of the motives behind the rejection of memory in today's movement. While in America it focuses on the Depression, in Italy it has hinged
primarily on the hard times of the war years and on class exploitation before and after. A young man in Terni commented, "[My father] asks, 'What
do you have to complain about? You have bread, you have everything. When
I was fifteen I ate meat once a week,'" and he answers, "He's right in his
way, but it makes no difference. Things have changed, there's no war on
now, there are more problems and less problems."[21]

The blackmail of past hardships turns the family into a channel of political conformity: "It's very Calvinistic: work, suffer, take twenty lashes
a day, and you can have a bowl of bean soup." Because the parents'
utopia was a world where "everybody eats," material abundance seems
to leave nothing to be desired: "Our quality of life, character, and tone
since the Thirties has been determined by the Depression: the buck is
almighty."[22]

Well-meaning parents who had hard lives and wish a better future for
their children transmit a message of subordination and obedience: "My
parents tell me: you must study, work, raise a family, earn some money,
buy an apartment, just like we did." says Andrea, a factory worker's son
from Milan.[23] Francesco Boccia, from the Christian Democrat electoral
stronghold of Amaseno in rural Southern Latium, recalls, "Recently, we
made a protest because the Christian Democrats had sold to a private spec-
ulator an ancient church in Amaseno. When I went home, my father
whipped me because by going to the demonstration I had destroyed my
chances of a job. In fact, I am still unemployed."[24] The link between class
memory and repression could not be more direct: aside from the police
and the control of public employment, the Christian Democrat politicians
can count also on concerned working-class parents with a history of hardships to stop their children from getting involved in struggles against the
new hardships of the present.

This attitude is also reproduced in working-class politics and organizations. Remembering the great farmworkers' struggles (and the heavily
mafia-ridden present) in the Calabria hill town of Guardavalle, a young
Communist activist explains: "It's not that older people are against us,
but they want recognition for their struggles and say we must continue
them. But times change, and they think the struggle should still be the

same. . . . They don't know whether we are irresponsible hotheads who want to blow up everything at once or change everything in one blow, or revolutionaries like they were in their days."[25]

Family and politics come together in one discourse of generational resentment. As Aldo Galeazzi, steelworker from Terni, put it in a startling metaphor, the children who complain about the house he built with his own hands are doing to him "like Khrushcev did to Stalin": in private life as in politics, they are literally rejecting their heritage.[26] Gaetano Bordoni, a barber in the anti-Fascist neighborhood of San Lorenzo in Rome, combines political history and the history of private life, past hardships and past struggle, hunger and the Resistance, in his criticism of the younger generations. His phrase, "What should *we* say?" is the older generation's answer to Bruno Andreoli's "What about us?"

> I say, young people complain, and they're right to complain, but then what should *we* say, who were young and had nothing, now we're getting old and still have nothing—at least we did something for the young, didn't we? I, when I was ten years old, I carried a machine gun, in the hills of Frosinone, along with my father, shooting it out. He told me, here, this is your gun, learn to use it if you want to save your life. I mean, now at age ten you have a toy; I had a machine gun, and I remember killing Germans and taking their clothes and their boots. We needed them, this is what life was like then, when I was ten. Now I am forty-three, I had so many hardships, I'm getting old, look at my white hair—the fear, the air raids, the Germans . . .
>
> And this is what I can't understand. I have a married daughter, and often we talk at home, because I like family discussions. But when she leaves her steak half uneaten on her plate—I won't stand for that! I didn't know what a steak was until I turned eighteen; I used to eat cat meat, whatever I could lay my hands on, what my father gave me. Nowadays they reject it—all this youth rebellion. I'm not saying it isn't right, but it should be done properly, because you can't be all the time fighting, brawling all the time. Times have changed, they've matured differently, and in a democracy—you can say the Communist Party has become bourgeois, but it isn't true: the party is always the same, only it has adapted to the times. You must go along with the times if you want to do what is right in a democracy, the way democracy is today. Otherwise, you have centuries of struggle ahead of you—and today's rebel youth, who do they owe, for having the chance to rebel? Those seventy thousand people, my father among them, who got killed for freedom. But, they say, this isn't freedom; yet, it's a step forward, toward democracy, toward freedom, isn't it? You don't make freedom with a magic wand. . . . We ought to change

everything now, soon; I wish we could, myself. But it can't be done, it
can't be done.[27]

If, as Bruno Andreoli said, socialism meant food for everybody, then
by leaving her steak uneaten on her plate, Bordoni's daughter is rejecting
all the achievements of her father's life: the higher standard of living and
the democracy that goes with it. By claiming that "this isn't freedom" and
calling for more radical forms of struggle, the younger generation questions both the achievements of the anti-Fascist struggle and the current
politics of the working-class Left.

This is a sore contradiction for men like Gaetano Bordoni. On the one
hand, his party's current politics are legal, electoral, basically moderate,
but he sees this moderation as the achievement of the armed struggles of
the past, which is essential to his own self-image as a machine-gun-toting
revolutionary. Armed struggle is often a shorthand for revolution; therefore, Bordoni cannot reject it in theory (and in the past), while denying it
viability and necessity in practice (and in the present). It was all right when
his father gave him his gun; it is antidemocratic today when other weapons
are available.[28]

Bordoni claims that he would be ready to do it all over again, if the
time came; but it never comes.[29] Meanwhile, he enjoys his democracy and
his steak, and can't understand his daughter's dissatisfaction. As another
of Studs Terkel's interviewees puts it, "They say, 'You have it soft now.'
The point is, *they* have it soft now," and can't see that their children are
going through hard times of their own.[30]

Occasionally, however, an older worker may learn a lesson from a young
man's estranging viewpoint, and a daughter may be able to relate to a father's story. In September 1979, I was interviewing Terni steelworker Santino Cappanera. He was talking about how the younger workers in the
factory are frightened by the violence of the environment and can't keep
up with the pace of production. Instead of criticizing them, however, he
questioned his own assumptions: "Perhaps I am slower than those who
came before me. And now I see that I keep a faster pace than the newly
hired boys. Not because I like work more than they do . . . but it's been
in my bones since I was a child." He talked about a student who visited
the steelworks and was shocked at the violence of some of the pranks that
workers played on each other.

> What joke is that? He, as a student, wondered; What kind of
> relationship can these people have, who work in such an environment,
> with their families? And I was surprised by this question: I even wrote

it down. I asked myself; Am I missing something; is there something I don't see? I've been working here thirty years—what difference has this made between me and my family?[31]

While Cappanera told this story, his daughter was listening to him, perhaps for the first time. Step by step, she drew nearer. By the end of the interview, she was sitting in the parlor, and I was interviewing *her.*

MEMORY OF PRICES PAID

"The Beatles, long hair, house parties, nonconformist dress," concluded Raffaele Marchetti, "all these things broke the silence, and coagulated a generation of young people who are more active, aware, open, even more politically alert. But now I feel the limitations of all this. It was a break from village culture, and all it meant in terms of closure, authoritarianism, conformity. But now that I am partly out of it, I feel I need to go back to our local history, to the traditions, the memories of struggle, the world of peasant culture, to reestablish an identity, to make myself whole again." For now, his peers call him "nostalgic," because they believe his is only a regret for things that are past.

He is only one of the growing number of young people who are becoming aware that knowledge of cultural history and traditions is a part of seeking for their own place in history and their own cultural contribution. It may be only an accident, but meaningful nevertheless, that the demonstration for which Francesco Boccia was whipped by his father was about preserving an ancient church: a symbol of the past, a site of memory (and even a source of alternative employment, were Italy's politicians able to develop the huge economic potential of our cultural and artistic heritage). Sometimes, however, it is only through outside influences that young people in rural and working-class environments become aware of their cultural heritage. Francesco Boccia explains,

> The interest [in] folk music was brought back by those who were
> politically engaged, who had been away, in Rome; but they don't
> relate to the music that local folk still sing and play, mostly for their
> own peers, ex-farm workers who now work in construction or car
> repair shops. Those who became politicized by going away are not
> interested in the town's heritage of history and folk culture. They
> know all about Del Carria[32] or the Black Panthers, but nothing about
> the struggles that have taken place here at Amaseno, which were very
> tough indeed.

On the other hand, urban radical movements develop their own forms of folklore and tradition, though they hardly recognize it as such. Movement slogans, songs, and graffiti are often similar to equivalent folk forms. The topical parodies of pop songs created by the movement of 1977 reproduced a widespread working-class practice in the late 1940s and early 1950s. Slogans were created, spread, changed, and memorized in collective contexts like *stornelli* or blues verses.[33] In greater depth, the movement's search for usable community values and forms parallels certain aspects of traditional, preindustrial folklore. In a seminar in 1977, the anthropologist Alberto M. Cirese remarked,

> I may be going too far, but if we are looking for actual tension toward change, rather than for bureaucratic alchemy, we must study these [movements]. The bureaucratization of life, the fact that we are all boxed in, lined up, televised, and that this is taking place also in the unions, in the historical parties of the Left, even in some of the New Left groups, this is what generates a desire for participation, an active peripheral spontaneity, a return even to forms associated with childhood. And it is a consequence also—I will never tire of repeating this, because it comes from Marx—of the nostalgia for the prices that have been paid. The return to the village holiday, to an immediate sociability that has been broken by the industrial life in the city, by emigration; the desire to meet again, to come together if only around a lamb chop or a glass of wine . . .[34]

Two young men from Sardinia, stranded as university students in Florence, improvised verses about lamb chops and bottles of wine and sang them in their native Sardinian language to folk verses and *organetto* accompaniment: "I know you're thinking of lima beans cooked in grease and our homemade bread dipped in it, chestnuts roasting on the fire, drinking with your friends, always keeping in mind the illustrious poetry of your mountain grandfather."[35] Ambrogio Sparagna, who came from a hill village in Southern Latium, got a degree in ethnomusicology, and went back to learn the *organetto* from his village's shepherds (and on to a brilliant musical career), opened his first album with a song about the real story of a folk musician who leaves the "bitter" land he was raised on to make a scant living in the city and lose his voice and his songs there, until he takes a train back to attend a village holiday, and "all the words we've spoken, all the songs we've sung, they all came back."[36] Alberto Cirese explained,

> It's about finding yourself when you've been torn to pieces. Marx says that workers became able to sell their labor force on the market when they broke the chains of serfdom and corporations; and this is the only

side that bourgeois historians see. But while they were losing those chains, they were also losing the guarantees that went with the chains: and this other side is written in history, Marx says, in traits of fire and blood. . . . Better living conditions, the passage from traditional agriculture to industry, council flats and water closets, all these things were heavily paid for in terms of the expropriation of earlier forms of associative life. Inevitably, hence arises the awareness—distorted, to be sure—of the price paid, in the form of nostalgia. An ambiguous sentiment; but we should be careful not to throw everything away too soon. We must make some extra effort to understand.

More violently and desperately, Tommaso Di Ciaula, a factory worker from Modugno, near Bari (Puglia), writes about this in his remarkable factory novel, *Tuta Blu (Blue Overalls)*: "This morning, I, mechanical worker, son of the unions, grandson of the steel workers' federation, as I laid my hands on my lathe I felt like a piece of shit, I began to scream like a madman that I wanted to die, that I wanted to go back to hoeing the land, go back to charming snakes, to pouring poisonous herbs, to dancing *pizzica pizzica* and *tarantella,* that I wanted to go back to fucking goats."[37] (In the 1990s, a blend of *pizzica pizzica, tarantella,* reggae, rap, and dialect verse created the music of a group from southern Puglia, called Sud Sound System, one of the most innovative expressions of contemporary Italian music).

Industrialization and consumer culture have been liberating and emancipating processes, but heavy prices were paid, and these prices accompany the redefinition of the cultural features of social classes and of the boundaries between them. Changes in education and in the labor market opened the university to the children of the urban and rural working classes, but the university no longer guarantees them social mobility as it used to. A growing number of young people are acquiring an education less as a way of leaving their culture and their history behind, than as a tool with which to go back, appropriate them, make them grow. This is the case of a group of young people from Avezzano (Abruzzi) who contacted us recently to produce an oral history of the struggles for land reform in their province.

Recently (summer 1978) we held an oral history seminar for a Communist youth club in Rome. We talked about Giulianello and Amaseno, and we played tapes of working-class history from Genzano and Terni. At the end, a very young comrade asked, "What do the kids from Genzano know about this history, the ones who are my age and who come down to Rome to go dancing?" At this stage of our work, we may offer two tentative answers. First, they know little, but some are beginning to want to know more: the daughter of one of our earlier oral history informants in Genzano set up a historical research group of her own. Second, the reasons why and the ways by which they come to Rome to dance (as Rita used to go to Artena) are not separate from that history, but a new phase in it.

Twelve years after this chapter was written, that girl from Genzano turned up as a source for our history of foreign-language students in the university of Rome. One of those young people from Avezzano was among the leaders of the student movement in Pisa in 1990; with the help of those from the Circolo Bosio who are still around, he organized at the university of Pisa well-attended seminars on Giovanna Marini, Woody Guthrie, and Bruce Springsteen.

Chapter Fifteen

Conversations with the Panther
The Italian Student Movement of 1990

FINDING THE PANTHER

In the summer of 1989, a panther was reported to be stalking the countryside northeast of Rome, leaving a trail of slaughtered chickens and sheep.[1] Police, farmers, and newspeople started a search, but the panther remains at large to this day.[2]

Meanwhile, on November 9, the Minister for Scientific Research and the University, Antonio Ruberti, introduced a university reform bill. It called for modernization and rationalization in the guise of more financial autonomy for each university and more involvement of private enterprise. On December 6, the students of the university of Palermo (Sicily) sat down in the Facoltà di Lettere (School of Philosophy and Humanities) to protest the Ruberti bill, and called for the support of their colleagues in other universities.

After the Christmas break, demonstrations and occupations started all over Italy. On January 15, the Lettere (Humanities) and Education schools of the university of Rome were occupied.[3] Lettere has always been at the center of national student movements, if only because it is the political core of Italy's largest university (over 150,000 students), in the country's capital, near the centers of power and communication. By the end of the week, the occupations had spread nationwide. Fax messages ran on the wires from one university to the other, creating a net of communication, discussion, and solidarity. By then, the movement had also found its symbol and slogan: "The panther is us."

> My name is Fabio, Fabio and nothing else. Stefano, here, and I, thought we would do something for the movement. Because we work in advertising, we thought we would create an image for the movement, so we thought of the panther. . . . We had thought about

this thing walking around in the city, which basically everybody liked, which at first looked like an aggressive thing. But because there was this widespread solidarity, because it was fooling everybody—the police, the newspapers, and so on. . . . We thought maybe we should suggest it to the movement. So we sent a fax. . . . Although [the newspapers] are talking about it as a marketing ruse, because Stefano and I do work for one of the world's largest, most competitive advertising agencies, yet Stefano and I have our own minds, we did this on our own, and our agency doesn't have shit to do with it. I mean, yesterday I had to come up with some ideas for Pampers, for Ariel detergent powder; every day we've got to have ideas for this kind of things. So there's more gratification in having ideas for a mass movement.[4]

On January 26, Villa Mirafiori, seat of the departments of philosophy and of foreign languages in the school of Humanities, where I teach, was occupied.

> *Fabio Ciabatti:* One of the first nights [after the occupation], it must have been around three, three and a half in the morning, I was out patrolling the grounds with Luca, and I noticed a couple of lights in the sky. I thought they were airplanes flying in formation, because they seemed to be moving at a fixed distance, but it was actually the clouds that were moving. We looked up, and saw two more lights behind them, and we thought those were planes, too. So we kept looking and it was only after a while that we realized that these weren't airplanes, these were stars.[5]

On the metaphorical level, this is a story about the rediscovery of the imagination: in the movement, a generation whose minds instinctively run to technological images of the space age became once again aware that some of the things you see in the sky may actually be stars. On the literal level, it is a story about a place. If they had been occupying Lettere, or some other building in the main campus, they would have been inside, and would not have looked at the sky. But Villa Mirafiori is surrounded by a park and a garden. "You don't see the night sky in the city," says Sonia Di Loreto, "but here in the villa you could. Nights were beautiful here, during the occupation. And you could climb up to the roof and look at the sunset."[6]

EXPLAINING THE PANTHER

Just as the panther that roamed the countryside eluded capture, the panther that raised its head in the universities eluded definition and explanation. Less than a year after the explosion of the movement, a major news-magazine featured a cover story called "The Youth of the Eighties: The Indifferent Generation," and a respected conservative newspaper reiterated that today's young people "do not want to change the world, they only wish to integrate, be better off, consume more."[7] If this is what they were writing *after* the movement, it's easy to imagine what they said before. "No one knows where in the world these students came from," says a sympathetic observer, in retrospect: "The ideology of privatization rules the scene, from cabinet ministers to bus drivers—and here come a few thousand students who claim—perhaps also ideologically, perhaps without due consideration of facts—that privatization is dirty, the 'culture is not for sale,' that knowledge is, and must be, 'virgin.' These students were not, and are not, in harmony with the times, and this makes them extraordinary."[8]

There had been no noticeable political stirrings in the university for several years. A movement of high-school students in 1985 received paternalistic media endorsement for its moderate demands, and seemed to vanish quickly. Politics in the universities seemed to be in the grip of a clientelistic Catholic group, *Comunione e Liberazione,* that combined ideological fundamentalism with sharp business practices. The Left was in disarray after the East European events of 1989, and the Communist party was busy with internal feuding over changes of name and identity.

Ruberti (an independent socialist, a scientist, and former president of the University of Rome) seemed genuinely surprised that the students would not welcome his bill, which he conceived to be a very advanced and democratic one, codesigned and supported by prominent academics of the Left. No one doubted that the condition of Italian universities called for drastic change: mostly state-owned, they are affordable and open, but provide very poor services and an erratic and unpredictable education, ranging from extremely good to deplorable according to chance and to each student's personal resources.

The movement resented the project's underlying philosophy of relying on the invisible hand of the market and privatization. It failed, however, to agree on any alternative solutions: the four months it lasted can be seen rather as a time of exploration, a generation taking time off to think about its own identity and its relation to the rest of society, than a political confrontation in traditional terms, although an effort was made to draw local and national platforms and demands.

On the one hand, there was anger about the inefficiency of the system: even the reasonable demands for evening classes, extended library hours,

and more chairs to sit on at lectures, proved to be finally utopian in the
context of a social system that deems any expenditure for public services,
and especially education, as a waste of tax money, and of a university hierarchy that has no idea of service. On the other hand, there was a resistance to the concept that efficiency and modernity were synonymous with
the bottom-line mentality. Different "souls," agendas, and scenarios clashed
and coalesced, often on the same picket line—as in the case of these two
interviews made on the same day at Villa Mirafiori. Both speakers are occupation activists:

> *Fabiana Battisti:* I don't like the way things are [in Italy]. Too much
> chaos, too much anarchy, too much confusion . . . nobody does what
> they're supposed to do. I think Italy is a country where only the
> sharpsters get ahead; if you can make it, all right, else you don't. I
> think the laws they give us are not intended to set down actual rules
> but just to patch up things here and there and then tell us, you make
> do any way you want; if you want to cheat it's all right because you
> can, and everybody does, and this is something I don't like, I don't like
> it at all.[9]

> *Lodovica Mutarelli:* I mean, Italy—well, maybe in Japan it's different;
> in Italy, we have a culture, a way of life, whatever, which is not exactly
> under the auspices of efficiency, technology, hyperactivism—to the
> contrary. So, I mean, it [the competitive pressure] tears people apart,
> and then conflicts, contradictions, explode. Which takes us back to
> why so many people in 1990 are still choosing to study humanities.[10]

The role of private enterprise in the Ruberti project achieved a symbolic
relevance beyond its actual short-term impact. Many students felt that this
was only a first step toward a subordination of the university to private
interests: "It's only in embryo there, but you can see what it leads to; it is
very narrowly sectorialized" (Pietro Rossini).[11] Others were concerned
that it would ultimately jeopardize the role of humanistic sectors and non-
marketable critical thinking.

Students also feared that financial autonomy for universities would
merely lead to an escalation of tuition fees according to the quality and
prestige of each institution. When one of the movement leaders at Villa
Mirafiori told me that "if this bill passes, I for one will be priced out of
the University," she was perhaps overstating the immediate danger but
thinking in terms of possible long-term consequences.[12]

Media and government criticized the students for being against progress and refusing to make the changes involved in "modernity." But all

students agreed that they had no stake in keeping things as they were; many, however, wanted to explore other ideas of modernity, rejecting the existing situation but refusing to accept the market ideology as the only alternative. They were, in fact, fascinated with technology. In the terms of Ciabatti's metaphor, they were now able to see the stars, but had no intention of giving up airplanes. The same symbology can be discerned in the two most widespread symbols of the occupation: the panther, with its connotation of exotic places, freedom, and nature; and the fax machine, which immediately acquired almost mythical status as the symbol and instrument of decentered, horizontal, dialogic communication technology. Videocameras were also very much on display, and the student productions looked more like rock videos than documentary realism; the music was hard rock and rap.[13]

"You felt like you were creating the world anew every day," a student put it. With a brilliant wordplay (on *faculty*, which means both "school" and "mental capacity"), students claimed that "the culture of the occupations" meant that they were now "in possession of all our faculties."[14] Politics was one of the things the movement felt it was recreating and repossessing. The excessive fear of being used by political parties and the refusal to be identified with earlier student movements of 1968 and 1977 (and with the "years of lead" of the terrorist offensive of the late 1970s) led the movement to insist on defining itself as nonpolitical—but also as "democratic," "nonviolent," and, with some misgivings over a political tag, "anti-Fascist." The main lecture hall of the Lettere building was renamed "Intifada-Tien an Mien Room." There was little reference to the revolutions of 1989 in Eastern Europe, in spite of the role played by students in them. Rather, the movement insisted that the collapse of "Communist" regimes in the East did not entail the pacification of radical opposition in the West: its response to theories about the "end of history" was the effort to "create the world anew." That it now appears that the task was too great for them is no reason to forget that they tried. Alone.

LISTENING TO THE PANTHER

One of the movement's demands concerned the possibility for the students to conduct their own seminars and receive credits for them. At a student-faculty meeting during the occupation, I suggested that one be dedicated to the history of the student experience at Villa Mirafiori, and the proposal was readily accepted.

I felt that oral history would highlight the students' role as producers rather than recipients of culture, and allow me to share my expertise with the movement in the role of a listener. I suggested we start with 1981, when the villa was acquired by the university,[15] in order to investigate what threads of resistance had run through the apparently pacified 1980s, coming to fruition in 1990, and that we concentrate on Villa Mirafiori in order to give the project a time and space focus. Most of the ongoing discourse on youth culture is hopelessly vague and ideologically loaded; a tightly focused field research project on a specific segment of young people might not lead to great illuminations, but would be at least a small piece of solid ground.

Though youth culture has been identified with lack of memory and rejection of history, young people and their culture do have a (sometimes reluctant, often untold) history and a memory of their own. I saw my participation in the project as part of a continuing effort to document the historical dimension of contemporary youth and mass culture and politics. This movement was more historically conscious than its precursors, precisely because it resisted identification with them; it was also very much image-conscious, both because it was part of an image-conscious era, and because it had to deal with the many distortions wrought by the media.[16] It was my idea that oral history could integrate the historical consciousness and provide further means of self-representation.

This, of course, was my agenda. The students who joined the project had other motives and concerns. In a preliminary report, they wrote that "the project arises from within a movement that has both continuity with and otherness from the past. Therefore it is part of the search for a meta-language—forms of self-narrative and self-representation—based on a memory that has coalesced during the occupation as a synthesis (or, at least, a comparison) of individual and collective moments, of analysis of the present and memory of the past." "The very fact of interviewing," they went on, is made possible by "assuming that the protest arises from a need to communicate and is part of a process of self-education and self-legitimation to speech."[17]

They were also concerned with the legitimation of the movement, which included only a fraction of the student body, as a representation of the whole—a theme on which the media had harped at length. "At Villa Mirafiori as elsewhere," the report stated, "a majority of the students were not actively involved in the movement, and allowed the others to represent them. The creation of an oral history takes place in the gap between a mass movement that stands for shared ideas and values and achieves the power to speak for itself, and the 'silent majority' that does not participate in this conquest of speech but must be postulated as part of collective memory."

The five students who joined the project, and later worked at the collective writing of a book, were all involved in the occupation, in different forms, and from different political and cultural backgrounds (none of them, however, could be said to have been "politicized" in the strict sense of the term at the beginning of the occupation). Some had helped create a student literary magazine (called *Babele*), and tried their hands at poetry and fiction.

They all had some awareness of the methods and problems of interpretation of oral sources through my Appalachian culture seminars; this, however, was their first experience as interviewers. After a couple of desultory training sessions, we decided that the best thing was to learn by doing, discussing method as problems arose during the research. They are all English majors; since they had already filled their quota of history and anthropology courses, they knew they would not receive any credit for this work. They did it only because they needed to understand their own environment and history, and themselves.

FLYING

Let me start with the story that Francesca Battisti (a member of the project) told us one night over pizza, as I remember and reconstruct it from my mental notes at the time:

> I met this guy who worked on a sailboat in Sardinia, during a summer
> vacation, and he said, why don't you come with me to work on boats
> in the South Pacific? I was nineteen, and a week later I was on a plane
> on my way to the Vanuatu Islands. I spent about a year working on the
> sailboats, and then I went to New Zealand. Spent a summer working
> on a farm, and I thought I'd go to the university. When I got to
> Auckland, I looked around: it was a big city. And I thought, if I'm
> going to live in a city and go to the university, I might as well go
> home. Which I did.[18]

A foreign language department attracts a large share of young people with international horizons and backgrounds. The impulse to leave home and explore alternate worlds is a leitmotif in our interviews: "I thought [that taking foreign languages] might make it easier for me to learn how to travel, allow me to break away from home, travel on my own."[19] To a few, traveling means exotic places like the South Pacific or the Far East (the original home of the panther); to many more, it meant England and America, so intricately tied to the mythic stature of the English language in youth culture. Most dreamed of combining traveling as experience and as a living: a huge proportion of girls joined foreign language departments with the idea that they would become airline hostesses—airplanes again, both as a job and as a way to fly to the stars. Chiara Midolo, a very visible opinion-maker and sometime punk-icon in the early 1980s at Villa Mirafiori, recalled,

> I was in love with the Beatles![20] I mean, actually I had caught this passion for English as a synthesis of everything I was not, everything Italy was not, everything my adolescence was not. So it was tied with certain musical myths, with that whole range of imagination, this rather ignorant cult of America and England—they were the same thing at the beginning, you know. So I landed at foreign languages to try to find out more about it all. And look, the situation was bleak, I mean, you'd talk to eighty percent of the people and what they had in mind was that this was where you'd train to become an airline hostess—which of course I had in mind too; they didn't take me because I was too short—and most people were upset, because, they said, where does all this literature come from?[21] The top was when I went to England and I was still in my first year—very reckless, because I didn't know a word of English, and I went alone, I may have known three or four words, it's God's truth: I could say "Love me," "Kiss me," and I could say "I wanna hold your hand." A year later I went back, I was more sophisticated, and I managed to stay a few weeks longer. I stocked up on breakfast cereals, and lived on them for a week. Actually, I was attending classes. I've always been a good bourgeois little girl. I was going to school, taking the toughest and most intensive courses, and then in the afternoon I'd hang around, and I'd go to concerts, not many, because I didn't have much money. And then, punk came on the scene, and I painted my hair pink all over . . . I never was a real punk: I liked the way they wore their clothes and hair, but I mean, I'd go home to mama's nice warm little soup, forget about punk. I just wanted to shock people; you like it, when they turn around and say, "Look at that!" And finally I gave it up because it turned out my folks weren't shocked at all—not a bit. The last straw came the day I was all purple and leather and everything, and I came home and my grandmother says, "How pretty!"[22]

To Chiara Midolo, adopting the punk image was an experiment in alternate identities; Caterina Duranti thought of foreign languages as a way of trying on theatrical masks and roles; Alessio Trevisani had a complex relationship with the Palestinian kefiah he wore, as a sign of non-conformity on the one hand, and as a way of conforming to a political image on the other; Gabriele Guerra wore his identity as a lone radical in the 1980s very much as a "Superman" role.[23] Like traveling, "masking," or speaking another language, wearing another look and another face, is another way of expressing at least a *desire* for difference, for—as Chiara Midolo puts it—"a synthesis of everything I was not." On the other hand, traveling, being on one's own away from home, also becomes a way of finding out what one is. Tiziana Petrangeli describes it as an initiation into self-reliance:

> Well, this was an experience that really changed me. You go away, you understand so many things, and then a year later you come back and fall back into the same vicious circles, the same situations, and perhaps the same mistakes all over again. For a moment there you stand naked, really naked; you have no shelter, you don't have a family, you're away from home, from your mama, from your daddy, from the money, from all the safety nets you have there. It's a way of measuring yourself, because you understand what your limits are. It's like starting everything all over again, by yourself, and in a more difficult situation because you don't know the language, you don't know anyone. And I was lucky, in that in measuring myself I was also able to improve myself—I had set myself a goal, to learn enough English to pass the written exam, and I did it. For me it was important; it made me trust myself, because I did it with nobody's help.[24]

Like others, Tiziana combines the student and the immigrant experience: "[In England] I did a bit of everything. I was a dishwasher, I was a waitress, I was a charwoman, I worked as a cook's helper in a fast-food, I was unemployed, I was drawing social security, I was a squatter—I mean, all the things that Italians in London do." In fact, traveling has been synonymous with emigration for generations of working-class Italians, and some of that historical experience contributes to the international outlook and backgrounds of several present-day university students.

Lucia Rossi grew up in Rochester, NY, and came back kicking and screaming to her family's native village in rural southern Italy; twelve years later, she still spoke with an American accent, wore American-style makeup, and played bass guitar in a "glam" heavy metal band with local young people. Marinella Bucetti's ancestors moved to Egypt in 1908, after the disastrous Messina earthquake; they lived there for two generations, and came back after World War II, spending two years in a refugee camp. Though Marinella was born here, she has an intense family memory of the Middle East as an international environment.[25]

Thus, the international horizon as escape from home and family mingles with international background as family heritage. While Lodovica Mutarelli reminisces about her New Caledonia childhood as a source of alternative values, Fabiana Battisti attributes her yen for traveling and her utopian ideas of foreign efficiency to her middle-European upbringing (one side of her family is Austrian): "I expected [the university] to be a little more orderly, and this may have something to do with my protestant descent." During the occupation, students who had studied abroad testified about their experiences of more comfortable and efficient systems.

Carlo Martinez also attributes his broad outlook to his father's stories about his travels with a TV news crew, but he also refers to another form of student travel: commuting. "I live three days at home, and three days in Rome: you're always temporary, always on the move," he says.[26] Most of the seasonal and commuting population, especially from small-town or rural South, is less economically privileged than the urban resident students. The hardships of commuting ("By the time classes started at eight," recalls Caterina Duranti, "you had already been up and going for several hours. . . . I remember that when we started from home, in the winter, it was still dark") mingle with the dreams of travel to fuel dissatisfaction:

> *Alessio Trevisani:* I think I am one of the thirteen percent of Italian young people who attend the university, but within this [privileged] thirteen percent I am one of those who do not have a well-to-do family, so you need to work your way, [which I did] ever since I got out of high school. People here are eternal children, eternal children, because you have to continue living at home anyway. I, too, I wish I could leave home, but then—I want to go to Germany to study the language or something, but I can hardly pay for books [here], pay for tuition, and maybe save some money for a train ticket and, if things get really bad, get my folks to send me a money order from home. So leaving home, living your own life, here, in the university, is impossible: if you break with your family, you break with school, too. And being here, taking part in this occupation, is essentially a political decision: it is evident that there was a lot of dissatisfaction here, very strong. From the very first day I came in here the message was that the university was not for you, that not everybody was going to graduate in the end.[27]

SOLITUDE

One early summer day, I stayed in my office after most people had left, and as I was preparing to leave I noticed a tiny, wide-eyed, dark-haired girl wandering helplessly through the empty corridors, trying to decipher notices on the professors' doors. I asked if I could help her, and she turned out to be a new student, from a village in Central Sardinia. She had long dreamed of coming to Rome to study English and be an airline hostess, but the only secondary education available in her area was a vocational school for chemical technicians. With that diploma in hand, she made her way to Rome, to find out that her starting class that year was a lecture course entitled "Figures of agnition and anagnoresis in medieval English literature." I explained what it meant, but I have never seen her again.

> *Luca Capparucci:* It's like, you don't know how to swim and they
> dump you into a swimming pool and say, "Go ahead and swim."
> Nobody tells you anything; you must find out everything by yourself,
> so the first impact is kind of tough. I remember the first class I went
> to. I didn't absolutely know what to do, where to go, and so on and so
> forth, and about a month later I was perfectly at home, or at least, I
> knew how this place worked. It didn't give me any big traumas, except
> you must do it all by yourself, catch the teachers, find out the books,
> everything. It seems natural now, but in retrospect, it isn't right—I
> mean, I see so many people quitting the university, or staying away,
> or dropping out, and when I ask them how come, it's because they
> couldn't make it, see? You've got to do it all by yourself, they don't tell
> you anything, and some people feel this pressure more than I did.
> Sincerely, it's hard to believe how many people just stayed away or
> dropped out because they could get no counseling, no orientation.[28]

Italian universities are among the world's most user-unfriendly institutions. "I mean, why don't they ask themselves a question: How come so many people drop out along the way? There was a moment, in my second year, when I seriously wanted to give up. Mostly, I wasn't looking for personal help; all I wanted was for someone to be there if they said they would meet me and talk to me. How many times I went to the university, to go to class—I was commuting from Grottaferrata—and no teacher showed up!" (Giulia Bartolomei).[29] "I spent the first four months running frantically from door to door trying to figure out what was going on, what was a study plan, what was an exam. I mean, to me the fact of speaking up in class was absolutely normal; after five or six times, everybody looked at me as I were from Mars or something. I thought, Well, I guess things are different in the university" (Beatrice Dondi).[30] Ultimately, in spite of ever-fashionable complaints about the "permissiveness" of the Italian school system, Italy has one of the highest drop-out rates and one of the lowest percentages of university graduates in Europe.

Although the system does not emphasize competition, many complained of excessive individualism among students. "Books are expensive, and you can't always come to class," says Alessio Trevisani: "There were notices on boards—'Class notes for sale'—and I always wrote in, 'Give them away, you shit!' Give them away, that's the least you can do!"

> *Luca Capparucci:* I felt different from most people. There was a lot of showing off, from a lot of them—I have this much money, I make so much, I go skiing, I go places—this aristocracy, sort of, and it bothered me. I felt I didn't have much in common with the people I went to class with, and I'd run off right after class. I mean, if you go skiing, if you can afford it, all right; what bothered me was that people just didn't give a damn about anything, it bothered me to hear people say things like—"Well, if they raise taxes who cares, my father's paying for it anyway"; or, "Great, if they occupy the university, I'll stay home and do something else." I mean, your social background is not a crime, or the money you have is not a crime, but what I couldn't stand was this not giving a damn you'd sense in a lot of people.

"What is missing," says Alessio Trevisani, "is a human relationship between people, and this is a huge problem of, you know, of schizophrenia, between what you study and what your life is." While some manage to turn this enforced solitude into self-reliance (like Tiziana Petrangeli, proud of learning to pass her English exam "all by myself"), others internalize it and blame themselves: "Here, in theory it's easy to socialize, but in practice there's my, my introversion, which makes it very hard for me to have [friends], or at least made it very hard, and before [the occupation] I had made very few friends" (Gabriele Guerra). Fabiana Battisti also explains that she didn't make many friends because of "a matter of personal character," but goes on to say that the occupation changed her, made her "more sociable." Others, finally, responded by creating their own small cliques, running around with a bunch of friends, often from the same high school and most frequently from the same social background.

The Villa Mirafiori and foreign language environment favors the re-creation of high-school conditions. Foreign language students attend classes more regularly, and are more attached to specific departments and teachers, than their colleagues at other schools; they have contact with intermediate figures (such as the native-speaking foreign language instructors) who bridge the status and age gap between students and professors. Their experience is, therefore, more homogenous, less impersonal, but also less independent, than that of other university students.

At Villa Mirafiori, this is reinforced by the characteristics of the space. The villa is separate from the main campus, which tends to throw people more together; on the other hand, it is inside a public park, which offers certain neutral spaces outside the building (such as the coffee bar) where students and faculty meet as citizens, theoretical equals, by the university but not really in it. Students therefore respond to the anomic conditions generated by the impact of the university by creating a mixture of regression to earlier communities, and embryos of a new one.

YEARS OF WAX, OR LENIN AT THIRTEEN

Alessio Trevisani: You can feel the burden of the eighties all over you. But they were not just a backlash among the people, or a lack of idealism. History was being rewritten, and even we who are occupying the university know next to nothing about the sixties, and we wind up sharing in the theory that movements, people, people's participation are useless; that you all need is management, and the manufacturers' association tells you that you have to be your own manager, your own entrepreneur, and that studying is a way of storing up capital for investment. So people come to the university with one goal: I must get ahead, make a career, and then it's fighting and struggling; you don't talk to your neighbor, you sell your class notes [instead of giving them away]. But I wonder if people are ultimately satisfied with this life, and I don't think they are.

"Yes, those years [the eighties] were years—years of silence, because the problem of terrorism was so recent, and people were still afraid to even think about meetings, politics . . . I mean, look, those were years—not of lead, but of wax, wax in our ears, because we weren't listening to any-thing" (Caterina Duranti). In a way, the rebellion of 1990 happened not "in spite" of the climate of the eighties, but precisely because of it: silence, individualism, competitive conformity generated their own antibodies. "All this bombardment from TV and everything, in the long run it drives you mad. I mean, it gives you no alternative: either you comply, or you're out. I mean, you don't live, you don't get a good job, you don't have enough money, you don't make a living, and this kind of language in the long run, drives you mad. You feel like you're in a race where either you are the winner or you are automatically last, and this is one reason why you finally explode" (Lodovica Mutarelli).

This helps interpret the movement's ambivalent relationship to history. On the one hand, students felt they had been deprived of a past, of a tradition of opposition and struggles. On the other, they recognized that media attempts to recast them in the mold of those earlier movements were one way of burdening them with a past that had become tainted with "ideology" and "terrorism," and depriving them of the right to make their own history.

Thus, there was no continuity with the sixties and seventies, but there was an awareness of the fact that there had been rebellions and occupations before. In Villa Mirafiori, "survivors" were few and scattered, and never organized in political groups, but there were always a few around. Their narratives are woven with threads of irony and defeat; none felt they were entitled to set themselves up as experts and models. In the movement, they contributed as individuals: through them, the occupation had access to memory, but very little organized memory encroached upon it.

Paolo Giacomelli: [My last years of high school], '77–'81, those were strange years: the years of political fervor, a rebirth of the so-called political element, including the violent forms, which I think started, at least in my personal history, after [the murder of] Walter Rossi [a high school student killed by Fascists in 1977]. It happened in the north side of town, near where I used to live, and there was a great deal of emotion, a huge response. Picketing, a number of Fascists were beaten up; it looked like Russia in the '50s, purges, a moment of terror. I wasn't much worried because I was on the side of the majority. . . . And then, all these demonstrations, one hundred thousand people, seventy thousand people, you know—impressive. And it was the beginning of a thread of violent politics in schools—not in terms of underground groups, Red Brigades, or such. But people were using Molotov cocktails; those who walked in the first ranks at demonstrations were armed, whether it was guns or bats I don't know. Anyway, each demonstration was an occasion to fight the police. I wasn't interested, because I had other myths—the American sixties, *Easy Rider*—and besides, I've always followed fads and fashions.[31]

Gabriele Guerra: When I was in high school, my classmates thought I was this fierce militant activist of Democrazia Proletaria [a small Left party]. And I basked in this, because it allowed me to set myself up above the mass. It felt good, at a time when this was absolutely unfashionable, to be the one who kept up the values of '68, of political involvement, so to speak. In fact, I was not alone, but I liked to think I was, because that way I stood titanically against this total darkness, the gray gloom of modern times. Very superman. Now I think I've grown out of it—aside from the occupation—because at the time I was very young; it was the result of things I'd read too quickly and superficially, Lenin at thirteen . . .

Lodovica Mutarelli: I must have been a difficult child, a naughty child or something, so that when I was thirteen I was sent to a boarding school. I didn't mind, because my parents placed me in what they thought was one of the better schools, but there were things in it which to a thirteen-year-old girl were sort of shocking. I mean, this was the typical school where rich families placed their children who were perhaps on drugs, or Fascist hoodlums. I mean, you'd see those crises of abstinence, people rolling on the floor—you weren't prepared for this sort of thing. Or swastikas. Anyway, the situation outside was very good, because this was one of those ultramodern schools were you had a great deal of freedom, 40 kilometers from Milan, so I'd go out, and this was 1977—occupied houses, politics everywhere. . . . I got interested, I began to read, like many, Lenin . . .

After I got out of school, I got a job [in 1984]. I was feeling these very heartrending contradictions, how could I be the daughter of an industrial manager, and a Left person at the same time? So, to prove that it was possible, I went to work in a factory. And it was a dreadful experience, every way you look at it. The pace of work was a nightmare; I just couldn't take it, and I had no experience of manual labor, so eight hours of it were killing me. As soon as you caught up with the pace, it speeded up. You never made it; as soon as production was up to a certain level, they wanted you to do more. There were eleven of us: no contract, forty-five thousand a week.[32] So I lasted seven months, after which one of my kidneys broke down, and I had to give up.

But the worst thing about it is that, like many others I guess, we had this myth of the working class. And instead, living inside, in there— the war of the poor against the poor, I mean. I was the last comer, so the woman who had just enough seniority to be above me gained some little power by me being last . . . they did all they could to make me make mistakes, so they could look good. . . . And it was terrible. [Enrolling in the university] to me was a defeat. I tried to tell myself that, well, after all, you grow up, you make choices; but really I went through it as a defeat. I mean, everything I believed in fell over me. But I have realized that, somehow, the principles that moved me since I was thirteen are still strong. When I found that my myths had collapsed, it would have been easy to say, "I don't give a damn," but I

just couldn't. I guess it means that deep inside I believed in those
things, and I still do.

THE POETICS OF SPACE: THE GARDEN

> *Caterina Duranti:* I started in '79–'80. And I remember with pleasure
> the shift from the Sapienza [the main campus] to Villa Mirafiori in
> '81–'82. It was as though at last we were finally seeing the places we
> studied about in literature, you know what I mean? With a bit of
> imagination. . . . And the eye rested upon this villa of classical forms.
> And the park—it was a public park, so you no longer felt like you
> were in a ghetto and all you saw were students: there were children
> around, old people strolling . . .

Caterina Duranti's perception of Villa Mirafiori as a place of the literary
imagination is emblematic: "It really projects the image of the '*locus
amoenus*'" (Pietro Rossini). Her view of the villa as an open space, however, reflects her early 1980s experience of leaving the crowded university
"ghetto"; later, most students, while still sharing the pastoral view, have
come to see Villa Mirafiori as another enclosed space. The vision of the
public park is replaced by idylls of enclosure, the garden or the island:
"We live in this beautiful villa," says Lodovica Mutarelli, "surrounded by
this garden, somewhat apart from the world. And, I don't know, perhaps
[if we were in the main campus] we would feel more in solidarity, more
in touch with the others, in the midst of university life. But from another
point of view, this is a fine place, the villa is beautiful, this garden is beautiful. And I think the others look at us in the same way: we are part of
Lettere in a way, but we are also the lucky ones who live in this sort of
green atoll." Another of Lodovica's definitions of the villa is "a bell jar on
velvet."

The pastoral perception was geared to the ambivalent views of community. As Northrop Frye has explained, the pastoral imagination is rooted
both in visions of the distant future and of the mythical past, of utopia
and of the golden age.[33] In our case, it supported the movement's utopian
ideal of the university as a future community of equals in search of disinterested knowledge, but it also implicitly evoked a golden age of childhood and ideal family. This was reflected in the occupation. The struggle
was less politically radical than at Lettere, but in some ways more successful: Villa Mirafiori was one of the few places where faculty recognized
and negotiated with the movement, agreeing (against the dean's and president's guidelines) to resume classes while the occupation was on. The in-

ternal politics were more personal and social than ideological, as people knew one another on other than political bases: "Villa Mirafiori is small; we know one another aside from meetings. The politicians are the ones you go to classes with, the ones you see at the bar . . ." (Carlo Martinez). There never was a total break with ordinary space and time: the park stayed open; teachers were able to continue using their offices. Cleaning and security personnel kept coming to work, keeping some cleanliness and order, quarreling and fraternizing with the students ("With the cleaning ladies we do have some conflicts—sometimes they're right, I mean—we do clean up, but [not as much as we should]. But sometimes they bring us coffee, when they come in, at six-thirty in the morning," said Lodovica Mutarelli; "As to the security, it's idyllic; we're great friends, we pass the nights away together watching the gates.")

As a consequence, the students were not forced to be entirely responsible for the space they had liberated: the garden was still protected and enclosed. The occupation was an experience of socialized growth; but the space in which these "eternal children" (Alessio Trevisani) attempted to "grow up all together" (Lodovica Mutarelli) was still "more like home" (Caterina Duranti), and the process was conducted "sort of like in a family" (Carlo Martinez). Even some of the teachers who sympathized with the movement had a visible maternal-paternal attitude (which the students duly resented). While cherishing the oppositional dream of leaving home, they found themselves at times in a surrogate home and alternative family. "Of course no one wants to leave Villa Mirafiori," says Laura Lombardi,[34] who has been sitting on her dissertation for two years while working at a variety of secretarial jobs: "as soon as you step out of here, they bite your ass off."

THE POETICS OF SPACE: THE BRONX

"I have gone back to Lettere a couple of times" during the occupation, says Fabiana Battisti, "and I always felt like I was entering the Bronx." Villa Mirafiori and the Lettere building on the main campus (La Sapienza) are most often described in the form of a binary opposition of literary genres: pastoral for the villa, and urban realism or naturalism for La Sapienza. If Villa Mirafiori is the Vanuatu Islands (the panther, the stars), then Lettere is Auckland (the airplane, the fax).

> *Elisa Fabbri:* The first day I came to Villa Mirafiori, I was surprised to find it was in the middle of this, this garden, sort of like a British college, and it was a pretty good impact, if you compare it to the

Sapienza—this inhuman crowd always coming in and out of these
huge buildings.[35]

The main campus was conceived in the 1930s precisely as an urban concentration, and was accordingly named Città Universitaria (University
City).[36] Negative urban connotations dominate the students' references
to Lettere and to the Sapienza: the dust, darkness, concrete, crowds of
urban peripheries. "Villa Mirafiori is smaller; there's more room for human
relationships. The Sapienza is more impersonal, it's sad, it's squalid. Villa
Mirafiori has trees . . ." (Tiziana Petrangeli). During the occupation, while
Villa Mirafiori remained a protected utopian-pastoral space, Lettere was
literally invaded by and absorbed into the reality of the city, as it became
a shelter for the homeless and for marginal figures from immigrant ghet-
toes, gypsy camps, and the dangerous streets around the railroad station.
It was hard for the students, in the name of solidarity, to keep these people out; it was also hard to manage them once they were inside. After a
while, vigilance in the building tended to deteriorate. The dean and conservative faculty members made a big deal out of the "damage" and "desecration" suffered by the building.

On the other hand, a city is infinitely more exciting and challenging
than a garden: the Bronx has a mythic status in Italian youth culture as a
metaphor of modernity. There was no writing on walls, no defacing slogans or obscene scrawls at Villa Mirafiori—but also none of the art work
and very little of the poetic, graphic, musical self-expression that deco-
rated Lettere. Politics at Lettere was more grown-up: abstract, impersonal,
sectarian—and full of ideas, of real decisions. You could see the stars and
the trees at Villa Mirafiori, but you had to go to Lettere to deal with airplanes and immigrants.

THE POETICS OF SPACE: THE LABYRINTH

Pietro Rossini: One other thing I like about Villa Mirafiori is the
inside. What I mean is, it's a labyrinth, which drove me crazy in my
first year, and later on gave me some gratification instead, because
I would take the sophomores around and show them the different
places. If you don't enjoy losing your way in a labyrinth, you don't
know the pleasure of reaching room 34 [the photocopy service]
utilizing both stairs, especially the one that goes through French up
to Philosophy, and then you have to come out onto the open terrace,
open the door, which seems closed but actually it's open, go down to
the end of the corridor. . . . I am quite sure that there are meanders,

although I'm an exceptional explorer, which I haven't explored yet.
Take the subterraneans below the stairs to room 7: I didn't get around
to them. I went once and I found a cellar with a closed door and went
no further.

According to rumors, confirmed by the villa's caretakers, the closed door
at the end of the stairs below room 7 opens onto an underground passage
leading to the early Christian catacombs two blocks down the street.
Villa Mirafiori used to be a convent, a natural for the gothic imagination.
Even jokes about the building have a gothic tinge: one story has it that the
cellar behind that door is used to store the corpses of dead instructors
whose turnover is unusually high due to low job security. Foreign language
students, used to the crowded first and second floors, get an eerie feeling
from the dark, resonating silence and emptiness of the Philosophy floor
above. "It was two years before I scraped up enough courage to climb the
central staircase," says Francesca Battisti: "I was scared. There's another
staircase up there, which I don't know where it goes. I was terrified." Laura
Lombardi recalls vague rumors of a ghost around the clock tower, but
admits that she may be making it up.

According to Paolo Borgognone, the back stairs that go up to the English department are commonly known as the Via Crucis (the Way of the
Cross), both because the nuns who occupied the building chose to ornament the rail with crosses, and because you climb them to take your oral
exams and be crucified.[37] By those stairs, students leave the horizontal
communal space of the garden and enter the vertical space of a highly hierarchic and stratified institution. The gothic imagination is closely linked
to all kinds of feudal environments, real or imaginary, and the university
is essentially a feudal institution (full professors are known as "barons").
Beyond its pastoral aspect and classical facade, when you really go into
it, Villa Mirafiori is another piece of this feudal universe. Its labyrinthine
shape is but an architectural correlative to the average student's sense of
being lost at the first contact with the university.

OBSERVING THE OBSERVERS

Describing the inside of the villa, Marinella Bucetti said it reminded her
of the description of the school in Edgar Allan Poe's "William Wilson."
I congratulated her on this brilliant insight, and asked her how she came
upon it. "I heard it from you in class," she said.

In the dialectics of fieldwork, what you get is always related to what
you put in in the first place and this is even truer when your "field" is the

place where you ordinarily live and work. By feeding back to me my forgotten remark about Poe and the villa, Marinella Bucetti showed that I
also shared in the gothic perception: there is a link between the gothic
and fear, but there is also one between the gothic and guilt. By making
that point, and proceeding to forget about it, I proved that I projected
upon the villa's gothic forms the anxiety, alienation, and guilt generated
by being situated at the wrong end of a feudal hierarchy of power rather
than inside a warm, pastoral community of knowledge.

"Nothing in the world more dangerous than a white schoolteacher,"
says a character in Toni Morrison's *Beloved*.[38] The more I got involved in
this project, the more I saw myself in the image of Morrison's school-
teacher-cum-slave-overseer, who goes around with a notebook and takes
anthropometric measurements on his slaves with a view to writing a book
about them. Though students are the same color as I am, and citizens
rather than slaves, yet a hierarchy of power is still involved. I theorized
about the oral history interview as an "experiment in equality," but I had
already "interviewed" (and "interrogated") most of my informants, and
would again do so, in the very unequal context of an oral examination.[39]

One of the most articulate student narrators was very vague and per-
functory when asked to speak about her exam experiences. Later, it turned
out that her most negative experience had been with me: she did not mention this on tape, and finally chose to tell me, not inside the building, but
in the neutral space of the coffee bar in the park. The hierarchical relationship, in fact, intruded not only in the interviews that I did myself, but
also in those which were carried out by student researchers, because the
speakers were aware that I would eventually see the interviews—one more
way for a professor to judge them and access their minds. I was always
present as an "implicit" interviewer: one girl, interviewed by a student,
yet addressed her replies to me.[40]

The perfectly frank interview, of course, is only a myth: our case is
only a more radicalized and transparent case of a general experience, which
makes it methodologically interesting. In fact, as is often the case, while
the awareness of a dimension of power determined silences and self-
consciousness, it also made narrators more reflexive and aware. While
much went unsaid about the student-faculty relationship, interviewees
were also prevented from sliding toward gossip and exclusively personal
grievance. Because they felt it would be safer to speak in general terms,
they had to seek general causes and explanations: the political inequality
between interviewer (explicit or implicit) and interviewees generated
more political responses.

The experience of the student interviewers also taught us, however, that there is no such thing as an "inside" researcher. By taking the role of researcher, in fact, every insider becomes an outsider, or at least a mediator. In this case, they appeared at one level to mediate between the students and me (as "spies"); at another, to mediate between the students and the public, and thus were assimilated to media people, one of the nemeses of a movement obsessed with fears of misrepresentation. At still another level, if I was suspect because I was a not student, they were suspect because they were, and therefore did not have the authority (which was, ironically, accorded to me) to observe their own equals.

On the other hand, they *were* insiders: one of the interesting stratifications in this project was that the "native anthropologists" were in turn being observed by a "stranger," myself, who looked at them as both coworkers and highly qualified informants. In other words, they were precisely the kind of informants against whom—as Dennis Tedlock reminds us—Franz Boas used to warn: smart natives who have their own theories about their society.[41]

I felt, however, that the best solution was to turn this supposed liability into a real asset. After all, in the tribe we were investigating everybody was supposed to be, if not smart, at least literate. Rather than insisting on detachment and objectivity, I suggested, therefore, that the interviewers contribute to the interviews as much of their own input as they wanted. This would, on the one hand, give us more data, drawn from comparing the interviewers' own descriptions of their experiences with those of the interviewees. On the other hand, it helped to ease some of the informants' misgivings about the role of the interviewers, reinstating the actual equality between them. While every interview is a conversation, these were emphatically so.

It's not as if we paid no price for this. Conversations tend to be more fragmentary and less elaborate than formal interviews; much was left unsaid that the interviewers didn't get around to asking because they already knew it (and forgot that what we wanted was not the rough information, but the informants' verbal representation on tape), or simply because so much was shared that neither participant realized that it was problematic. These gaps were filled partly by the sessions in which we discussed the interviews (some of the quotes in this paper are from remarks made by the interviewers in that context), which sent them back to another round of interviews with an increased awareness. For instance, everyone seemed to take the language of the movement for granted; it was only after I raised the question at one of our sessions that, first, the group made some very perceptive remarks on how it had changed during the occupation, and second, they began asking questions about it in the interviews.[42]

The dialogic quality of the project was compounded after we first completed a semifinal draft of the manuscript. It was at that point that we felt the need both to "give back" our work to the student community, and to verify our interpretations with our sources. Therefore, we gave copies of the manuscript to a number of people whose interviews we had used, and called a meeting. It was quite an experience.

Most of those who attended had positive things to say about the manuscript, in terms of the stories it told, but were concerned about its "literary" approach ("It may be a good thing, but it seems to me that the people you interview are more characters in a book than the people that occupied Villa Mirafiori," said Lodovica Mutarelli). What especially seemed to bother them was the fact and nature of our interpretations: "I read it at the beach, in a very lyrical situation, and I liked it very much, especially some [interviews] that were very lyrical, I liked them a lot. But the comments do not seem to connect very well with the interviews. The comments seem somewhat juxtaposed" (Tatiana Petrovich).[43]

Aside from factual misinterpretations that we were able to correct, what intrigued us in this discussion was the paradox whereby these young people—philosophers or literary critics in training, that is, specialists in interpretation—resisted being interpreted themselves. If nothing else, this contradiction reveals that interpretation is always part of a power relationship: to interpret is one thing; to be interpreted is another. As Sebastiano Calleri (a peculiar observer, because he attended the discussion but had not been interviewed before, and therefore saw it with some detachment) pointed out,

> Probably none of the populations that have been studied by
> anthropologists or sociologists would have agreed with more than
> 2 percent of what sociologists, anthropologists, wrote about them,
> which does not mean that there is no evidence to support [those
> writings]. Actually subjectivity in this book is only partially there,
> because what it wants to foreground is a sort of regularity in feelings
> and impressions, which return in all of the interviews. Somehow,
> dissatisfaction with the interpretation is inherent in a collection like
> this one.[44]

The "natives" to which Calleri refers are hardly ever in a position to respond to the anthropologists' interpretations. The inhabitants of Villa Mirafiori, on the other hand, were able to react to the monologic unilateralism of textual and anthropological critical discourse upon them. In this case, the *interpretees* possess the tools to resist and *interpret back* their own interpreters. While both Petrovich and Calleri recognize that the distance between the narrator's self-interpretation and the researcher's analysis is inevitable and almost natural, yet they seemed to resent the fact that interpretation and generalization diminished their individuality by including it in a collective narrative. Though our collective theorized oral history as an art of the individual and a practice of difference, yet our interviewees still felt that we insisted too much on "regularities" and patterns: we had flattened them into exemplarity.

Ultimately, this is a contradiction inherent in the social sciences: two points of view on the same reality, from inside and outside, that are both limited and responsible, neither of which can claim a superior authenticity and authority. One stresses the person's protagonism, individuality, personal motivations, and the other attempts to identify shared cultural traits and place them within the systematic discourse of the group's culture.

This contradiction was highlighted by the discussion of the ruling metaphor of our book, the airplane and the stars. Not only had we liked the story so much that we opened our manuscript with it, but we had found that the metaphor made sense of a whole paradigm of binary oppositions that became our interpretative grid: airplane and stars, fax and panther, pastoral and urban, Europe and Asia, travel and work, and so on. Now the original source begged to disagree:

> *Fabio Ciabatti:* As far as I'm concerned, since the book begins with my quote, I wanted to point out one thing, that is that, by telling that story my intention was only to tell tales of ordinary mental dissolution caused by the occupation, a very early senile madness, and it was only the second day, so you can imagine what the following days must have been. . . . All the interpretation that is given, I don't know, it might be true, but it's not what I was trying to say. . . . I simply wanted to tell a story because I had been asked to tell interesting, particular episodes, and this seemed nice enough simply to show how lucidity all but vanished in certain moments.

Ciabatti does not reject our interpretation outright, but resists the possibility that his narrative may yield more complex and general meanings than those that are "simply" occasional, personal, and explicit.[45] However, his counterinterpretation is itself a cultural act that may be interpreted in turn. Thus, while he claims full control over his utterance by stressing intention, yet he described precisely a breakdown of control

("lucidity all but vanished"). Even in this version, the episode of the airplane and the stars would not be the first occasion in which "senile madness" and loss of "lucidity" allow the emergence of visions, dreams, symbols.[46] Also, Ciabatti insists that, though it describes a general condition,
yet his is an *individual,* idiosyncratic statement, and he resists our effort
to make it "representative" by finding in it the "regularities" of a shared
symbolic pattern. Yet he does so by using a narrative genre shared by many
narratives of youth movements, the heroicomic and autoironic form,[47]
and a familiar quotation ("tales of ordinary mental dissolution") from a
book that was very popular in Italian youth culture, Charles Bukowski's
Tales of Ordinary Madness.[48]

While this does not make our narrator's self- (counter-) interpretation
less cogent and plausible, it confirms his use of shared patterns of discourse even as he tries to deny it. Thus, his response does not erase our
interpretation, but rather shifts it to a different level and function. While
he claims the individual meaning and control that are necessary to everyone's sense of personal subjectivity, we hear in his words the shared cultural meanings and the implications that are beneath explicit awareness
and that make the work of the historian and the cultural critic significant.
The two levels of interpretation, and the counterinterpretations that follow, carry on a conversation with each other in the endless spiral of the
search for a necessary and unattainable meaning.

Chapter Sixteen

The Apple and the Olive Tree
Exiles, Sojourners, and
Tourists in the University

I am fond of writing, or saying, that I am an olive tree, an olive tree torn from
its native ground and planted by force in another.
—Thamer Birawi, Palestinian immigrant, poet[1]

The apple breaks away from the tree, and so does the young man, or the animal
that can fly. At a certain age, one breaks away from one's parents, catches a
plane and goes, all the way to the North Pole. There is a time for breaking away
from the family: a violent impulse, I must go, I don't know where but I must. I
don't want my mother to control me, I don't want my father to control me . . .
—Gifi Fadi, Syrian immigrant, graduate in medicine[2]

My ideal? To travel, what else? To roam about the world freely, contentedly . . .
—Valeria Landolfi, Italian student of foreign languages[3]

One thing I noticed is how travel-oriented Islamic culture is, how much it is
inclined towards traveling, going around, going out . . .
—Omar Nasser Miludi, Italo-Libyan student of foreign languages[4]

AN INTERNATIONAL GROUND

This chapter is a spin off of the project on the oral history of the students
of foreign language departments at the Villa Mirafiori campus of the University of Rome "La Sapienza," begun in the context of the student movement of 1990.[5] Departments of foreign languages and literature are, by
definition, places where people gather to learn about other cultures and

This paper was coauthored with Francesca Battisti. It was published in Rina Benmayor
and Andor Skotnes, eds., *Migration and Identity*, vol. 3 of the *International Yearbook of
Oral History and Life Stories* (Oxford: Oxford University Press, 1994). It is included here,
with minor changes, with my coauthor's consent.

273

forms of expression; they are, therefore, almost natural places to look for signs of a multicultural imagination. Indeed, a central theme highlighted by our research was the students' desire for "otherness," the myth of travel, and cultural and linguistic multiplicity.[6] On the other hand, the university, and foreign language departments in particular, also have a multiethnic and multicultural constituency: they attract both a number of foreign students and of Italian-born students with nationally or ethnically mixed backgrounds, who wish to take advantage of their native knowledge of languages or to keep in touch with their roots. We decided to investigate these groups more deeply and to compare their stories with those of other young, Third World intellectuals and educated migrants, to explore aspects of what we perceived less as a dimension of the international the labor market, than of the multiplicity and fragmentation of subjectivity in the international youth culture.[7] This chapter therefore, is concerned less with patterns of migration than with aspects of subjectivity: point of view and visibility; displacement and estrangement; language and aphasia; memory and synchretism; family, origins, and ambivalence.

In our time, people, especially young people, travel for many reasons. Tourism and exile, violence and choice, the trauma of emigration and the fascination of seeing the world and seeking an identity are often less the terms of a binary opposition than polarities along a continuum. The same individual may identify both with the uprooted olive tree and with the free-floating apple. Thamer Birawi, who describes dramatically the conditions under which he left Palestine, also speaks proudly of his explorations across three continents: "Italy is where I am now, but before coming here I had to take a long detour. I went to Jordan; from Jordan I went to Iraq, then I went back to Syria, to Lebanon, to Egypt. I wanted to know, to feel, to master another world." Another exile, Ribka Sibhatu, left Eritrea "for one thing, to save my life, but what really motivated me was the search for myself." She sums up both motivations under one heading: "freedom."[8]

In this regard, though our migrant interviewees tend to be older than the average student, yet shared generational tensions may be as relevant as national or ethnic differences. Both the exiled Gifi Fadi and the student Caterina Duranti use the same verb—*staccarsi*, "breaking away"—to account for their travels. The desire to "go away, out" that motivates a student to learn foreign languages and to travel abroad may be typical of contemporary, Western, middle-class culture, but it also resembles the "inclination toward going out, going around" that Caterina's classmate Omar Nasser Miludi identifies in his father's Islamic background.[9]

Of course, we cannot ignore the differences. Both Thamer Birawi and the student Chiara Midolo wanted to get away, but while Chiara sought some undefined cultural alternative ("everything I was not, everything Italy was not, everything which my adolescence was not"),[10] Birawi had to get away from the Israeli occupation. The perspective of return also differs: the voluntary traveler goes home at the end of the trip, while exiles and migrants may never be able to return, at least not to their homes as they left them. Indeed, the sheer duration of absence creates a dramatic qualitative difference in experience. Yet the differences stand out more clearly when seen against a background of emotions and desires which are shared or, at least, comparable.

Comparability is heightened by social background. Although all of our foreign interviewees support themselves by what Ribka Sibhatu describes as "the little jobs that suit my color" (she "does for" a lady in exchange for rent; Birawi works in a pub, and Gifi makes a living by teaching Arabic in spite of his medical degree, and so on), yet they come from middle-class families and received a higher education before leaving home. Like the Italian students (and unlike the vast majority of immigrants), their motivations for going abroad were not primarily economic: "When I came here in '69," says Gifi, "Syria and Italy had the same standard of living; my father made good money, so until he died I didn't have to work to support myself here." Omar Miludi, son of a Libyan journalist and a middle-class Italian mother, is very much aware of the cultural and economic difference between himself and the black immigrants:

> A friend told me once, "People can tell you're not an immigrant:[11] you wear dreadlocks, you look good." For the immigrants it's different. All right, I'm colored, but I go to the university, I speak good Italian; if someone says something to me on the bus I can talk back. She told me, they don't look at you the way they look at the immigrant who wipes windshields at the traffic light. People don't see color so much as the image of that person that they think is here up to no good, maybe he's pushing dope, while you're the guy who goes to the university, studies, makes no trouble.

On the other hand, these privileged migrants, exiles, and ethnics interact with the larger immigrant working-class communities and feel involved in their destiny: "It's important to me to see how other colored people are seen" says Miludi. While not representative in statistical terms, they represent a shared subjective horizon of possibilities and desire. They stand for the fact that not all non-European presences in Italy can be summed

up in the stereotypes of the victim or the peddler-beggar-pusher. In admittedly varying degrees, all migrants are bearers of knowledge, and all
struggle to retain a degree of choice and control over their lives. This is
also why this chapter does not attempt to generalize from a broader sample, but focuses on the horizon of possibilities, the meanings and implications of a few significant narratives.[12]

In the continuum between exile and tourism, therefore, roles and out-
looks may overlap and reverse. Student travelers may experience, by choice
or necessity, the condition of the emigrant, while the emigrant may take
on the *persona* of the tourist. "The other day," says Gifi Fadi, "I was stroll-
ing in the Roman Forum, beneath the arch of Septimius Severus, with a
young lady from Asmara [Eritrea]. . . ." In a book of stories and poems,
the "young lady from Asmara," Ribka Sibhatu, writes, "Between myself
and the Rome of the Republic, of Nero, of Saint Peter's, we have established a marriage in chaos. The ruins whisper a mysterious and moving
language to me. . . . Rome has so many eternal tales for the exiles. . . ."[13]
On the other hand, middle-class Italian students may support themselves
abroad by working at immigrant jobs: "I was a dishwasher, I was a waitress, I was a charwoman, I worked as a cook's helper in a fast-food, I was
unemployed, I was drawing social security, I was a squatter—I mean, all
the things that Italians in London do."[14]

Yet, the mixing of roles highlights the different backgrounds and histories. For Gifi and Sibhatu, acting as tourists is a way of holding on to
their originary membership in the educated middle class; for student travelers whose middle-class status is not in question, the "immigrant" experience is part of their strategy of seeking new selves by getting away, albeit temporarily, from their families and countries, and from their classes
as well.

ON THE MARGIN: DIFFERENCE AND DISPLACEMENT

Manuela Bagnetti, a part-Chinese student, told us of the girl who ap-
proached her in the women's rest rooms of the University and told her:
"I've been noticing you. Are you colored, or are you normal?"[15] This introduces a theme that is shared by all of our interviewees: the question of
visibility and vision, seeing and being seen. Italy has not yet grown ac-
customed to the presence of ethnic difference in its midst: "I grew up in
Italy, my mother is Italian, I went to school here," says Omar Miludi; yet,
because he is black, "I'm the one people turn around to look at. After all,
you're not the conventional person people expect to meet. Sometimes I

wonder—if I were to go into a building and ring the wrong bell, how would I feel if I were the person that opens the door and sees me?" Highly visible strangers in their own country, Manuela and Omar are made to feel at times estranged and displaced, as if they were standing "on the parapet, dangling between two worlds," as Lucia Rossi, daughter of returned Italian emigrants to the United States, puts it.[16] As Franco Esposito, who is part-Indonesian, says, "It used to bother me, when they ask me, 'Where are you from?' I'd say I was Italian, and they didn't believe me."[17]

Student travelers also experience displacement and liminality. In their case, however, it results from a voluntary departure from the native context; therefore, rather than feeling exposed to other people's gaze, these intellectual questers (as opposed to conventional mass tourists) turn their own gaze inwards, generating a sort of inner estrangement. "There are three thousand different ways of living and being, and when you're traveling you become aware of this. You can really be other than you normally are, understand?"[18] "For a moment," says Tiziana Petrangeli, "you stand naked, really naked," away from the shelter and safety net of home and family: "It's a way of measuring yourself, because you understand what your limits are."

Since identity and personal growth are the main objects of this type of travel, however, the perception of the new contexts remains often rather conventional: they are seeking less a confrontation with otherness than a discovery of self. Essentially, young travelers seek in the places they visit an alternative to their ordinary experience: "everything I was not, everything Italy was not." Thus, in Germany or Britain they find Western efficiency, modernity, user-friendly universities ("a huge library . . . comfortable armchairs and gardens, clean bathrooms, available teachers, a laundry service"); in the Third World, they discover alternatives to Western competition and consumerism.[19] Paolo Giacomelli sees in Thailand a "kindness" to which "we are completely unaccustomed," and "a strength, a courage which we have all but forgotten, with our running hot water, mom and dad, our clothes washed and ironed in the closet." Lodovica Mutarelli remembers New Caledonia, where she grew up, as a "paradise" of communal solidarity and sharing, inhabited by "truly mild people."[20]

Exiles and migrants, on the other hand, experience both outer and inner estrangement. They are the object of other people's gaze because of their ethnic difference, but they also see themselves in a new light. Most important, the fact that their estrangement is more involuntary and less temporary allows them to view their new environment differently from the local people. "I know Rome very well," says Birawi. "I hate it and love it. I am

an immigrant, I work at night, and I suffer from the cold—I ride my mo-
torbike home each night, to a cold-water flat on a seventh floor; there is
also an inner cold, not physical, but one of the things I dislike about Rome
is the cold, the cold weather." He writes poems about the cold nights of
the migrants in this supposedly warm city:

> In Rome at night the graves open up
> In Rome at night the dead rise
> they walk around
> hands on their heads
> in the rain
> shoeless
> toothless
> without a ticket
> undocumented[21]

Seeing Rome differently may be a way of finding themselves in it. In
his strolls around the Forum, Gifi Fadi identifies a Middle Eastern presence at the very roots of Roman civilization: the word "Arabicus" in the
arch of Septimius Severus, the traces of the "Syrian cult of the sun" and
of "the priests, the singers, the architects of the Syrian school" under emperors Caracalla and Eliogabalus. "Fifty percent of the Italian people have
Syrian blood in their veins: we find Syrians around Tarquinia, toward
Abruzzi, all around Etruria . . . The Roman legend of Romulus and Remus
. . . Romol means sand in Aramaic." Credible or not, this version of Italian origins combines effectively the estranged self-recognition of the traveler and the estranging vision of the migrant and exile, establishing continuity and legitimacy for this Syrian-born Italian citizen.

Indeed, a plurality of modes of perception is the most frequent case,
especially for persons of multiple roots. Omar Nasser Miludi is made to
feel like a stranger in Rome, but when he visits his father, who lives in
Malta, he perceives the difference that his Italian upbringing makes:

> My father keeps Ramadan, has been to Mecca; he prays, and I don't.
> And at times it happened that it was Ramadan when I was down there
> with my father. And you see yourself seated at the table, you eat and he
> does not. It's ironic. It used to be a shock [to visit my father] and find
> Arabic visitors, Libyans or Islamic, or whatever, all squatting on the
> ground eating kouskous, and I didn't speak Arabic, so I couldn't
> speak, I could only say three or four words. Ironic—I was dressed
> different, I had different rituals—I didn't know how to eat kouskous, I
> didn't even know whether I liked it or not. And my father introduced
> me, saying, "This is my son, who has been living in Italy."

"I feel completely Chinese," says Manuela Bagnetti—and five minutes later she speaks of "us Italians." According to where she is, in Italy or China, she shifts to an outsider's position. Thus, the tea-taking scenes in Henry James's *Portrait of a Lady* remind her of "the darkest period of China . . . because tea is a reminder of the colonial period" of which she heard in her mother's stories. On the other hand, while she fears that the tourist may replace the colonizer, and is proud of riding the trains with the Chinese rather than in the compartments reserved to foreigners, she inevitably shares the traveler's way of looking at people and landscapes through the glass of a train window, a camera eye, a nostalgic imagination: "I took so many pictures. . . . And then this land, cultivated inch by inch . . . it's a very rich land, with the river flowing by. . . . The adults, there, live together with the children; the houses are made of one big room." Again, her image of China includes a projection of a desired alternative to her ordinary, Italian environment: the commune she visited "seemed truly an ideal community because the people work and share what they raise, equally—it's not like here, where everything is calculated, a race to see who is, or has, more. . . . There, you see all that we don't have in Italy."

Franco Esposito goes back to Indonesia ("the place of my mythic childhood") in a disappointing search for the "exotic" part of himself: "You come from Europe, and Indonesia, which happens to be a part of me, appears to you through exotic eyes—this terrible thing of every European who goes to these places and thinks he's God because he has money, and is looking for these [exotic] things and is disappointed because they are no longer to be found. He finds color TV, he finds parmesan cheese, all the comforts." It's a good thing, he says, because "people are no longer starving"; yet when he reclaims his status as a native, he finds that he has become a tourist:

> It's not even the color of your skin, it's the way you act that identifies you. People can tell right away who is a tourist. Last summer, my girlfriend and I—she is Italian—and other friends went back down to Indonesia and we were walking along the beach, and these children who peddle things spoke to me in Italian! I got mad, and I asked them, "Don't you see that I am like you, that I am Indonesian?" He looked at me and said, "No, I don't."

LANGUAGUE AND SUPERLANGUAGE

Manuela Bagnetti: When we were small, we lived for ten years in Switzerland, with my mother. We returned to Italy around 1979–80, and my brother had a language problem, because in Switzerland we spoke French or English, also at home, with my mother, and my father now wanted my brother to speak Italian right away, immediately, and for a year and a half he did not speak at all. My father thought French was a secret language between us.

The reconstruction and creation of identity finds in language, and in culture in general, a crucial battleground, especially in the case of young people who make the study of languages their specific avocation. Manuela Bagnetti refers to studies and stories of aphasia, such as Roman Jokobson, Maxine Hong Kingston's *The Woman Warrior*, N. S. Momaday's *House Made of Dawn*:

> My brother's inability to express himself reminded me of Abel in the Los Angeles ghetto. . . . Momaday explained that Abel's problem is that he is a man without a voice. For us Italians, language is just a way of communicating, while for blacks or Indians in America there is more attention to language at the stage of birth—dialect is the stage of birth—and then the study of aphasia is language in dissolution, and this applies to every language.

What she is dealing with is the linguistic consequences of displacement: aphasia on the one hand, and internal Babel on the other; too many languages, or no language at all. The multiplicity of languages is primarily a symptom of possibility: "Languages fascinated me as a different way of communicating, as formal instrument, a sort of mask, you know. I mean, let's see, if I played the part of an English person, what would the result be?" (Caterina Duranti). This sense of possibility, however, is rooted in the fact that their membership in their native linguistic community is never threatened or questioned. For migrants and exiles, foreign languages are a matter of necessity as much as choice; holding on to their native language becomes a matter of protecting and preserving their innermost identity. "My diaries and my poems," says Sibhatu, "I often write them half in Italian and [half] in Tigrinya. It depends: when I think of my mother, my words flow in Tigrinya." The tie of language and roots takes a different twist in the case of Italians of mixed descent. Omar Miludi had to study Arabic in order to speak with his father, and Manuela Bagnetti is studying Mandarin with her mother. Learning a foreign language becomes a search for a part of one's roots.

Migrants and exiles exhibit their mastery of languages as evidence that they are educated and world-wise: "I think I have a very great advantage, in that when I want to write in Arabic I write in Arabic, when I want to write in English I write in English, or in Italian, and I can find the right ways and words. Languages are almost like clothes, when you feel you have mastered something, you use it instinctively," says Birawi. Like Sibhatu, he takes pride in his virtually accentless Italian; in fact, most contemporary immigrant writing stresses mastery of the host language rather than linguistic syncretism (when I detected some slight errors in Sibhatu's prose, I suggested she let them be as a reminder of her identity, but she insisted on correcting them). Linguistic signs of otherness must be sought, rather, in certain metaphors drawn from a pre-urban, village paradigm, especially for Gifi and Birawi: language as "a garden" or "clothes"; identity as apple, olive tree, "fruit," bread (the Israeli occupation as "the oven which matured my generation").

Franco Esposito gives a vivid description of multilingualism as possibility: "In my house we speak a very strange language, a sort of patois. I speak to my sister in Indonesian, English, and Italian. I say the things that come to my mind in the language which has the more appropriate words." For instance, he refers to hard cheeses in Italian and to soft ones in Indonesian, because "cheese is always soft in the Orient." On the other hand, he remembers his father speaking Neapolitan dialect at the dinner table, and says—*in English,* "He reared me up as an Italian." The use of English to describe an Italian upbringing in a part-Indonesian family reveals a fracture at the root of his linguistic identity. In fact, the price for polyglotism can be the nostalgia for a truly satisfying language of one's own, or the utopia of a higher synthesis:

> Q: What language do you think in?
> *Gifi:* Right now, in Italian; when I must think of something I
>   studied in English, I think in English.
> Q: What about feelings?
> *Gifi:* More often in Italian. In Arabic, only the children's tales I
>   studied in Arabic: Aladdin and the flying carpet. . . . Years ago,
>   I wrote books both in Italian and in Arabic, and it was a waste
>   of energy, because I am not satisfied with languages as they are
>   spoken today. There will have to be a superlanguage, one
>   which conveys most information with least energy.

A similar process concerns another deep layer of identity: religion. Being exposed to more than one religion, in a context of displacement, can result in having none: "My father was a nonbelieving Moslem, who lived in a Christian neighborhood. Really, after studying everything, I can no longer believe in any religion, because they are all the same" (Gifi). As is to be expected from intellectuals in an intellectual environment, the place of religion is filled often by culture. Knowledge is often presented as an antidote to racism: "I had a hard time, in the beginning, until I understood that racism is ignorance. Yes, studying helped me through many of the difficulties that a foreigner faces" (Sibhatu).

Thus, all describe the university as a friendlier environment, where "there is less ignorance, or at least, there should be; there is more information, much more politics" (Miludi). Ribka Sibhatu writes,

> The University adopted me. My teachers are my parents, and the students my sisters and brothers. When I first started going to classes, I couldn't understand what was said, and Daniela happened to sit next to me. One day, when the professor began to talk about Joyce's *Ulysses*, I asked her, "Who are Penelope, Thelemacus. . . ?" She was agape, but she explained it. . . . Later, she corrected my history paper six times, and she even gave me money for books, trying not to hurt my feelings, when I had to stop doing "the little jobs that suit my color."

Sibhatu describes "self-knowledge" as the most important aspect of both her travels and her studies, and compares her exile with literary precedents: "It's easy to talk about exile and silence, as Joyce does. But talking about it, and living it, are two different things." Likewise, Omar Miludi reconstructs his identity through the study of history and literature, drawing especially on Malcolm X's presentation of African history: "Culture has been a great help to me. First of all, it has helped me claim what it means historically to be black. A few years back, if someone had asked me how come I am in Italy, I would have answered it was because my father married my mother. It is still the main reason, but now I know there's more than that."

If racism is identified as ignorance, culture becomes a weapon. "I study anthropology for self-defense" says Gifi, and he means it literally. His anthropology is of the nineteenth-century positivistic type, not exempt from risks of anti-Jewish prejudice ("international Zionism will win in the end, because it holds the world economy in its hands . . ."). But it also helps to make knowledge and language parts of a strategy of physical survival:

> Once I was stopped by Nazi skinheads, the Fascist youth movement, near the Colosseum: "Foreigner," they said, *"quo vadis?"* ["where are you going?"]. And they were doing the Fascist Roman salute. So I told them, I may be more Roman than you are: look at the Colosseum, it was celebrated by an emperor named Philip the Arab; I have an Italian last name, and if you want to know, it was the Syrians that built up

Rome. They wanted to invite me to dinner that day, I didn't go, but I gave them a lot of information they didn't have. There are three emperors of Syrian descent; I learned that for reasons of self-defense, of survival.

SYNCRETISMS

"I come from a family that has two different views of the world. My father was more linked to his culture, more attached to the land; my mother, she said, 'The world is changing; it is a world of education, not land.'" Cultural syncretism has always been part of Ribka Sibhatu's environment, as a consequence of Italian colonialism in her native country, but it is also a part of the experience of all the interviewees. We will see in the following paragraphs how it is perceived as a source of both empowerment and fragmentation.

Sibhatu makes a determined effort to recover and preserve her grandfather's mythical stories ("He said that the West would be the origin of the loss of man. Mankind will get lost on its way to the West"), yet she received from her grandmother a more practical example of how to deal with colonialism, in terms of selective appropriation, economic gain, cultural mediation, and a sense of historical rather than mythical time:

> During Italian colonization, in '35, she was the first to learn the language. She was an orphan, so she had to make her own way, and she had the most contacts with Italians. I mean, normally Italians were seen as devilish sorts of creatures; the very fact of being easily angered was typical. Among us, when one is angry, one does not show it; one checks oneself. Our grandmother, however, had no choice if she were to survive. So she worked as a babysitter. Later she became an interpreter; she was twice here in Mussolini's residence, to interpret. So they had discussions between them, and she supported colonization—she had a great deal of money; my grandparents were well off. After all [she said], sooner or later they will have to go away, they shall not live here forever. One day we shall have our independence. Meanwhile, until we are free, let us take what they know.

Mussolini's residence where her grandmother worked as interpreter is two blocks away from the Villa Mirafiori campus where Sibhatu is now studying foreign languages. So when she came to Italy, she was not a total stranger: Italians had invaded her country, and now she is traveling to theirs, bringing back some of their impact on her homeland. This syn-

cretism has deep historical roots in Africa and the Mediterranean: as Gifi
Fadi says, "I'm not the first Syrian who comes to Italy. Migrations didn't
begin yesterday." And they went in more than one direction: after all, Italy
is historically a country of emigrants.

> *Marinella Bucetti:* I was born in Cairo, Egypt, from Italian parents,
> children themselves of Italian parents who had moved there to work.
> My grandparents were from Messina [in Sicily], and after the [1908]
> earthquake they settled in Egypt to stay. They had been there
> temporarily before. Since the beginning of the century, there is this
> flux of emigration toward everywhere. I have relatives scattered all
> over the world. I have relatives in Egypt, I have relatives in Lebanon,
> relatives in South Africa, Yemen, people who speak Italian, French,
> English, and Arabic. If Nasser had not chased all us foreigners out of
> the country in '66 we would have stayed in Egypt.[22]

This history of multidirectional migrations, ethnic mixing, and cultural
syncretism allows Gifi Fadi to claim Italian roots for his family just as he
claims a Syrian presence at the roots of Italian civilization: "I bear an Italian surname, Giffi—half the people in Abruzzi bear this name. In Arabic,
the double consonant falls. These unusual surnames in Syria always intrigued me: like Morelli, which I find both in my hometown and here."
On this basis, he imagines a story of Abruzzi fishermen landing on the
Syrian coast a century and a half ago, and concludes: "My family was
Italian, Gifi, back in 1830, my great-grandfather was Christian, then my
grandfather was Moslem. . . ."

In most interviews, ethnic and cultural syncretism is described as a source
of strength. Gifi, again, takes it very literally: "My father used to say, the
more you mix the stronger you become; all the ancient peoples who were
unable to mix grew weaker and died." Omar Miludi insists on the possibility for self-creation that derives from combining in an individual way
the different pieces of his multiple identity, adopting the black images of
the Jamaican Rastafarian and the American blues singer—though, perhaps, more through Italian youth culture than through his African origins. He thus turns the enforced visibility and marginality of his otherness into an empowering vision of his unique self:

> From this point of view, I am glad, sincerely glad that I am black. I am
> pleased with my experiences, with what it has brought to me. I mean,
> if I had lived my life in Africa among so many other blacks, I could
> not have appreciated it, I would not have been as glad as I am now.
> Because on certain things you always have to choose, you must always

choose something which is much more personal, which others do not share. So you can create a strong identity. If this identity also contains insecurity, it's not important. What counts is that it also contains something strong within you; you are strong inside.

The postmodern sense of fragmentation as possibility, however, combines in these stories with a sense of fragmentation as the result of violence. "When you have a cultural identity that has been shattered," says Marinella Bucetti, "it's harder to know what you are." Thus, Miludi concludes the discussion of his multiple and open self with a recognition of the historical paradox on which it is based:

> It makes me kind of sad—everybody says, "How nice, a black boy who speaks with a Rome accent." I used to like it; now I don't like it so much. Because after all, a black who speaks Roman, I see it simply as something that has been violated. Not negatively, or positively, either. A course which has been changed.

MEMORY AND LOSS

> *Thamer Birawi:* Yes, I'm talking about '66, the six days war, the six years, the six centuries, I don't know. That event was the oven which matured a generation which is mine, which throughout Palestine had almost the same influences, the same handicaps, the same broken dreams, that is, of going home one day to sleep on that pillow, in that corner—forget what happens in the world, whether I have accomplished anything in life or not. . . . In a way, we are still anchored, we are still bound, something in us has been broken.

This final section is concerned with the memory of the cultural and physical violence and loss, personal and historical, which is implicit in the histories of exile and migration, but also, as Miludi reminds us, in the roots of mixed ethnicity. We will also look at the ways in which the narrators deal with this memory and turn it into a source of strength and identity through the use of imagination and symbolism. Let us start with the most dramatic story, that of Ribka Sibhatu:

> I was sixteen when I was arrested. Just because an officer was courting me, and I didn't want him. He accused me; he said that I was in touch with the guerrillas. I didn't know anything about these guerrillas. So, the first thing—torture. They cover your eyes, tie your arms around your back, I don't know what they did to me, but torture is the first thing; my back still aches. Actually I was lucky, because I was only

tortured twice. I think that the foremost torture for someone who is in
prison is psychological: facing death. There is no trial, so every night,
each time we heard those feet coming, we thought they were coming
to take. . . . Every day life is in danger, in tension, because they take
you one by one. So when we hear the handcuffs and the feet—"It's
my turn." And at night, it's not our cellmate we're afraid for, it's
ourselves. It's the next day that we weep for the girl who was taken.

In a poem, Sibhatu evokes her friend, Abeba, who was killed in jail. She
explained that the dots between two verses represented both the silence
of absence, and the shape of the bullets that killed her. But we might also
read them as a metaphor of what was broken within herself:

> For the world to understand,
> while they were digging her grave,
> wrapped in the mystery of death,
> I weave an *aghelghl*
> and send it without *hmbascia.*
>
> In an intense night
> they took her from me in handcuffs!
> . . . .
> Each day she is absence,
> but in the dark she is omnipresent![23]

Cultural memory, concentrated in powerful symbols, is the only way
to overcome the trauma. This is the function of the *aghelghl* and the
hmbascia (a palm leaf basket and the ritual bread it usually contains) in
Sibhatu's poem. Birawi's story of the Israeli occupation of his native village also focuses on three symbols: the mother, the loss of vision and
meaning, and the physical destruction of the land:

Of that day, I remember only my mother. And I remember that she
was nervous; she kept coming and going around the house, looking in
all directions. And then she goes out into the garden and begins to
look down a road, the only paved one, that came in from the village's
north gate. She wasn't saying anything, but I knew something big was
happening. We couldn't open the door, but there was a hole in it, and
I used to kneel at the hole and look outside; that day I went, out of
curiosity, and saw military machines, armed men. The village was
dead, no one around, a heavy air. I saw these cars come and turn and
go. Then we went out to see the signs of this visit, this change, this
event. The first thing that struck me—as children, we used to play
beside the street, or in the street itself. And when I went out on the

street, it was all ground up. I saw the street ground up, where we used
to play, because the tanks had torn it with their wheels.

The earth torn by the tanks is a powerful metaphor for the loss of homeland. Exiles and migrants, as opposed to tourists, know that the home
they left will not be waiting for their return: "I used to miss my village,"
says Gifi. "I went back twice, and the village I used to miss is gone. My
world is dead. It was painful, and later on I was afraid to go back." "We
went back to Egypt ten years ago, and Egypt was completely changed,"
says Marinella Bucetti. This makes for a different shape of memory: travelers remember being abroad, migrants and exiles remember being home.
Ultimately, it is always a memory of absence, of where one is not: "In a
way, I have never left, though I am away from the place where I was born,"
says Birawi. "Nablus is a town I love very much also because I am far
away from that town."

The loss of home is also cultural loss: the violence of history silences
the transmission of culture. Awaiting the invasion, Birawi's mother looks
in all directions, but does not speak; afterwards, "Even the adults could
not explain what was happening." It is up to the younger generations both
to make sense of these events and to attempt to preserve—through memory, writing, storytelling—what is left of the culture of their ancestors.
"We had to learn by ourselves that there was an occupation, that there
was an army, that this army was our enemy; we had to see the dreadful
fear in the eyes of our neighbors, of our brothers and our parents. Our first
battle was a battle against the fear of what had happened, to get rid of this
fear, and recognize this reality, understand it, and finally control it."

Ribka Sibhatu says that she is studying African literature in Rome "in
order to keep my grasp on this ephemeral culture which is being lost with
all its wise men." While Sibhatu holds on to her oral tradition, Gifi gives
preference to book learning and written culture ("I was born 16 kilometers from Ugarit, which is where the alphabet was born"). Writing is rooted
in absence and loss: Sibhatu sees her work as a writer as an alternative to
participation in the liberation struggle ("I mean, I cannot go back, because now I want to write books. And those books will be censored. So,
how can I go back? Maybe I ought to fight, but I don't know, I don't believe that my struggling would be of much [use]. It is more useful to write
it").[24] Birawi writes hundreds of letters and has sent his first writings home
for a friend to keep until he returns. His poems turn obsessively on a
word—"without"—and on a symbol, the moon, which is both an image
of the cold nights of Rome, and the memory of a lost, powerful emblem

of Arabic and Moslem culture: "The moon in Rome is no moon," for those who are "on the sidewalk" and "outside the walls without clothes without fear."[25] These writings of absence, in Italian by foreigners, are the contribution of these intellectual migrants and exiles to the creation of a multicultural literature in Italy.

The theme of loss is implicit in the effort to recover historical and family origins. Manuela Bagnetti begins as follows:

> My mother's mother was half French [and half Italian]. At eighteen,
> she left everything, because she had fallen in love with this Chinese
> soldier who had come to the Mediterranean to learn the art of war.
> He went to military school in Turin. Then he met my grandmother
> and they left, without marrying. He took her to China where he had
> his concubines; then he left her there alone and went to war.

These stories, however, also include the awareness of the irretrievable distance that now separates them from these origins. While young tourists and students travel temporarily away from their families, exiles, migrants, and "ethnics" travel back and forth between the memory and nostalgia of the olive tree, and the desire for selfhood and difference of the apple detached from the branch.

Often, this dual attitude is expressed by references to the mother as a signifier of "descent," as opposed to the father as a token of difference, change, choice, and "consent."[26] Omar Miludi muses, "My father is dark; he is darker than me. Between my father and me there has always been this thing, that after all I am whiter than him; or perhaps he is blacker than me." Franco Esposito describes an emblematic scene: "All the family at the table, with my father at the head, almost as the white patriarch. . . ." It is not a matter of color, since both the Indonesian and the southern Italian extended families are patriarchal, "but with the eyes of memory [he sees] this family scene, this terrible connotation" of the racial, colonial difference between his colored self and his beloved, white, father.[27]

On the other hand, Ribka Sibhatu evokes her mother as the focus of her wish to return, the subject and addressee of her writing. And Thamer Birawi sums up the ambivalence that is the basic undercurrent in all these stories, in a deeply touching final scene:

> The very morning I left home, I say goodbye to everyone, and then I
> say, "Mother?" No one can tell me where she is. The taxi was waiting,
> so I go into the house, I look in the room—we had a single room—she
> isn't there. Where can she be? Then I think of the orchard, the same

orchard where she stood beside me when the Israelis came, and I say, "What's the matter?" "Why, are you really leaving?" She seemed like a historic hero trying to destroy a whole story. In a word, she says, "Are you really leaving?" And so I left, with these words of hers that still ring in my mind and in my life, "But are you really leaving?"

Notes
Index

Notes

INTRODUCTION

1. Ian McEwan, *Black Dogs* (London: Picador, 1992), pp. 164–65.

2. Edoardo Succhielli, interview quoted in Giovanni Contini, "La memoria divisa: Osservazioni sulle due memorie della strage del 29 giugno 1944 a Civitella Val di Chiana," paper presented at the international conference "In Memory: For a European Memory of Nazi Crimes after the End of the Cold War," Arezzo, June 22–24, 1994. See also "The Massacre at Civitella Val di Chiana (Tuscany, June 29, 1944): Myth and Politics, Mourning and Common Sense," chapter 10 in this book.

3. Richard Slotkin, "Introduction," in James Fenimore Cooper, *The Last of the Mohicans* (New York: Penguin, 1986), p. xi.

4. Alistair Thomson, *Anzac Memories: Living with the Legend* (Melbourne: Oxford University Press, 1994), p. 1.

5. Alessio Trevisani, quoted in M. Arcidiacono et al., *L'aeroplano e le stelle. Storia orale di una realtà studentesca prima e dopo la Pantera* (Rome: Manifestolibri, 1995), p. 196.

6. Alessandro Portelli, *The Death of Luigi Trastulli and Other Stories: Form and Meaning in Oral History* (Albany, N.Y.: State University of New York Press, 1991).

7. Gianni Bosio, "I canti della Prima Internazionale in Italia. Prime ricerche e chiarimenti sulle fonti scritte. Lettera aperta a Roberto Leydi," in *L'intellettuale rovesciato* (1965; Milan: Edizioni Bella Ciao, 1975), p. 89: "The activity of [certain] researchers is exclusively addressed to field collecting; each recording is therefore a *hermetic discovery*," lacking context, background, and interpretation.

8. Alistair Thomson, "The Memory and History Debates: Some International Perspectives," *Oral History* (Autumn 1994), pp. 33–35; Paul Thompson, letter to the editors, *Oral History* (Autumn 1985), pp. 27–29. Luisa Passerini also confirms this vision: "At the international oral history conference at the University of Essex in 1979 . . . the theme of memory had been introduced, significantly, by the Italian contributions. But it was only the following year, at Amsterdam, that a real discussion developed concerning the relationship of memory and forgetting, narrative and silences. Until then, in fact, the factual approach of British oral history, that sought primarily the contents of memory and merely claimed it as a legitimate source along with traditional ones, had prevailed." See "Il dibattito ra-

diofonico come fonte," in *Storia e soggettività. Le fonti orali, la memoria* (Florence: La Nuova Italia, 1985), p. 167. At Amsterdam, it was Luisa Passerini's opening paper that introduced the discussion on memory. For some of the Italian contributions on memory at the Essex conference, see Paul Thompson, ed., *Our Common History: The Transformation of Europe* (London: Pluto Press, 1982).

9. Pietro Clemente, "Debate sobre las fuentes orales en Italia," *História y fuente oral* 14 (1995), pp. 81–94.

10. To my surprise, *L'aeroplano e le stelle* was used a textbook for the sociology course at the university of Salerno in 1995–96, together with Giovanni Contini and Alfredo Martini's introductory handbook to oral history, *Verba manent. L'uso delle fonti orali per la storia contemporanea* (Rome: La Nuova Italia Scientifica, 1993). It is the only case of which I am aware.

CHAPTER 1. ORAL HISTORY AS GENRE

1. This essay is based on a paper presented at the international workshop, "Methodology and Methods of Oral History and Life Stories in Social Research," L'viv, Ukraine, September 5–7, 1994.

2. Elizabeth Tonkin, *Narrating Our Pasts: The Social Construction of Oral History* (Cambridge, U.K.: Cambridge University Press, 1992). Among the papers presented at the L'viv conference, this approach is brilliantly illustrated in Hana Hlosková's "Oral History and Folklore Studies," which classifies oral history, within the system of oral literature, as a type of "legend narrative," based on the belief in the veracity of the narrative.

3. Mikhail Bakhtin, "Discourse in the Novel," in *The Dialogic Imagination* (Austin: University of Texas Press, 1984), pp. 259–422; Eva McMahan and Kim Lacy Rogers, *Interactive Oral History Interviewing* (Hillsdale, N.J.: Lawrence Erlbaum Associates, 1994).

4. Excerpts from this interview are included in "Absolutely Nothing: Wartime Refugees," chapter 8 in this book.

5. See my *"Absalom, Absalom!:* Oral History and Literature," in *The Death of Luigi Transtulli: Form and Meaning in Oral History* (Albany, N.Y.: State University of New York Press, 1991), pp. 270–72.

6. I use *text* here to indicate the words that make up the discourse. Strictly speaking, of course, there is no such thing as an oral text; see Walter J. Ong, *Orality and Literacy: The Technologizing of the Word* (London and New York: Methuen, 1982), p. 13; and *"Maranatha:* Death and Life in the Text of the Book," in *Interfaces of the Word* (Ithaca and London: Cornell University Press, 1977), pp. 230–71.

7. I borrow this expression from Albert Lord, *The Singer of Tales* (Cambridge, Mass.: Harvard University Press, 1960), who uses it to describe the work of oral epic poets. In less formalized terms, it applies to all unrehearsed forms of discourse. On incremental repetition, see Gordon Hall Gerould, *The Ballad of Tradition* (1932; repr. New York: Oxford University press, 1957), pp. 105–10.

8. Jean-Marie Schaeffer, *Qu'est-ce qu'un genre littéraire?* (Paris: Seuil, 1982); I am quoting from the Italian translation, *Che cos'è un genere letterario?* (Parma: Pratiche, 1992), p. 73, trans. Ida Zaffagnini. Both in the French original and in the translation, the sentence quoted here is in English.

9. See "There's Gonna Always Be a Line: History-Telling as a Multivocal Art," chapter 2 in this book.

10. See Portelli, *"Absalom, Absalom!*: Oral History and Literature."

11. Eugenia Meyer, Elena Poniatowska, and Eva Salgado Andrade, "Documenting the Earthquake of 1985 in Mexico City," *The Oral History Review* 16, no. 1 (Spring 1988), pp. 1–31. A number of papers presented at the L'viv conference exemplify this approach in their very titles: e.g., Katia Foteeva, "Well-to-Do Families Meet the Challenge of Revolution"; Daniel Bertaux, "From Families' Case Histories to the Understanding of Social-Historical Processes."

12. This is not to belittle the work of elite oral historians, but rather to point out that, as oral historians, they are after the distinctive individual personality of their narrators as well as their public role. For a discussion based on elite oral history projects at the CPDOC (Documentation Center) of the Fundaçao Getulio Vargas in Rio de Janeiro, see Marieta de Moraes Ferriera et al., *Entre-vistas: abordagens e usos da história oral* (Rio de Janeiro: Fundaçao Getulio Vargas, 1994).

13. Published in 1881, rev., 1891; repr., New York: Collier's, 1962.

14. Some examples of this motif appear in *The Death of Luigi Trastulli*, pp. 102–3, 134–35.

15. Antonio Gibelli, "Per una storia dell'esperienza di guerra dei contadini," in *La cultura delle classi subalterne fra tradizione e innovazione*, proceedings of the conference on "Subaltern Cultures between Innovation and Tradition," Alessandria, May 14–16, 1985 (Alessandria: Edizioni dell'Orso, 1988), pp. 85–102.

16. Irene Guidarelli, born in 1896, interviewed in Terni, July 16, 1980; quoted in A. Portelli, *Biografia di una città. Storia e racconto: Terni 1830–1985* (Turin: Einaudi, 1985), p. 247.

17. Eric Leed, *No Man's Land: Combat and Identity in World War I* (Cambridge, U.K.: Cambridge University Press, 1979); Paul Fussell, *The Great War and Modern Memory* (Oxford: Oxford University Press, 1975); Nuto Revelli, *La guerra dei poveri* (Turin: Einaudi, 1962); Alistair Thomson, *Anzac Memories: Living with the Legend* (Melbourne: Oxford University Press, 1994); Gabriele Rosenthal, "Narración y significado biográfico de las experiencias de guerra," *História y fuente oral* 4 (1990), pp. 119–28; John Limon, *Writing after War: American War Fiction from Realism to Postmodernism* (New York: Oxford University Press, 1994).

18. Prue Chamberlaine and Annette King, "Carers' Narratives as Genre: An East-West German Comparison," submitted for the unpublished vol. 5 of the *International Yearbook of Oral History and Life Stories*. Kristine Popova and Peter

Vodenicharov's "The Stories of Death in the Stories of Life: Corporality and Individuality in the Narratives of Bulgarian Moslems," presented at the L'viv conference, shows in fascinating detail the continuity between war and hospital stories in the narrative of one (male) informant.

19. Giuseppina Migliosi, b. 1900, interviewed in Terni, October 17, 1980;
Debbie Spicer, b. 1907, interviewed in Blackbottom, Harlan County, Ky., October 10, 1988.

20. Even in this chapter, I have always used the term *speaker* to refer to the
interviewee, not the interviewer. See Ronald J. Grele, "History and the Languages
of History in the Oral History Interview: Who Answers Whose Questions and
Why?" in McMahan and Rogers, eds., *Interactive Oral History Interviewing* pp.
1–17, and his afterword, ibid., pp. 163–64. On interviewing and fieldwork, see
also Elliot G. Mishler, *Research Interviewing: Context and Narrative* (Cambridge, Mass.: Harvard University Press, 1993); Bruce Jackson, *Fieldwork* (Urbana: University of Illinois Press, 1987), pp. 79–101; Sidney W. Mintz, "The Sen-
sation of Moving While Standing Still," *American Ethnologist* 16, 4 (November
1989), pp. 786–96; Kathryn Anderson and Dana C. Jack, "Learning to Listen: Interview Techniques and Analyses," in Sherna Berger Gluck and Daphne Patai,
eds., *Women's Words: The Feminist Practice of Oral History* (New York: Routledge 1991) pp. 11–26.

21. Michael Palmer et al., "'I Haven't Anything to Say': Reflections of Self
and Community in Collecting Oral Histories," in Ronald J. Grele, ed., *International Annual of Oral History 1990* (New York: Greenwood, 1990), pp.
167–90.

22. The distinction between self-authorization and authorization from others
is especially important in the genre of slave narratives, some of which are taken
down by white editors while others are written directly by the ex-slaves themselves. See John W. Blassingame, "Using the Testimony of Ex-Slaves: Approaches
and Problems," and Robert B. Stepto, "I Rose and Found My Voice: Narration,
Authentication, and Authorial Control in Four Slave Narratives," both in Charles
T. Davis and Henry Louis Gates, Jr., eds., *The Slaves' Narrative* (Oxford: Oxford
University Press, 1985), pp. 78–98 and 225–242.

23. Mary Jones, *The Autobiography of Mother Jones* (Chicago: Charles H.
Kerr, 1972); Riziero Manconi, b. 1984, Terni, July 7, 1980.

24. "[The interviewer] spoke only once or twice while she talked. Margaret
Jones didn't need him, care for him. She was permitting him to overhear what she
told the machine": John Wideman, *Philadelphia Fire* (1990; repr. London: Picador, 1995), p. 9.

25. Maggiorina Mattioli's narrative technique is discussed in Portelli, *"Absalom, Absalom!: Oral History and Literature."*

26. Most projects, of course, use intermediate techniques, or both. See Dean
Hommer and Aaron Wildavsky, "La entrevista semi-estructurada de final
abierto. Aproximación a una guía operativa," *História y fuente oral* 4 (1990),

pp. 23–77; William Cutler III, "Accuracy in Oral History Interviewing," in David K. Dunaway and Willia K. Baum, eds., *Oral History: An Interdisciplinary Anthology* (Nashville, Tenn.: American Association for State and Local History, 1984), pp. 79–106.

27. Dennis Tedlock, "The Analogical Tradition and the Emergence of a Dialogical Anthropology," in *The Spoken Word and the Work of Interpretation* (Philadelphia: University of Pennsylvania Press, 1983), p. 334.

28. Annamaria Di Marco, b. 1964, int. Rome, July 16, 1992. See chapter 5 in this book, "Deep Exchange: Roles and Gazes in Multivocal and Multilateral Interviewing."

29. See "Research as an Experiment in Equality," in Portelli, *The Death of Luigi Trastulli*, pp. 29–44.

30. Zora Neale Hurston, *Mules and Men: Negro Folklore and Voodoo Practices in the South* (1935; repr. New York and Evanston: Harper & Row, 1970), p. 24.

31. A classic of the form, of course, is *The Autobiography of Malcolm X*, written by Alex Haley. In most cases, the actual writers tend to be journalists (paid for the task), rather than historians; professional attitudes and power relationships play an important role in shaping the genre.

32. In fact, the main difference was that, though he repeated his mythic version of the death of Luigi Trastulli (see "The Death of Luigi Trastulli: Memory and the Event" in Portelli, *The Death of Luigi Trastulli*, pp. 1–36), he was now aware through contact with me that it was factually "wrong."

33. See Joel Gardner, "Oral History and Video in Theory and Practice," *The Oral History Review* 12 (1984), pp. 105–11; Silvia Paggi, "A propósito de la entrevista filmada en la investigación antropológica," *História y fuente oral* 12 (1994), pp. 163–71; Giovanni Contini and Alfredo Martini, *Verba Manent. L'uso delle fonti orali per la storia contemporanea* (Rome: La Nuova Italia Scientifica, 1993), pp. 23–27.

34. There is a justifiable reason for this: the *linguistic* aspect of the interview is usually perceived to pertain more directly to the linguistic and verbal behaviour of the speakers, rather than to the visual and gestural exchange; also, appearing in video tends to be perceived as a more narcissistic act on the part of the interviewer than reporting the questions in a paper. Whether these perceptions are correct is another question.

35. These remarks also apply to various aspects of aural media; in fact, they are in part derived fom my experience in documentary records and radio broadcasts. I skip here the discussion of another visual means of presentation, photography. Michael Frisch discusses "the picture book genre" in "Get the Picture? A Review Essay," in *A Shared Authority: Essays on the Craft and Meaning of Oral and Public History* (Albany, N.Y.: State University of New York Press, 1990), p. 203–14. He also contributes to a splendid example of the genre, *Portraits in Steel*, photographs by Milton Rogovin, interviews by Michael Frisch (Ithaca and

London: Cornell University Press, 1993). Both Frisch and Rogovin, and Judith Modell and Charlee Brodsky, "Envisioning Homestead: Using Photographs in Interviewing (Homestead, Pennsylvania)," in McMahan and Rogers, eds., *Interactive Oral History Interviewing,* exemplify the use of photographs as a technique for generating memories and narratives in interviewing.

On multimedia and radio, see Charles Hardy III, "Aural History and the Digital Revolution," unpublished manuscript, July 1996; on video, Pamela H. Henson and Terri Schorzman, "Videohistory: Focusing on the American Past," *The Journal of American History* (September 1991), pp. 618–27; on museums, John Kuo Wei Tchen, "Creating a Dialogic Museum: The Chinatown History Museum Experience" in Ivan Kemp, Christine Mulleer Kreamer, and Steven D. Lavine, eds., *Museums and Communities: The Politics of Public Culture* (Washington D.C.: Smithsonian Institution Press, 1992), pp. 285–326.

36. Paula Rabinowitz, "Introduction," to *They Must be Represented: The Politics of Documentary* (London: Verso, 1994), p. 12.

37. Not, however, by "microhistorians" themselves. Although some influential oral history work was published in the Microstorie series of which he was general editor, Carlo Ginzburg omits all mention of oral history from a recent review essay and methodological discussion of microhistory: "Microstoria: due o tre cose che so di lei," *Quaderni storici* 86, no. 2 (August 1994), 511–39.

38. Theodore Rosengarten, *All God's Dangers: The Life of Nate Shaw* (New York: Knopf, 1974); Ronald Fraser, *Blood of Spain: An Oral History of the Spanish Civil War* (New York: Pantheon, 1979).

39. Cristina Borderías, *Entre Líneas. La compañia telefónica 1924–1980* (Barcelona: Icaria, 1993); Liliana Barela et al., *Barrio y memoria* (Instituto Histórico de la Ciudad de Buenos Aires, 1992); Tamara Hareven, *Amoskeag: Life and Work in an American Factory City* (New York: Pantheon, 1978); Ronald Fraser, ed., *1968: A Student Generation in Revolt* (New York: Pantheon, 1988).

40. Rosanna Basso, "Myths in Contemporary Oral Tradition: A Children's Strike," in Raphael Samuel and Paul Thompson, eds., *The Myths We Live By* (London and New York: Routledge, 1990), pp. 61–69; András Kovács, "The Abduction of Imre Nagy and His Group: The 'Rashomon' Effect," in *International Yearbook of Oral History and Life Stories,* vol. 1, *Memory and Totalitarianism,* ed. Luisa Passerini (Oxford: Oxford University Press, 1992), pp. 117–24. On the other hand, my *Biografia di una città* stretches over 150 years.

41. See for example, Carlos Sebe Bom Mehy, *Canto de morte Kaiowá, Historia oral de vida* (São Paulo: Loyola, 1991); Philippe Joutard, *La légende des Camisards* (Paris: Gallimard, 1977).

42. Raphael Samuel, *East End Underworld: Chapters in the Life of Arthur Harding* (London: Routledge and Kegan Paul, 1981), an individual life story; Bianca Guidetti Serra, *Compagne. Testimonianze di partecipazione politica femminile* (Turin: Einaudi, 1977), a series of interviews with women in the Resistance; Anna Bravo and Daniele Jalla, *La vita offesa dei Lager nazisti nei racconti*

di duecento sopravvissuti (Milano: Franco Angeli, 1987), a polyphonic montage of interviews with survivors of the Nazi concentration camps.

43. Mark Baker, *Nam* (London: Abacus, 1982); Wallace Terry, *Bloods: An Oral History of the Vietnam War by Black Veterans* (New York: Ballantine, 1984). See chapter 11 in this book, "As Though It Were a Story: Versions of Vietnam."

44. Nuto Revelli, *Il mondo dei vinti. Testimonianze di vita contadina* (Turin: Einaudi, 1977), and *L'anello forte. La donna: storie di vita contadina* (Turin: Einaudi, 1985). The use of "testimony" and "lives" in the titles underlines the effect of objectivity; Revelli goes so far as to incorporate his own questions into the informants' answers, so as not to appear to intrude: "Do I believe they sent a man to the moon?" Revelli uses a very different, dialogic and self-reflexive approach in his recent *Il disperso di Marburg* (Turin: Einaudi, 1994), which focuses on the history of a research and on his own responses to the problems it raises.

45. Luisa Passerini, *Torino operaia e il fascismo* (Milan: Feltrinelli, 1984).

46. Maurizio Gribaudi, *Mondo operaio e mito operaio* (Turin: Einaudi, 1987).

47. Contini and Martini, *Verba Manent* p. 47 n.

48. According to Luisa Passerini, the combination of montage and narrative contextualization in this book causes "a seeming disappearance of the subject, or, rather, an ambiguity as to who is the subject in this game of re-writing and extrapolation—who plays which role in the piling up of quotations" ("Il programma radiofonico come fonte," in *Storia e soggettività*, pp. 172–73). Ultimately, as the name on the cover indicates, the speaking subject, responsible for the overall statement, is the historian himself. See Portelli, *Biografia di una città*.

49. Luisa Passerini, *Autoritratto di gruppo* (Florence: Giunti, 1988).

50. For another Italian example of transition from oral history to theater, see Domenico Starnone, "Scuola, ricerca e teatro. Per riprendere la parola," *I Giorni Cantati* 4 (1983), pp. 52–65.

51. See chapter 4 in this book, "Tryin' to Gather a Little Knowledge: Thoughts on the Ethics of Oral History."

52. Michael Frisch, *A Shared Authority* (especially ch. 13, "The Presentation of Urban History in Big City Museums"); Paul Thompson, *The Voice of the Past: Oral History* (Oxford: Oxford University Press, 1978), ch. 1. One of my best experiences with oral history was the writing and staging, together with my students at the University of Rome, of a play with music based on my oral history interviews in Harlan County, called *Quilt*. The play was presented at schools and at movement and union venues in different parts of Italy several times in 1990–92.

53. Paul Bowles, *Without Stopping: An Autobiography* (1972; repr. London: Peter Owen, 1987), p. 347.

54. Bill Haywood, *Big Bill's Book: The Autobiography of Big Bill Haywood* (1929; repr. New York: International Publishers, 1969); Jones, *Autobiography*; Woody Guthrie, *Bound for Glory* (1943; repr. New York: Dutton, 1970); Jack

Conroy, *The Disinherited* (1933; repr. New York: Hill and Wang, 1963). An immediately visible difference is that Haywood or Jones say very little about their private lives and their childhoods, while these form the bulk of Conroy's and Guthrie's books. Of course, what is presented as a factual autobiography may contain less actual truth than what is presented as a novel. What counts, however, is the quality of the "pact" stipulated between the writer and the reader; see Philippe Lejeune, *Le pacte autobiographique* (Paris: Seuil, 1975).

55. John G. Neihardt, ed., *Black Elk Speaks* (1932; repr. Lincoln: University of Nebraska Press, 1979), pp. 5, 66.

56. Interview with Dante Bartolini, b. 1910, Castel di Lago (Terni), April 4, 1972.

57. Tedlock, "Learning to Listen: Oral History as Poetry," in *The Spoken Word and the Work of Interpretation*, pp. 107–23. I had transcribed it in this fashion also in the manuscript of *Biografia di una città*, but my editors wouldn't hear of it, and compelled me to falsify the passage by printing it as prose.

CHAPTER 2. HISTORY-TELLING AS A MULTIVOCAL ART

1. A different, shorter version of this paper appeared in *The Oral History Review* 20, nos. 1–2 (Spring–Fall 1992), pp. 51–66. The present version is a revision of the text published in Geneviève Fabre and Robert O'Meally, eds., *History and Memory in African American Culture* (New York and Oxford: Oxford University Press, 1994), pp. 164–78, as "History-Telling and Time: An Example from Kentucky."

2. Neihardt, ed., *Black Elk Speaks*. This is a common practice, for instance, in Native American narrative: see Arnold Krupat, *The Voice in the Margin* (Berkeley: University of California Press, 1989), pp. 159–60; Virgil Lucullus McWhorter, *Yellow Wolf: His Own Story* (1940; rev. and enlarged ed., Caldwell, Idaho: Caxton Printers, 1991), pp. 34, 193.

3. The interview took place in Lexington, Kentucky, September 28, 1983. It is quoted here as transcribed by Ms. Julia Hairston.

4. See "The Death of Luigi Trastulli: Memory and the Event," and "'The Time of My Life': Functions of Time in Oral History," both in a Portelli, *The Death of Luigi Trastulli and Other Stories;* see also, "Form and Meaning of Historical Representation: The Battle of Evarts and the Battle of Crummies (Kentucky: 1931, 1941," chapter 7 in this book.

5. See "Life and Times of Valtèro Peppoloni, Worker," in Portelli, *The Death of Luigi Trastulli,* pp. 117–37, for several stories of this kind told by Italian steelworkers.

6. For another Harlan Co. example, compare the interview with Mr. James Hall, a black miner from Lynch, Ky.: "I went into the mines when I was sixteen years old." "Q. What year were you born in?" "A. I was born in 1917. When I went in the mine . . ." (int. Lynch, Ky., October 8, 1986).

7. Pierre Nora, "Between Memory and History: *Les Lieux de Mémoire,*" in

Fabre and O'Meally, eds., *History and Memory in African American Culture,* pp. 284–300, English translation Marc Roudebush. The book (in which the present chapter first appeared) was a series of responses to and applications of Nora's essay from the point of view of African American research.

8. The mantrip is the vehicle that carries miners in and out of the mine.

9. Toni Morrison, *Beloved* (London: Chatto & Windus, 1987), p. 266.

10. Isabel Hofmeyr, "'Nterata'\'The Wire': Fences, Boundaries, Orality, Literacy," in Ronald J. Grele, ed., *International Journal of Oral History* (New York: Greenwood Press, 1990), pp. 69–91. An example of "fluid" boundaries in paraliterate societies is the case related by Harlan County lawyer Sidney Douglass (int. July 13, 1987) of the land deeds in which the boundary between two properties is marked by "a snowbank," which of course melts in the summer.

11. W. E. B. Du Bois, "Of the Dawn of Freedom," from *The Souls of Black Folk,* in Du Bois, *Writings,* ed. Nathan Huggins (New York: The Library of America, 1986), p. 372.

CHAPTER 3. MEMORY AND RESISTANCE

1. Gianni Bosio, *Diario di un organizzatore di cultura* (Milan: Edizioni Avanti, 1962). On Gianni Bosio, see my "Research as an Experiment in Equality," in *The Death of Luigi Trastulli and Other Stories: Form and Meaning in Oral History* (Albany, N.Y.: State University of New York Press, 1991), pp. 40–43.

2. The journal had several incarnations, from mimeographed bulletin to semischolarly research journal, to bimonthly magazine. Every time we changed format and publisher, the numbers started again, which is why the footnote references may look confusing. *I Giorni Cantati* was finally declared dead in the spring of 1995.

3. The traditional day for the gathering of crops and the division between croppers and landlords.

4. Mark Twain, *The Adventures of Huckleberry Finn* (Harmondsworth, Midds.: Penguin, 1967), p. 244.

5. This article is written in the plural because it gathers a history that involved many people. Not all of the individuals who worked with the Circolo Gianni Bosio were involved with all of its activities and discoveries. Perhaps I am the only one who experienced *all* the things related in this article, but none of them was experienced by me alone.

6. This version of the ballad is included on the record. *La Sabina. Canti, balli e riti* (Milan: Dischi del Sole DS 517/19). It bears number 1 in Costantino Nigra's classic collection, *Canti popolari del Piemonte* (1888; repr. Turin: Einaudi, 1967), pp. 3–34.

7. Ernesto de Martino, "Note lucane" (1950), in Pietro Clemente et al., eds., *Il dibattito sul folklore in Italia* (Milan: Edizioni di cultura popolare, 1976), pp. 370–82.

8. Jurij M. Lotman and Boris A. Uspenskij, "Sul meccanismo semiotico della cultura" (1971), in *Tipologia della cultura* (Milan: Bompiani, 1973), pp. 46–48, Italian translation by Remo Faccani.

9. Alessandro Portelli, "Riccardo Colotti: 'Sarebbe 'sto comunismo.' Una lectura Dantis contadina," *I Giorni Cantati*, I, 1, nos. 2–3 (July–December, 1981), pp. 25–33.

10. See my "Typology of Industrial Folk Song," in *The Death of Luigi Trastulli*, pp. 161–92.

11. A volume of *I Giorni Cantati* (1, nos. 2–3 [July–December, 1981]) was devoted to "L'improvvisazione e la regola: la spontaneità possible" ("The rules of improvisation: possible spontaneity").

12. A. Portelli, "Bruce Springsteen: Working-Class Hero?" *I Giorni Cantati* 0 (1986), 3–8, and "Cristiani che bevono birra. La country music e le ambiguità della cultura operaia in America," *I Giorni Cantati* 5 (Spring 1984), pp. 61–67; Filippo La Porta, "Salsa: Musica di un continente," *I Giorni Cantati* 1, no. 1 (January–March 1987), pp. 3–6; Massimo Canevacci, "Suoni malesi e sincretismi planetari," *I Giorni Cantati* 2, nos. 7–8 (December 1988), pp. 8–10; Felice Liperi, "Talking Heads, Gabriel, Prince," ibid., pp. 5–7.

13. Two of Ambrogio Sparagna's folk operas are *Trillillì. Storie di magici organetti e altre meraviglie* (Rome: Sudnord Records SNCD 0021) and *Giofà il servo del Re* (Rome: BMG Ariola 743211 64412). Both are about the liberating power of memory and music.

14. Alberto M. Cirese, *Cultura egemonica e culture subalterne* (Palermo: Palumbo, 1973). While learning much from this standard manual of folklore (written by one of the original founders of the Istituto De Martino, the Circolo Gianni Bosio's *alma mater*), we never accepted the title's rationalistic and ethnocentric implication that there are many "subaltern cultures" but only *one* "hegemonic culture."

15. I take this figure from Paula Gunn Allen, *The Sacred Hoop: Recovering the Feminine in American Indian Traditions* (Boston: Beacon Press, 1986).

16. Gianni Bosio, "Uomo folklorico/uomo storico," in *L'intellettuale rovesciato* (Milan: Edizioni Bella Ciao, 1975), pp. 254–63.

17. Paolo Pietrangeli, "Contessa," on the record. *Mio caro padrone domani ti sparo* (Milan: Dischi del Sole DS 197/99).

18. A. Portelli, "I metalmeccanici e la funzione poetica. Espressività orale di base nella manifestazione nazionale del 2 dicembre 1977," *I Giorni Cantati* 1, nos. 2–3 (July–December 1981), pp. 43–60; and "La classe operaia e la Santissima Trinità," *I Giorni Cantati* 7 (1976).

19. Lodovica Mutarelli, b. 1965, in M. Arcidiacono et al., *L'aeroplano e le stelle. Storia orale di una realtà studentesca* (Rome: Manifestolibri, 1995) p. 155. See chapter 15, "Conversations with the Panther," in this book.

20. At the time, I was working as a clerk in a government office: a secure, tenured job, with decent pay.

21. See chapter 2, "There's Gonna Always Be a Line," in this book.

22. Annalucia Accardo et al., eds., *Un'altra America: Letteratura e cultura degli Appalachi meridionali* (Rome: Bulzoni, 1991).

23. Frank Adams, with Myles Horton, *Unearthing Seeds of Fire: The Idea of Highlander* (Winston-Salem, N.C.: John F. Blair, 1975); Myles Horton, "Le avventure di un montanaro ribelle," interview with C. Mattiello and A. Portelli, *I Giorni Cantati* 5 (Spring 1984), pp. 36–41. Domenico Starnone was also one of the speakers at the seminar to which the present essay was the introduction. One of his novels, *Segni d'oro* (Milano: Feltrinelli, 1990), was also the story of an oral history project first presented in our journal: Domenico Starnone, "La Santa e le polveri. Antinfortunistica sacra alla SNIA di Colleferro," *I Giorni Cantati* 1, no. 1 (June 1981), pp. 46–68.

CHAPTER 4. SOME THOUGHTS ON THE ETHICS OF ORAL HISTORY

1. This chapter is based on two talks given at the conference entitled "Oral History and Ethics," organized by the Catholic University of São Paulo and the Research and Documentation Center (CPDOC) of the Fundaçao Getulio Vargas in Rio De Janeiro, Brazil, October 14–26, 1995.

2. Although I am a professional academic, my professional position is not in the field of oral history (or, for that matter, history). Therefore, I cannot rely on a structure designed for this type of work, which to a certain extent remains for me a volunteer activity. I am not sure I would want it differently. The thing I regret most is that, in more than twenty years, I have not been able to find an archive that will keep my tapes and transcripts, possibly index them correctly, and make them available to other researchers.

3. For an early critique of the "bureaucratization" of oral history, see Luisa Passerini, "Conoscenza storica e fonti orali," in *Storia e soggettività. Le fonti orali, la memoria* (Florence: La Nuova Italia, 1988), pp. 35–36. For discussions of ethics in oral history, see Valerie Yow, "Ethics and Interpersonal Relationships in Oral History Research," *Oral History Review* 22, 1 (Summer 1995), pp. 51–66; Daphne Patai, "Ethical Problems of Personal Naratives, or, Who Should Eat the Last Piece of Cake?" *International Journal of Oral History* 8, 1 (February 1987), pp. 5–27. The most articulate effort at shaping a professional ethics for oral history are the 1992 *Guidelines and Principles of the Oral History Association*.

4. Olaudah Equiano, *The Interesting Narrative of the Life of Olaudah Equiano, or Gustavus Vassa, the African. Written by Himself* (1785), in Henry Louis Gates, Jr., ed., *The Classic Slave Narratives* (New York: Penguin, 1987), p. 11.

5. In some of my earlier writing, I used this expression occasionally and uncommittedly, and was criticized for it (Luisa Passerini, "Per una critica storica dell'oralità," in *Storia e soggettività*, p. 115). I only thought it was a handy expression, designating not a "group" memory outside the individual, but rather recol-

lections "shared" (the term I later adopted) by many individuals in a given social environment.

6. See chapter 6 in this book, "Philosophy and the Facts: Subjectivity and Narrative Form in Autobiography and Oral History."

7. Luisa Passerini, "Diritto all'autobiografia," in *Storia e soggettività*, p. 8.

8. "Research as an Experiment in Equality," in Portelli, *The Death of Luigi Trastulli and Other Stories: Form and Meaning in Oral History* (Albany, N.Y.: State University of New York Press, 1991), pp. 29–44; "There's Gonna Always Be a Line: History-Telling as a Multivocal Art," chapter 2 in this book.

9. Christopher Bigsby, *Hester: A Romance* (1994; repr. London: Phenix, 1995), p. 96.

10. For early discussions of this quandary, see Annie Borzeix and Margaret Marzani, "La duplicité incontournable du métier de sociologue" and Mary Chamberlain, "Power and Authority in the Collection and Presentation of Oral History Material," both in *V Col•loqui Internacional d'Historia Oral. "El Poder en la Sociedad"* (Barcelona, March 29–31, 1985), pp. 65–72, 163–74. The essay by Borzeix and Marzani is also reprinted as "La memoria como un objectivo de poder y la duplicidad insoslayable del oficio del sociólogo, "in Mercédes Vilanova, ed., *El poder en la sociedad. História y fuente oral* (Barcelona: Antoni Bosch, 1986), pp. 109–19.

11. Mildred Shackleford, b. 1950, Evarts (Harlan Co.), Ky.; int. Nov. 2, 1990, at New Market, Tenn.

12. Gianni Bosio, "Lettera a Giuseppe Morandi" (1967), in *L'intellettuale rovesciato* (Milan: Edizioni Bella Ciao, 1975), p. 186.

13. Calvin Trillin, "A Stranger with a Camera," *The New Yorker*, April 29, 1969; reprinted in David S. Walls and John B. Stephenson, eds., *Appalachia in the Sixties: Decade of Reawakening* (Lexington, Ky.: The University Press of Kentucky, 1972), pp. 193–201.

14. See "There's Gonna Always Be a Line: History-Telling as a Multivocal Art," and "Deep Exchange: Roles and Gazes in Multivocal and Multilateral Interviewing," chapters 2 and 5 in this book.

15. Mildred Shackleford did not know (and it did not occur to me at the moment) that there are coal mines in Appalachia that are owned and operated by Rome-based energy conglomerates. Being from Rome might have made a difference in Martin County, Kentucky—just as it did make a difference in Terni.

16. See my "Two Peripheries Talk to Each Other: Italy and Appalachian America," *Appalachian Journal* 12, no. 1 (Fall 1984), pp. 31–37. I derive the concept of the periphery of the empire both from Umberto Eco's *Dalla periferia dell' impero* (Milan: Bompiani, 1975) and Helen M. Lewis, Linda Johnson, and Donald Askins, eds., *Colonialism in Modern America* (Boone, N.C.: Appalachian Consortium Press, 1978).

17. My first awareness of Appalachia came from a rudely racist joke about an anthropologist who goes to Kentucky and interviews a young mountaineer. It

turns out he has a moonshining father, his mother is his father's first cousin, and he has one brother in jail and one at Harvard. "At Harvard? And what is he studyin'?" "He ain't studyin' nothin'. They're studyin' him" (incidentally, the story is also told in Italy about a Neapolitan with a two-headed brother at the Milan Polytechnic).

18. Micaela Arcidiacono et al., eds., *L'aeroplano e le stelle* (Rome: Manifestolibri, 1995). For a discussion, see "Conversations with the Panther," chapter 15 in this book.

19. Luisa Passerini, "Antagonismi nella storia sociale," *Storia e soggettività*, pp. 100–101.

20. Claudio Pavone, *Una guerra civile. Saggio sulla moralità nella Resistenza* (Milan: Bollati Boringhieri, 1992).

21. See Portelli, "Uchronic Dreams: Working-Class Memory and Possible Worlds," in *The Death of Luigi Trastulli*, pp. 99–116.

CHAPTER 5. DEEP EXCHANGE

1. Based on Micaela Arcidiacono, Francesca Battisti, Sonia Di Loreto, Carlo Martinez, Alessandro Portelli, Elena Spandri, eds., *L'aeroplano e le stelle* (Rome: Manifestolibri, 1995), pp. 231–36. See also chapter 15 in this book, "Conversations with the Panther: The Italian Student Movement of 1990."

2. Annamaria Di Marco was 28 years old; the interview took place on June 6, 1992.

3. In English. These are English language and American literature majors, and it shows.

4. The phrase "national-popular" comes from Antonio Gramsci, who used it to speak of the need for a cultural bridge between intellectuals and "the people." in Italy, he argued, "There is no common world view between 'writers' and 'the people'; that is, the feelings of the people are not shared by the writers as their own, nor do writers perform a 'national educational' function, that is, they do not deal with the problem of elaborating upon the feelings of the people after making them their own." See *Letteratura e vita nazionale* (Rome: Editori Riuniti, 1971), pp. 135–36. The popular TV announcer Pippo Baudo, probably unaware of the source, used the expression to describe TV programs with a wide mass appeal, with no intellectual or "educational" intention whatsoever. This is what Di Marco, who is aware of Gramsci, means by the "derogatory" sense of the expression.

5. Battisti was 26, two years younger than Di Marco.

6. See Carlo Martinez and Elena Spandri, "Authority, Dialogue and Self-Awareness," in *Memory and Multiculturalism*, papers presented at the Eighth International Oral History Congress, Siena-Lucca, February 25–28, 1993, pp. 1061–67, 1127–32.

7. See chapter 15 in this book, "Conversations with the Panther: The Italian Student Movement of 1990."

8. Gerald Prince, "Introduction to the Study of the Narratee," *Poétique* 14 (1973), pp. 177–96.

9. A less intense form of this split between questioner and narratee takes place when neighbors or family members suggest stories they've heard and that the interviewee might tell to the interviewer: "Why don't you tell him about that time, in the service, when . . ." (Lucilla Galeazzi to her uncle Aldo Galeazzi, Terni, October 10, 1979). In these cases, these members of the audience act as supplementary questioners, enhancing the role of the interviewer as narratee.

CHAPTER 6. PHILOSOPHY AND THE FACTS

1. This chapter is based on a paper presented at the conference on "Subjectivity and the Social Sciences," Granada, Spain, April 12–16, 1993; it was published as "La filosofia y los hechos. Narración, interpretación y significado en las evocaciones y las fuentes orales," *Fundamentos de antropología* 3 (Granada, Spain, 1994), pp. 33–39.

2. Frederick Douglass, *The Life and Times of Frederick Douglass* (1892; repr. New York: Collier, 1962), p. 217.

3. Dennis Tedlock, "The Analogical Tradition and the Emergence of a Dialogical Anthropology," in *The Spoken Word and the Work of Interpretation* (Philadelphia: University of Pennsylvania Press, 1983), pp. 321–38.

4. On the reluctance to being interpreted, displayed even by interpreters-in-training (students of philosophy and literature at the university of Rome), see M. Arcidiacono et al., *L'aeroplano e le stelle* (Rome: Manifestolibri, 1995), pp. 239–41.

5. William Labov and Joshua Waletzky, "Narrative Analysis," in June Helm, ed., *Essays on the Verbal and Visual Arts* (Seattle: University of Washington Press, 1967), pp. 12–44; William Labov, "The Transformation of Experience in Narrative Syntax," in *Language in the Inner City: Studies in the Black English Vernacular* (Philadelphia: University of Pennsylvania Press, 1972), pp. 354–96.

6. Frederick Douglass, *Narrative of the Life of Frederick Douglass, an American Slave. Written by Himself* (1844), in Henry Louis Gates, Jr., ed., *The Classic Slave Narratives* (New York: Mentor, 1987), p. 261. In *Life and Times,* Douglass explains that "Though he sometimes wielded the lash, it was evident that he took no pleasure in it and did it with much reluctance" (p. 53). In this final version of his autobiography, he spells the other overseer's name as Sevier; the spelling used in the first edition may have been an allegorical interpretation produced by the slave's imaginative ear.

7. *The Life of Olaudah Equiano, or Gustavus Vassa, the African,* 1789, in Gates, ed., *The Classic Slave Narratives,* p. 40.

8. As such, the "reluctant overseer" may be a distant relative of the "good German," discussed in chapter 10, "The Massacre at Civitella Val di Chiana," in this book.

9. Toni Morrison, *Beloved* (London: Chatto & Windus, 1987), p. 190.

10. Above all, see Luisa Passerini, *Storia e soggettività. Le fonti orali, la memoria* (Florence: La Nuova Italia, 1988).

11. Robert William Fogel and Stanley D. Engerman, *Time on the Cross: The Economics of American Negro Slavery* (Boston and Toronto: Little, Brown, 1974), vol. 1, p. 145.

12. For further discussion, see my "The Best Garbage Man in Town: Life and Times of Valtèro Peppoloni, Worker," in *The Death of Luigi Trastulli and other Stories: Form and Meaning in Oral History* (Albany, N.Y.: State University of New York Press, 1991), pp. 117–37.

13. Stephan Feuchtwang, "Distant Homes, Our Genre," article submitted for vol. 5 of the *International Yearbook of Life History and Life Stories*, 1995. The *Yearbook* ceased publication before the volume was issued.

14. Ferruccio Mauri, b. 1926, civil service worker, April 8, 1983; quoted in A. Portelli, *Biografia di una città. Storia e racconto. Terni 1830–1985* (Turin: Einaudi, 1985), p. 241.

15. Likewise, describing his native community, Equiano writes: "I can speak from my own knowledge, throughout our vicinity" (*Life*, p. 20): he knows only what he sees *(vicinity)*, but knows it first-hand *(my own knowledge)*.

16. Stefania Piccinato discusses the interaction of story and discourse in Douglass's *Narrative* in "Autobiografia ed esemplarità," in A. Accardo et al., eds., *Identità e scrittura. Studi sull'autobiografia nord-americana* (Rome: Bulzoni, 1988), pp. 145–56.

17. I have discussed Douglass as a representative man in my introduction to the Italian translation of his *Narrative: Memorie di uno schiavo fuggiasco* (Rome: Manifestolibri, 1992). See also chapter 2 in this book, "There's Gonna Always Be a Line: History-Telling as a Multivocal Art."

18. Ralph Ellison, "The Essential Ellison," interview with Steve Cannon, *Yardbird Magazine* (1978), p. 155; Ian McEwan, *Black Dogs* (London: Picador, 1992), pp. 164–65.

19. Beniamino Placido makes this point in his critique of *Time on the Cross* in *Le due schiavitù. Per un'analisi dell'immaginazione americana* (Turin: Einaudi, 1975), p. 130.

20. Rita Cappanera, b. 1963, student, steelworker's daughter, September 12, 1979. On this interview, see chapter 1, "Oral History as Genre," and chapter 8, "Absolutely Nothing: War Refugees in Terni," in this book.

CHAPTER 7. FORM AND MEANING OF HISTORICAL REPRESENTATION

1. Presented at the International Oral History Conference, Essen, Germany, March 1990; published as "Forma y significado de la representación histórica. La batalla de Evarts y la batalla de Crummies (Kentucky: 1931, 1941)" in *História y Fuente Oral* 4 (Barcelona, Spain: 1990), pp. 79–100.

2. George J. Titler, *Hell in Harlan* (Beckley, W. Va.: BJW Printers, no date), p. 205; W. C. Stump, "The Bloody Harlan Legacy: Harlan County History—Like

It Or Not" (Harlan, Ky.: privately printed pamphlet, 1988). Paul E. Taylor mentions the Battle of Crummies in the "Epilogue" to his *Bloody Harlan: The United Mine Workers of America in Harlan County, Kentucky, 1931–1941* (Lanham, N.Y.: University Press of America, 1990), p. 238, but gives Titler as his source. An indirect reference is perhaps in Lee Smith's novel, *Fair and Tender Ladies* (New York: Ballantine, 1988), in which the heroine writes that "four people have been killed already in the Harlan strike. . . . There is a war on and a big strike at Harlan right across the state line" (p. 244). Note the ambiguity of "war," which may refer both to World War II (the date is 1942) and to the union "wars" in Harlan.

3. Frances "Granny" Hager, b. 1914, nurse, union activist; interviewed by Mike Mullins, Lothair, Kentucky, January 31 and March 28, 1978, in the Appalachian Oral History Collection at Alice Lloyd College. Other quotes from Granny Hager are from my own interview with her in Hazard, Kentucky, September 11, 1973.

4. Bob Hall, untitled comment on an interview with Florence Reece, *Southern Exposure* 4, nos. 1–2 (Spring/Summer, 1976), p. 91.

5. John Ed Pearce, Louisville *Courier-Journal,* Sunday supplement, October 6, 1985, p. 6.

6. John Hevener, *Which Side Are You On?* (Urbana, Ill.: University of Illinois Press, 1978), pp. 33–34.

7. Quoted in Bill Bishop, "1931: The Battle of Evarts," *Southern Exposure* 4, nos. 1–2 (Spring/Summer 1976), pp. 92–101.

8. William D. Forester, *Harlan County—The Turbulent Thirties* (Harlan, Ky.: privately printed, 1986), p. 9.

9. My interview with Granny Hager, Hazard, Ky., September 11, 1973.

10. Mullins interview, March 28, 1978.

11. Titler, *Hell in Harlan,* pp. 205, 163.

12. "C. K. W.'s 'Mind Run,'" *Harlan Daily Enterprise,* April 16, 1941. I wish to thank Kate Black, of the University of Kentucky Libraries, for helping me locate this source.

13. Born 1917, retired coal miner, Barbourville, Ky., July 18, 1987.

14. B. 1917, coal miner's wife, Louellen, Ky., October 28, 1988.

15. B. 1917, retired coal miner, Harlan Sunshine, Ky., October 28, 1988.

16. Mike Mullins interview, March 28, 1978.

17. Remark made during interview with Plennie Hall, July 18, 1987. Annie Napier, b. 1942, coal miner's wife, who is related to Hall and introduced me to him, was one of the persons who told me the story of the battle while driving by the commissary store.

18. Born 1921, Highsplint, October 24, 1989.

19. "Roadhouse on Mountain Burns," *Harlan County Daily Enterprise,* April 3, 1941 p. 1: "The Top of the Mountain roadhouse . . . was burned to the

ground last last night. . . . The roadhouse is located atop the mountain between Crummies Creek and Viginia state line."

20. Titler, *Hell in Harlan,* p. 206; *Harlan Daily Enterprise,* April 16, 1941.

21. This analysis builds on a theoretical framework developed in earlier articles: "The Death of Luigi Trastulli: Memory and the Event," and "The Time of My Life: Functions of Time in Oral History," in *The Death of Luigi Trastulli and other Stories: Form and Meaning in Oral History* (Albany, N.Y.: State University of New York Press, 1991,), pp. 1–26, 59–76. See also "There's Gonna Always Be a Line: History-Telling as a Multivocal Art," chapter 2 in this book.

22. Melvyn Dubofsky and Warren Van Tine, *John L. Lewis: A Biography* (Urbana and Chicago: University of Illinois Press, 1986), p. 240.

23. Forester, *Harlan County—The Turbulent Thirties,* p. 262; see also Taylor, *Bloody Harlan,* p. 230.

24. On the Battle of Stanfill, see Hevener, *Which Side Are You On?* pp. 167–68.

25. Walter Benjamin, "Theses on the Philosophy of History," in Hannah Arendt, ed., *Illuminations,* English translation by Harry Zahn (New York: Schocken, 1969), p. 257.

26. In my 1973 interview with Hager, the shuttlework has a broader scope. She shifts back and forth from the Thirties to the Roving Pickets movement in the 1960s, to the Miners for Democracy and the Black Lung Movement in the 1970s, creating the paradigm of her life as—to modify a phrase from a folk song popular in Harlan—"a girl of constant struggle."

27. W. C. Stump's pamphlet dates the Battle of Crummies on April 15, which is, instead, the date of the Battle of Fork Ridge. On the earlier episode at Crummies, see Hevener, *Which Side Are You On?* p. 49.

28. Forester, *Harlan County,* p. 10.

29. Hevener, *Which Side Are You On?* p. 47; Forester, *Harlan County,* p. 10.

30. John M. Robsion to John L. Lewis, President of the United Mine Workers of America, UMWA Correspondence Files, Dec. 1, 1931.

31. Theodore Dreiser, *Harlan Miners Speak* (New York: Da Capo, 1970). A sample of Left-wing reports on the Harlan strike of 1931–1932 is in *Harlan and Bell 1931–32: The National Miners Union. As Reported at the Time in "The Labor Defender"* (Huntington, W.Va.: Appalachian Movement Press, 1972). On the role of the NMU in Harlan, see also Theodore Draper, "Communists and Miners," *Dissent* (Spring 1972), pp. 371–92.

32. John Gaventa, *Power and Powerlessness: Rebellion and Quiescence in an Appalachian Valley* (Urbana, Ill.: University of Illinois Press, 1980), pp. 106, 116, 109.

33. United States Senate, *Conditions in Coal Fields, Harlan and Bell Counties, Kentucky: Hearings before a Subcommittee of the Committee on Manufactures,* May 11–19, 1932.

34. Mullins interview, January 31, 1978.

35. On theater and the judicial system, see Milner S. Ball, "The Play's the Thing: An Unscientific Reflection on Courts under the Rubric of Theater," *Stanford Law Review* 28 (November 1975), pp. 81–113; and my "The Oral Shape of the Law: The 'April 7' Case," in *The Death of Luigi Trastulli*, pp. 241–69.

36. This charge is made systematically, and with some plausibility, in *Bloody Harlan: Facts from the Court Records in the Harlan Frame-up Trials*, a pamphlet published by the Kentucky Miners Defense in New York, 1937. The pamphlet is copied almost wholesale by Titler in *Hell in Harlan*, pp. 22–35. Titler, who is ideologically hostile to the Miners Defense Committee, fails to credit this source.

37. The description of the Battle of Evarts in Hevener's *Which Side Are You On?* gives as references only the courtroom testimony of the company guards and deputy sheriffs who were in the motorcade and appeared as witnesses for the prosecution (Orville Howard, E. M. Cox, George Dawn, Sherman Percival), and the testimony given to the Costigan Committee hearings by Colonel Daniel M. Carrell, who commanded the National Guard in Harlan. This is not due to prejudice on his side (on another question—whether the defendants had conspired to ambush the guards—he quotes both sides and leaves conclusions open), but to the inevitable pull of the available official sources. The brief description of the battle in Tony Bubka, "The Harlan County Coal Strike of 1931," *Labor History* II no. 1 (Winter 1970), pp. 41–57, is also based mainly on courtroom testimony. Needless to say (but usually unrecognized), these are all oral sources to begin with.

38. Florence Reece, "They Say Them Child Brides Don't Last," interview in Kathy Kahn, *Hillbilly Women* (Garden City, N.Y.: Doubleday, 1973), p. 31.

39. Forester, *Harlan County*, p. 10; Jim Garland, *Welcome the Traveler Home: Jim Garland's Story of the Kentucky Mountains*, ed. Julia S. Ardery (Urbana, Ill.: University of Illinois Press, 1983), p. 141. Garland, an NMU organizer, did not take part in the Battle of Evarts. Forester also notes that "On May 23, 1932, the body of a fifth man believed to have been killed in the 'Battle of Evarts' was found. He was unidentified. This added credence to Sheriff Blair's claim that more people than were reported had been slain in the fight" (p. 14).

40. H. C. Brearley, *Homicide in the United States* (Chapel Hill: The University of North Carolina Press, 1932), p. 105; *Knoxville News Sentinel*, January 4, 1934, a banner front-page headline.

41. Ample evidence is assembled in the hearings of the LaFollette Committee: U.S. Congress, Senate, Committee of Education and Labor, *Violations of Free Speech and Rights of Labor*, 1937. John H. Blair is quoted in Bishop, "1931: The Battle of Evarts."

42. Everette Tharpe, b. 1899, interviewed by Guy and Candie Carawan, September 1973, in Guy and Candie Carawan, eds., *Voices from the Mountains* (Urbana: University of Illinois Press, 1975), p. 9. In the same context, Tharpe speaks of the "rugged individualism" of the mountaineers.

43. Brearley, *Homicide in the United States,* pp. 51, 52. Brearley explains lower homicide rates in New England by the fact that it is farther in time from frontier conditions (pp. 24–25).

44. Titler, *Hell in Harlan,* p. 163.

45. See Gaventa, *Power and Powerlessness,* pp. 85–96.

46. "The union miners have been characterized as 'violent,'" wrote a coal miner's wife during the Pittston strike in Virginia, in 1989; "My uncle died a violent coal miner's death, and the absentee owner reaped the profit": Dolores Booker, of St. Paul, Virginia, letter to the *UMWA Journal* 100, no. 7 (July–August 1989), p. 3.

47. See my "Patterns of Paternalism: From Company Town to Union Shop," in *The Death of Luigi Trastulli,* pp. 195–215.

48. "Report of Governor Laffoon's Investigation," Frankfort, Ky., June 7, 1935, Berea College Library, file on Miners (Harlan and Bell).

49. One informant, whom I asked to tell me about the Battle of Evarts, thought I was referring to another multiple killing that occurred in 1936 over some stolen ballots during a local election. On electoral politics in Harlan, see Forester, *Harlan County,* pp. 147–91; Titler, *Hell in Harlan,* pp. 156–65.

50. Hevener, *Which Side Are You On?* p. 45; Garland, *Welcome the Traveler Home,* p. 141; Titler, *Hell in Harlan,* pp. 163, 207; Taylor, *Bloody Harlan,* p. 238.

51. Tillman Cadle, b. 1902, Townsend, Tenn., July 15, 1987.

52. *The New York Times,* September 28, 1931. The article is the first of a series of reports from Harlan by Louis Stark.

53. Mark Baker, ed., *Nam: The Vietnam War in the Words of the Men and Women Who Fought There* (London: Abacus, 1982), p. 140. See also chapter 11 in this book, "As Though It Were a Story: Versions of Vietnam."

54. "An old miner," quoted by John Ed Pearce in the Louisville *Courier-Journal,* October 6, 1985, p. 6. Pearce's original source is an unspecified article in *Mountain Life and Work,* published at Berea, Kentucky.

55. Louis Stark implied as much, when he remarked that he was writing his story in a Chicago office "overlooking the comparative peace of Michigan Boulevard, where racketeers 'shot it out' the other day." See "Harlan Coal Fields Face Civil War," *The New York Times,* September 28, 1931.

56. Lynda Ann Ewen, *Which Side Are You On? The Brookside Strike in Harlan County, Kentucky, 1973–1974* (Chicago: Vanguard Books, 1979), pp. 81–83. The meeting is also documented in Barbara Kopple's film, *Harlan County, USA,* 1977.

57. Ewell Balltrip, newspaper editor, October 14, 1987.

58. Ewell Balltrip; Delbert Jones, retired coal miner, Highsplint, Ky., October 24, 1988.

59. Harold Dutton and Tommy Meade, striking coal miners, St. Paul, Virginia, December 27, 1989.

60. "They've got us down—their martial lines enfold us. . . . / I only want the

leaves to come and hide me, / To cover up my vengeful wandering . . . / I want to use this GUN from under cover— /. . . O, Buddy, how I'm longing for the spring!" Ralph Chaplin, "When the Leaves Come Out," 1914, now in Joyce Kornbluh, *Rebel Voices, An I.W.W. Anthology* (Ann Arbor: The University of Michigan Press, 1972). Chaplin wrote this poem during a miners' strike in West Virginia. He is also the author of the song "Solidarity Forever," which is one of the anthems of the Pittston strike. According to a witness in the Battle of Evarts trial, in a meeting before the battle, an orator told the miners, "The leaves are getting green and now is a good time to go squirrel hunting" (Philip Kinsley, "Witnesses Give Word Picture of Unrest in Mines," *Knoxville News-Sentinel,* November 26, 1932). "They'll put on camouflage or bush-fighting stuff, and they'll go in the hills," said a miner and preacher from Harlan County, in 1986, discussing the possibility of a strike (Tommy Sweatt, coal miner, preacher, 1948, Lynch, Ky., October 7, 1986).

61. "Violence in Coal Strike Is Increasing," *The New York Times,* September 5, 1989.

62. On "gatekeeping" and "mobilization of bias," see Gaventa, *Power and Powerlessness,* pp. 14–15, 106.

CHAPTER 8. ABSOLUTELY NOTHING

1. Born 1933; steelworker; Terni, September 12, 1979. See chapter 1 in this book, "Oral History as Genre."

2. A shorter version of this chapter was presented at the conference "L'altro dopoguerra: Roma e il Sud 1943–1945," organized by the Rome Institute for Italian History from Fascism to Resistance (IRSIFAR), Rome, June 4–6, 1984, and published in the proceedings, edited by Nicola Gallerano (Milan: Franco Angeli, 1985), pp. 135–44.

3. Libero Fornaci, "Dieci giorni di bombardamenti a Terni nel diario di un ufficiale medico," *Terni. Rassegna del Comune* 3 (May–June 1965), pp. 31–43. The same issue of the magazine includes a list of 783 identified victims. Elia Rossi Passavanti, *Terni* (Terni: Alterocca, 1974), lists 1,018 victims.

4. Born 1913; ex-textile worker; June 26, 1979.

5. Born 1924; retired steelworker; September 8, 1982.

6. "A Narrative of the Captivity and Restoration of Mrs. Mary Rowlandson" (1676), in Nina Baym et al., eds, *Norton Anthology of American Literature* (New York: Norton, 1989), p. 151. She also wrote, "The first week of my being among them, I hardly ate anything: the second week, I found my stomach grew very faint for want of something: and yet it was very hard to get down to their filthy trash: but the third week, though I could think how formerly my stomach would turn against this or that, and I could starve or die before I could eat such things, yet they were sweet and savory to my taste."

7. Vincenzo Padiglione, *Il cinghiale cacciatore. Antropologia simbolica della caccia in Sardegna* (Rome: Armando, 1989) describes such feasts in the boar-

hunting culture of Sardinia, whose function is to ritualize the hunter's relationship to the animal world.

8. Alberto Moravia, *La ciociara* (1957; repr. Milan: Bompiani, 1990), p. 29. See also the huge alimentary feast on page 70. Another theme in common is the experience of dwelling in spaces fit for animals: "'Back where I come from, these huts are for beasts' . . . 'Here, instead, we put Christians in them'" (p. 78).

9. B. 1932; housewife; interviewed in 1979 by Marcello Ricci.

10. B. 1899; steelworker; September 3, 1982.

11. B. 1925; merchant; interviewed in 1979 by Marcello Ricci.

12. Studs Terkel, *Hard Times: An Oral History of the Great Depression* (New York: Random House, 1970), pp. 37–43; see the narrative of Gaetano Bordoni in "Luigi's Socks and Rita's Makeup: Youth Culture, the Politics of Private Life, and the Culture of the Working Classes," chapter 14 in this book.

13. Born 1912; steelworker; June 26, 1979.

14. Margaret Mitchell, *Gone with the Wind* (London: Pan, 1974), p. 418.

15. B. 1925; steelworker; December 30, 1980. For more information on Petrini, including the story of his father's work accident, see my *The Death of Luigi Trastulli: Form and Meaning in Oral History* (Albany, N.Y.: State of New York University Press, 1991) pp. 272–73.

16. B. 1919; carpenter; September 16, 1980.

17. For ampler discussion, see my "La classe operaia ternana tra cultura contadina e vita di fabbrica," in Renato Covino and Giampaolo Gallo, eds., *L'Umbria* (Turin: Einaudi, 1989), p. 739–69.

18. "For these people in Fondi, and in my home village, too, eating and drinking was as important as in Rome it is to have a car or an apartment. . . . They dressed in rags but were as proud of their eggs and their lard as the ladies in Rome of their evening dresses." See Moravia, *La ciociara*, p. 70–71.

19. B. 1924; Office worker, former factory worker; Rome, January 7, 1981.

20. B. 1901; former railroad and factory worker; Terni, October 18, 1982.

21. B. 1921; office worker, city councilman; Terni, September 9, 1984.

22. B. 1926; steel worker, city councilman; September 17, 1980.

23. The day of Italy's separate peace with the Allies and the dissolution of the Italian army.

CHAPTER 9. THE BATTLE OF POGGIO BUSTONE

1. B. 1913, steelworker; interviewed in Terni, June 21, 1981.

2. Dante Bartolini, "Il traditore Tanturi," recorded April 8, 1972; on the record *La Sabina*, ed. Alessandro Portelli (Milan: Dischi del Sole DS 517/19).

3. Silvio Micheli, "A Poggio Bustone partigiani e popolo fermarono la Hermann Goering e le SS," in Sergio Bovini, ed., *L'Umbria nella Resistenza* (Rome: Editori Riuniti, 1972), p. 340.

4. This paper is an example of incremental repetition through oral performance. Its written core is in pp. 277–82 of my *Biografia di una città. Storia e rac-*

conto: Terni 1830–1984 (Turin: Einaudi, 1985). It was elaborated through different presentations at an Oral History Office seminar at Columbia University, New York, November 1983; at a seminar at Avila, Spain, April, 1992; at the conference on oral history organized by the National Institute of Anthropology and History (INAH) at Mexico City, August 1992; at the conference for the fiftieth anniversary of Resistance and Liberation from Fascism, organized in Rome, October 1995, by the Institute for Italian History from Fascism to Resistance (IRSIFAR). Each presentation was significantly different from the previous one. Research trips to Poggio Bustone and later the "discovery" of the song and its author, Dante Bartolini, were foundational episodes in my personal and intellectual history. Perhaps this is why this story haunts me so. Publishing it may be a way to put it at rest.

5. Since this paper was written and presented, in 1991 and 1992, revisionism has come a long way. After the name change and dissolution of the Communist Party, the neo-Fascist MSI also changed its name to Alleanza Nazionale and announced that it now supported democracy. The increasingly common sense in the country is that, while anti-Communism is still usable, anti-Fascism is no longer relevant.

6. Claudio Pavone, *Una guerra civile. Saggio sulla moralità nella Resistenza* (Milan: Bollati Boringhieri, 1992).

7. Mario Sabatini, b. 1925, chemical worker, Marmore (Terni), July 7, 1973.

8. Ezio Ottaviani, "Ferro e fuoco a Poggio Bustone," in S. Bovini, ed., *L'Umbria nella Resistenza*, p. 349.

9. S. Micheli, "A Poggio Bustone partigiani e popolo," p. 342.

10. Giorgio Pisanò, *Storia della guerra civile in Italia,* quoted in S. Bovini, ed., *L'Umbria nella Resistenza*, p. 398.

11. Mario Filipponi, b. 1924, steelworker, September 3, 1982. A sign of the contamination is that Micheli's account names Enzo Cerroni as the partisan who climbed the roof of the house where the Fascist officials were barricaded.

12. Beniamino Placido, "La storia americana dalla 'Tesi della frontiera' (1893) a *Birth of a Nation* (1915)," in *Materiali di documentazione* (Venice: Biennale Cinema, 1975).

13. See the testimony of the partisan commander Edoardo Succhielli, in Ida Balò, *Giugno 1944. Civitella racconta* (Cortona: Etruria, 1994), pp. 174–75. For a discussion, see chapter 10, "The Massacre at Civitella Val di Chiana (Tuscany, June 29, 1944): Myth and Politics, Mourning and Common Sense" in this book.

14. *L'Unità* (Umbria edition), January 10, 1944. One of the victims was the father of a high school friend of mine (later, he became a neo-Fascist local politician). I was always impressed by the mark the event had left on this boy.

15. See chapter 1 in this book, "Oral History as Genre."

16. Comunardo Tobia, b. 1920, chemical worker, December 29, 1982.

17. Bruno Zenoni, b. 1908, barber, June 24, 1980.

CHAPTER 10. THE MASSACRE AT CIVITELLA VAL
DI CHIANA

1. This paper is based on remarks made at the international conference, "In Memory: For a European Memory of Nazi Crimes after the End of the Cold War," Arezzo, June 22–24, 1994, and developed upon request and suggestion of the conference organizer, Leonardo Paggi. It has appeared in Italian in a slightly different version, in Leonardo Paggi, ed., *Storia e memoria di un massacro ordinario* (Rome: Manifestolibri, 1996). I attended the conference, a welcome and uncommon opportunity to contribute the oral history approach to a discussion of historians and anthropologists, as a respondent. Rather than giving a paper, my task was to participate in the discussion. This chapter, therefore, reflects the papers and documentation as they were presented at the conference, and uses the documentation made available there.

2. In Romano Bilenchi, *Cronache degli anni neri* (Rome: Editori Riuniti, 1984), p. 254. The written testimony of the widows and survivors of Civitella was collected by Romano Bilenchi in 1946, and originally published in *Società* 2, nos. 7–8 (1946). This collection is henceforth referred to in the text with the initials RB and page numbers. The women of Civitella use proudly the old-fashioned naming practice of prefixing the word *widow* to the name of their dead husbands. Beside keeping their memory alive, it also immediately identifies them as survivors of the massacre. It is retained in this article.

3. Giovanni Contini, "La memoria divisa. Osservazioni sulle due memorie del la strage del 29 giugno 1944 a Civitella Val di Chiana," paper presented at the international conference, "In Memory: For a European Memory of Nazi Crimes after the End of the Cold War," Arezzo, June 22–24, 1994. In this chapter, I refer to papers and documentation as they were presented at the conference: drafts of papers; a number of interviews collected in 1993 (I will refer to those recorded by Paola Calamandrei and Francesca Cappelletto by the interviewees' initials in the text and other information in the footnotes); the 1946 testimony collected by Romano Bilenchi (see note 2); and the written testimony collected in Ida Balò Valli, *Giugno 1944. Civitella racconta* (Cortona: Editrice Grafica L'Etruria, 1994), published immediately after the conference (I will refer to this book in the text with the initials *CR* and page numbers).

4. M.C., woman, 66, int. July 7, 1993.

5. Interviewed by Giovanni Contini, Aug. 27, 1993.

6. In all accounts of the partisan attack on the Germans, the moral and narrative center of the story hinges on the question, "Who fired first?" (Ida Balò, *CR*, 35), a defensive construct found both in Western literature and cinema and in other Resistance narratives (see chapter 9 in this book, "The Battle of Poggio Bustone: Violence, Memory, and Imagination in the Partisan War"). Both the partisan commander Edoardo Succhielli and the partisan Vasco Caroti, who took part in the action, describe—contradicting each other in important details—a scene in

which a German soldier reaches for his weapons, but the partisans are faster and kill him in self-defense. All the variants of the partisan versions are collected in *CR* and discussed in Contini's paper.

7. Valeria Di Piazza, "Civitella della Chiana 50 years after the massacre," paper presented at the Arezzo conference.

8. Pietro Clemente, "Ritorno dall'apocalisse," paper presented at the Arezzo conference.

9. For instance, the Communist journalist and politician Rossana Rossanda writes, "The irrationality of illness and death, of the illusion of happiness, of solitude, these are all things that the workers' and revolutionary movements bracket out of their perspective. . . . Hard, but adult, would be to admit that the human condition, suspended between life and death, this biological, a-historical datum, the indestructible remnant of individuality in human suffering, is the dark boundary that limits the road of political emancipation"; see "Bergman: un dolore senza storia," *Il Manifesto,* Nov. 8, 1973.

10. Paola Calamandrei and Francesca Cappelletto, "La memoria lontana di paesi diversi: i massacri nazi-fascisti nei racconti," paper presented at the Arezzo conference.

11. The expression "grey zone" was formulated by Primo Levi to describe the concentration camp prisoners who collaborated or mediated with the Nazi authorities: see "La zona grigia," in *I sommersi e i salvati* (Turin: Einaudi, 1991), pp. 25–52. More recently, the writer Stefano Levi Della Torre (from whom I quote here) has applied the concept to the part of the Italian people who "did not take sides" between Fascism and the Resistance. See S. Levi Della Torre, *Mosaico. Attualità e inattualità degli ebrei* (Turin: Rosenberg & Sellier, 1992), p. 66.

12. Giorgio Bocca, *Storia dell'Italia partigiana* (Bari: Laterza, 1970), p. 288.

13. When I studied the narratives of the workers of Terni (Umbria), who dated the police killing of their comrade Luigi Trastulli in 1953, I was able to recognize them as *representations* (or at least, to recognize what kind of representations they were) because I was also aware of the *fact* that the event had taken place in 1949 instead. See my "The Death of Luigi Trastulli: Memory and the Event," in *The Death of Luigi Trastulli and other Stories: Form and Meaning in Oral History* (Albany, N.Y.: State University of New York Press, 1991), pp. 1–26.

14. Uliana Merini, widow Caldelli, in *Società,* 1946, quoted in Clemente, "Ritorno dall'apocalissi"; Lara Lammioni Lucarelli (*CR,* 271). I have intentionally selected examples from different times (the postwar years and the present) and different media (oral narrative and written testimony), in order to show the pervasiveness of this approach. Contini, "La memoria divisa," also comments (critically) on the killing of the Germans as narrative beginning.

15. Man, 67, July 7, 1993.

16. Ida Balò (*CR,* 3, 9–10); Don Daniele Tiezzi, "Paese mio," poem (*CR,* no page number); Teresa Milani widow Bernini (*CR,* 365).

17. One of the few testimonies that mention Cagnacci is also one of the few that do not confirm the image of the idyll: "From the early months of 1944, we at Civitella lived in the anxious anticipation of an imminent, fearful future of war." This anxiety was communicated to the narrator (eleven years old at the time) by the fact that his father had to show his papers as he crossed the ammunition depot zone to go to work each day. "A few months earlier, in this area, Gino Cagnacci had been killed . . .": Dino Tiezzi (*CR*, 292).

18. Man, 62, Sept. 11, 1993.

19. The figure of paradise lost is also functional to questioning the need for the partisans' presence: "They shouldn't have done it because they ought to have realized that even if they were Germans they were not people that bothered anybody" (A.M., man, 64, Sept. 9, 1993). Several narrators belittle the meaning of the partisans' struggle by attributing to them opportunistic or dishonest motives: they stole, or they only did it to escape the draft (that is, to avoid having to fight for the Fascists and the Germans). These are widespread, commonsense accusations.

20. Man, 63, Oct. 4, 1993.

21. Woman, 86, July 9, 1993.

22. Enzo Droandi, "I massacri avvenuti attorno ad Arezzo dei documenti della 'Wehrmacht,'" paper presented at the Arezzo conference.

23. The partisan Vasco Caroti claims (but all the survivors deny) that the action was carried out also because people in town complained that the partisans were doing nothing.

24. As a collaborator of the Nazis recalls, precisely the insistence that the town was harmless and pacified accentuated the Germans' feeling that they had been "betrayed" (Costantino Civitelli, *CR*, 265). V.C.'s formula—"they had done nothing"—is the same that the workers of Terni repeated in frustrated anger recalling that they had "done nothing" when of one of their comrades, Luigi Trastulli, was killed by the police (Portelli, "The Death of Luigi Trastulli"). Terni is a large industrial town, Civitella a small rural community, and it would be absurd to expect the same reactions. Yet it is ironic that what is shameful in one place becomes a virtue in another. I cannot but wonder (although there is no trace of it in the interviews) whether the antipartisan resentment at Civitella does not also include a trace of unease at having done nothing against the Fascists and the Germans. The only traces are the passages in which the survivors claim that "we would have defended the town" if only the partisans had helped (Ml. C., M.C.).

25. Herman Melville, *Moby Dick*, (Harmondsworth, Midds.: Penguin, 1986), pp. 261–62.

26. See RB 256, 258, 268, 276, 279–81. "If we stoop to trace a separation almost in terms of species between 'us' and 'them,' as if Nazism was an 'alien' phenomenon, we would only be practicing a reassuring exorcism": S. Levi Della Torre, *Mosaico*, p. 72.

27. Woman, 68, July 7–8, 1993. The narrator also claims that the Germans were "under orders," and that "they were betrayed."

28. Ida Balò gives the priest's offer to sacrifice himself for his flock as a fact. The story is confirmed also by Bishop Luciano Giovannetti, who stood near the priest as an altar boy, and by the priest's niece, Lina Rossi. The temporal sequences of these narratives, however, do not coincide. The story is not mentioned in Bartolucci's testimony to the English inquest in 1944 nor in his daughter's recent testimony (*CR*, 100, 123). On the other hand, offering himself in exchange for the others made little sense when the Germans were clearly intent on killing both him and the rest. Both Lina Rossi and Father Daniele Tiezzi testify that the priest might have escaped, but returned willingly to die; their versions, however, differ in that Tiezzi says that it was a German soldier who pointed out the way of possible escape, which Rossi does not confirm.

29. Woman; no data supplied by interviewers.

30. Father Daniele Tiezzi says that he has forgiven the partisans "with great difficulty."

31. The officer in charge of the German detachment that had been attacked by the partisans in Rome was exonerated for religious reasons from carrying out the retaliation. One soldier fainted during the mass execution of the 335 victims. "It was said about him," writes Giorgio Bocca, "that he refused to fire for religious reasons. It is false: no German hesitated" (*Storia dell'Italia partigiana*, p. 285). Eric Priebke, one of the officers who carried out the massacre, claims that the Vatican helped him get safely out of Italy at the end of the war: *La Repubblica*, May 9 and 10, 1994.

32. Ivano Sabatini, Terni, Jan. 25 1976, int. by Valentino Paparelli; quoted in Portelli, "The Death of Luigi Trastulli," p. 9. In a speech in parliament (April 2, 1949), the Socialist representative Tito Oro Nobili claimed that a policeman was about to fire on the crowd from a window and one of his comrades stopped him: see Francesco Bogliari, *Tito Oro Nobili* (Perugia: Quaderni Regione dell'Umbria, 1977), pp. 219–28.

33. Gennara Magini Gualdani (*CR*, 433–34), whose father was helped to reach safety by a German soldier during the Cornia massacre, also suggests that the "good German" was killed by his comrades. Other local variants of the "good German" theme are found in the narrative of M.C. (she was spared by a German soldier whom her father had asked for mercy on his knees) and in Father Daniele Tiezzi's version of Father Lazzeri's death. The idea of the one righteous person who redeems a community of sinners also has Biblical roots: see Genesis, 18:23–33.

34. Primo Levi, "Lettere di tedeschi," in *I sommersi e i salvati* (1986; rept. Turin: Einaudi, 1991), p. 139.

35. Nuto Revelli, *Il disperso di Marburg* (Turin: Einaudi, 1994), p. 165.

36. There is no mention of the "good German" in the testimony given to the British commission of enquiry in 1944 by Gino Bartolucci. Bartolucci was shot with the other men, but he was only wounded and survived by feigning death. He was, therefore, in a position to witness the whole mass execution. His daugh-

ter's testimony also makes no mention of the story (Ilva Bartolucci Saletti, *IB*, 323).

37. It was an informal conversation, so I did not think of taping it. I am using the notes I jotted down immediately after it was over. The discussion in this paper is based on the comments I made at the conference; Mrs. Balò was in the audience, and I later asked her whether I had distorted what she had told me. She said I had reported it correctly.

38. Actually, Father Biagini dates the episode at 1983, that is, eleven years before my conversation with Ida Balò. However, the fact that an authoritative narrator like Mrs. Balò uses the same formula for both events suggests she sees them as roughly contemporary.

39. Woman, 55, July 7, 1993.

40. "A providential help was given us by the then young congressman A-mintore Fanfani, who took the town's condition to heart and was active, among other things, in the construction of the aqueduct and low-rent housing, as well as in securing pensions for the widows": Ida Balò Valli (*CR*, 167). I am not sure whether, in such a sincerely religious witness, the word "providential" is to be taken as a mere colloquialism, shorn of its sacred implications. The next paragraph begins: "Civitella slowly *resurrects*" (my italics). M.C. recalls that "later, they built the low-rent houses, the Fanfani houses . . . at the time, he was in charge. It must have been '48, when they made a celebration for Fanfani's water." A.M. recalls that Fanfani was "the only one who went [to Civitella], he secured the funds for the monument through some organizations—he's from Arezzo." Again, the narrators project themselves in a passive historical role. The Fanfani houses and Fanfani's water are neither their right, nor the consequence of any action of theirs, but the gift of a powerful intermediator.

41. Maurice Halbwachs, *La mémoire collective* (Paris: Presses Universitaires de France, 1968). On forgetting as a mechanism of memory, see Jurij M. Lotman and Boris A. Upsenskij, "Sul meccanismo semiotico della cultura," in *Tipologia della cultura* (Milan: Bompiani, 1973), pp. 46–47, Italian translation by Remo Faccani.

42. I taught at the Arezzo campus of the university of Siena from 1975 to 1981.

43. See the passage from Succhielli's interview quoted in the introduction to this book, p. viii.

44. Contini, "La memoria divisa."

45. *La Repubblica*, June 4, 1996, p. 17; *Il Messaggero*, June 5, 1996, pp. 1, 9; *La Repubblica*, June 8, 1996, p. 3.

46. In January, 1996, a stone commemorating the German "victims" and extolling Priebke was placed at via Rasella (where the partisan action had taken place) by unidentified neo-Nazi activists. It was later removed by the authorities. The struggle for memory continues. In July 1966 the military court found Priebke guilty, but granted him extenuating circumstances and ordered him freed on a statute of limitations.

CHAPTER 11. VERSIONS OF VIETNAM

1. Born in 1924; interviewed in Terni, Oct. 9, 1982; quoted in Alessandro Portelli, *Biografia di una città. Storia e racconto. Terni 1830–1985* (Turin: Einaudi, 1985), p. 203.

2. B. 1916; int. Terni, April 25, 1981; in Portelli, *Biografia di una città,* p. 239. About Peppoloni, see also my "The Best Garbage Man in Town: Life and Times of Valtèro Peppoloni, Worker," in *The Death of Luigi Trastulli and Other Stories: Form and Meaning in Oral History* (Albany, N.Y: State University of New York Press, 1991), pp. 117–37.

3. This chapter first appeared in Stefano Ghislotti and Stefano Rosso, eds., *La "guerra sporca." Il Vietnam nel cinema, nella letteratura, nella letteratura e nel teatro* (Bergamo: Marcos y Marcos, 1996).

4. William Least Heat Moon, *PrairyErth* (Boston: Houghton Mifflin, 1991), p. 55.

5. Malcolm X, "Message to the Grassroots," in *Malcolm X Speaks* (New York: Grove Press, 1965), p. 7.

6. Antonio Gibelli, "Per una storia dell'esperienza di guerra dei contadini," in *La cultura delle classi subalterne fra tradizione e innovazione* (Alessandria: Edizioni dell'Orso, 1988), pp. 85–102.

7. Henry David Thoreau, "Resistance to Civil Government," in Nina Baym et al., eds., *The Norton Anthology of American Literature* (New York: Norton, 1989), p. 1620.

8. Mark Baker, *Nam: The Vietnam War in the Words of the Men and Women Who Fought There* (London: Abacus, 1982), p. 14. Further references are indicated by the initial *N* and page numbers in the text.

9. Philippe Lejeune, *Le pacte autobiographique* (Paris: Seuil, 1975).

10. Chuck Rosenberg, "Boony Rat Song," from the compact disc *In Country: Folk Songs of Americans in the Vietnam War,* published by the Vietnam Veterans Oral History and Folklore Project (Flying Fish records, 1991, FF 70552).

11. Wallace Terry, *Bloods: An Oral History of the Vietnam War by Black Veterans* (1984; repr. New York: Ballantine, 1992), p. 109. Further references are indicated by the initial *B* and page numbers in the text.

12. For another case of ambiguity between impersonal and personal *you,* see chapter 2 in this book, "There's Gonna Always Be a Line: History-Telling as a Multivocal Art."

13. Elena Spandri, "Non puoi sempre dire tutto a tutti. Storia di un'intervista," in M. Arcidiacono et al., *L'aeroplano e le stelle. Storia orale di una realtà studentesca* (Rome: Manifestolibri, 1995), pp. 220–26.

14. Malcolm X, "Message to the Grassroots," p. 12.

15. Ibid.

16. *The Life of Olaudah Equiano, or Gustavus Vassa, the African. Written by Himself* (1789) in Henry Louis Gates, Jr., ed., *The Classic Slave Narratives* (New York: Penguin, 1987), pp. 57, 59, 60.

17. Frederick Douglass, "Black Regiments Proposed," in Philip S. Foner, ed., *The Life and Writings of Frederick Douglass* (New York: International Publishers, 1950), vol. 3, pp. 94–95. See also David Blight, *Frederick Douglass's Civil War: Keeping Faith in Jubilee* (Baton Rouge: Louisiana State University Press, 1989), pp. 148–74.

18. W. E. B. Du Bois, "An Essay Toward a History of the Black Man in the Great War" (1919), in *Writings* (New York: The Library of America, 1986), p. 881.

19. On free indirect speech as the expression of a divided self, see Henry Louis Gates, Jr., *The Signifying Monkey* (New York and Oxford: Oxford University Press, 1988), p. 215.

20. On the other hand, see Archie Biggers: "The enemy would do anything to win. You had to respect that. They believed in a cause. They had the support of the people. That's the key we Americans don't understand yet" (*B*, 133). Though he respects the Vietnamese, yet Biggers speaks of "we Americans": his perception of the Vietnamese remains impersonal; they are "the enemy."

21. Malcolm X, *The Autobiography of Malcolm X*, with the assistance of Alex Haley (Harmondsworth, Midds.: Penguin, 1968), p. 392.

22. Mario Filipponi, b. 1924, steelworker, Terni), March 9, 1982. See chapter 9 in this book, "The Battle of Poggio Bustone: Violence, Memory, and Imagination in the Partisan War."

23. Leslie Marmon Silko, *Ceremony* (1977; repr. New York: Penguin, 1986), p. 60.

24. Silko, *Ceremony*, p. 252.

25. Interestingly, the "pop" of the flashbulbs in this narrative is the same sound as that of the eyeball plucked out from a Vietnamese prisoner in the passage quoted above.

26. Valtèro Peppoloni showed me a picture he kept in his Spanish War album of Fascists holding the cut-off head of a dead enemy, with the same expression of festive pride.

27. Herman Melville, *Moby Dick* (Harmondsworth, Midds.: Penguin, 1986), pp. 276, 534.

28. A similar theme is explored in Bruce Springsteen's "Galveston Bay," a song about Vietnam veterans and Vietnamese refugees, in *The Ghost of Tom Joad* (Columbia COL 481650).

CHAPTER 12. INTERVIEWING THE MOVEMENT

1. This chapter is a revised and enlarged version of an essay published in Bruce Jackson and Edward D. Ives, eds., *The World Observed: Reflections of the Fieldwork Process* (Urbana and Chicago: University of Illinois Press, 1996), pp. 44–59. A different version of the first three paragraphs appeared as "Intervistare il movimento: il '68 e la storia orale," *I Giorni Cantati* 10–11 (September 1989), pp. 27–32.

2. Phil Ochs, "I'm Going to Say It Now," in *I Ain't Marching Anymore* (Elektra EKS 7269) and in *Chords of Fame* (AM Records SP 6511).

3. Peppino Ortoleva, *Saggio sui movimenti del 1968 in Europa e in America* (Rome: Editori Riuniti, 1988).

4. Luisa Passerini, *Autobiografia di gruppo* (Florence: Giunti, 1989); Ronald Fraser et al., eds., *1968: A Student Generation in Revolt. An International Oral History* (New York: Pantheon, 1988), pp. 248–60; Alessandro Portelli, *Biografia di una città. Storia e racconto. Terni 1830–1985* (Turin: Einaudi, 1985), pp. 330–34.

5. On recent improvements in the archive situation, see G. Barrera, A. Martini, and A. Mulè, eds., *Fonti orali, Censimento degli istituti di conservazione* (Rome: Ministero per i Beni Culturali e Ambientali, 1993).

6. Cesare Bermani, "Dieci anni di lavoro con le fonti orali," *Primo Maggio 5* (1975), pp. 35–50; Gianni Bosio, *L'intellettuale rovesciato* (Milan: Bella Ciao, 1975); Rocco Scotellaro, *Contadini del Sud* (Bari: Laterza, 1954).

7. Walter J. Ong, *Orality and Literacy: The Technologizing of the Word* (London and New York: Methuen, 1982).

8. The catalogue of the Istituto De Martino contains thirty-eight tapes recorded in 1968 during the student movement in Milan. Rather than a specific research project, these tapes represent an effort at documentation. They consist almost entirely of recordings of public events such as demonstrations and mass meetings. See Franco Coggiola, ed., *Fonti orali per la storia e l'antropologia: Testimonianze e documenti del mondo contadino e operaio* (Milan: Istituto Ernesto de Martino and Urbino: Istituto di Filosofia dell'Università degli Studi, 1988), pp. 48–9, 53.

9. Ernesto de Martino, *Furore simbolo valore* (1962; repr. Milan: Feltrinelli 1980); this is a collection of his earlier essays on the anthropology of contemporary urban societies.

10. P. Boccardo, G. Bosio, and T. Savi, eds., *Addio padre. La guerra di Belochio, di Palma e di Badoglio* (Dischi del Sole, DS 116/18); Gianni Bosio, ed., *La Prima Internazionale* (Dischi del Sole DS 301/3/CP); A. Portelli, ed., *La borgata e la lotta per la casa* (Dischi del Sole SdL/AS/10).

11. Carmela Luci, Rome, Oct. 28, 1973.

12. Gianni Bosio, ed., *I fatti di Milano* (Dischi del Sole, SdL/AS/7).

13. Paolo Pietrangeli, "Valle Giulia," *Canzoniere della Protesta 6* (Milan: Edizioni Bella Ciao, 1977); on record, Paolo Pietrangeli, *Mio caro padrone domani ti sparo* (Dischi del Sole DS 197/99).

14. A. Portelli, "I metalmeccanici e la funzione poetica. Espressività orale di base nella manifestazione nazionale del 2 dicembre 1977," *I Giorni Cantati 2–3* (1982), pp. 43–60.

15. A commemoration of the thirtieth anniversary of the murder of Paolo Rossi, organized by the Rome Institute for the History of Resistance and Fascism in April 1966, was the occasion of my writing the essay on youth culture in Harlan, included in this book (chapter 13).

16. Color TV was introduced in Italy in 1976. I have made a little experiment

of asking people if they remember the date; in most cases, they move it back from five to ten years, as if to suggest that it has always been there.

17. This was the central issue in the conference organized by the Istituto Ernesto de Martino and the journal *Primo Maggio* in Mantova, October 23–25, 1981, "Working-Class Memory and New Class Composition: Problems and Methods of Historiography of the Proletariat." In the published proceedings, *Memoria operaia e nuova composizione di classe. Problemi e metodi della storiografia del proletariato* (Rimini: Maggioli, 1986), see Cesare Bermani, "Introduzione," pp. ix–xlii; Valerio Marchetti, "Rivoluzione e follia," pp. 59–68; and the discussion remarks by Claudio Pavone, Bruno Cartosio, and Valerio Marchetti.

18. Paolo Pietrangeli, Rome, June 19, 1996. All other interviews used in this section were collected by Andrea Colombo, a journalist for *Il Manifesto*, on the occasion of a 1968 twentieth-anniversary supplement, April 1988.

19. At the time of the events, Massimo Pieri was a student in physics, and is now a researcher.

20. Lucio Castellano was a sociology student; he later became a sociologist.

21. Raul Mordenti, university professor, interviewed by me in Rome, March 1988. He was a literature student and now teaches Italian literature in the university.

22. In the April, 1988, supplement to *Il Manifesto*.

23. Roberto De Angelis, interviewed by Andrea Colombo, was then a sociology student and is now a socioanthropologist, specializing in youth cultures.

24. Maria Rossi is a pseudonym. She was a philosophy student and later became a psychoanalyst. She also was interviewed by Andrea Colombo.

25. Alessandro Portelli, "Uchronic Dreams: Working-Class Memory and Possible Worlds," in *The Death of Luigi Trastullli and Other Stories* (Albany: State University of New York Press, 1991), pp. 99–116.

26. Walter Mazzilli, b. 1948, interviewed by me in Terni, July 7, 1983. Mazzilli was at the time Culture Officer for the Terni city administration.

27. For another example of mock-heroic style in movement narratives, see chapter 15 in this book, "Conversations with the Panther."

28. Oreste Scalzone is from Terni. The analogy with the Terni partisans' peace offer to the Fascist chiefs in the battle of Poggio Bustone ("If you come out peacefully—maybe—you will be spared": see chapter 9, "The Battle of Poggio Bustone: Violence, Memory, and Imagination in the Partisan War") may be more than a coincidence.

CHAPTER 13. IT WAS SUPPOSED TO BE HAPPENING
IN BERKELEY

1. David Walls, formerly on the staff of the Appalachian Volunteers and then of the Appalachian Center at the University of Kentucky (Lexington), is now a college administrator in California. This interview was recorded in Rome, July 19, 1992.

2. Gurney Norman, b. 1937, Grundy, Va., writer, professor at the University of Kentucky, interviewed by Ronald Grele for the Columbia University Oral History Office, New York, September 27, 1986.

3. "Vista [Volunteers in Service to America] was a program that was part of the war on poverty, part of the Office of Economic Opportunity; it was essentially a one-year volunteer program on the model of the Peace Corps. Vista was a one-year domestic volunteer program that first drew from the same sort of recent college graduate type that the Peace Corps at that time drew primarily from, although Vista later moved to local persons being recruited as volunteers and paid by Vista. Originally it drew from a wide range of recent college students or graduates" (David Walls).

4. Johnny Woodward, Cumberland (Harlan Co.), Southeast Community College, November 1, 1990.

5. Merle Travis, "Nine Pound Hammer," on the record *The Best of Merle Travis* (Capitol SM-2662).

6. Elizabeth Blum, b. 1942, interviewed October 19, 1996, on a Delta flight from New York to Rome.

7. "The AVs had by then split from the Council of Southern Mountains and had their headquarters in Bristol, Tennessee. The AVs started as one kind of organization and very quickly became another kind, and that created a great tension with the new organization. The Council of Southern Mountains is a sort of traditional community development organization which operated on a sort of a consensus model of social change, not a conflict model, and that's how the AVs began in the very early sixties, as a project from some students, first from Berea College, going out to work in very poor communities which had one- and two-room school houses, and they would help repair these old school houses, and they collected books, they even did a national book drive they've called Books for Appalachia. This is around 1962–1963, right after the disastrous flood in Hazard that Henry Caudill describes at the end of his *Night Comes to the Cumberlands*" (Henry M. Caudill, *Night Comes to the Cumberlands: A Biography of a Depressed Area* [Boston and Toronto: Little, Brown, 1963], p. 194.) (David Walls). On the Council of the Southern Mountains and its evolution during and after the Sixties, see John Glen, "The Council of the Southern Mountains and the War on Poverty," in *Now and Then* (published by the Center for Appalachian Studies and Services/Institute for Appalachian Affairs, East Tennessee State University, Johnson City) 5, no. 3 (Fall, 1988), pp. 4–12.

8. Seminar at the Fourth Appalachian Project Conference, University of Rome, January, 1990.

9. Gurney Norman, *Divine Right's Trip* (New York: Dial Press, 1972), pp. 294–302.

10. Paul Good, "Kentucky's Coal Beds of Sedition" (*The Nation*, September 4, 1967), in David Walls and John B. Stephenson, eds., *Appalachia in the Sixties: Decade of Reawakening* (Lexington: University Press of Kentucky), pp. 184–193.

The population of Harlan County had dropped from 71,751 in 1950 to 50,765 (71.2 percent) in 1960; the figures for Perry County were from 47,626 to 38,889. The two counties ranked respectively 119 and 115 out of 120 Kentucky counties in negative population trend for the decade. If one counts only migration, without considering the natural increase, Harlan retained 53.1 percent of its population, and Perry 53.4 percent; the two counties rank 119 and 118. See Willis A. Sutton, Jr. and Jerry Russell, *The Social Dimensions of Kentucky Counties* (University of Kentucky, Lexington: Kentucky Community Series Number 29, September, 1964), tables 6, 10.

11. See Brit Hume, *Death in the Coal Mines: Rebellion and Murder in the UMW* (New York: Grossman, 1971).

12. Peg, "A Letter from Perry County, Kentucky," in Jim Axelrod, ed., *Growin' Up Country* (Clintwood, Va.: Council of the Southern Mountains, 1973), pp. 40–41.

13. Dan Wakefield, "In Hazard" (*Commentary,* September 1963), reprinted in Walls and Stephenson, eds., *Appalachia in the Sixties,* p. 11.

14. See chapter 7, "Form and Meaning of Historical Representation: The Battle of Evarts and the Battle of Crummies (Kentucky: 1931, 1941)."

15. "I couldn't understand why, all of a sudden, my next door neighbor who'd always had a new car, always bought new clothes for the kids and painted [the] house every summer, was all of a sudden standing on the welfare line with me drawing food stamps" (Johnny Woodward).

16. James Goode, teacher at Southeast Community College in Cumberland, Ky., Benham (Harlan Co.), Ky., October 27, 1988.

17. In 1960, only 11.3 percent of all dwellings in Harlan were occupied by their owners; the county ranked 119 out of 120 in Kentucky (Perry County ranked 103). See Sutton and Russell, *The Social Dimensions of Kentucky Counties,* table 45.

18. "We had the best of instruction, at the company school, and the reason we did was because all of the bosses, foremen, superintendents' sons and daughters attended the school, and they had control of the budget, so they hired the best that they could find so that their own sons and daughters would benefit. While all the peasants, all the working class people would benefit from that, everybody went to the same school" (Goode).

19. Hal Ketchum, "Small Town Saturday Night," on the CD *Past the Point of Rescue* (Curb Records D2-77450). Harlan stations played this song almost obsessively in 1992.

20. Gurney Norman, "Night Ride," in *Kinfolks* (Frankfort, Ky.: Gnomon, 1977), pp. 37–38.

21. Lydia Surgener, b. 1930, Cawood, Harlan Co., December 25, 1989 (conversation notes).

22. Mildred Shackleford, 1950, New Market, Tenn., February 11, 1990.

23. George Ella Lyon, b. 1949, interviewed by Annalucia Accardo, Lexing-

ton, Ky., November 1988. Unless otherwise indicated, quotes from Lyon come from this interview.

24. Gurney Norman, *Kinfolks,* p. 68.

25. George Ella Lyon, *Braids: A Play* (1984); typescript, courtesy of the author, in Appalachian Project Collection, University of Rome, p. 15. Appalachia, says George Ella Lyon, has "a very antifemale culture. It's very patriarchal, the culture as a whole. . . . It may be more hidden in some places; I think in the mountains there's a particularly strong notion of silence, particularly for women."

26. George Ella Lyon, interviewed by Alessandro Portelli, Lexington, Ky., November 2, 1988.

27. Peg, "A Letter from Perry County, Kentucky," pp. 28–29, 46.

28. Sidney Douglass, b. 1943, lawyer, Loyall, Harlan Co., July 13, 1987.

29. Rev. Tommy Sweatt, b. 1948, Lynch, Ky., July 10, 1986.

30. Shaunna Scott, *Two Sides to Everything: The Cultural Construction of Class Consciousness in Harlan County, Kentucky* (Albany, N.Y.: State University of New York Press, 1995).

31. Mary [a pseudonym], b. 1969, interviewed at the adult literacy center, Harlan, October 24, 1988.

32. George Ella Lyon, Portelli interview.

33. Gurney Norman, "An Interview with George Ella Lyon," *Appalachian Heritage* 12, 1–2 (Winter–Spring 1985), pp. 54–68.

34. If I may insert a personal note, I might very well have been one of George Ella Lyon's around-the-world correspondents: I too was reading *Sing Out!* in Italy, and would not have been in that room interviewing her, nor would I be writing this book, if one day in 1969, at the house of *Sing Out!*'s editor Irwin Silber in Brooklyn, Barbara Dane had not sung for me a song by Harlan County's Sara Ogan Gunning: "I Hate the Capitalist System." My recording of Dane's rendition of the song is included in the record *L'America della Contestazione,* ed. Alessandro Portelli and Ferdinando Pellegrini (Dischi del Sole: DS 179/81/C1). See also Barbara Dane's album, *I Hate the Capitalist System* (Paredon P 1014).

35. See Jean Ritchie, *Singing Family of the Cumberlands* (New York: Oxford University Press, 1955).

36. Anthony Scaduto, *Bob Dylan* (New York: Grosset & Dunlap, 1971), pp. 164, 167.

37. Josh Dunson, *Freedom in the Air: Song Movements of the '60's* (New York: International Publishers, 1965), pp. 80–81. Tom Paxton's report of the trip first appeared in *Broadside,* n. 45.

38. Phil Ochs, "Hazard, Kentucky," on the record *The Broadside Tapes 1* (Smithsonian Folkways SF 4 8); Eric Andersen, "The Blind Fiddler," in Guy and Candie Carawan, eds., *Voices from the Mountains* (Urbana: University of Illinois Press, 1982), p. 160; Tom Paxton, "The High Sheriff of Hazard," on the record *The Folk Box* (Elektra EKL-BOX).

39. From *Progressive Labor News*, January 1963; reprinted in Guy and Candie Carawan, eds., *Voices from the Mountains*, p. 164.

40. Malvina Reynolds, "Mrs. Clara Sullivan's Letter," in *Little Boxes and Other Handmade Songs* (New York: Oak, 1966).

41. Linda Hairston, b. 1954, store clerk, Lynch, Ky., October 7, 1986.

42. Edward J. Cabbell, "Black Invisibility and Racism in Appalachia: An Informal Survey," in William H. Turner and Edward J. Cabbell, eds., *Blacks in Appalachia* (Lexington: The University Press of Kentucky, 1985), pp. 3–10.

43. On race in Harlan County history, see also my "No Neutrals There: The Cultural Class Struggle in the Harlan Miners' Strike of 1931–32," in *The Death of Luigi Trastulli and Other Stories: Form and Meaning in Oral History* (Albany, N.Y.: State University of New York Press, 1991), pp. 216–38; also my "From Sanctified Hill to Pride Terrace: Urban Ideals and Rural Working-Class Experience in Black Communities in Harlan County, Kentucky," *Storia Nordamericana* 7, 2 (1990), 51–64.

44. Earl Turner, retired mine foreman, Lynch, Ky., October 1986. "My brother taught for about fifteen years here, to white kids and black kids. Every white kid here in their twenties, or early thirties, that went to Evarts high school knew my brother because he was their teacher, Mr. Blue" (Dallas Blue, b. 1925, Coxton, Harlan Co., October 29, 1988).

45. [William H. Turner], untitled editorial, *Sojourner Memorial Calendar* (Lynch, Ky.: Eastern Kentucky Social Club, 1988), n.p.

46. "Some of the teachers, some of the black teachers had to go elsewhere to find jobs. To get knowledgeable people out of the community hurts. That seems to be the basic criteria of Harlan County" (Dallas Blue); "Before the schools were integrated, our teachers pushed us to go and do and learn. . . . I tell you how I feel, I feel like after integration, the teachers that we had didn't care, the majority of our teachers were white teachers. When I went to school it was all black. We were always pushed to go and do and be something. They would teach us even if you were gonna be a garbage man, you be the best garbage man you can be. This is what we were taught. If you can't learn to do anything but haul garbage, you be the best garbage man you can be. Always excel at what you're doing—and we weren't taught that after integration" (Willetta Lee, Cumberland, Ky., October 7, 1986).

47. Mrs. Julia Cowans, Lexington, Ky., September 28, 1983.

48. The sense that these changes were part of a broader framework over which local forces had little control influenced also the behavior of the whites: "From what I gather, during that period the [white] people here were smart. They just went along with the president's program. Whatever the president said, the higher ups [said] it would be better to do this because they are going to do what they want anyway. So they went right along and there was no impact at all. Keeping kids out of school or what have you, it was just a matter of transition" (Dallas Blue).

49. Ed Cabbell, "Black Invisibility and Racism in Appalachia: An Informal Survey"; A. Portelli, "From Sanctified Hill to Pride Terrace."

50. Mildred Shackleford wrote an article in the school paper about the confrontation with the racist teacher and was threatened with expulsion. She had a Vista legal aid call the principal and stop the sanction, but the teacher gave her an F in the course, which ruined her chances for college.

51. Mrs. Julia Cowans, Lexington, Ky., Sept. 28, 1983.

52. See chapter 2, "There's Gonna Always Be a Line," for more context about this episode.

53. "I was a good ballplayer, so the companies were anxious to have me come and play. That way I stayed in touch with the union and always stayed active in the organizing. Since they recognized me as a ballplayer, I could walk into any camp any time. I was never once bothered by the thugs. No other organizers could ever get into the camps." Bill Worthington, quoted in Kennet Warren Mirvis, *A Phenomenological Analysis of Two Appalachian Coal-Producing Counties*, Ph.D. diss., Boston University, School of Education, p. 218 (typescript in Highlander Center library).

54. In Harlan County in 1960, only 27.7 percent of dwellings were defined as "in good condition" (that is, with hot running water, inside toilets, private bath, and not dilapidated); the percentage was similar (27.2 percent) in Perry County. The two counties ranked 81 and 85 out of 120 Kentucky counties. See Sutton and Russell, *The Social Dimensions of Kentucky Counties*, table 46.

55. Harlan and Perry ranked 108 and 120 out of 120 in "Valuation of Education" in Kentucky Counties in 1960 (that is, in "the ratio of educational to other expenditures" in the county). See Sutton and Russell, *The Social Dimensions of Kentucky Counties*, table 65.

56. Former AV staff member David Walls was one of the first to discuss the "internal colonialism" model in the Appalachian context; see "Internal Colony or Internal Periphery? A Critique of Current Models and an Alternative Formulation," in Helen M. Lewis, Linda Johnson, and Donald Askins, eds., *Colonialism in Modern America* (Boone, N.C.: Appalachian Consortium Press, 1978).

57. "To see the devastation caused by strip mining, to see the terrible rock slide and mud slide that took place at the very end of Johnson's Creek, I think in that winter of 1967, certainly brought it very close to home to me that surface mining was going on without regard to what was happening to the land and that it was going to endanger lots of people" (David Walls). Former AV members were also instrumental in forming the Appalachian Group to Save the Land and People, who were especially active in Knott and Perry Counties in the struggle against strip mining, often in terms of direct action.

58. Loyal Wagner, b. 1941, Benham, Ky., October 16, 1996.

59. A Harlan businessman, quoted by Shaunna Scott, says, "The school superintendent had more jobs to give than any other one person in the county and that's the reason [politics] got so involved [in schools] in the hills. Back in the 1930s, if you could give out 150 to 200 jobs during the Depression, you talk

about *power* . . . and it's stayed the same." "In no place," notes Scott, "was nepotism more evident than in the Harlan County education system": Scott, *Two Sides to Everything*, pp. 117–18.

60. T. N. Bethell, Pat Gish, and Tom Gish, "Kennedy Hears of Need," *The Mountain Eagle*, February 15, 1968; reprinted in *Appalachia in the Sixties*, pp. 62–68.

61. Curtis Snow, son of black coal miners from Lynch, quoted in Bob Hill, "Black Home in Appalachia," Louisville *Courier-Journal Magazine*, June 28, 1987, p. 12.

62. Don West, "Romantic Appalachia," in Walls and Stephenson, eds., *Appalachia in the Sixties*, pp. 210–16. For a fiercely critical account, see also Bruce Jackson, "In the Valley of the Shadows: Kentucky," *Transaction* (June 1971).

63. Gladys Hoskins, Harlan, Ky., October 17, 1996.

64. Paul Good, "Kentucky's Coal Beds of Sedition," *The Nation* (September 4, 1967); reprinted in Walls and Stephenson, eds., *Appalachia in the Sixties*, pp. 184–93.

65. James Goode made it clear in the interview that his criticism of his father's anti-Communism did not imply that he had any Communist leanings himself.

66. In 1970, at the end of the War on Poverty, the population of Harlan County had dropped to 37,370; on a national ranking, Harlan ranked 2,934 out of 3,097 U.S. counties in socioeconomic status; 2,929 in health status; 2,765 in family status; 2,022 in "alienation." (The corresponding rankings for Perry were 2,986; 2,640; 2,349; and 1,326. Population in Perry County was 25,714.) See U.S. Department of Agriculture: Economics, Statistics, and Cooperative Services, *Indexes and Rankings for Indicators of Social Well-Being for U.S. Counties* (Statistical Supplement for Rural Development, Research Report No. 10), 1979.

CHAPTER 14. YOUTH CULTURE, THE POLITICS OF PRIVATE LIFE, AND THE CULTURE OF THE WORKING CLASSES

1. "Cultura operaia, condizione giovanile, politicità del privato: ipotesi per una ricerca sul campo," *Rivista di storia contemporanea* 8, no. 1 (January, 1979), pp. 56–83.

2. While the influence of the women's movement was crucial in these developments, there was little explicit awareness of gender issues as such in the movement at the time. Part of the original text of this paper dealt with these issues; I have left them out because there was nothing in them that has not been said over and over, and in part also left behind, by the women's movement and feminist thought.

3. Gianna Pajetta and Adriana Nannicini, *I consigli,* magazine of the Federazione Lavoratori Metalmeccanici (mechanical and steelworkers' federation), April 1977, p. 32.

4. Pier Paolo Pasolini, "Studio sulla rivoluzione antropologica in Italia" (June 10, 1974) and "Il vero antifascismo e quindi il vero fascismo," in *Scritti corsari*

(Milan: Garzanti, 1990), pp. 39–44, 45–50. Pier Paolo Pasolini, writer and film-maker, was one of the "prophetic" voices of the 1970s.

5. Alberto Melucci, "Dieci ipotesi per l'analisi dei nuovi movimenti," *Quaderni Piacentini* nos. 65–66 (February 1978), pp. 9–11.

6. Pasolini, *Scritti corsari,* p. 48. This statement must be taken metaphorically; indeed, a commonplace of the times was that too often the option of Left or Right was reduced to opposing dress codes.

7. Giovanna Marini, *I Treni per Reggio Calabria* (Dischi del Sole DS 1066/68; repr. Bravo Records CD 070).

8. Pier Paolo Pasolini, "Il genocidio," in *Scritti corsari,* p. 228.

9. In another controversial article, Pier Paolo Pasolini attacked long hair, saying that it had gone from a statement of protest to a fashion in which "the subculture of power has absorbed the subculture of opposition" ("Il 'Discorso' dei capelli" in *Scritti corsari,* p. 10). Behind this process, however, Raffaele Marchetti reveals a history of struggle, and perhaps what counts now is not the hair, but the memory of the struggle and its continuation in new forms.

10. "Marriage is still often arranged by mediators. A few years ago my mother introduced me to a girl: 'She's a good girl, where you put her she stays.' And I: 'What is she, a piece of furniture?'" (Francesco Boccia, from Amaseno, a village near Frosinone, Southern Lazio, in a seminar at the Circolo Gianni Bosio in Rome, March 1977).

11. Silvano Spinetti, "La signorina America," recorded in Genzano (Rome), March 9, 1970. Silvano Spinetti's songs are included in the anthology *I Giorni Cantati. Cultura operaia e contadina a Roma e nel Lazio,* ed. Circolo Gianni Bosio (Milan: Mazzotta, 1983).

12. Blind Alfred Reed, *How Can a Poor Man Stand Such Times and Live?* (Rounder Records, 1001).

13. Unidentified young man, interviewed by Susanna Cerboni, Guardavalle (province of Catanzaro, Calabria), July 1977; see Susanna Cerboni, "Ruoli generazionali e cultura tradizionale a Guardavalle," *I Giorni Cantati* 13 (1979), pp. 22–28, and "Guardavalle, Calabria. Trasformazioni di una ricerca," *I Giorni Cantati* 4 (1983), pp. 22–28.

14. Nuto Revelli, *L'anello forte. La donna: storie di vita contadina* (Turin: Einaudi, 1985).

15. The only institution concerned is the Church, which exercises moral supervision over the trade, while often the local priests act as (unpaid) mediators themselves. For a recent, excellent work filling the gap in feminist sociology on the rural women of Calabria, see Renate Siebert, *"E' femmina però è bella": Tre generazioni di donne al Sud* (Turin: Rosenberg & Sellier, 1991).

16. Bruno Andreoli, Modena, San Cataldo public library, May 31, 1977.

17. "When I say 'my,'" Andreoli explains, "I do not mean it individually, but in terms of class: it is a way of relating myself to others, to place myself inside a class."

18. Cesare Bermani writes that in the fifties there was "a real gap in the creation of social songs" and "mass creativity seems to come to a halt, along with the stagnation of mass struggles" (booklet enclosed with the album *Sventolerai lassù. Antologia della canzone comunista in Italia 2*, ed. Cesare Bermani [Milan: Dischi del Sole DS 1078/80]).

19. The Fiat 500 was a cheap compact car that made automobiles available to working people—Italy's equivalent of the Model T.

20. Diane, in Studs Terkel, *Hard Times: An Oral History of the Great Depression* (New York: Avon, 1970), p. 39.

21. Interview with a group of football fans, Terni, May 25, 1981, quoted in Alessandro Portelli, *Biografia di una città. Storia, memoria e immaginario. Terni 1830–1985* (Turin: Einaudi, 1985), p. 350.

22. Diane, in Terkel, *Hard Times*, p. 39; Michael, ibid., p. 43.

23. Pajetta and Nannicini, *I Consigli*, p. 44–45.

24. From notes taken during a a seminar at the Circolo Gianni Bosio, Rome, June 23, 1977.

25. Interviews recorded at Guardavalle Marina (Catanzaro, Calabria) by Susanna Cerboni, August 4, 1977, with a group of workers and students, ages 18 to 27.

26. Quoted in A. Portelli, "Dividing the World," in *The Death of Luigi Trastulli: Form and Meaning in Oral History* (Albany, N.Y.: State University of New York Press, 1991), p. 93–94.

27. Gaetano Bordoni, b. 1933, barber; interviewed in Rome by Alfredo Martini and Silvana Mattei, April 8, 1976; the complete interview is in Circolo Gianni Bosio, *I Giorni Cantati*, pp. 10–14.

28. An episode in Bordoni's narrative summarizes this attitude. When the police questioned him about a Molotov cocktail hurled at the local station, he replied, on the one hand, that he had nothing to do with it, because he was not a Fascist; on the other, that if he had planted the bomb, it would have done a lot more damage. Thus, bomb-throwing is a Fascist act in a democratic state, but a revolutionary act in the abstract.

29. A Communist song from Guardavalle outlines the same contradiction, in the form of an alternative between the ballot and the bullet: on election day, the song says, we shall win for the sake of all those who went before us; but if we don't, "we are always ready to seize the knife." Of course, when the election was lost, very reasonably, they did nothing but prepare for the next one; but singing about armed struggle was essential to their image. The song was composed by Riitano Fioravante (b. 1902, farm worker), and recorded by Marco Muller at Guardavalle, Nov. 16, 1974. The full text is in *I Giorni Cantati* 11–12 (April 1978), n.p.

30. Tad, in Terkel, *Hard Times*, p. 21.

31. Santino Cappanera, 1933, Sept. 12, 1979. See chapters 1 and 8 in this

book, "Oral History as Genre" and "Absolutely Nothing: Wartime Refugees," for other references to this interview.

32. Renzo Del Carria, *Proletari senza rivolutione* (Rome: Edizioni Oriente, 1970); this was a popular history of the Italian working class, a sort of primer for 1960s activists.

33. See my "I metalmeccanici e la funzione poetica. Espressività orale di base nella manifestazione nazionale del 2 dicembre 1977," *I Giorni Cantati* 2–3 (1982), pp. 43–60, and "Typology of Industrial Folk Song," in *The Death of Luigi Trastulli,* pp. 170–74.

34. Alberto M. Cirese, seminar at the Circolo Gianni Bosio, Rome, March 21, 1977 (subsequent extract is also from this source).

35. Davìde Peddìo and Antonangelo Casùla (Desolo, Nuoro, Sardinia), recorded in Florence by Francesco Giannattasio, July 6, 1977; the full text with musical transcription and analysis is in F. Giannattasio, "Fiore raro d'altura. Due fuorisede sardi a Firenze," *I Giorni Cantati* 1 (1981), pp. 149–56.

36. Ambrogio Sparagna, "Canzone pe' Iacuruzingaru," *I Giorni Cantati* 2, no. 5 (April 1988), p. 2; it is included also in the record *Il paese con le ali* (Sud-nord Records SN 0010).

37. Tommaso Di Ciaula, *Tuta Blu. Ire, ricordi e sogni di un operaio del Sud* (Milan: Feltrinelli, 1988), p. 146.

CHAPTER 15. CONVERSATIONS WITH THE PANTHER

1. A shorter version of this paper was presented at the Oral History Association Meeting in Baltimore, October 1991, and published in *International Annual of Oral History,* ed. Ronald J. Grele (Summer 1990), pp. 145–66. Although I am responsible for the analysis and conclusions, this paper is part of a collective work in progress. It was written in preparation for what became a book edited by Micaela Arcidiacono, Francesca Battisti, Sonia Di Loreto, Carlo Martinez, Elena Spandri, and myself, *L'aeroplano e le stelle. Storia orale di una realtà studentesca prima e dopo la Pantera* (Rome: Manifestolibri 1995). All of the ideas presented here were discussed—and some originated—with them. See also Carlo Martinez and Elena Spandri, "Authority, Dialogue and Self-Awareness," in *Memory and Multiculturalism,* papers presented at the Eighth International Oral History Congress, Siena-Lucca, 25–28 February, 1993, pp. 1127–32.

2. On the possibly legendary nature of the animal and its apparitions, see Cesare Bermani, *Il bambino è servito. Leggende metropolitane in Italia* (Bari: Dedalo, 1991), pp. 244–48.

3. The Facoltà di Lettere e Filosofia (School of Humanities and Philosophy) of the University of Rome, usually shortened to "Lettere," includes the schools of Humanities (modern and classic literatures and history), geography, philosophy, and foreign languages. In this article, I will use "Lettere" to refer both to the Facoltà as a whole, and to the 1930s building in the Città Universitaria in which

most departments (with the exception of philosophy and foreign languages) are located. Context will clarify the individual references.

4. Unidentified, interviewed by Marco Capitelli, in M. Capitelli, ed., *La Pantera siamo noi* (Rome: C.I.D.S.—Instant Book, February 1990), pp. 22–23.

5. Fabio Ciabatti, b. 1968, interviewed by Micaela Arcidiacono, May 8, 1990. Unless otherwise noted, all interviews were done at Villa Mirafiori.

6. Sonia Di Loreto, b. 1969, int. July 27, 1991 by Alessandro Portelli.

7. *Panorama,* Nov. 30, 1990; Giampaolo Martelli, in *Il Giornale,* December 4, 1990.

8. Livio Quagliata, "Il sonno agitato della Pantera," *Il Manifesto,* December 15, 1990.

9. Fabiana Battisti, b. 1966, int. March 1, 1990, by A. Portelli.

10. Lodovica Mutarelli, b. 1965, int. March 12, 1990, by A. Portelli.

11. Pietro Rossini, b. 1967, int. February 1990, by Elena Spandri.

12. It has become a commonplace recently to point out that student fees only cover less than 15 percent of the costs of the university. What these commentators fail to notice is that, (1) the university is not intended to be a service aimed only at the social promotion of the students who attend it, but to the country at large: it is the tax-supported universities that provide teachers for free elementary schools; (2) the cost of the university also includes activities not directly related to the students, such as research, which it would be absurd to expect the students to pay for; and (3) the actual cost of a university education is much higher than the tuition costs, due to the poor quality of services (e.g., the near-total lack of library facilities compels to students to buy their own, expensive books; almost nonexistent dormitory facilities increase the cost for out-of-town students, etc.).

13. Roberto De Angelis, "Osservatori osservati. Il video e la Pantera," *I Giorni Cantati* 15 (December 1990), pp. 51–65.

14. Carlo Martinez-Elena Spandri, "Siamo in possesso di tutte le nostre facoltà, ovvero, la cultura dell'occupazione," *I Giorni Cantati* 13 (March 1990), pp. 3–5.

15. Villa Mirafiori used to be a convent; before that, King Victor Emmanuel II, the first king of united Italy, kept his mistress there after the country's capital was moved to Rome in 1870.

16. *I mass media e la Pantera,* mimeographed research report by the Collettivo Studentesco Romano, no date (May 1990).

17. "Il movimento ascolta: rapporto su una ricerca in corso," unsigned, *I Giorni Cantati* 14 (June 1990), 5–11 (written by Elena Spandri and Carlo Martinez, after group discussion).

18. I later got Francesca to tell the story in more detail on tape, and the transcript is included in Arcidiacono et al., *L'aeroplano e le stelle,* pp. 69–72. See chapter 5 in this book, "Deep Exchange: Roles and Gazes in Multivocal and Multilateral Interviewing."

19. Caterina Duranti, b. 1960, int. Feb. 18, 1990, in Genzano (Rome) by Carlo Martinez.

20. On the political impact of the Beatles in the history of Italian youth culture, see chapter 14 in this book, "Luigi's Socks and Rita's Makeup: Youth Culture, the Politics of Private Life, and the Culture of the Working Classes."

21. One frequent misunderstanding, caused by lack of counseling and alternatives, is that most students believe they are going to learn foreign languages, only to discover that what they are joining is actually a literature department, where languages are taught—when they are at all—only as an adjunct to advanced literary study. The sense that they are getting something other than what they bargained for is part of the sense of alienation—heightened by the fact that those who came with these expectations are the less academically and politically informed and socially privileged members of the student body.

22. Chiara Midolo, b. 1962, int. March 19, 1990, by Francesca Battisti.

23. Gabriele Guerra, b. 1968, int. March 1, 1990, by Micaela Arcidiacono.

24. Tiziana Petrangeli, b. 1965, int. Sept. 11, 1990, by Sonia Di Loreto.

25. Marinella Bucetti, b. 1964, int. May 31, 1990, by A. Portelli.

26. Carlo Martinez, b. 1966, int. May 30, 1991, by A. Portelli.

27. Alessio Trevisani, b. 1966, int. Feb. 5, 1990, by Micaela Arcidiacono.

28. Luca Capparucci, b. 1967, int. Oct. 15, 1990, by Sonia Di Loreto.

29. Giulia Bartolomei, b. 1964, int. March 8, 1990, in Genzano (Rome), by Carlo Martinez and Elena Spandri.

30. Beatrice Dondi, b. 1966, int. March 12, 1990, by Micaela Arcidiacono.

31. Paolo Giacomelli, b. 1963, int. June 26, 1990, by A. Portelli.

32. Firms with less than fifteen employees are exempted from applying the union contract (which has force of law in Italy). Two hundred thousand lire, at the mid-eighties exchange rate, were less than $150.

33. Northrop Frye, *The Stubborn Structure: Essays on Criticism and Society* (1970), Italian translation by Riccardo Terzo: *L'ostinata struttura. Saggi su critica e società* (Milan: Rizzoli, 1975), pp. 124–34.

34. Laura Lombardi, b. 1962, conversation notes, February 1990; Lombardi was later interviewed by Francesca Battisti, March 17, 1990.

35. Elisa Fabbri, int. March 30, 1990, by A. Arcidiacono, C. Martinez, and E. Spandri.

36. The opposition between the urban and the pastoral vision is also implicit in the adoption, also in Italian, of the word *campus* to designate university grounds. Although it was imported from English, this was originally a Latin word meaning "field." Italian students are aware of this connotation, which reinforces the pastoral vision (along with the tree-lined paths and smooth lawns of the idealized American college), and heightens the implicit contradiction in the phrase "university city."

37. Paolo Borgognone, b. 1963, int. May 25, 1990, by A. Portelli.

38. Toni Morrison, *Beloved* (London: Chatto & Windus, 1987), p. 266.

39. See "Research as an Experiment in Equality" in my *The Death of Luigi Trastulli and other Stories: Form and Meaning in Oral History* (Albany, N.Y.: State University of New York Press, 1991). On the dialectics of "interview" and "interrogation," see "The Oral Shape of the Law," ibid.

40. See M. Arcidiacono et al., *L'aeroplano e le stelle*, pp. 214–15, 227–31.

41. Dennis Tedlock, "The Analogical Tradition and the Emergence of a Dialogical Anthropology," in *The Spoken Word and the Work of Interpretation* (Philadelphia: University of Pennsylvania Press, 1983), pp. 282–301.

42. See chapter 5 in this book, "Deep Exchange: Roles and Gazes in Multivocal and Multilateral Interviewing."

43. Tatiana Petrovich, b. 1966, October 3, 1993, meeting; Petrovich had been interviewed on Dec. 20, 1990, by Micaela Arcidiacono. The discussion that follows is based on pp. 238–40 of *L'aeroplano e le stelle*, materially written by me but collectively authored.

44. Sebastiano Calleri, b. 1965, was later (January 28, 1994) interviewed by Sibilla Drisaldi, who contributed the tape to our project.

45. While the resistance to interpretation of these particular interviewees is shaped by their intellectual profession and aspirations, yet they reflect a more generalized attitude. In my Harlan County fieldwork files, I find a loose note, dating perhaps from 1989, which says that, while I made an effort to understand the meaning of what I saw and heard, yet "What amazed me was, in interviews and conversation, the explicit denial that any meaning was there, or the lack of a metalanguage." A further note describes this attitude as "coverup," which may be only part of the explanation.

46. See the narrative of Alfredo Filipponi in Portelli, "Uchronic Dreams: Working-Class Memory and Possible Worlds," in *The Death of Luigi Trastulli*, pp. 100–105.

47. See chapter 12 in this book, "I'm Going to Say It Now: Interviewing the Movement."

48. *Storie di ordinaria follia* is the title of the Italian translation of Charles Bukowski's collection of short stories *Erections, Ejaculations, Exhibitions, and General Tales of Ordinary Madness* (1972), Italian translation by Pier Francesco Paolini (Milan: Feltrinelli, 1975).

CHAPTER 16. EXILES, SOJOURNERS, AND TOURISTS
IN THE UNIVERSITY

1. Interviewed in Rome by Alessandro Portelli, February 15, 1992. Unless otherwise noted, all interviews were conducted at Villa Mirafiori, seat of the English Department of the University of Rome "La Sapienza."

2. Interviewed in Rome by Francesca Battisti and Alessandro Portelli, March 16, 1992.

3. Interviewed in Spain, on the train from Salamanca to Madrid, by Francesca Battisti, Aug. 1991.

4. Int. by Francesca Battisti and Alessandro Portelli, March 31, 1992. In quoting Middle Eastern names, we have followed the usage of the informants themselves; thus, while Gifi Fadi still follows the Middle Eastern form of putting the family name before the given name, the others have Italianized the form and reversed the order. In the course of the essay, we will refer to them mostly by family names.

5. See also chapters 5 and 15 in this book, "Deep Exchange: Roles and Gazes in Multivocal and Multilateral Interviewing" and "Conversations with the Panther: The Italian Student Movement of 1990"; Micaela Arcidiacono, et al., *L'aeroplano e le stelle: Storia orale di una realtà studentesca* (Rome: Manifestolibri 1995); Micaela Arcidiacono and Sonia Di Loreto, "Precious Memories: On the Historical Background of the Italian Student Movement of 1990," and Carlo Martinez and Elena Spandri, "Authority, Dialogue and Self-Awareness," in *Memory and Multiculturalism,* papers presented at the Eight International Oral History Congress, Siena-Lucca, 25–28 February, 1993, pp. 1061–67, 1127–32.

6. Francesca Battisti, "Another Country: Multiculturalism and Imagination in Foreign Language Students," in *Memory and Multiculturalism,* pp. 1068–75.

7. The narrators discussed in this paper also include two persons who are not students at Villa Mirafiori (Thamer Birawi and Gifi Fadi). However, they were contacted through Villa Mirafiori students, and interviewed there. They may be considered as part of the social network that radiates from the foreign language departments.

8. Int. by Alessandro Portelli and Maria Antonietta Saracino, January 24, 1991.

9. Caterina Duranti, int. in Genzano (Rome) by Carlo Martinez, February 18, 1990; Sonia Di Loreto, int. by Alessandro Portelli, May, 1992. For a discussion of travel myths and practices of Villia Mirafiori students, see also chapter 15 in this book, "Conversations with the Panther."

10. Chiara Midolo, int. by Francesca Battisti, March, 1990.

11. The expression used is *extracomunitario,* meaning "a non-European Community national." Although technically the term would also apply to Swedes or to U. S. citizens, it is intended to refer euphemistically to Third-World or Eastern European immigrants.

12. On the concept of "horizon of possibility" as a form of representativity in oral sources, see Alessandro Portelli, in Paul Thompson et al., "Responses to Louise A. Tilly," *International Journal of Oral History* 6, no. 1 (February 1985), pp. 32–39.

13. Excerpted in *I Giorni Cantati* 23–24 (December 1992), p. 3. Sibhatu's book, *Aullò: Canto-poesia dall' Eritrea,* a bilingual collection of stories, tales, and poems, traditional and written by herself, was later published (Rome: Sinnos, 1993).

14. Tiziana Petrangeli, int. by Sonia Di Loreto, September 11, 1990.

15. Manuela Bagnetti was interviewed by Alessandro Portelli, March 27, 1992. This remark was made later in conversation.

16. Lucia Rossi, int. by Alessandro Portelli, May 17, 1990. Rossi draws the metaphor of the parapet from her reading of Norman Mailer's *An American Dream* in my class.

17. Franco Soekardi Esposito, int. by Alessandro Portelli, April 30, 1992.

18. Anna Gatti, int. by Elena Spandri, March, 1990.

19. Fabio Ciucci, int. by Micaela Arcidiacono, March 26, 1990.

20. Int. by Alessandro Portelli, September 26, 1990, and March 12, 1990.

21. 'Portoghesi,' unpublished poem; manuscript supplied by the author. "Portoghesi" ("Portuguese") is vernacular for "gate-crashers."

22. Marinella Bucetti, int. by Alessandro Portelli, May 31, 1990.

23. R. Sibhatu, *Aullò*, p. 38.

24. Since she was interviewed, the political situation has changed, and she was able to go back.

25. 'Lettere,' in Thamer Birawi, *Un po' di poesie* (Roma: Ed. Raggio Verde, 1992), p. 18.

26. Werner Sollors, *Beyond Ethnicity: Consent and Descent in American Literature* (New York and Oxford: Oxford University Press, 1989).

27. This tension of identity and difference is accidentally but emblematically embodied in the speaker's Italian surname. A very common name in Naples ("It shows we don't come from the aristocracy"), Esposito is an indication of regional origins; on the other hand, it is one of the surnames that the Church imposed on children abandoned ("exposed") at convents. Thus, it stands both for paternal roots and for ultimate fatherlessness.

Index

Names in bold indicate oral narrators whereas names in italics indicate oral narrators quoted from written sources.

Abernathy, Ralph (civil rights leader), 215
Abruzzi, Italy, 284
Aesthetics, 19–23, 47
Africa, 46, 166–67, 282–85 *passim*, 287
African Americans, 25; in Appalachia, 30–39, 214–20; and black English, 36; and the Black Panther Party, 245; and civil rights, 35, 168, 203, 215–20, 224; in the Civil War, 150; and the Nation of Islam, 169; and oral history, 58; in Vietnam, 167–71. *See also* Cowans, Rev. Hugh; Cowans, Julia; Douglass, Frederick; Equiano, Olaudah; Race; Slavery
Agee, James: *Let Us Now Praise Famous Men*, 100
Alabama, 32
Alighieri, Dante: *Divine Comedy*, 45, 86
Amaseno, Lazio, Italy, 242, 245
America. *See* United States
American studies, xiv, 47
Anagnoresis, 259
Anecdotes, 4, 5, 161, 186
Anderson, Eric (singer, songwriter), 212
Anderson, Sherwood (author), 100
Andreoli, Bruno (factory worker, researcher), x; on alienation, 240–41; and workers' culture, 239–40
Anthropology, xiv, 6, 13, 57, 70, 143, 255, 282. *See also* Native anthropology
Appalachia, 8, 11, 14, 63, 199–231; African Americans in, 24–39, 214–20; and Appalachian Project (at Rome Uni-

versity), 42; and culture, 201, 211–13, 221–22, 225–26, 228–29, 255, 271; and literature, 205–6, 209, 211–12; and music, 210–13; and the sixties, 100–201, 220–31; and stereotypes, 304–5; and time and space, 205–9; and the War on Poverty, 99, 200–204, 212, 221, 223–30, 233
Appalshop media cooperative, 213
Arabic language, 280–81
Archives, xvi, 17, 44, 52, 64, 65, 68, 104, 184, 187
Arezzo, Tuscany, Italy, 140, 142, 158, 238
Argentina, xiv
Ariosto, Lodovico (poet), 45
Artena, Lazio, Italy, 236, 248
Auschwitz, 154
Autobiography, xiii, 5, 9–10, 13, 18–19, 24, 58, 79–84, 164, 168, 185, 190. *See also* Douglass, Frederick; Equiano, Olaudah; Interviewing; Narrative; Oral history
Avezzano, Abruzzi, Italy, 247–48

Bagnetti, Manuela (student): on China, 279; on color, 276–77; on family, 288; on languages, 279–80
Baker, Mark: *Nam*, 16, 162, 164, 168, 172, 175
Ballads, 44, 187, 234
Balltrip, Ewell (journalist): on Harlan, Brookside strike, 112

339